T0392088

Brahmins and Kings

Brahmins and Kings

Royal Counsel in the Sanskrit Narrative Literatures

JOHN NEMEC

OXFORD
UNIVERSITY PRESS

OXFORD
UNIVERSITY PRESS

Oxford University Press is a department of the University of Oxford.
It furthers the University's objective of excellence in research, scholarship,
and education by publishing worldwide. Oxford is a registered trade mark of
Oxford University Press in the UK and certain other countries.

Published in the United States of America by Oxford University Press
198 Madison Avenue, New York, NY 10016, United States of America.

© Oxford University Press 2025

All rights reserved. No part of this publication may be reproduced, stored in a retrieval system, transmitted, used for text and data mining, or used for training artificial intelligence, in any form or by any means, without the prior permission in writing of Oxford University Press, or as expressly permitted by law, by license or under terms agreed with the appropriate reprographics rights organization. Inquiries concerning reproduction outside the scope of the above should be sent to the Rights Department, Oxford University Press, at the address above.

You must not circulate this work in any other form
and you must impose this same condition on any acquirer

CIP data is on file at the Library of Congress

ISBN 978-0-19-779199-8

DOI: 10.1093/oso/9780197791998.001.0001

Printed by Marquis Book Printing, Canada

FSC www.fsc.org
MIX
Paper | Supporting responsible forestry
FSC® C103567

For AJ, who loves stories.

Contents

Acknowledgments ix

Introduction 1

1. When the *Paramparā* Breaks: On Gurus and Students in the *Mahābhārata* 33

2. The Perfect King: Rāma's Suffering, and Why His Story Must Be Told Anew 66

3. Kingship in Kashmir: Brahminical Norms in Kalhaṇa's *Rājataraṅgiṇī* 104

4. Wizards and Kings, or "Tantra beyond the Tantras": The Śaiva-Brahminical Narrative of the *Kathāsaritsāgara* 141

5. The King in the Garden: Pleasure in Dramatic Imagination 176

6. The Wisdom of Animals: Kingship and the *Pañcatantra* 221

Conclusion 259

Bibliography 277

Index 299

Acknowledgments

The majority of this book was written in Philadelphia during the coronavirus "lockdowns" that brought the world to a halt in 2020 and 2021. A number of the chapters have their roots in earlier work, however, which I pursued in fits and starts and presented in various venues over the course of a number of years.

Chapter 1 was first hatched as a talk in 2005, entitled "Gurus in the Great Tradition" and delivered in the weekly seminar of the South Asia Center of the University of Virginia. Thanks to the generous invitation and editorial work of H. L. Seneviratne, it was subsequently published in a *festschrift* honoring Gananath Obeyesekere, this time under the title "When the *Paramparā* Breaks: On Gurus and Students in the *Mahābhārata*" (for which see Nemec 2009 in the Bibliography). I am particularly thankful to H. L. for encouraging me to work on the narrative literatures, which got me started in earnest down the interpretive path that brought this book to fruition.

First steps into the worlds of the *Rājataraṅgiṇī* and the *Kathāsaritsāgara*, respectively examined in Chapters 3 and 4, first came to fruition in 2010 with a presentation at the South Asia Center of the University of Wisconsin, Madison: "The River of Kings and the Ocean of Rivers of Stories: Brahmins, Kṣatriyas, and Tāntrikas in the *Rājataraṅgiṇī* and the *Kathāsaritsāgara*." I thank Don Davis for inviting me to give this lecture and both him and Gudrun Bühnemann for their hospitality during my visit.

In 2012, I gave a lecture at the University of Pennsylvania, my alma mater, in the South Asia Colloquium and under the title "History and Narrative in Kalhaṇa's *Rājataraṅgiṇī*." In anticipation of this event, I offered the same talk with the same title to the South Asia Seminar of the University of Virginia. I am thankful to Daud Ali, Deven Patel, and Ramya Sreenivasan for making the Philadelphia visit possible and to Daud and Deven for their responses to my work. I also thank my former Penn teacher, now a friend, Michael Meister, who helped me to develop my thinking by sharing his own work on the Kashmir region.

Another trip to Madison, this time for the Annual Conference on South Asia in 2017, occasioned a new presentation of the work that is found in

Chapter 4: "Tantra Beyond the Tantras: The Śaiva-Brahminical Narrative of the *Kathāsaritsāgara*." The paper was included in a panel co-organized by Srilata Raman, the late Anne E. Monius, and myself, entitled "Śaivism in New Contexts." I am thankful to Srilata and Anne for collaborating in this way, and to both for their sheer brilliance, exemplary scholarship, and friendship.

Finally, a visit to the Department of Asian Languages and Cultures at Northwestern University in 2018 offered the opportunity to deliver a lecture entitled "Three Kings, a Wicked Queen, and a Garland of Gnomic Wisdom: On the Brahminical Narrative of Kalhaṇa's *Rājataraṅgiṇī*, 1149 CE." I thank Mark McClish and Laura Brueck for all they did for me around this visit.

Several colleagues and friends read individual chapters of this book and offered helpful comments, for which I am grateful. Frank Clooney did so for both Chapters 1 and 2. I thank Patrick Olivelle for reading Chapter 6 and offering both detailed and instructive comments and encouragement regarding the same. I also thank the two anonymous peer reviewers who offered thoughtful and constructive reviews of the manuscript, and I owe a particular debt of gratitude to Gregory M. Clines, who read Chapter 2, furnishing perspicacious comments that led me more deeply to think through the issues addressed therein. Greg also joined my graduate seminar on a weekly basis in the spring of 2023 at the University of Virginia, where he spent a part of his sabbatical leave, which enlivened the discussions and led to many insights that would not have been possible without his participation.

The seminar was dedicated to premodern Indian political works and scholarship thereon, and the students in the class initiated or engaged numerous conversations that advanced my thinking about politics and religion and much else, which is reflected in the Introduction to the present volume. I thank all the seminar students, including Mahati Agumamidi, Eva Frohnhofer, Daniel Gordon, Brian Johnson, Arya Mack-Gilson, Abhyudaya Mandal, Josh Novick, Sergio Sastre Salgado, Jack Schwartz, Pema Sherpa, and Tulku Sangye Tenzin.

Also at Virginia, I thank Bob Hueckstedt for talking to me about Sanskrit literature and some of these stories in particular; Geeta Patel for a number of deeply insightful conversations around concepts of realism, film theory, and a host of other ideas and concerns; and Indrani Chatterjee for her stellar intellectual company. All three are ideal colleagues and friends. I also thank Mark Juergensmeyer for sharing in a number of discussions of this book project and the various concerns it addresses, usually over a meal or a drink at the American Academy of Religion Annual Meeting, always, somehow—or so it seems to me—in San Diego. Sometimes Julie Ingersoll joined us as well, and I always learned much from our conversations.

This project would not have been possible without the support and guidance of Cynthia Read, my former editor at Oxford University Press, who took on the project. Her retirement led me to Theo Calderara, who put the book through peer review and did everything to make its publication possible. I am deeply grateful to both Cynthia and Theo for all that they did and do. Thank you.

Finally, and most of all, I thank Carmen, my wife, who helped me conceptualize the models of inequity charted in this book, and AJ, our teenager, who works wonders with words. Both believed in me and supported me through the writing of this book, and much more. This project would have been impossible for me without them and, more than this, hardly worth doing.

Introduction

The Counsel of Stories

Religions deal in equal measure with transcendent concerns and worldly affairs, and when it comes to the latter, it is vital that practitioners and scholars of religion alike ask how one may move another to act in principled ways. What can change another's mind? How can one exert influence or prevail upon others to do as one wishes and believes they must? Simply put, what renders counsel effective, and when does it fail to persuade?

One answer to these questions is offered by way of example in the Sanskrit narrative literatures, which often tell stories that engage or represent principles elaborated in the Sanskrit language, technical treatises concerned with proper conduct and political affairs. Inasmuch as persuasive advice inevitably requires not just a convincing message but also a compelling medium for its delivery, narrative—the telling of stories—presents itself as a likely candidate for conveying good counsel. A good story, if aptly chosen and compellingly and opportunely conveyed, is perhaps unique in its capacity to persuade.

Consider, for a moment, what stories can do. They present not merely abstracted principles and ideals but the dynamic movements of personal, cultural, social, and religious life, all in their mutual relation and evolving constitution. Stories animate doctrines, ideas, and ideals. They place "mere" thoughts in context; they put flesh, as it were, on the bare bones of doctrine by elaborating various circumstances in which individual choice and predisposition, or the vicissitudes of luck or fate, can define ideas and ideals by turning events in ways that abstract maxims or logical syllogisms sometimes fail to capture in equal contextual detail. Meaning needs action, which can readily be found in story.[1]

[1] Thus, Todorov [1973] 1975: 166 states that the very definition of narrative is an event that modifies a previously existent equilibrium, ultimately eventuating a new equilibrium that has both a social and a literary function and consequence. Indeed, he says ([1973] 1975, 163), "*all narrative is a movement between two equilibriums which are similar but not identical.*" Stephen Neale (1980: 20) similarly states in his famous booklet on the ordering of cinema that "narrative is always a process

Brahmins and Kings. John Nemec, Oxford University Press. © Oxford University Press 2025.
DOI: 10.1093/oso/9780197791998.003.0001

Something intimate is offered in narrative because stories are emotionally resonant. They are often told to please or to entertain, and they therefore must easily capture the imagination of those who hear or read them, or see them performed. Stories draw their audiences into an imagined world that is palpable—is felt, heard, and seen. They draw their audiences into the dreamworld of the story. The spell a story casts, if it is a good story, is rarely broken by inconsistencies, incoherent turns of events, or inaccurately represented social, cultural, or other practices, just as good stories draw one to and keep one in their ambit by leaving out what their audiences wish, or would not notice, to be absent. Whether of the acts, feelings, and ideas of agents accurately remembered from history or of those of fictionalized characters placed in contrived circumstances, the very narration of a story reveals something of the values, implicit assumptions, and preferences of storytellers and their audiences.

To engage a story is thus to participate in the storyteller's expressive act. To hear, watch, or read a story, that is, is to imbibe and impart—perhaps even implicitly to accept or to endorse—its values, preferences, and presuppositions, passing them on as the story passes through from hearer to hearer, reader to reader, audience to audience. Stories evoke acceptability in their audiences—unless they are turned away. Thus are stories culturally situated, and thus do they not only reveal and depict the social, political, religious, emotional, and affective contexts in which they are situated but also help to form and perpetuate the same.

It is in these senses that stories—in their telling, in their being shared—may be said to be "grounded" in the reality of their contexts and "realistic" in their expression. And yet, good stories simultaneously traverse cultural

of transformation of the balance of elements that constitute its pretext: the interruption of an initial equilibrium and the tracing of the dispersal and reconfiguration of its components. The system of narrative characteristic of mainstream cinema is one which orders that dispersal and refiguration in a particular way, so that dispersal, disequilibrium, is both maintained and contained in figures of symmetry, of balance, its elements finally re-placed in a new equilibrium whose achievement is the condition of narrative closure." While the media and modes of narration in Sanskrit literature are in important ways dissimilar, comparison with modern film, I argue, is implicitly vital to this book, because movies are designed to reach a wider audience, just as many of the works examined in this book were and did, and because, as Neale (1980, 19) put it, cinema is "a constantly fluctuating series of signifying processes, a 'machine' for the production of meanings and positions, or rather positionings for meaning: *a machine for the regulation of the orders of subjectivity*" (emphasis mine). To explore this type of social influence and social effect in Sanskrit narrative literatures defines the purpose of this book. See also Doniger O'Flaherty 1984: 127–132, which, though focused on myth rather than the types of stories examined in this book, meditates on the argumentative, even philosophical, dimensions of narrative.

boundaries and reach across generations. They speak not just of and to the historical moments of their authors and inaugural audiences but by capturing something of the human condition can reach—for good or ill—across the globe and over the course of millennia. Well-made stories, in a word, are human stories and may be read as such.

Finally, and thus, stories have power. They shape how those who share them see themselves, their social lives, their values and sense of being in the world. Indeed, it is axiomatic to say that "we are the stories we tell about ourselves," for stories often are and certainly can project self-fulfilling prophesies: those who engage them or hold them subconsciously in mind may tend toward living out the logical courses of actions and choices patterned in the stories that define a community's social sense of self.

Political Themes in the Sanskrit Narrative Literatures

The present volume consists in a series of close readings of major works of the Sanskrit literatures of India's premodernity. Six chapters are dedicated to the examination of some of the most significant, widely circulated, and best-known narratives composed in the language in question, including the two Sanskrit epics, the *Mahābhārata* (Chapter 1) and the *Rāmāyaṇa* (Chapter 2); the chronicle of the lives of the kings and queens of Kashmir, what has sometimes been counted as the "first historical work" written in Sanskrit, Kalhaṇa's *Rājataraṅgiṇī* (Chapter 3); Somadeva's encyclopedic, nested compendium of fictive narratives, the *Kathāsaritsāgara* or "Ocean of Rivers of Stories" (Chapter 4); two of the most celebrated dramas in the history of Sanskrit literature, Kālidāsa's *Abhijñānaśākuntala* and Harṣa's *Ratnāvalī*, which are read together with Dāmodaragupta's narrative poem, the *Kuṭṭanīmata* or "Bawd's Counsel" (Chapter 5); and, finally, Viṣṇuśarman's animal fables, which is the first work of its kind in world literature, the *Pañcatantra* (Chapter 6).

Reading for their framing narratives and with attention to their mutual resonances and intertextual markings, I argue that a central storyline may be identified in these landmark literary works, one that involves the nature and functioning of political authority in South Asia's premodernity. I further propose that something may be known thereby of the implicit assumptions and values that were held and cultivated by those who composed, circulated, and engaged these works, which articulated normative terms regarding the power of kingship and its proper exercise.[2] The narratives examined in this book all express a distinct cultural understanding of political authority and action, which may be summed up in a single sentence: a political ruler must be good to do well in the world (and beyond it).[3] "Being good" means disciplining emotions and controlling desires, and keeping the company of those (Brahmins) who maintain the same disciplines and counsel others to do so as well. All the stories in question present discipline in thought and action and the controlling and channeling of desire as precisely what permit those with political authority to cultivate the lawful order of society (*dharma*); to offer direct means for securing political power, fame, an honored reputation, and material wealth (*artha*); to open the way to the myriad pleasures of worldly existence (*kāma*), be they somatic, intellectual, artistic, or otherwise; and even to achieve felicity in the hereafter, be it spiritual emancipation (*mokṣa*), a heavenly afterlife (*svarga*), or, as we shall see in Chapter 4, immortality as a *vidyādhara*.[4]

[2] As is well known, premodern South Asia knew of at least one form of political formation apart from kingship, namely, that of federation. Yet, the Brahmins who authored the works on Hindu law, the Dharmasūtras and in particular the Dharmaśāstras, as well as the books on statecraft and governance, the *Arthaśāstra* and like works, favored kingship as the normative model of governance. On confederation see, e.g., Thapar [1984] 2002: 70–115 and *passim*; Thapar 1978b (at, e.g., p. 22, where tribal forms of government are contrasted with kingship); R. S. Sharma 1989; and Roy 1994: 1, fn. 2 and 208, fn. 34. See also the eleventh book of the *Arthaśāstra*, which is dedicated to conduct toward confederacies.

[3] Far from offering a model of action that sets material gain (*artha*) against *dharma*, then, the narrative literatures examined in this book—at least in their major and framing stories—emphasize their synchrony. See Doniger 2018 for a study that argues that the core messages of the *Kāmasūtra* and the *Arthaśāstra* oppose the *dharmic* strictures emphasized in the Dharmaśāstras and related works. See also a similar idea regarding the indispensability of *dharma* to all pleasure and success, expressed (as it so often is) in the *Mahābhārata*, in this case—it is but a single exemplar among hundreds (cf., e.g., *Mahābhārata* 5.122.32–36)—uttered by Balarāma in the Śalya Parvan, MBh 9.59.17–18: *dharmaḥ sucaritaḥ sadbhiḥ saha dvābhyāṃ niyacchati | arthaś cātyarthalubdhasya kāmaś cātiprasaṅginaḥ ||* 9.59.17 || *dharmārthau dharmakāmau ca kāmārthau cāpy apīḍayan | dharmārthakāmān yo 'bhyeti so 'tyantaṃ sukham aśnute* || 9.59.18 ||. "*Dharma* is properly practiced by the virtuous. But two things cause it to fail: the pursuit of wealth by those who desire it too strongly, and the pursuit of pleasure by those who are addicted to it. The person who pursues *dharma*, wealth and pleasure, all three, without suppressing two of them, whether *dharma* and wealth, or *dharma* and pleasure, or pleasure and wealth, he is the one that finds the greatest happiness." (This translation is a very slight modification of that of John Smith 2009: 555. Reference here is to the enumeration of verses found in the Pune Critical Edition of the epic.) Cf. also, e.g., *Nītisāra* 4.3ab: *ātmānam eva prathamam icched guṇasamanvitam* |. "He should first of all wish for himself and no other to be endowed with good qualities." This, as with all references to the *Nītisāra*, cites the edition of the Murty Classical Library of India that is found in Knutson 2021. Cf. also Ali 2004: 90–91.

[4] So much suggests a certain conservatism of the narrative literatures in that the same model is offered in the *Mānavadharmaśāstra* (at, e.g., 1.108–110) (and also the *Nītisāra* at, e.g., 1.51), which suggests that following *dharma* produces not only the results of the Veda but also the "full reward" of proper conduct (this being the translation of Olivelle 2004b: 20). Similarly, the entire "triple set" of *dharma*, *artha*, and *kāma* are said to be conducive to "welfare" at *Mānavadharmaśāstra* 2.224 (cf. Olivelle 2004b: 40). *Mokṣa* or spiritual release, or else an analog thereto such as a heavenly reward in

More than this, the narratives in question further suggest that these disciplines not only effect both the royal sovereign's individual ends but also align them with those of the kingdom's subjects, personal successes being achieved when and while the needs of others are served by way of virtuousness.[5] It is this concern above all that is presented in these narratives when they relate stories of kings and princes (and sometimes queens) living their daily lives or prosecuting the obligations of their political offices.

The understanding of the political conduct in question is similarly recommended in key works of the Dharmaśāstras and Arthaśāstras, which state that it is by way of restraint of the senses that the king may accomplish his aims.[6] The personal disciplines involved include the admonition to guard against addictions, particularly those of gambling, drinking, womanizing, and hunting, four vices repeatedly identified in works on statecraft and elsewhere as of perennial temptation to the king.[7] But the fundamental form of restraint described in the narrative literatures is characterized as that of the application of a dispassionate good judgment, an unselfish discretion in action born from *dharmic* restraint. It is by developing self-restraint that one

the afterlife (*svarga*), is also associated with the *dharmic* action of the king in the narrative literatures, as is examined, for example, in Chapter 4 of the present volume.

[5] See, e.g., *Arthaśāstra* 1.19.34, which suggests the king's happiness is to be found in that of his subjects, a concept referred to as well in Aiyangar 1935: 85. (This and all references to the *Arthaśāstra* in this book cite the enumeration of verses and passages found in Kangle 1969 and also followed, with several emendations, by the translation of Olivelle 2013.) Cf., e.g., Ghoshal 1923: 182–187; Pollock 1984b: 525 and *passim*. Finally, note that the same sentiment is repeatedly conveyed in the *Mahābhārata*, as at, e.g., 2.12.6–7, which describes Yudhiṣṭhira as considerate of what would help all his subjects and as showing kindness to all of them without exception: *bhūyaś cādbhutavīryaujā dharmam evānupālayan | kiṃ hitaṃ sarvalokānāṃ bhaved iti mano dadhe || anugṛhṇan prajāḥ sarvāḥ sarvadharmavidāṃ varaḥ | aviśeṣeṇa sarveṣāṃ hitaṃ cakre yudhiṣṭhiraḥ ||*.

[6] Thus, for example, the sixth chapter of the *Arthaśāstra* is devoted to mastery over the senses and the idea that without just that, nothing can be accomplished. Aiyangar 1935: 114–115, fn. 207 further mentions that Kauṭilya suggests the king should refrain from vice. See also *Mānavadharmaśāstra* 2.88–100, where control over the eleven organs is said to lead to success (and cf. *Mānavadharmaśāstra* 4.15–16). Another example: subduing his organs, a king is able to control his subjects, says *Mānavadharmaśāstra* 7.44 (and see Olivelle 2004b: 109 for his rendering of the same. Cf. *Mānavadharmaśāstra* 8.173 and Olivelle 2004b: 135). The same is expressed also in Kāmandaki's *Nītisāra* in the first chapter, entitled "Discussion of Conquering the Senses" (*indriyajayaprakaraṇa*). See esp. *Nītisāra* 1.21–22. Finally, see *Mahābhārata* 12.220, this section of the Śāntiparvan being dedicated to the importance of self-restraint (*dama*).

[7] See *Arthaśāstra* 8.3, conterminal with topic 129 of the text, which deals with human vices. *Arthaśāstra* 8.3.38 lists hunting, gambling, women, and drinking as vices stemming from wrath. The *Nītisāra* similarly lists hunting, gambling, and drinking as "reprehensible for kings" (per Knutson's translation) at *Nītisāra* 1.56ab: *mṛgayākṣās tathā pānaṃ garhitāni mahībhujām |*. *Nītisāra* 15 in turn identifies seven vices and devotes dozens of verses to the four here noted. See also Ali 2004: 241–252 for a more general discussion of self-control and the anxieties over losing just that in the context of the royal court. Here, Ali distinguishes between attachment to and engagement with pleasurable concerns, with the former posing the danger rather than the latter per se.

may effectively practice wisdom and enact the care in action that permits successful endeavor in the world.[8] This means that one must check one's desires, tend to biases, and stall the inclination narrowly to serve one's immediate needs and wishes, for by doing so the royal sovereign is equipped to evaluate the concerns to hand, enabling judicious choice in action in the face of dynamic and ever-shifting social and material circumstances. Thus, while the core message of the *Arthaśāstra*, as Olivelle notes, is *atisaṃdhāna*,[9] a term he understands to refer to the "outwitting" of one's adversaries and opponents, the narrative literatures implicitly, explicitly, and repeatedly recommend that kings, princes, queens, and those who advise them cultivate personal rectitude above all. *Dharma* constitutes a kind of "higher law,"[10] an internal battle, and the narrative literatures suggest that only this could furnish one with the discretion and wisdom ever to "outwit" one's opponents at all—though, as we shall see in Chapter 5 and especially Chapter 6, outwitting or a realpolitik sometimes proves to be necessary.[11]

It is in this way that the major theme of the narrative literatures may be said primarily to be closer not to the clever cunning of Kauṭilya's *Arthaśāstra* but rather to the disciplining works on personal conduct and disposition, the Dharmaśāstras.[12] A "theology of ordinary life," to borrow a term coined by Donald R. Davis,[13] implicitly defines the major concerns of the narratives

[8] This is again as in the *Mānavadharmaśāstra*. See 2.2–5, where it is suggested that all people have desire, but that engaging desire properly leads one to attain both the world of immortals and all the objects of desire in the present world. Also, the "ten-point law" (*Mānavadharmaśāstra* 6.91–93) brings one to the highest state, but it is also what brings one reward in the world, as we see in the narrative literatures. The ten items include resolve, forbearance, self-control, refraining from theft, performing purifications, mastering the organs, understanding, learning, truthfulness, and suppressing anger. (These are the ten terms in question as translated by Olivelle 2004b: 105.)

[9] Olivelle 2013: 50.

[10] Aiyangar 1935: 104–106 cites the *Bṛhadāraṇyaka Upaniṣad* at 1.4.11–14 to suggest that *dharma* stands for more than mere civil law but may be properly identified with truth as such.

[11] Indeed, as the *Arthaśāstra* says of itself (at 1.6.3, here following the translation of Olivelle 2013: 71), the entire treatise boils down to mastery over the senses. Thus, the first chapter of the *Nītisāra* similarly is concerned with *indriyajaya*, conquering the senses.

[12] One may note, however, that the kind of virtue ethic recommended the king in the narrative literatures is clearly and prominently articulated in the *Nītisāra* of Kāmandaki, in contrast to the *Arthaśāstra* of Kauṭilya, on which it is nevertheless largely based in its contents and organization, as Kāmandaki himself states at *Nītisāra* 1.6. On the various models of ethics and governance modeled in the *Mānavadharmaśāstra*, the Śāntiparvan of the *Mahābhārata*, the *Nītisāra*, and the *Arthaśāstra*, see Nemec 2023.

[13] See Davis 2010: 1. Davis argues that law—in premodern South Asia "law" being defined principally by the writ of the Dharmaśāstras—involves a normative ordering of all of quotidian life. Indeed, a legal structure defines and shapes human endeavor and activity to a degree that requires one to think in legal terms about all religiously sanctioned activity and, conversely, to think with and through religiously imbued categories and concerns when defining and exploring the full and proper ambit of the law. "If law is the theology of ordinary life," Davis 2010: 6–7 explains, "then religion is not a phenomenon directed solely at otherworldly ends, at God or gods, or at escaping or circumventing the

examined in this book, more so than, if not entirely to the exclusion of, the ruthlessness and cold calculation that largely characterizes Kauṭilya's political advice. A kind of virtue ethics—a code of conduct that shapes how members of the court are to engage both quotidian affairs and the obligations of their government offices—defines the moral principles of the narrative literatures, though it is, in fact, tempered by a certain Kauṭilīyan consequentialism. In fact, the narratives elaborate ordered and chastened manners of action in daily life, what constitute an ethical formulation that stands in contrast both to the ruthless and unapologetic consequentialism of the *Arthaśāstra*[14] and to the tendency toward deontology that often characterizes ethics in the Dharmaśāstras. If we can boldly generalize and suggest that Kauṭilya's *Arthaśāstra* in effect argues that being good is unimportant if one does well in the world, and that the *Mānavadharmaśāstra* intimates both that one must be good if one is properly to take one's place in the world (and beyond) and that being thus is of intrinsic value and reward, then the narrative literatures, taken together, rather suggest that inasmuch as doing well results from being good—being chastened in desire and emotion—there is no conceivable reason to be otherwise, with the caveat that being good in this sense sometimes also involves deploying acts of cunning. This is to say that in putting metaphorical flesh on the proverbial bare bones of Hindu law (Dharmaśāstra) and the science of statecraft (Arthaśāstra), the narratives in question intimate a way of action that synthesizes and in practice transforms the messages of both:[15] political action as depicted in the narratives in

practices of ordinary life. In this way, transcendence does not have to imply denial of or disengagement from the world. Law is both a means and an end for giving ordinary life meaning and value through a worldly transcendence. This is why law is often connected with other human goods such as order and justice." It is in my view also why, as Davis 2010: 37 notes, "Hindu jurisprudence . . . concentrates on law in its fulfillment," while, by contrast, "modern legal theory," with its more narrowly defined ambit, "tends to focus on law in its breach, the violations of law that expose how rules work in practice and how contraventions of the law are punished." And this is in error, he argues, for Davis 2010: 12 makes the strong claim that "it is not that *Hindu* law is the theology of ordinary life for *Hindus*. It is that the specifically religious foundations of all legal systems can be revealed through an examination of the Hindu legal tradition." On Hinduism as a legal tradition, see also Davis 2007.

[14] Kāmandaki, I argue, works a virtue ethics into his *Nītisāra* that fits neatly with the position one finds in the narrative literatures, in a palpable contrast with the *Arthaśāstra*—at least regarding their respective ethical orientations. See also Nemec 2023.

[15] This book does not offer a thorough reading of all Arthaśātric works. There are differences between them, of course. Kāmandaki's text, though it adopts Kauṭilya's to a significant degree, as Ghoshal (1923: 214–215), Knutson (2021: vii–xvi), and many others have noted, does express the kind of virtue ethics emphasized in the narratives in question and to a degree not found in either the *Mānavadharmaśāstra* or the *Arthaśāstra*. (Knutson 2021: xiii suggests it "presents spiritual self-control as the model for rule.") It is my view that, of all the technical works examined for this book, it is the closest in spirit to the disposition of the narrative literatures.

question consists in performing a highly cultivated personal virtue, which leads one to act in ways that produce measurable and favorable results, sometimes ruthlessly but always with discretion, control, and self-restraint.

Royal Counsel and Counsellors in Sanskrit Narrative Literatures

brāhmaṇenaidhitaṃ kṣatraṃ mantrimantrābhimantritam |
jayaty ajitam atyantaṃ śāstrānugam aśastritam || *Arthaśāstra* 1.9.11 ||

Royal power (kṣatra) prevails that is ignited by a Brahmin and consecrated by the counsel (mantra) of counsellors (mantrin); it is ever and always unsurpassed, unconquered, so long as it accords with the treatise [that is the *Arthaśāstra*].[16]

Kings, then, are said to do well for themselves and their subjects by being good. *Dharma* produces *artha*, *kāma*, and even liberation along the way.[17] But kings and princes are hardly asked to act alone. To develop and act out a wisdom born from self-restraint, these narratives explicitly and implicitly argue that the royal sovereign must engage and adopt the considered counsel of trusted advisors.[18] Just as is recommended in various Dharmaśāstras and in the later redaction of the *Arthaśāstra* and other Arthaśāstric works, the kings and princes who are almost invariably the protagonists of the narrative literatures deeply engage with Brahmins as their companions and advisors.[19]

[16] This translation is an adaptation of that of Olivelle 2013: 75. See also Schetelich 1997/1998 for a treatment of the same, which is attentive to its complex polysemy and reviews both Kangle's and Meyer's translations thereof.

[17] To offer but one example from the technical literature, see *Nītisāra* 1.51ab: *dharmād artho 'rthataḥ kāmaḥ kāmāt sukhaphalodayaḥ* |. "*Dharma* produces wealth (*artha*); wealth, pleasure (*kāma*); [and] pleasure produces the fruits of happiness."

[18] This is, of course, a central feature of political culture in South Asia, one known even since the time of the early Greek encounters with India, for which see, e.g., Halbfass [1981] 1988: 12.

[19] On types of ministers in the king's ministry and the royal sovereign's dependence thereon, see, e.g., Altekar [1949] 1962: 160–186. McClish 2019 charts the formation of a Brahminically influenced redaction of the *Arthaśāstra* overlaying Brahminical norms on the text (about which see also Olivelle 2013: 6–25); Kāmandaki at *Nītisāra* 1.61–68 suggests those (kings) who are of chastened senses should serve a wise guru, whether in seeking political or spiritual accomplishment. The *Mahābhārata* repeatedly claims kings need their Brahminical counselors, as, for example, at *Mahābhārata* 3.110.19–21, which suggests that King Lomapāda, a friend of Daśaratha, was abandoned by his Brahmins for acting unfaithfully and untruthfully toward them, and because he lost his household priest (*purohita*) he found that Indra ensured it would not rain on his kingdom. See also *Nītisāra* 1.61–71, which suggests that a king who has mastered his senses may properly engage wise men for counsel. Finally, see also, e.g., *Mānavadharmaśāstra* 7.54–59, which recommends the king

Kings, as Adheesh Sathaye has noted, are told to honor the "*a priori* social superiority of Brahmins" if they wish to be "good" *kṣatriyas*.[20] Brahmins are held to make for good company, moreover, precisely because they are themselves said habitually to develop the very personal virtues that cultivate clear thinking and effective decision-making. Simply put, the narrative literatures implicitly and explicitly communicate the claim that Brahminical counsel and company intrinsically serve to cultivate the virtues necessary for members of the royal court to achieve their ends.

These stories thus may be said to lend themselves to a study of the culture of political power in premodern South Asia precisely because they so regularly tend to the mutual relations of the paradigmatic agents of the royal court—Brahmins and kings. Indeed, the first, foundational claim of this book is precisely that the narrative works examined herein invariably affirm the vitality of the famed *brāhmaṇa-kṣatriya* alliance to which Sanskrit-language theoretical and scriptural works repeatedly attest.[21] All the narratives examined herein evoke the relationship in question by presenting framing stories that feature the alliance, by recommending it as conducive to proper conduct in

obtain some seven or eight counselors (*saciva*, on the meaning of which see Olivelle 2005: 295, note at 7.54, which also refers the reader to Scharfe 1993: 125–137), from one among whom, a Brahmin, he should seek the highest counsel regarding the sixfold strategy of dealing with other kingdoms by making peace, war, and so forth.

[20] See Sathaye 2015: 92.

[21] See Ghoshal 1923: 44–45, 46–47, 47–50, 52–54, 62–63 and 66–67, and 108–110 respectively for discussions of the *brāhmaṇa-kṣatriya* bond in the Vedic Saṃhitās and Brāhmaṇas; the joint divinity of the two classes as expressed in the *Taittirīyasaṃhitā* and the *Śatapathabrāhmaṇa*; their mutual relations recommended in the Brāhmaṇas more broadly; Vedic conceptions of Brāhmaṇas' divinity; their mutual relations in the Dharmasūtras; and the doctrine of "joint lordship" as expressed in the *Arthaśāstra*. On sacerdotal links between the two, see, e.g., Roy 1994: 127–129.

There are, of course, exceptions, as Brian Collins (2020) has illustrated in his study of the "other" Rāma, the core thesis of his book being that the Paraśurāma myth serves to negotiate such social tensions and explore and negotiate the place of violence in forming, maintaining, and challenging the same, with particular attention to the *brāhmaṇa-kṣatriya* alliance. See Collins 2020: 215, 217, 254–255, and *passim*. See also Roy 1994: 143–150 on the competitive nature of the alliance, expressed in ritual in, among other works, the *Śatapathabrāhmaṇa*. Shulman's outstanding study (Shulman 1985), in turn, on which Collins's book appears to be modeled, also examines the agonistic dimensions of the *brāhmaṇa-kṣatriya* relationship, mapping the contravening tendencies of kingship, its *pravṛtti* and *nivṛtti* movements, in South Indian, Tamil literature, both past and present. Shulman not only centers mythology more than I do here in the present volume, which is significant because myth explores such fissures and tensions more readily than do the works examined herein, but also takes in the Vedic ritual models of social relation and tensions, for example, as examined by Jan Heesterman (I think the concerns are best represented in Heesterman 1985 and 1993), which also more readily explore tensions and ruptures in the *brāhmaṇa-kṣatriya* alliance. Finally, note that Sathaye 2007 similarly maps certain rifts in the *brāhmaṇa-kṣatriya* bond through an analysis of the figure of Viśvāmitra. The present volume instead charts the ways in which the narratives here placed under study, *in their core narratives and framing tropes*, emphasize the productive, implicitly beneficial nature of the relationship between the (*kṣatriya*-caste) king and his (*brāhmaṇa*-caste) advisors, and this rather emphatically so.

the administration of the state, or by favorably deploying the *brāhmaṇa-kṣatriya* bond in their narratives as an element that shapes positive turns of events in their stories.

A pervasive emphasis in narrative on royal counsel and the fruits of the *brāhmaṇa-kṣatriya* relationship should come as no surprise. They in fact present as the likeliest of possible tropes given what the theoretical literatures have to say about the same.[22] The king and his ministers are counted as the first two of, and the first and second in importance among, what are identified as the seven fundamental constituents of a kingdom, for example, according to Kauṭilya,[23] a position also echoed by Kāmandaki, who repeatedly admonishes kings to take good counsel.[24] The *Arthaśāstra* similarly identifies good advice as one of the three fundamental strengths of the king, or as Olivelle succinctly put it in the introduction to his landmark rendering of this landmark work on statecraft, "all undertakings presuppose counsel."[25] Trusted ministers were the king's eyes, Kauṭilya further declares;[26] and good counsel, as Aiyangar noted, would have been indispensable to a king who sought to understand and perpetuate the laws and local customs pre-existing his reign, a practice of continuity that was generally recommended and followed by new kings upon gaining power.[27]

Good counsel is indispensable most of all for measurable, knowable reasons. Indeed, it is vital to underscore the singular quality of good advice as identified in the narratives here examined. *All good counsel is efficacious.* Virtue produces results, and good counsel must facilitate the same. Thus,

[22] Thus, Aiyangar (1935: 75) on Kauṭilya says the following (here citing in summary form what he counts as *Arthaśastra* 1.6, found in Kangle's edition and in Olivelle's translation at *Arthaśāstra* 1.7.9): *sahāyasādhyaṃ rājatvaṃ cakram ekaṃ na vartate | kurvīta sacivāṃs tasmāt teṣāṃ ca śṛṇuyān matam* ||: "Thus Kauṭilya does not hold that the king could see and do everything personally for his kingdom. As a wheel cannot turn itself, so a king cannot govern by himself. He accordingly needs ministers." Cf. Spellman 1964: 69.

[23] See *Arthaśāstra* 6.1.1. After the king himself (*svāmi*) and his ministers (*amātya*) are enumerated the kingdom (*janapada*), forts and fortifications (*durga*), the treasury (*kośa*), the army (*daṇḍa*), and allies (*mitra*).

[24] See *Nītisāra* 7.1, where the list includes a slightly different terminology: *svāmi, amātya, rāṣṭra, durga, kośa, bala*, and *suhṛt*.

[25] See *Arthaśāstra* 1.15.2, cited too by Olivelle 2013: 40 in his introduction to his translation of this text.

[26] See Aiyangar 1935: 88–89.

[27] See Aiyangar 1935: 91 and 103–104. Related to this is the fact that the *Arthaśāstra* reflects a general cultural value around the royal court in suggesting that it is vital to a king's success for him to cultivate satisfaction among his subjects (at *Arthaśāstra* 1.4.11–15, e.g., Kauṭilya suggests punishment properly ordered is conducive to *dharma, artha*, and *kāma*, but improperly applied it leads forest dwellers and ascetics—and householders—to violent revolt, an endeavor that requires the very eyes and ears—and institutional memory—of good counselors).

while the pathway to success in action is the cultivation of virtue, the measure of choice in action, of effective counsel, is ultimately consequentialist. The implicit claims of the narratives are *both* that only the virtuous can offer good counsel and put it to proper effect and that the proof of the quality of the counsel given is visible in its results—success in pursuing *dharma*, *artha*, *kāma*, and *mokṣa* or *svarga* or immortality.

Theological, Doctrinal, and Religious Justifications of the Brāhmaṇa-kṣatriya Alliance

Though virtue and the counsel that effects and is affected by it are said to produce measurable results, the narratives in question and various Sanskrit theoretical works on *dharma* and statecraft also offer more plainly theological and doctrinal justifications for the *brāhmaṇa-kṣatriya* alliance. Take, for example, the claim that Brahmins were created before all other humans and are innately superior, which is found in the Śāntiparvan of the *Mahābhārata*,[28] this book, as is well known, offering a foundational statement on the nature of the *dharma* of the king. Elsewhere therein it is suggested that Brahmins stand as the source or origin of *dharma* itself.[29] The *Mānavadharmaśāstra* similarly depicts the life of Brahmins in terms that are applicable to all the four *varṇas*, because they are said uniquely to embody *dharma* and therefore to serve as the normative model thereof.[30]

The Śāntiparvan further states that Brahmins and *kṣatriyas* are right to rely on one another, because when they honor one another the people prosper.[31] It also claims that the link between the two social classes is self-made and self-reinforcing: without the preserving force of *kṣatriyadharma*

[28] See *Mahābhārata* 12.329, esp. 12.329.5, where Brahmins and Kṣatriyas are ranked in a hierarchical order, the former superior to the latter, and this in a manner that corresponds to stages of the creation of the universe.

[29] See *Mahābhārata* 12.91.19ab, where Bhīṣma in explaining the ways in which a king may rule virtuously tells Yudhiṣṭhira that kings must honor Brahmins: *dharmasya brāhmaṇā yonis tasmāt tān pūjayet sadā* |. "Brahmins are the well-source of *dharma*. Therefore [the king] must always honor them."

[30] This is the observation of Olivelle 2004b: xxxi–xxxii, which further indicates (2004b: xxxii–xxxv) that the *Mānavadharmaśāstra* represents the life of *kṣatriyas* in terms that are specific to the tasks of that class, in particular those of the king, who is featured in the section on the *dharma* of *kṣatriyas* and essentially identified with them. This is to say that the conduct of Brahmins, unlike that of *kṣatriyas*, is uniquely written in Manu as paradigmatic for *all* the *varṇas*, meaning it only follows that one should cultivate their company.

[31] See *Mahābhārata* 12.74, esp. 12.74.4cd: *brahmakṣatrasya saṃmānāt prajāḥ sukham avāpnuyuḥ* |.

there would be no Brahmins at all, no *dharma*, no classes of society, and no stages of life.[32] It is similarly stated in the Anuśāsanaparvan that honoring and protecting Brahmins should be the royal sovereign's first priority, because they are intrinsically both dangerous and powerful, able to make and break kings.[33]

The consequences of the alliance too are sometimes spoken of in what can be labeled theological terms. It is repeatedly stated, for example, that the king himself creates the cosmic eon in which he and his family and subjects will live out their time in the world, be it the pristine Satya age or the Tretā, the Dvāpara, or the most decrepit one—that of the present day, the Kali Yuga—each being manifested by way of the royal sovereign's capacity or incapacity to act well.[34] So too is the king said quite literally to make it rain: he himself can guarantee a bountiful harvest simply by maintaining personal virtue, while the opposite results from his transgressing of *dharma*.[35]

Theoretical works on kingship further claim that the king himself embodies the gods, the parts of his person manifesting various powerful deities who effect particular results in the world.[36] Brahmins are of course also repeatedly called to support *kṣatriya*s in sacerdotal ways, by performing rituals and deploying magical spells that counteract poisons, stop enemy activity, or address like concerns. This suggests that desired ends can be produced not merely by the kind of (rationally ordered) wisdom in action that is featured in the narrative literatures but also by way of what may be described as supernatural or supernormal interventions as well, with Brahmins offering kings access to just that.

Most importantly—this fact is reprehensible and will be discussed further in the conclusion to this book—both Dharmaśāstric and narrative works sometimes claim that kingship properly engaged effects what they (wrongly and deplorably) count as a social good: the perpetuation of caste hierarchy and caste discrimination. The Śāntiparvan of the *Mahābhārata*, for one, notes that the chastened king stops caste miscegenation, and it understands separation by caste identity (*varṇa*) to be a desired

[32] See *Mahābhārata* 12.64.23–29. As is tragically so often the case in Sanskrit literature, this reference counts the preservation of *varṇa*-based differences—caste-based hierarchy—as an innately desirable social force.

[33] See *Mahābhārata* 13.33.2.

[34] See *Mahābhārata* 12.70.6d (*rājā kālasya kāraṇam* |) and following.

[35] See, e.g., *Mahābhārata* 1.58.14. *Nītisāra* 5.60 similarly compares the king to a rain cloud.

[36] See Ghoshal 1923: 94–95, citing there *Mahābhārata* 12.68.41*ff*. The king is also said to be possessed of the nature of being a god on earth (*bhūtaladevatva*) at *Nītisāra* 4.4.

end.[37] The king elsewhere is regularly lauded as the very power that perpetuates distinction in the social classes, by which is meant the preservation of distinct and limited social roles defined by *varṇa*.[38]

All of this clearly indicates that the narrative literatures work in a cultural context in which their audiences would have implicitly understood the social influence and therefore importance of the principal characters of their stories. The theological and doctrinal praise of kings, their Brahminical advisors, and their mutually beneficial relations would have been known to those who engaged the stories that we shall examine in the following pages. The thoughts and actions of the characters in these stories, then, were all but inevitably to have been received as of interest and importance to worldly affairs.

Choice of Focus in the Narrative Literatures

Though a particular emphasis in narrative on the importance of the *brāhmaṇa-kṣatriya* alliance is to be expected, it nevertheless also involves choice, and a honing of focus, for Sanskrit-language technical works that deal with kingship, the royal court, and statecraft address a truly staggering range of concerns beyond merely the value of Brahminical company and good royal counsel, any of which could be set as central features in narratives about princes and kings. Consider, first, that the key topics extensively addressed in Kauṭilya's *Arthaśāstra* include the cultivation of economic activity; taxation; government administration; the maintenance of a powerful military and the construction and operation of defensive installations such as forts and fortified outposts; spying and other intelligence efforts; negotiating peace treaties; the forming of alliances and sowing of dissension among neighboring polities; and the functioning of the legal system and systems of corporeal and other types of punishment.[39]

Within the ambit of the science of statecraft itself is singled out the particular matter of the administration of justice, or *daṇḍanīti*, an emic category of such importance that it is discussed at length in the Dharmaśāstras,

[37] See, e.g., *Mahābhārata* 12.49, where caste mixing is described in the context of telling the story of Rāma Jāmadagnya. Cf., e.g., *Nītisāra* 2.18–35, which enumerates the proper social roles by caste status.

[38] See *Mahābhārata* 12.68.29.

[39] As is well known, the Kauṭilīya *Arthaśāstra* begins with a summary account of its contents, for which see *Arthaśāstra* 1.1–17.

in the Arthaśāstras, and elsewhere.[40] The *Nītisāra*, for example, echoes the *Arthaśāstra* in stating that kingship is punishment, full stop,[41] just as punishment also figures prominently in the *Mānavadharmaśāstra*'s treatment of the duty of kings.[42]

One similarly could render specific attention to the disciplined practices of women (*strīdharma*), or those appropriate for war (*dharmayuddha*) or emergencies (*āpaddharma*), as these are other emic areas of analysis and practice that constitute significant subcategories of concern in the Dharmaśāstras and, sometimes, the Arthaśāstras. One even could meditate on the semantic differences between *nītiśāstra* and *arthaśāstra*, respectively the sciences of good political conduct and of wealth or power or success, each fundamental to royal disciplines but offering nuanced emphasis in describing the same.

Beyond this array of concerns in governance stand issues of personal discipline and personal relations, which were as much constitutive of premodern political theory or political philosophy as they often are of modern and contemporary forms of the same, be they either South Asian or Western. Gender relations and sexuality, for example, were of central concern, minimally in the sense that whom one married could determine who could inherit power. To appreciate fully premodern political philosophy in South Asia thus requires one also to tend to the various concerns addressed in the Kāmaśastra, the science of pleasure.

Finally, and perhaps most conspicuously, at least when it comes to thinking of the intersection of "religion and politics" in premodern South Asia, one must consider the functioning of the royal sovereign vis-à-vis sacerdotal matters, what might be counted under the broad category of the disciplined practices of kings (*rājadharma*). The fact, for example, that Kauṭilya's *Arthaśāstra* and other Arthaśāstric works frequently mention the religious officiants of the Atharvaveda, so too the power of spells and like concerns, suggests an explicitly religious theme that could have framed and defined the storylines of the narratives in question.[43] And yet, I argue, the major and organizing narrative trope that is found in all of the landmark narrative works examined in this book, as well as in other narratives beyond

[40] So much is discussed in all the secondary literature on kingship and the science of governance as defined in Sanskrit sources. See, e.g., Spellman 1964: 5 and *passim*.

[41] See *Nītisāra* 14.37c: *daṇḍaprāyo hi nṛpatir*.

[42] See esp. *Mānavadharmaśāstra* 7.14–31.

[43] But one of a host of possible examples thereof may be found at *Arthaśāstra* 4.3.17, spells from the *Atharvaveda* there being used to kill snakes.

them, articulates, evokes, and supports the dogma that virtue in personal conduct is conducive to measurable, material success in the world of affairs.

To be clear: the aforementioned—and many other—themes are addressed, sometimes at length, in both the narrative literatures generally and the individual works that will be examined in this book. The *Mahābhārata* in particular might fruitfully be read as an exhaustive compendium of stories about kingship and statecraft in all their dimensions. Other narratives examined herein also take up some of the concerns cataloged above, for example, the quest to win wives in the *Kathāsaritsāgara* or the nature of love in the *Rāmāyaṇa*.[44] Nevertheless, the *brāhmaṇa-kṣatriya* alliance regularly frames and substantially defines the narratives in question, presenting itself as a highly—perhaps even uniquely—prominent trope thereof, and this in the context of *dharmic* advice being imparted, explicitly and implicitly, by learned Brahmins counseling the royal sovereign on conduct in affairs of the state. This is to say that while many concerns that are defined in Sanskrit-language political-philosophical works and are addressed in the texts here examined are largely left out in the chapters that follow this introduction, this is so not only for the elected focus of this study but also because the narrative literatures examined in question themselves privilege the theme in question, emphasizing as they do in their narrative framing and in many of their major narrative developments the (frankly male-centered and upper-caste-focused) dynamic between princes and kings, on the one hand, and Brahminical political counselors, on the other hand.

The Selection of Texts

But how were the narratives examined in this book chosen for review and why? What justifies their selection from among the vast and heterogenous narrative literatures written in Sanskrit? What does one accomplish by reading them as a set?

On the one hand, the collection of works analyzed herein is surely incomplete when measured against the canon of extant Sanskrit-language narrative writings, composed as it is of hundreds of texts that are often mutually

[44] Reading Sanskrit narratives *primarily* in light of the *Kāmasūtra* as well as the *Arthaśāstra* promises to be a fruitful proposition. A path forward would be assisted by tending to the claims made in Doniger 2018, which weighs these two works in mutual relation and considers their common, adversarial disposition vis-à-vis the more Brahminically conservative, Dharmaśāstric tradition.

constituted and mutually referential in their narrative contents. Selection, on the other hand, is inevitable in any scholarly account that seeks to find patterns of interaction among multiple Sanskrit literary narratives, simply because no single monograph—perhaps no single academic career—could explore the entire range of works written in Sanskrit that narrate stories of one kind or another. One can hardly imagine a more expansive—and creative—tradition of narrative literary production in the premodern world, and it would be a fool's errand to endeavor comprehensively to examine "Sanskrit narratives," broadly conceived—at least, that is, if one wishes to do so with a greater attention to detail than may be found in the major extant surveys of Sanskrit literature.[45]

I will say more presently about the (1) thematic coherence, (2) intertextuality, (3) prominence, and (4) literary realism of the works examined in the following chapters, all of which serve as criteria for narrowing the selection of texts to be examined in this volume. Consider first, however, the wide variety and number of items written in Sanskrit that one may properly count under the etic and general category of "narrative literature."[46] Among them are the numerous, often but not exclusively "mythological," works that are emically classed as Purāṇas, an in fact ranging genre that includes localized as well as trans-local works of great variety in their contents, which were written over the course of hundreds of years.[47] Included as well are the two major Sanskrit epics, written in verse and classed within the tradition as Itihāsa, traditional accounts of heroic historical events (examined here and following in Chapters 1 and 2). Also composed in Sanskrit were numerous dramatic works of various types (*rūpaka*), conceived of as ten in number in the *Nāṭyaśāstra*.[48] Still other, poetic narratives include not only the famed Mahākāvyas but also a host of other works such as narrative poetry, for example, the *Kuṭṭanīmata* of Dāmodaragupta, which is to be examined, as noted already, in Chapter 5.

Still other works are counted in the Indian tradition as story literatures proper, including both what are emically labeled as fictive narratives, the

[45] See MacDonell [1900] 1962; Keith [1920] 1966; Krishnamachariar [1937] 1974; Warder [1974] 1990 and 1990; and Winternitz 1908, 1927, 1933, and [1963, 1965] 1985.

[46] Such an etic category is of course a heuristic. Maurice Bloomfield famously innovated one of his own, "Hindu fiction," which, while imperfect, captured a literary direction in Sanskrit, just as, I would argue, the label "narrative literatures" does as well. See, e.g., Bloomfield 1917 and 1924; cf. Silk 2020: 281.

[47] For a detailed survey of this genre of literature see the well-known study of Rocher 1986.

[48] See, e.g., Keith 1924: 345–351. Eighteen subsidiary types or *uparūpakas* also exist in the normative classification of dramatic works, as is well known.

kathā literature, or alternatively as more historically grounded stories, the *ākhyāyikās*.[49] Selected texts of the *nīti* literature are similar to the *Pañcatantra*, in turn, for their narrative articulation of political ideas; and the *Pañcatantra* is ultimately something of a genre of works unto itself, rather than a single title,[50] one that nests stories within stories about animals that are narrated for explicitly didactic purposes. Then there are works that describe royal lineages and local geographies, the Vaṃśāvalī literature, which may be said to be similar to the *Rājataraṅgiṇī* in that they narrate history as story and therefore could have been included in a volume such as the present one.[51] Finally, even the narrowing of works examined to those written in Sanskrit involves selection, there of course being countless narratives from premodern South Asia written in a host of other languages and representing both Brahminical and non-Brahminical traditions along the way.

With such a diversity of narrative textual material in view, I have narrowed the selection of texts first and foremost by including works that can and must be read together inasmuch as they relate the very concern described, above: a culture of kingship and the royal court existed in South Asian premodernity that was fundamentally directed toward the cultivation of successful human endeavor. One needs this array of texts, because it captures a key sensibility articulated in narrative concerning the proper acts and roles and ways of being that are deemed appropriate for the royal sovereign and the counsellors to the crown; it captures the virtue ethic of the Sanskrit narratives. Thematic coherence is thus the first reason to assemble the works included in this volume, which tell an important story about normative views of political action in premodern South Asia.

Second, the selected works merit inclusion because they exhibit an explicit and intricate intertextuality,[52] albeit of varying directionality and

[49] The distinction in question is of course well known. See, e.g., De 1924: 512: "The *ākhyāyikā* was more or less a serious composition dealing generally with facts of actual experience with an autobiographical or semi-historical interest; while the *kathā* was essentially a fictitious narrative—which may sometimes (as Daṇḍin contends) possess an autobiographical form, but whose interest chiefly resides in its invention."

[50] The existence of two Jain versions of the text, in particular, demands further investigation into their particularities. On the various recensions that influenced Pūrṇabhadra's twelfth-century version of the tales, see Hertel 1912: 5–21. See also M. Taylor 2007.

[51] On the relation of Vaṃśāvalī works to the *Rājataraṅgiṇī* see Witzel 1990.

[52] The formation and function of textual authority in the context of multiple textual sources require further reflection and theorization, though I have made an effort at just this in Nemec 2020a. Generally speaking, to read texts in mutual relation is indispensable to the study of Indian culture and religions, which have always been textually pluralistic and intertextually embedded. From the time of the Vedas, scriptural authority has been defined by the presence of multiple texts, no singular "Bible" defining the scriptural landscape. One similarly sees in the *Mahābhārata*, to offer a second

degree. Thus, the *Rāmāyaṇa* and the *Mahābhārata* are thematically mutually formed and implicitly mutually referential, and the *Rājataraṅgiṇī* is explicitly said to be modeled on the latter.[53] Kālidāsa's famed play, the *Abhijñānaśākuntala*, in turn, repeatedly echoes the *Rāmāyaṇa* (as I shall argue in Chapter 5), and Dāmodaragupta's brilliant and entertaining poetic narrative, the *Kuṭṭanīmata* or "Bawd's Counsel,"[54] narrates a performance of the other of the two plays examined in this book, the *Ratnāvalī*. The *Ratnāvalī* in turn offers a narrative plot that is echoed in the *Kathāsaritsāgara*, while the *Kathāsaritsāgara*, itself a retelling of the *Bṛhatkathā* (by way of an intermediary, Kashmirian version of the story), in turn is both modeled on the plot of the *Rāmāyaṇa*[55] and includes within it a full narration of the *Pañcatantra*.[56] Finally, the *Pañcatantra* echoes the *Kathāsaritsāgara* and cites the two epics, all while it encapsulates the culture of the royal court as one requiring the cultivation of wisdom in action, which is explored in depth in the *Kathāsaritsāgara*, the *Rājataraṅgiṇī*, the epics, and across the gamut of Sanskrit-language narrative works.[57] Simply put, these texts are deeply mutually cognizant, and it is a fundamental argument of this book that to know them well requires one to read their stories in mutual relation. Indeed, to

example, a habit of reading across texts—plural—to find the proper source of authority (regarding *dharma* and proper action in the present instance). In a word, textual authority has always been multiple in the Indian context, and how this has been and is so merits further scholarly reflection.

[53] Kalhaṇa's masterwork has come in for significant new analysis of late, in particular in a special issue of the *Indian Economic and Social History Review* of 2013 in which are found contributions of Whitney Cox, Yigal Bronner, Daud Ali, Luther Obrock, Chitralekha Zutshi, and Lawrence McCrea, with a guiding preface, revising too his own view of the text, of David Shulman. Also of note is a recent monograph of Shonaleeka Kaul (2018). These items are examined in Chapter 3. Finally, see, e.g., Hopkins [1901] 1969: 58–84 for a relatively early view of the intertextuality of the two epics.

[54] See Dezső and Goodall 2012 for a new edition and translation of this striking poem.

[55] See Lacôte 1908: 230, cited also in Nelson 1974: 321. Cf. Lacôte 1908: 276.

[56] Note also that Kṣemendra himself associated the *Kathāsaritsāgara* with both the *Mahābhārata* and the *Rāmāyaṇa*, these being the three narratives for which he writes "Bouquets" or *Mañjarī* retellings, as Lacôte 1908: 10 remarked some time ago.

[57] In fact, the *Pañcatantra* echoes the message of the *Arthaśāstra*—success is its own reward—but only while also representing the fundamental concern of the other works examined in this book, namely, the need to act efficaciously and with virtuosity in matters of kingship and the state. What distinguishes it from the *Arthaśāstra* is a sensitivity to trust one's judgment of others, even if doing so sets one to trust against the evident "true nature" or objective circumstances of the person in question. The *Arthaśāstra* is more directly strategic and tactical than this, viewing the world through the lens of measurable categories—a weak king, an unpopular king, and so forth—and with a more single-minded ambition for the king to increase his influence, sovereignty, and wealth. In a word, while both texts share a kind of consequentialism in their ethical orientation, the *Pañcatantra* implicitly and explicitly acknowledges the virtuosity of the royal sovereign to a degree not evinced in the *Arthaśāstra* (on my reading of that work, at least), and in doing so the *Pañcatantra* also captures something of the spirit of the core message of the narrative literatures as I have identified it in this monograph.

tend to the mutual relation of stories is the natural mode of reading in premodern South Asia.

Third, I narrowed the selection by tending toward narratives that would have been widely circulated in the subcontinent, but with an emphasis too on what would have had currency in my own regional area and period of specialization: the Kashmir Valley in the centuries around—in the present study, just after—the turn of the second millennium. It is my contention that the vision of the culture of the royal court that is highlighted by reading the selected materials is likely to have been well known there by the time all the works in question were composed and sufficiently circulated. This claim is of course inferential and speculative in nature, however, as the history of the premodern reception of these works "on the ground" will never be more than only partially known. Nevertheless, the very prominence, the widespread citation and internal and external references of and to these works, warrants the claim that these texts and their stories, read together, represent a well-understood, though of course idealized, model of thinking about kingship in the time and place in question.

Fourth and finally, the selected texts speak in a realist voice. The realism I see in these works is not a simple, mimetic one that reflects invariable correspondence to contemporaneous quotidian realities, however. These texts offer a window into the premodern literary *imaginaire* around political office and the court,[58] the culture of which Daud Ali examined insightfully in a striking monograph-length study,[59] and they do so precisely inasmuch as they present verisimilitudinous representations of contemporaneous attitudes and expectations. Specifically, I understand the works in question to speak in voices of genric verisimilitude, which I argue reflect a cultural verisimilitude that is dateable to the time when the texts had all been composed and were widely circulated and engaged.[60]

[58] The concept of the *imaginaire* is well known in the study of religion. The foundational notion that corporate or social identity is in part constructed, imagined, and no less real for being imagined may be found with Anderson 1991 (about which see also, e.g., Asad 2003: 194). Anderson, in turn, owes much to the fundamental work of Gellner 1983. Sympathetic with the same (though *mutatis mutandis*) is Bellah 1975. Application of these approaches to culture and religion may be found in ways implicitly and explicitly informative—and expressive—of my understanding of the concept and functioning of an *imaginaire* in Lincoln 1999, Nemec 2020a, and Schilbrack 2010. Finally, like Pollock (1989: 604, esp. fn. 7), I am influenced in my thinking about narrative and history—and the construction and articulation of a culturally formed and reiterated consciousness by and around the same—by the writings of Paul Ricoeur, esp. Ricoeur 1979 and Ricoeur 1981; see also Ricoeur 1990.

[59] Ali 2004.

[60] The distinction between genric and cultural verisimilitude is represented in Neale 1980. Differentiating realism from verisimilitude on the basis of the notion that what is represented in artistically ordered narratives is ever and always constructed, Neale understands the verisimilitude of

Genric verisimilitude can simultaneously reveal a degree of cultural verisimilitude in popular works of art. This can be so even in instances when creative works present their audiences with what is fantastic or even magical, because the characters and events of such stories continue to conform to cultural norms within the confines of the given narrative's genric conceits. Superman could fly, for example, while mere mortals cannot; but he fell in love, worried about justice, helped the helpless, and cared for innocent strangers in ways that regular people inside and outside the narrative did and would do. The animals who speak and act in the *Pañcatantra*, to offer another example, find no literal correspondence in the world outside the text, where birds and deer and lions do not speak as humans do; yet, within the bounds of the genre, the characters in question behave in ways that are explicitly meant to reflect contemporaneous attitudes and possibilities in engaging the political concerns of the day.

Selecting works that speak in this mode excludes whole numbers of texts,[61] but it also promises access to a cultural verisimilitude by way of genric verisimilitude, for three principal reasons. First, all the works examined grapple with real-life concerns, even if in sometimes contrived or even fantastical contexts. The texts examined in this book realistically represent human choices, actions, and the considered reflection of the major agents in their

works of art to lie not primarily in their simple correspondence with what is actually the case in the world outside the works in question but in their correspondence with what dominant cultural views maintained was, and accepted as, real. Genric verisimilitude refers in particular to representations that conform to the expectations of the genre of art in question, whereas cultural verisimilitude refers to the correspondence of the same with the norms, mores, and ideals and expectations outside the work in question. This, anyhow, is how Hall [1997] 2003: 360–361 summarizes the matter. See Neale 1980: 36–41, esp. 37, where he deals with the fetishism of film (the refusal to recognize the difference between reality and the representation of the cinematic production), suggesting that genres more directly engaging "realism," on the one hand, such as historical narratives, and those that are "more fictional" and engaged in fantasy, on the other, such as horror films, engage their audiences in accepting their authenticity in differing ways, this according to genric norms.

[61] Many of the Purāṇas are excluded by this standard, for example, for while they often convey a cultural verisimilitude, they also can be more difficult to interpret when they engage largely or nearly exclusively with the extra-human—the worlds of the gods. This is so because to interpret such works one must read metaphorically and not analogically. This is *not* to argue that such works are less revealing of the kinds of cultural attitudes and preferences that are probed by way of literary analysis in this book, however. It is only to say the interpretive challenges with mythologically oriented Purāṇic works are sometimes significant and are not set within the ambit of the present volume.

Similarly excluded on this criterion are Vedic works that speak allegorically or in terms deeply embedded in the syntax of ritual. Such sources can offer much in the way of insight into contemporaneous cultural attitudes, particularly those related to kingship and the exercise of political power, as scholars such as Jan Heesterman have illustrated in abundance. They nevertheless can present with real interpretive complications, which the realist narratives examined in this book can avoid (not to say completely) for presenting with a markedly closer correspondence of representation with quotidian life.

narratives in a manner that must reflect contemporaneous preferences and ideals if they were to have had any narrative appeal at all.[62]

Second is the very frequency with which the primary concern of this book is represented in the literatures in question. Brahmins and kings and princes caper together from adventure to adventure so frequently and in a manner so regularly conducive to successful action as to compel one to see the phenomenon as an expected—and a wished-for—ideal outside the texts.[63]

Third and most importantly, the narratives in question work implicitly or explicitly to minimize the differences or lower the boundary between the characters internal to the narratives and the audiences who received their stories.[64] While this is more or less true of almost all good stories, the degree to which internal and external persons are set in mutual relation or are mutually identified in the selected texts is sometimes simply astounding. (I shall have more to say about this in what follows in the section of the Introduction entitled "The Lives of the Texts: Internal and External Audiences, Normative and Constructive Modes.") So much, what is a distinctly dialogical quality of the works examined in this book, directly suggests that the stories in question offered prescriptions for and descriptions of idealized practice in the world outside the texts: by homologizing the narrative characters with the texts' audiences, they suggest their stories are for their audiences precisely inasmuch as they ultimately are also stories about their audiences.

[62] Seeking to marry, for example, would have been a realistic ambition for any prince, reflecting the real concerns to marry well, enjoy life, and perpetuate the lineage of royal sovereigns through the birth of sons. So much is literally (and literarily) represented in the *Kathāsaritsāgara*, for example (as examined in Chapter 4), even while its narrative includes moments of interaction among the gods in heavens, travel via a magical tunnel under the sea, conversations with undead *vetāla*s, and similar extraordinary phenomena. Even so, the text depicts the value of maintaining the *brāhmaṇa-kṣatriya* bond, the need clearly to discern whom one can trust and against whom one must guard oneself, and other, similar concerns around kingship. Simply, the story, despite its extranormal narrative elements, fairly and clearly represents human concerns of the day. And within the logic of the narrative—*vetāla*s by the mores of the genre can teleport themselves to a tree in the cremation ground—the characters in question act with a degree of reason in choice that reflects contemporaneous norms and possibilities. The famed animal fables of India, the *Pañcatantra* (examined in Chapter 6), offer a second and perhaps more direct example of verisimilitude, as noted already. They show a deep and sophisticated reflection on kingship and the administration of the state even while doing so by way of fictitiously personifying various species of animals and setting them in mutual contact.

[63] This is not to claim any historical accuracy to the narrative rhetoric of these texts, however, only to suggest that they convey attitudes and sentiments about a sociological institution that did indeed exist and function outside the narratives and in the daily lives of their audiences.

[64] Indeed, a mode of instruction is found in the texts examined in this book, which mirrors that of the *Mānavadharmaśāstra*. As Olivelle 2004b: xxvi has noted, that work seeks to fuse internal and external audiences of the text in its narrative framing, where he finds five layers of " 'telling', 'hearing', and re-telling," the last of which consists of the readers or hearers of the text itself as the audience.

Modes of Reading, Historical Location, and the Synchrony of the Present Analysis

By representing ideals that could have been or, *mutatis mutandis*, still could be put into place in the cultural worlds in which the texts in question had a purchase on their audiences, these stories may thus be said to offer lessons for real-world action in a manner that reflects the recommendation of Kauṭilya's *Arthaśātra*, that political learning may be gained by way of reading narrative.[65] To capture these lessons, I argue that one must first of all read "with the grain," as it were, of the major narrative themes of these works.[66] Examining how the authors of the stories in question frame their narratives and shape the primary arcs of their stories is an effective mode of reading if one wishes to infer what these stories reveal of their audiences' habitual and implicit values and expectations, because the very framing and narrating of the major plotlines fundamentally drive attention and engagement with the stories in question. Such a mode of reading may not regularly furnish documentary evidence of historical realities contemporaneous with their composition, and I seek to make no empiricist historical claims with this study; but it does offer access to what were acceptable or at the least intuitively recognized attitudes and ideals regarding an elite subculture of Indian antiquity.

It also, however, produces an admittedly synchronic analysis of the cultural ideals presented. Despite the limitations thereto, I argue that there is nevertheless a certain value in capturing these ideals even if they are, as it were, somewhat frozen in time, and I have sought to do so in a manner that is perhaps comparable to that of Don Davis's study of the "spirit" of Hindu

[65] Reference there is specifically to the *ākhyāyikās*, however. See Olivelle 2013: 70. We note, moreover, that narratives of the kind examined in this book presented an ideal, and this for an elite audience. See, e.g., Thapar 1978b, which argues that the narrative of the *Rāmāyaṇa* served to justify class difference, the elite for whom it was written being reinforced in their identity, which was supported by their accumulation of land ownership; specifically—and here (1978b: 21) following D. D. Kosambi—she further argues that this epic poem symbolizes the landlord's dominance over peasants by way of Rāma's clear superiority over Hanumān. Cf. also, e.g., Marriott 1976, esp. 125–126 and 128–129, where he speaks of the ways in which *kṣatriyas* and Brahmins engaged modes of transaction that were based in "a unitary Indian concept of superior value" (p. 137), engaged by "dividual persons" (p. 111), who "absorb heterogenous material influences."

[66] Effective as it can be to read "against the grain" of a work to find incidental references or allusions that can date or locate particular peoples, phenomena, religious orders, ideas, or geographies adventitiously and/or inadvertently indicated in text, this book seeks to examine what are self-consciously and primarily issued as the core ideas and concerns of the narratives in question. Rather than mining texts for "data," that is, I here examine the narrative themes, framing, and major plotlines of the selected stories, simply because these are the very elements of story that most capture the imagination and emotions of their audiences. See also Davis 2010: 162–163 for his distinction of "sympathetic" from "transgressive" forms of reading, which is close to the distinction I here wish to make.

law.[67] A certain synchrony of analysis is called for in reading the narratives in question given the consistency and frequency with which they represent what is one of their closest concerns (and is the central focus of this book): the efficaciousness of a virtue ethics for royal sovereigns, who are supported by Brahminical counsel.

The perennial appearance of this core message is indeed striking given the long historical span in which the texts in question were produced. The *Mahābhārata* was likely composed over the course of a few centuries on each side of the advent of the Common Era,[68] while the early core of the *Rāmāyaṇa* likely predates the *Mahābhārata*, though its final composition occurred roughly contemporaneously with it or perhaps just slightly later.[69] The *Pañcatantra*, in turn, is datable to around 300 CE.[70] Both Kauṭilya's *Arthaśāstra* and the *Mānavadharmaśāstra* were composed in the first couple of centuries of the Common Era.[71] Kālidāsa's *Abhijñānaśākuntala* is datable to the fifth century, while Harṣa, author of the *Ratnāvalī*, lived in the seventh century.[72] The *Nītisāra* of Kāmandaki, another technical work that

[67] See Davis 2010: 20–22. While I remain somewhat uneasy with the conceptual emphasis this approach engenders, I, like Davis, can justify it by noting that it "permits us to see the remarkably stable conceptual frameworks of the tradition" (p. 22). One in fact does witness a high degree of consistency in the presentation of this idealized doctrine, offered as it is as timeless Brahminical advice to kings and members of the royal court, and I understand this to suggest there was some desire to make the world reflect this representation in whatever reception of these texts was engendered "on the ground." This, then, is to say that I have much more patience for studying the idealized representation of the *brāhmaṇa-kṣatriya* bond in the Sanskrit narrative literatures than Bisgaard (1994: ix) expresses, for example, in his fascinating study of the social critique of the Brahminical sacerdotal order from within the Sanskrit tradition.

[68] Some scholars have argued for a multiple-staged development over some eight hundred years, from 400 BCE until 400 CE. More recently, Hiltebeitel has argued for a narrower period of composition between 200 BCE and the year zero. On dating this epic see Hiltebeitel 2001: 10–35, esp. 18.

[69] Hiltebeitel 2001: 10–35 examines the scholarly views of the dating of the *Rāmāyaṇa* and suggests (2001: 19) it was composed perhaps slightly later than the *Mahābhārata* but largely within the two-century timeframe he identifies for the latter work's composition, about which see the immediately preceding footnote. Goldman 1984: 14–23 also surveys various views of and approaches to the possible dating of the *Rāmāyaṇa*, noting (1984: 14) a divergence of scholarly views, such that the text's composition has been placed as early as into the sixth millennium BCE and as late as into the fourth century CE.

[70] See Olivelle 1997: xii, which also notes that the translation of the *Pañcatantra* into Pahlavi sets the *terminus ante quem* at around 550 CE and that the scholarly consensus around the 300 CE date is "only an educated guess."

[71] Olivelle 2013: 28–29 suggests a *terminus post quem* for the "Kauṭilya Recension" of the *Arthaśāstra* of the middle of the first century CE and concludes "with some confidence that Kauṭilya composed his treatise sometime between 50 and 125 C.E." A "Śāstric Redaction" of the work, Olivelle (2013: 29–31) further argues, may be dated "not . . . too far off the mark . . . to 175-300 C.E." The *Mānavadharmaśāstra* may be dated to circa the second century CE, though it could be as old as the first century BCE, about which see Olivelle 2004b: xx–xxiii. Cf. Olivelle 2005: 18–25, esp. 25, which suggests a date for the text in the second to third centuries CE.

[72] See Doniger 2006: 15.

has informed this study, was likely composed between the fifth and eighth centuries,[73] while Dāmodaragupta and his *Kuṭṭanīmata* are datable to the Kashmir Valley of the late eighth to early ninth century.[74] Somadeva's *Kathāsaritsāgara*, in turn, is a product of the latter half of the eleventh century,[75] and, finally, Kalhaṇa's *Rājataraṅgiṇī* was completed in the Kashmir Valley in 1148/49 CE.[76] That there is an abiding thematic consistency in these works, then, speaks to the very prominence, vitality, and cultural significance of the major theme examined herein.

The Lives of the Texts: Internal and External Audiences, Normative and Constructive Modes

Still greater confidence may be secured in there having been a welcoming interest in the fundamental theme of the narrative literatures that is identified in this book, if one considers their most dynamic compositional quality. The works here examined dialogically fuse, in greater or lesser degrees, the worlds of their narratives with those of their audiences. They in their very structures and modes of presentation make a narrative place for those who read, hear, or watch them; they even negotiate the entrance of narrative personages into the world outside the texts.

This fusion is evident in the *Rājataraṅgiṇī*, to begin, with the implicit tone in which it is written. It is composed *entre nous*, as it were: the work's inaugural audience included the direct descendants of those about whom it was written, including Brahminical families whose very *agrahāra* lands were endowed by the kings of the chronicle, and many of the members of the royal court who might have encountered the *Rājataraṅgiṇī* were descended from those who were of influence in the same political circles.[77]

[73] See Knutson 2021: vii.

[74] This may be said to be so on the basis of the fact that the *Rājataraṅgiṇī* mentions he was the chief minister to King Jayāpīḍa, who ruled in the Kashmir Valley circa 779–813 CE, about which see Dezső and Goodall 2012: 21.

[75] See Bühler 1885: 558, cited in Slaje 2019: 6, fn. 39; cf. Silk 2020: 263, 297, where the author is dated to the "last third of the 11th century."

[76] See Stein [1900] 1989 (vol. 1): 14–21, esp. 15.

[77] A decidedly Kashmiri geography also defined terms by which the text's audiences could (and can) identify with the text. This localized quality above all else can explain the narrative value found in the fact that the preponderance of the history recounted is recent history. (It has long been understood that Kalhaṇa's historical sources would have been more numerous and reliable for the recent history of the Kashmir Valley, but the narrative value of the same has to my knowledge gone more or less unnoticed. It is, simply, that the audience was familiar with the subjects of the narrative.)

The *Rājataraṅgiṇī* thus offers a more historically located example of the narrative model of the *Mahābhārata*, the quasi-mythological frame story of which genealogically ties the audience to the narrative's major players. The audience outside the text is informed in the epic's framing narrative that a hearer of the tale standing within the narrative—Janamejaya—is told stories about the acts of his ancestors, who are neatly placed at least three generations prior to him: Arjuna was Janamejaya's great-grandfather, living therefore at or just beyond the natural limits of human memory.[78] When he hears the Bhārata story, the text's external audience does as well, and both receive the same ancestral wisdom thereby, for—this is the point—it is represented as their wisdom: the epic tells the story of the Bhārata lands and people, recounting a past that is of value and relevance down through time and extending to the external audiences who lived (and live) in the territory where the events of the epic narrative transpired.

Audience and narrative are even more seamlessly fused in the *Pañcatantra*. This is so because the text is framed by a story that conveys the narrative to an audience inside the text but outside the worlds of the particular stories it relates: it is for three princes that the wise and aged Brahmin Viṣṇuśarman is said to narrate the didactic animal fables. Those who read or hear the *Pañcatantra* are positioned aside this internal audience and listen simultaneously to what the princes themselves are told. In setting the frame for the text in this way, both the three princes and the audience external to the text equally are called to puzzle out the sometimes dislocating, didactic lessons that may be gleaned through story.

The *Kuṭṭanīmata* is similar to the *Pañcatantra* in that it offers advice for a character within the work while simultaneously communicating its lessons to its external audiences. The poem features an older bawd teaching a young prostitute the ways of the trade by narrating a pair of braided stories, one exemplary and the other cautionary. As with the *Pañcatantra*, the audience external to the narrative is simultaneously given occasion to absorb the stories, hearing in this case either instruction for conducting the "oldest profession" (if the text's historical audiences included women of that world) or

[78] Hegarty 2006 also considers the role of the *Mahābhārata* in examining the "significant past" but with an emphasis on Vedic ritual forms. As he puts it (2006: 83): "the construction of the significant past in the Sanskrit *Mahābhārata* is marked by a sustained, deliberate, and creative engagement with Vedic religious and social self-understandings." See also Hegarty 2009, which makes a similar argument for place making by the epic, also in relation to Vedic ritual formations; finally, cf. Hegarty 2012.

else lessons for men who might need them to negotiate the dangers of falling for a professional lover.[79]

The two Sanskrit dramas examined in this book do not pull their audiences into their stories as coequal hearers of their tales, nor are their audiences practitioners in their narratives, and they do not easily allow their dramatic characters agency in the everyday world outside the texts. They do, however, interact with their audiences in one notable, affective manner.[80] By the conventions of the Sanskrit drama the plays set the charming worlds they represent apart from everyday life.[81] It is this very separation that activates the dramas' emotional resonance with their audiences. Sanskrit dramas famously offer only happy endings, and they thus may participate dynamically with the sentiments of their audiences by presenting in story what is emotionally consonant with the happy occasion of their performance. The dramas, as I shall argue in Chapter 5, can end happily precisely because the kings they feature as *dramatis personae* are safe to play, blissfully untroubled by the many dangers that the technical works on statecraft suggest always can threaten them. In contrast to the Rājadharmaparvan of the *Mahābhārata*, which states that *nīti* or statecraft may be summed up in a single word—nontrusting[82]—the two dramas examined in this book (and many like them) depict an implicit trust between the sporting king and his ever foresighted and reliable ministers, this or it is fate and the vicissitudes of luck and chance that ever work in the dramas ultimately to favor the king, the queen, and members of the royal court. Thus, the joyful escape offered in watching an entertaining dramatic performance is mirrored in their contents.

The *Kathāsaritsāgara* participates in the lives of its audiences in a manner similar to that of the Sanskrit dramas. We are told in the epilogue to this massive, nested set of narratives that it is conveyed to Sūryamatī, the queen of king Ananta, to please her in a moment of particular despair,[83] and it is therefore no coincidence that the stories are fantastical, somewhat whimsical, and most of all thoroughly entertaining. Readers are delighted by stories of

[79] I will have more to say about the purpose and possible audiences intended for this text in Chapter 5.

[80] This is not, however, to make an argument excessively based in *rasa* theory, as Tieken 2000 argues contemporary scholars have been wont to do.

[81] Indeed, one of the first events in many Sanskrit dramas involves a preamble introduction to the spectacle by the stage director, an explicit and performed separation of the play from the "real world" occupied by its spectators.

[82] See also *Nītisāra* 5.90a, which states that Bṛhaspati says that "suspicion" or *aviśvāsa* should define the king's primary attitude. (See also the translation of Knutson 2021: 73.)

[83] On this episode see Slaje 2019: 6–7. Cf. Bühler 1885: 553, cited also by Slaje.

adventure, including horror-like stories of vampire-like *vetālas*, all wrapped in a playful framing narrative with a happy ending, involving a prince who wanders the world to win brides in marriage and ultimately achieve immortality as a *vidyādhara* wizard. The tone of the narrative defines the emotions it means to cultivate in its audiences, intended as it is for a respite, an escape.

If the *Kathāsaritsāgara* is perhaps the least robust in fusing the world of the text with that of its audience, the *Rāmāyaṇa* most completely accomplishes this feat. It does so, in fact, to a degree and with a quality I dare say is unsurpassable by any other work of religious or cultural concern in world literature, for it places the very act of hearing the text for the first time not in a framing story but within the narrative itself. The hero, Rāma, is told the story of the future events of his life at the same time the audience hears the same: he comes to know his future acts by way of the predictive narration of his sons-become-bards. The words offered to him about himself shape his actions, and they are words that the audience hears simultaneously. The external audience is thus set side by side with the god-king of the epic, who becomes the primary audience of his own story, and Rāma and the external audience are equally called to live up to the merits of the same. More than this, the narration also positions Rāma as an active agent in the world outside the text, a world that can be made by hearing the narrative ever and again, or broken by failing to heed its perennial message. This astounding quality of the *Rāmāyaṇa* will be explored in greater detail in Chapter 2.

All the texts examined in this book thus make themselves a part of the cultural world they depict by narratively forging a dialectic between their representations and reality. The representations themselves are meant as models for and of appropriate action, precisely because these stories do not easily allow their audiences to live outside their narrative mores. It is thus an explicit argument of this book that narrative was intended to shape the very subjectivity of the texts' audiences, calling them to identify and engage with their stories. The stories present themselves, that is, as precisely the kind of didactic tool that the *Arthaśāstra* suggests they can be.

Counsel and Agency: Freedom to Act

If these texts thus offer counsel, then it is only proper to ask as to what influence they wished to exert. Ultimately and finally, I argue that these texts, taken together, narrate a model of political authority that advocated for restraint of the royal sovereign and a conservation of a particular social order. It is the political agent's subjectivity above all that their authors wished to form. They define a permissible mode of action available to princes, kings, queens, and royal ministers deployable in pursuit of the gamut of human ends. The counsel crafted for the royal sovereign (primarily) and his courtiers (secondarily and along the way) assumes not that royal power is hollow, agonistically unstable,[84] but potent, truly capable. Indeed, taken together, the counsel of the texts in question intimates a palpable sense that the texts' authors felt to be true what one scholar has recently argued, that the king gained the upper hand in the *brāhmaṇa-kṣatriya* alliance at a certain early point in its history (not, of course, to say invariably so).[85] Emphasis is rendered on virtuosity in the narratives' counsel, because these works implicitly recognized that kings and princes and queens were often largely free to do as they pleased. They needed convincing if they were to play by any rules but their own; the texts thus suggest there is real incentive in doing so, namely, the material gain that the *Arthaśāstra* suggests is the fundamental end of political power.

I wish to argue, that is, that a virtue ethic is emphasized because a pure consequentialism would present too free a hand to the royal sovereign, and any advocacy of a straight deontology would necessarily presuppose what could not be presumed, namely, an implicit willingness of those with political authority to conform to the (Brahminically devised) ethic in question. These narratives suggest counsel is vital to the royal sovereign and that his (or sometimes her) bond with Brahmins is sacrosanct and can furnish pragmatic, results-oriented advice, because by doing so they could forestall the catastrophic consequences of an essentially unbridled *kṣatriya* power. The royal sovereign's ranging capacity—this unbridled freedom of agency—ultimately was seen not as an end to be cultivated in narrative but as a fundamental problem to be attenuated by the instructive didacticism that is textured in story.

Chapter Outlines

Six chapters of literary analysis are offered in the following pages, each of which focuses on a particular text (or in the case of Chapter 5, a trio of texts).

[84] This is to say I find the core theme and central tropes of these narratives to work against the model offered in Shulman 1985. See also footnote 21, above.

[85] As I read her, Roy 1994: 145 and *passim* make just this point.

They are intended to offer a unitary and extended reflection on the single concern elected for study in this book—that of exploring from the textured point of view of narrative the nature of royal counsel and its intended effects. Given, however, the demands this book makes on readers—more than passingly to know the many stories addressed—one also suspects some will prefer to read the chapters individually. The analyses are therefore composed so that this is possible, each intended alternatively to be read exclusively alongside the primary texts they analyze.

I argue that four elements define the narrative works that are examined in this book. First, all of the texts in question depict the *brāhmaṇa-kṣatriya* alliance as fundamentally of value. The alliance is implicitly and explicitly presented as constitutive of good advice and the success it brings, because Brahmins are said regularly to embody the kind of virtue that opens to wise counsel and judicious action thereby.

Second, the texts in question all offer their narratives as counsel. Put differently, the texts, following a distinction first made by Clifford Geertz, offer both models of and models for action in the world.[86]

Third, the texts examined in this book almost invariably narrate stories about princes and kings receiving counsel: the giving and receiving of advice make up the internal frames of the narratives in question, or the same is a major trope in their stories, or both.

Fourth and finally, the narratives in question all implicitly or explicitly convey the one fundamental piece of advice identified in this book as paradigmatic of these narratives, namely, the admonition that one should be good (in directing one's thought, intention, and action) in order to do well, to achieve one's ends in the world, and beyond.

The chapters are ordered along an emically sourced rubric of the goals of life or *puruṣārtha*s. First, the *Mahābhārata* (Chapter 1) is fundamentally concerned with *dharma*. It presents as a challenging work that engages the *brāhmaṇa-kṣatriya* alliance in the breach. The central narrative consists in conveying a grand exception that proves the rule, for the Bhārata story is offered (by Brahmin narrators) as a lesson (for a *kṣatriya* king) in support of the alliance, but it involves a baleful tale in which the discipline of virtue is breached, with dire consequences for those who fall from virtue and for the subjects of the kingdom at large. Key here is the incapacity of central figures of the epic narrative to curb their personal desire to favor their kin, this

[86] Geertz 1973: 87–125, esp. 92*ff*.

as opposed to maintaining a dispassionate disposition toward action in the world, their transgression proving disastrous for the kingdom's subjects and the royal agents who breach the discipline of restraint as they do.

The *Rāmāyaṇa* (Chapter 2) also deals principally with *dharma*, laying claim to the notion that virtuous action is innate to the constitution of good individuals in the world, excepting in momentary lapses of judgment. Rāma is shown to embody the innate qualities that kings and Brahmins regularly possess and ideally—and regularly—should uphold, this text-as-counsel itself serving to cultivate the same. Tending to Rāma's internal conflicts, his feelings around the strains of maintaining the self-disciplining that is upholding *dharma*, the narrative stands in contrast to the message of the *Mahābhārata* and self-consciously so. Keeping *dharmic* counsel is eminently possible and fruitful, the *Rāmāyaṇa* suggests, even if it is not always simple or easy to do.

Chapter 3 critically examines the major narrative theme of the *Rājataraṅgiṇī*. Like the two epics it explores a *kṣatriya* milieu, inasmuch as the work chronicles the history of the kings and queens of the Kashmir Valley; however, I argue—against the prevailing scholarly opinion—that the *Rājataraṅgiṇī* chronicles the lives of Kashmir's rulers not to recommend to its (probably largely Brahminical) audience to turn away from the world in a sentiment of "resignation" but to encourage that same Brahminical audience to work productively to model and counsel *dharmic* action, so as to effect the same in the lives of those in power. (In this sense, I read the *Rājataraṅgiṇī* in a manner consonant with my interpretation of the *Mahābhārata*, on which the former is clearly modeled.) This, then, is a story about kings that primarily is for Brahmins. Counselors can see that their advice is put to practice only if they can practice the same. *Dharma* is thus again the primary concern of the work, though its link to the pursuit of prosperity, *artha*, is implicitly enlaced through the entire narrative as well.

Next, the *Kathāsaritsāgara* (Chapter 4) narrates the pursuit of good fortune (*artha*), of pleasure (*kāma*) in the form of winning wives, and ultimately of felicity beyond this world, achieved in the form of immortality as a "wizard" or *vidyādhara*. Its milieu is heavily that of the third of the four *varṇa*s, the *vaiśya*s, but it is framed and organized by the *brāhmaṇa-kṣatriya* alliance and features both *varṇa*s as primary characters of the narrative. The tone of the text is decidedly less didactic than the works that deal with *dharma*, and therefore the message it offers is more implicitly conveyed, though equally clear. Kings and princes should keep the company of trusted ministers, who offer reliable counsel in times of duress, for—purely and simply—they are magically powerful. It is by way of Brahminical counsel that the hero of the narrative wins his way to his beloved and back home from an exhaustive journey, this by taking the counsel of his minister who can properly engage the services of a dangerous *vetāla* to achieve their desired ends, the *vetāla* stories standing, I argue, as the central fulcrum on which the entire narrative structure of the *Kathāsaritsāgara* pivots. Here we see the Brahmin advisor as a tantric and tantrism presented for a nontantric audience, all in a manner that overcodes the preexistent, vernacular-language (or at least non-Sanskritic) source story, the *Bṛhatkathā*, in a manner that centers the royal sovereign and his uniquely capable ministers.

Chapter 5 engages two of the most famous plays in Sanskrit literature and the *Kuṭṭanīmata* of Dāmodaragupta to illustrate the (again implicitly offered) narrative lesson that kings should brook company with Brahmins if they wish to do well in the world, and that pleasure is eminently available to those who implicitly are inclined toward *dharma*. Here, the goal of life—and the performance of the dramas—is pure pleasure, *kāma* start to finish, so didacticism recedes from narrative view. And yet, the texts implicitly present as counsel in that the royal protagonists who do well in the world innately follow the rules and/or keep good Brahminical counsel, even while they playfully sport in pursuit of pleasure. The *Kuṭṭanīmata*, which in part shows the potential pitfalls of falling in love and thus offers a clear contrast to the dramas, also depicts a Brahmin who, unlike his *kṣatriya* counterpart, escapes the worst of the professional lover's trap simply because he is able to take good counsel.

Finally, Chapter 6 offers a close reading of the *Pañcatantra*, that famed didactic work of wisdom literature, which frames its story as counsel offered by a learned Brahmin to princes in need of instruction. We end with this textual meditation on good judgment par excellence, because good judgment was held to be the preeminent quality to be nurtured by both those in positions of political authority and those positioned to direct them: good judgment is the premiere product of virtuous restraint and the means to the material ends promised by the same, and it is said to be guaranteed by a properly functioning *brāhmaṇa-kṣatriya* alliance.

Ultimately, the audiences for these works are invited into the worlds of the texts—and vice versa—because the lives of those narrated in the texts had much to say about their own. These are not mere stories, even as they are nothing less than stories that entertain; these are stories of consequence and possibility, depicting the range of human endeavor and possibly fruitful engagement in the political realm. They are fun, and emotionally charged, and they surprise and sometimes cause wonder, and they present the dangers and sorrows of life's failures. They paint in emotionally resonant terms the nature of the human condition—of the personal in a socially structured world—which, in a world in which the state is so fundamentally dependent on the personal constitution of a single royal sovereign, is precisely where one goes to find the nature of a politics shaped by religion: it is found in the life and person of the royal sovereign, guided to a virtue ethic by wise Brahmins.

Brahmins and kings; royal counsel and its consequences. Politics thus is personal in premodern South Asia, and everything of value in life—morality and order, power and wealth, pleasure, even ultimate felicity—may be derived from the personal, subjective modalities of life, the care in deeply felt and nurtured human dispositions, such that one is cultivated in efficacious action. And it is precisely because politics is personal that it must be elaborated in narrative, in affectively reaching works of story, which shape individuals and make and reflect social connections and public selves—the complexity of the human condition. And thus we turn now to the stories that explore the lives of sovereign rulers, their advisors and courtiers, and the advice they received and imparted, to see the ways in which the persons who could shape society were meant to be shaped in turn by such stories, such that they might act out and embody—day in and day out—their most vaunted and guarded ethics and mores.

1

When the *Paramparā* Breaks

On Gurus and Students in the *Mahābhārata*

śiṣyas te 'ham śādhi māṃ tvāṃ prapannam
I am your student. Teach me who supplicates you.
—*Mahābhārata* (Bhīṣma Parvan) 6.24.7d

Introduction

Our study begins with the great epic the *Mahābhārata*, which deals in its frame story and extensive contents with the question of how it is that proper knowledge of *dharma* informs action in the political realm. It would have been possible instead to initiate our close readings with an analysis of the *Rāmāyaṇa* rather than the epic that ushers in the Kali age, to take up the epic concerned with the exemplary approach to *dharma* rather than with *dharma* in the breach.[1] Yet Kṛṣṇa's epic here takes precedence because it will serve to inform our interpretation of Rāma's epic in a manner that would not be immediately possible if the order of analysis were inverted.

The *Mahābhārata* is, to be sure, a work composed both for and in important ways about *kṣatriyas*. It deals extensively and fundamentally with the question of how political sovereigns must accept learned counsel in the course of engaging political action, and more importantly how they so often—in this epic—fail to do so, leading to catastrophic consequences. To

[1] The *Mahābhārata* in its counsel of dispassion may be said to be more "scientific" than the *Rāmāyaṇa*. The latter, in its call to feel for the values and persons one loves and its explicit evocation of the emotion of grief (*śoka*) in the origin story of poetic verse (*śloka*) itself, may be said to be more "artistic" in orientation. The former deals with instances of reasoned calculation being blocked by emotional attachment; the latter deals with instances of emotion properly placed and deployed, as well as the social boundaries that are defined and drawn thereby. One is not better than the other, and they also reflect one another, for the *Mahābhārata*'s is a complex science, which, as I note in the Conclusion to this book, evokes a powerful emotional response of its own. The *Rāmāyaṇa* in turn also appeals not just to the heart but also (if secondarily) to the head, for it also figures moral quandaries on occasion in a *Mahābhārata*-like fashion, as we argue in Chapter 2.

Brahmins and Kings. John Nemec, Oxford University Press. © Oxford University Press 2025.
DOI: 10.1093/oso/9780197791998.003.0002

access just this, the present chapter takes as its purpose the work of illustrating the prevalence of guru-student relationships in the text.[2] I argue that not only are stories of teachers and their students central to the great epic, involving key characters and pivotal scenes of its narrative, but also this is so most of all because the guru-disciple relations in question are frequently marred by the shortcomings of the characters involved, confused by the circumstances in which they are formed, and morally complicated by the real virtues of some of the characters who nevertheless break the laws of *dharma*, as they are expressed in the *Mānavadharmaśāstra* (a.k.a., *Manu*). The *Mahābhārata* depicts what cannot but be described as failed teacher-student relationships and in doing so narrates the very deterioration of *dharma* that one would anticipate in this epic, or in other words nothing more or less than the slippery disintegration of the virtue ethic that defines Brahminical counsel in the Sanskrit narrative literatures.

The transgressions in question are notably defined by the misplaced, imprudent, and excessive preferences of major characters in the epic for loved ones or their own ambitions, this against *dharmic* counsel, which for good reason repeatedly demands restraint around the same: the transgressions that precipitate the Bhārata war are most starkly defined by instances when *kṣatriya* princes and kings, as well as the Brahmins who teach them, favor their loved ones or their own interests when the proper balance and functioning of the social order require the same be held in check. This, indeed, is precisely what Dhṛtarāṣṭra is admonishingly told and repeatedly so across the epic narrative, that the entire war could have been averted if he only could have denied his son Duryodhana, chief of the antagonist Kaurava clan, his unreasoned and excessive wishes.[3] Indeed, it is of no coincidence that the guru-student bond and its normative sociological manifestation in the *brāhmaṇa-kṣatriya* alliance has—as we shall see—its origins in the

[2] For the purposes of this chapter, I follow Hiltebeitel (1976: 14–15) in understanding the *Mahābhārata* "as a narrative continuum, as a 'work in progress,' rather than [choosing] one variant or portion of the epic as a fixed or original text." This is to say that I intend to examine the narrative and literary qualities of the epic in its present form, by which I mean the form canonized in the Poona Critical Edition, rather than to scrutinize the authenticity and/or relative antiquity of various passages and variant readings of the text.

[3] See, e.g., *Mahābhārata* 2.45.49, 2.72, 5.53, 6.61, 5.127.11, 6.73.1, 6.79, 6.85, 7.97, 7.110, 8.4, 8.22, 8.69, 11.1, and 15.5. Certainly there are other instances of the same, but these examples suffice to indicate that restraint was precisely what Dhṛtarāṣṭra failed to impose on his son(s). Notably, moreover, he is often told just this, by Saṃjaya, when trying to blame fate rather than his own involvement-by-neglect in the matter.

Sanskritic tradition with the father-son bond, by which Vedic learning historically was transmitted.

Yes, unrighteous transgression precipitated the tragedy of the Bhārata war, but it also ushered in an extraordinary renewal of the teacher-student bond, in the form of the innovation of the institution of the divinized guru. Kṛṣṇa in the form of a *kṣatriya* prince is God in human form, and he serves his allies only by way of counsel: he offers only advice in the epic, not his hand in battle. Those who follow him, moreover, succeed in turning back the forces that would leave *dharma* unheeded for all time to come, though this God-as-counselor manages to save the *dharmic* order only by breaking *dharma*, fighting fire, as it were, with fire, but precipitating collateral damage of catastrophic, indeed genocidal, proportions along the way. But his divine intervention, as we shall see, is narratively directed ultimately to a more conventional state of affairs: the very recounting of the epic story in which Kṛṣṇa's extraordinary acts of counsel are narrated serves itself to counsel Janamejaya, calling him dispassionately to honor the more workaday model of the *brāhmaṇa-kṣatriya* bond.

Finally, the *Mahābhārata* narrative clearly suggests that the tragedy of a world where virtuous restraint is eroded is inevitably reflected sociologically as well, for it is no coincidence that the pivotal counsel offered in the epic is conveyed from *kṣatriya* to *kṣatriya*, from Kṛṣṇa to his Pāṇḍava allies, the balance of the famed *brāhmaṇa-kṣatriya* alliance and its unique capacity to embed *dharmic* mores displaced by the unique alliance of a *kṣatriya* God serving in a time of peril as counselor to allied princes and kings.[4] This *Mahābhārata* alliance saves *dharma*, but it does so only by way of the protagonists prevailing in a context of uncontrolled violence, which is precisely what a world entirely governed by the mores of the warrior class promises: nothing more or less than "the law of the fishes."[5] This is what is at stake in preserving the guru-student bond, embodied as it also is in the father-son bond and guaranteed by the *brāhmaṇa-kṣatriya* bond: it promises a continuous tradition of prosperity by way of a tradition of virtuosic

[4] Similarly, virtually all of the famously expansive and didactic passages of the Śāntiparvan of the epic, which issues forth huge tracts of counsel, are offered by Bhīṣma to a victorious Yudhiṣṭhira, both of them of course being *kṣatriyas* by caste. (They are observed by the Brahmin Vyāsa, however.) On this massive and fascinating, if sometimes eclectic, chapter of the epic, see, e.g., Fitzgerald 2004, Bowles 2007, and John Smith 2009: 668–702.

[5] The "law of the fishes," or *mātsyanyāya*, as the idiom goes in Sanskrit literature, is a perfect analog to the "dog eat dog" world, the idea of course being that more powerful fish eat the smaller ones, no principle other than power defining choice in action.

restraint—the virtue ethic of the Sanskrit narrative tradition, preserved by the *paramparā* unbroken.

We proceed in what follows first by examining the normative model of the guru-student bond, by exploring its description in the *Mānavadharmaśāstra*. Doing so serves to illustrate the ways in which the *Mahābhārata* directly plays on Dharmaśāstric norms and expectations in elaborating the breaches in *dharma* that are so common to this epic, repairable as they are ultimately by a return to those same *dharmic* norms. This conceptual and doctrinal model in hand, we next examine the places where the major characters of the epic encounter the kinds of moral difficulties that define the narrative, breaking from *dharma* as they do out of a surfeit of preference for and loyalty to the ones they love or who serve their personal ambitions and interests. Finally, we review the passage with which the epic opens, namely, the dilemma faced by Janamejaya, which resolves by way of his honoring the counsel offered to him by wise Brahmin bards. In the end he chooses to practice a virtuous restraint in tending to his relationship with his father, because he can learn from the negative lesson of the fall from virtue ethics—from personal restraint—conveyed by the *Mahābhārata* narrative.

Ideals and Norms: Manu on the Institution of the Guru

Although the teachers[6] (*guru*, *ācārya*) described in *Manu*[7] are primarily teachers of the Veda rather than those principally concerned with the arts of war, the law book offers prescriptions for normative behavior and as such illustrates the ideal manner in which any teacher should be regarded. Even if the martial arts are not the primary subject of instruction there, however, *Manu* explicitly links Vedic study with the warrior's pursuit of power, the former leading to the acquisition of the latter,[8] and the text more generally suggests that knowledge of various kinds can be fruitfully acquired from members of any caste. It is even possible, in adverse times, to learn the Veda from a non-Brahmin, and *Manu* requires the student to afford such a teacher

[6] For definitions of the various types of teachers, see *Manu* 2.140–143. See also *Manu* 2.191, where the terms *guru* and *ācārya* are used synonymously. Finally, see Gonda 1965: 229–283 (esp. 237–241) for a discussion of the etymology of the Sanskrit term *guru*.

[7] All quotations of the *Mānavadharmaśāstra* in this chapter refer to the critical edition presented in Olivelle 2005.

[8] See *Manu* 2.37c, where we are told that a *kṣatriya* intent on gaining power should undergo the *upanayana* initiation in his sixth year, as opposed to the usual eleventh: *rājño balārthinaḥ ṣaṣṭhe*.

the same deference and respect due to his Brahmin exemplar, at least for the duration of the period of instruction.[9] The prescriptions for and descriptions of the institution of the *guru* in *Manu*, therefore, are to a large degree indicative of the normative standards by which to judge the teacher-student relationship in general and therefore are by no means inapplicable to the *kṣatriya* milieu of the *Mahābhārata*.

A caveat in reading *Manu* involves the degree to which it reflects contemporaneous social realities. It is perhaps impossible to know beyond doubt the degree to which the normative account of society presented in it reflects the facts of the day,[10] but one can be certain that the author(s) of the text set out to encapsulate a set of social ideals, legitimate particular customs, or even invention tradition; it is even possible that all of these ends were pursued simultaneously.[11] As such—and given that by all accounts *Manu* and the *Mahābhārata* were, more or less, contemporaneously redacted[12]—it is not inappropriate to presume that many, though certainly not all,[13] of the norms articulated in *Manu* were anticipated in the narrative of the *Mahābhārata* and, indeed, probably expected by its audience.[14]

[9] See *Manu* 2.238–242.

[10] In my view, Olivelle is right in suggesting an indirect and abstracted, but real, relationship between *Manu* and contemporaneous social life, it being a text concerned with ideal human behavior that nevertheless reflects, to some (significant) extent, the social realities of the day. According to Olivelle 2005: 65–66: "Although it presents the 'should' more often than the 'is' and may occasionally engage in pious wishes and wishful thinking, the amount of detail it presents with regard to diverse areas of human activity—ritual, food, marriage, inheritance, adoption, judicial procedure, taxation, punishment, penance—shows that it was not divorced from reality."

[11] As a *śāstra*, *Manu* can be said to constitute, quoting Pollock, "a verbal codification of rules, whether of divine or human provenance, for the positive and negative regulation of particular cultural practices." Pollock goes on to catalog the possible relationships of *śāstric* works to "actual social practices," as follows: "*śāstra* could be viewed as offering a real blueprint for practice; as merely describing, *ex post facto*, a cultural product and thereby explicating its components for the benefit of a cultivated public; as providing, in the guise of normative injunctions, something like a standard of taste and judgment to critics, that is as defining the 'classic'; even as functioning in some cases to invent a 'tradition'; as constituting, in the hegemonic manner of high cultures elsewhere, practices as 'sciences' for theoretical or actual control; or . . . as endowing a practice with the status, legitimacy and authority directly confirmed by any 'Vedic' charter, something most *śāstras* aspire to become." See Pollock 1990: 17–26, esp. 18 and 25–26. Olivelle quotes the latter passage in Olivelle 2005: 63.

[12] See Olivelle 2005: 20–25; Bühler 1886: xcii–cxviii; and Hopkins 1882–1885: 239–275, esp. 268.

[13] See Hopkins 1882–1885: 251.

[14] This is not to say that *Manu* was already a fully formed text that was directly quoted during the time of the composition of the *Mahābhārata*, but rather that the normative social vision articulated in *Manu*, by and large, would have been known to the authors of the epic and their audience. In other words, whether or not *Manu* was fully formed by the time of the completion of the great epic, both texts elicit a certain shared and received "common wisdom." Hopkins argues as much when he suggests that while the *Mahābhārata* was unaware of the *Mānavadharmaśāstra* as a complete, autonomous, and authoritative text, "the *śāstram* [i.e., *Manu*] was in great part collated between the time when the bulk of the great epic was composed and its final completion" and that "previous to its collation, there had existed a vast number of sententious remarks, proverbial wisdom" that "floated

Now, *Manu*'s account of the teacher-student relationship, as is the general tone of the work, is prescriptive, affirming certain norms and prohibiting a variety of actions. As the book is organized in large part on the basis of the chronology of an individual's life, the teacher is of primary interest in the section dealing with the first *āśrama*, which is the principle subject matter of *Manu*'s second chapter. After the teacher releases the student to enter into the householder stage of life (3.1–4; 4.1; cf. 2.245–246), his presence in *Manu* is greatly diminished, excepting intermittent reminders of the teacher's preeminent stature (e.g., 4.182)[15] and exhortations to respect and honor him.

Of paramount importance throughout is the student's respect for the teacher. He is regularly exhorted to revere and serve him (at, e.g., *Manu* 12.83),[16] and he should do so obediently in order to gain access to the knowledge he holds.[17] The student must not argue with his teacher (4.179–180),[18] nor may he even tread on his shadow (4.130). Controlling his thoughts and disciplining his body (2.192–193), the student must show him utter deference, whether by eating food and wearing clothes of lesser quality (2.194), by occupying a lower seat (2.198) or refraining from speaking to him while lying down (2.195), or by standing down from a vehicle before greeting him (2.202). He must never mock his teacher (2.199) and must never abandon him.[19] His loyalty is further measured by the company he keeps, for the student must avoid both his teacher's opponents (3.153) and those who mock him (2.200). Bearing all of these strictures in mind, it should also be obvious that *Manu* proscribes the student from harming his teacher (4.162).

The same respect, moreover, must be granted the teacher's teacher (2.205), as well as the teacher's family, and *Manu* is particular to proscribe lustful encounters with women of the latter (2.211–214).[20] The student is also linked ritually with the teacher and his family, for he must respect the rules of ritual

about in the mouths of people," and as such were "drawn from the hearsay of the whole Brahman world." See Hopkins 1882–1885: 268.

15 Bühler considers the verse in question to be an interpolation. Olivelle does not. See Bühler 1886: lxviii and Olivelle 2005: 54–55.

16 While Bühler considers the verse in question to be an interpolation, Olivelle does not. See Bühler 1886: lxxiii and Olivelle 2005: 60–62.

17 The analogy is with digging for water: "Just as a man, digging with a spade, finds water, so too does the one who wishes to learn find the knowledge contained in his teacher." See *Manu* 2.218: *yathā khanan khanitreṇa naro vāry adhigacchati | tathā gurugatāṃ vidyāṃ śuśrūṣur adhigacchati ||*.

18 Bühler considers *Manu* 4.180–185 to be an interpolation; Olivelle does not. See Bühler 1886: lxviii and Olivelle 2005: 54–55.

19 See *Manu* 11.60*ff.*

20 Bühler considers *Manu* 2.213–215 to be interpolated verses, though Olivelle disagrees. See Bühler 1886: lxvii and Olivelle 2005: 54–55.

purity when his guru or members of his family expire.[21] The same respect is granted to fellow students, although the period of ritual impurity is shorter.[22]

The teacher is associated with the student's father, and family, in various ways: *Manu* explicitly requires the student to treat his teacher in the same manner as members of his biological family (2.206); he is simultaneously instructed never to treat his parents, older brother, or teacher with contempt (2.225);[23] and, as is well known, the student should live with the teacher for the duration of his Vedic training (2.164). *Manu* further suggests that the second birth, into the Veda, is rather more valuable than the first, biological one that depends on mere *kāma*, the parents' sexual desire (2.147–148), and, notably, the teacher is even labeled the student's "father" in his second birth (2.169–171). In a word, and as Gonda suggests, the similarity of the father with the teacher is the result of the latter's institution having been developed on the model of the former: "According to *Manu* 2.142 and *Yājña[valkya Smṛti]* 1.34 the guru is the one who performs the *saṃskāras*, maintains the child, and imparts the Veda to it. This must show that at least in the first place or originally the father is meant."[24]

The aforementioned prescriptions are perhaps best summed up by the general injunction (2.191) that the student, whether enjoined by the teacher to do so or not, should recite the Veda daily and likewise always perform those acts that benefit his teacher:[25] the student should always offer him his loyalty, deference, and respect. Finally, *Manu*'s extensive treatment of student errancy is justified by the idea that the guru is responsible for the karmic consequences of his student's misdeeds, receiving the karmic fruits of his sins—what is of vital concern in the *Mahābhārata* epic, as we shall see.[26]

As will also be shown, truth-telling, whether by keeping a vow or uttering statements of fact, is a virtue of particular importance in the *Mahābhārata* and in particular in the guru-student relationships depicted therein.[27] *Manu*, however, does not explicitly associate this virtue with the institution

[21] See *Manu* 5.80–81. The impurity lasts for three days, while the impurity following the death of someone of the same ancestry (*sapiṇḍa*) lasts for ten days (or alternatively three or even only one), for which see *Manu* 5.59.

[22] It lasts for only one day in the case of the *sabrahmacārin*. See *Manu* 5.71ab.

[23] Bühler considers *Manu* 2.225–237 to be the innovation of a later redactor/compiler of the text, though he accepts the possibility that similar verses appeared in the original. Olivelle readily accepts the authenticity of these verses, however. See Bühler 1886: lxvii and Olivelle 2005: 54–55.

[24] See Gonda 1965: 241.

[25] See *Manu* 2.191: *codito guruṇā nityam apracodita eva vā | kuryād adhyayane yogam ācāryasya hiteṣu ca ||*. Of additional interest in this verse is the synonymous use of the terms *guru* and *ācārya*.

[26] See *Manu* 8.316–318.

[27] On vows, curses, blessing, and the like in the *Mahābhārata*, see Hiltebeitel 1976: 38–39.

of the guru, though the text clearly expresses the value of truthfulness[28] and indirectly associates it with the institution in question by identifying it particularly with Brahmins, the normative caste identity of gurus in the *Mānavadharmaśāstra*.[29]

Elsewhere, the text *is* explicit in linking to the institution of the guru another virtue of central concern in the epic, namely, conformity to the rules of *varṇāśramadharma*. While *Manu* reserves a certain subordinated position of respect for *śūdras* (2.136–137), the text also reviles the "husband of a *śūdra* woman" (*vṛṣalīpati*) (3.155) and is explicit in condemning those who teach, or are taught by, members of the fourth caste (3.156), going so far as to prescribe reviling (*jugupsita*) names for *śūdras* (2.31), though the injunction is immediately followed by another that recommends names connoting mere servitude (*preṣya*) (2.32). This is to note that caste-based taboos are recommended—deplorably so, it must be added—in *Manu*'s account of the institution of the guru.

It is worth remarking that, while cataloging a wide range of possible failures on the part of the student, *Manu* is relatively silent on the possible failures of the teacher. Apart from the aforementioned prohibition from teaching students of a low-caste status, the text merely suggests that the guru should not charge a fee for his teachings (3.156), aside from the final offering of student to teacher at the close of the period of study (i.e., the *dakṣiṇā*), and that he may not impart learning to those who have not asked for it or to those who have asked in an inappropriate manner.[30] It may therefore be observed that *Manu* employs a strategy of presuming the integrity of the teacher rather than explicitly articulating a full range of prohibitions regarding his potentially errant behavior. (To an extent, however, this may reflect the fact of the teacher's seniority in relation to his pupils, who very often would have been prepubescent, or perhaps not much older.[31]) One must further note that while the text has not yet reached the point of presuming the teacher's divinity,[32] it does assume his conformity to *dharma*

[28] See, e.g., *Manu* 1.29, a verse that Bühler thinks absent from the original form of the text but which Olivelle accepts as part of it. See Bühler 1886: lxvi; cf. Olivelle 2005: 52–54.

[29] For example, Brahmins must be made to take an oath in court on truth itself. *Kṣatriyas*, by contrast, must swear on their vehicles and weapons. See *Manu* 8.113ab: *satyena śāpayed vipraṃ kṣatriyaṃ vāhanāyudhaiḥ*.

[30] See *Manu* 2.110–111. Presumably, the latter violation entails the student's failure to show proper deference and respect to the teacher, or perhaps it involves the student lying to the teacher, examples of which appear in the *Mahābhārata*, as described later in this chapter.

[31] It also of course reflects the bias of the probably Brahmin authors of the work itself.

[32] Gonda suggests that the guru has always been considered to be divine, though he also acknowledges an increasing "deification" of the same in the history of the religion. Unnoticed is the

and further associates Brahmins, the teacher's unmarked caste status in *Manu*, with the liberating knowledge of *brahman*, provided the teacher is well versed in the Veda.[33]

The *Mahābhārata*, by contrast, narrates not an idealized form of the guru but rather the failures of both teachers and their students. It occasionally depicts the institution as an instrument through which to exercise power, both by dint of the moral shortcomings, personal idiosyncrasies, and private desires of the teacher and as a result of the moral shortcomings of his students, leading almost inevitably to ruinous ends. In other words, the anxiety illustrated in *Manu* over the integrity of the guru-student relationship, by way of the many rules prescribing the student's behavior toward the teacher, is further elaborated in the narrative of the *Mahābhārata*, a text that, insofar as it catalogs the deterioration of *dharma* at the dawn of the last and morally darkest of the cosmic eons, is ideally conceived for the exploration of such failings—the failure, that is, to maintain the very virtue ethic that is reflected in *Manu*'s treatment of the guru and defines the counsel of the Sanskrit narrative literatures, which is offered to the royal sovereign as the singular pathway to material, and spiritual, reward.

Of Loyalty and Caste: Ekalavya

Recall, for example, the story of the outcaste prince, Ekalavya.[34] Young, determined, devout, and the son of the king of the Niṣādas, Ekalavya set out to learn the art of archery from Droṇa, a Brahmin who also was the greatest guru of the martial arts. Droṇa, however, "who knew the law" (*dharmajña*), declined to teach the prince "out of respect" (*anvavekṣā*) for his students, the Pāṇḍavas and Kauravas, who were *kṣatriyas* and therefore loath to associate with the outcaste prince.[35] That Ekalavya nevertheless crafted and

great difference in tone and content of *Manu*'s presentation of the guru when compared with that of the epic. In *Manu*, while his integrity is assumed, the guru is depicted as rather more a learned elite than a divine being, quite a contrast from the epic's depiction of Kṛṣṇa. See Gonda 1965: 230–231 and 280–283.

[33] See *Manu* 2.242.

[34] See *Mahābhārata* 1.123.10–39. All quotations of the *Mahābhārata* in this chapter refer to the enumeration of verses found in the Poona Critical Edition, for which see V. S. Sukthankar et al. 1927–1959.

[35] See *Mahābhārata* 1.123.10–11: *tato niṣādarājasya hiraṇyadhanuṣaḥ sutaḥ | ekalavyo mahārāja droṇam abhyājagāma ha || na sa taṃ pratijagrāha naiṣādir iti cintayan | śiṣyaṃ dhanuṣi dharmajñas teṣām evānvavekṣayā ||*.

worshipped an image of the famous guru is testament to an unwavering loyalty, a virtue not only demanded of the student by *Manu* but also explicitly attributed thereto.[36] It is by this very loyalty, moreover, that Ekalavya was rewarded with an unsurpassed agility with bow and arrow.[37]

It is Ekalavya's steadfast devotion to his self-selected guru that makes him extraordinary and consequently evokes sympathy for his plight, but abundance of one virtue does not guarantee sufficiency in another. In Ekalavya's case, his exemplary devotion is presumptuous, because it renders him blind to his disqualifying caste status. And while caste is a deplorable cause for exclusion from a modern point of view, it was mandated under the strictures of *varṇāśramadharma* in India's premodernity: as mentioned above, *Manu* is reproachful of the teacher who deigns to instruct a *śūdra*, let alone an outcaste.[38]

Ekalavya's devotion is nonetheless admirable, for it is not opportunistic: he offers it not only in the quest to acquire Droṇa's instruction but also when the latter takes it from him, and the devotion that wins Ekalavya supremacy in archery consequently pales in comparison to his eponymous[39] display of loyal obedience in the face of his teacher's exacting command. I am of course referring to Ekalavya's run-in with the Pāṇḍava brothers and in particular their teacher. At some point following his austerities, the Pāṇḍavas enter the forest along with a dog that, barking incessantly, earns Ekalavya's wrath and is forced to swallow seven of his arrows, fired with lightning quickness in simultaneous succession.[40] The Pāṇḍavas were amazed at that feat of archery, and Arjuna in particular was dismayed to hear the outcaste prince claim as his guru none other than Droṇa, who had promised Arjuna he would remain unmatched in all the martial arts.[41]

Not to be made a liar, Droṇa quickly found Ekalavya, and upon being greeted appropriately by his "student," he promptly demanded the latter's thumb as his fee for instruction, his *dakṣiṇā*, which of course is always paid only once and in arrears, after the entire period of the guru's instruction has closed. Declaring, "There is nothing I will not give to my guru," Ekalavya,

[36] See *Mahābhārata* 1.123.14ab: *parayā śraddhayā yukto yogena paramena ca* |.

[37] According to Gonda 1965: 252, it is with Ekalavya that the concept of "the grace of the guru" is introduced.

[38] See *Manu* 3.156c and following.

[39] The name Ekalavya can be translated as "gets one cut off."

[40] See *Mahābhārata* 1.123.15–19.

[41] See *Mahābhārata* 1.123.25–28.

in an act of utter obedience to his teacher's "harsh" (*dāruṇa*) command, fulfilled his wish, but at the cost of his light touch in archery (for firing the bow requires use of the thumb).[42]

Droṇa's *dakṣiṇā* exhibits a ruthless efficiency, and not simply due to the uniqueness of the object he desires.[43] To accept the gift is to recognize Ekalavya as his student, and yet the nature of the demand presents the disciple with an exacting choice, for to defy the order of a teacher is strictly forbidden, but to lose a thumb is devastating for an archer. Thus, Ekalavya was forced to choose between the teacher and the fruits of his teaching, and while his decision exemplified his loyal allegiance—his adherence to the *dharma* of discipleship—it cost him precisely what his devotion and loyalty had earned him.

The story is touching and consequential, and the authors of the *Mahābhārata* therefore felt it necessary to justify the violence done to the prince: in the Droṇa Parvan, it is suggested that Ekalavya would have been dangerously undefeatable in battle had he retained his right thumb.[44] Still, if the episode evokes sympathy by contrasting Ekalavya's faith in his teacher with his failure to adhere to the laws of *varṇāśramadharma*, it also exhibits a second layer of conflicting virtues, the clash of the virtue of loyalty with that of truthfulness. Ekalavya's mastery of the art of archery put into doubt the veracity of Droṇa's promise to Arjuna, and so to guarantee his word Droṇa exploited the institution of the guru by nefariously leveraging the *dharmically* mandated loyalty (albeit misplaced given the biases of *varṇāśramadharma*) of his self-designated disciple.

What's more—and as is so often the case in the *Mahābhārata*—the incident is tainted by the cross-purposes of one of the characters involved, in this case the teacher, Droṇa. The Ekalavya episode is not the only occasion when Droṇa demanded an unusual *dakṣiṇā* of his disciples.[45] Indeed, the promise he made to Arjuna was not a benevolent one, for it was tied to his desire to prosecute a personal vendetta. Just prior to the encounter with Ekalavya,

[42] See *Mahābhārata* 1.123.29–39.

[43] On the nature of *dakṣinā*, see Gonda 1965: 198–228.

[44] See *Mahābhārata* 7.156.19: *ekalavyaṃ hi sāṅguṣṭham aśaktā devadānavāḥ | sarākṣasoragāḥ pārtha vijetuṃ yudhi karhi cit* ||.

[45] At least according to *Manu*, the *dakṣiṇā* is more commonly a material gift, for example, "land, gold, a cow, or a horse" (see Manu 2.245–246). It is unusual to demand as *dakṣiṇā* that one's students settle a personal vendetta, and it goes without saying that Droṇa's request of Ekalavya's thumb betrays the spirit of the institution.

Droṇa hinted at a forthcoming demand—the capture of Drupada—in return favor for his instruction in the martial arts, and while the other students responded to his appeal with silence, Arjuna enthusiastically assented to it.[46] Shortly thereafter, Arjuna's devotion to his teacher (juxtaposed in the narrative with, and therefore implicitly compared to, that of Ekalavya) won him his guru's preference,[47] the guru however again using his social office to further a personal aim.

At issue is a personal slight, suffered at the hands of a friend-become-king. Droṇa, a Brahmin, and Drupada, a *kṣatriya*, played together as children, but when the latter ascended to the throne he shunned the former, refusing to grant him a place of prominence in his kingdom. It is with this that Droṇa set off to the land of the Kurus to offer his teachings, carrying his grudge along with him.[48] Of course, he eventually pays the price for his vendetta: although the Pāṇḍavas capture Drupada, returning to him only half his kingdom, Droṇa acquires a lifelong enemy in the process,[49] and it is ultimately Drupada's son, Dhṛṣṭadyumna, who, having vowed revenge for the injustice done to his father, kills the vengeful teacher on the field of battle, despite an overwhelming appeal for mercy from both the Pāṇḍava and Kaurava camps.[50] A personal conflict mars what was a childhood *brāhmaṇa-kṣatriya* bond, with cascading consequences and a host of preamble causes all tied to the teacher-student bond. Doing the right thing, in the right way, and for the right reasons—virtue ethics—could have forestalled the same, if only Drupada had not shunned a Brahmin, if only Droṇa had not exploited his Brahminical office as guru to avenge a personal slight.

[46] See *Mahābhārata* 1.122.40cd–44.

[47] Similarly, it is perhaps no coincidence that the famous scene in which Droṇa tests his disciples (*Mahābhārata* 1.123.45–67) closely follows the Ekalavya episode (*Mahābhārata* 1.123.10–39). (It is in the scene in question that Arjuna famously sees only the head of a targeted bird and not its body, his concentration being so exact.) The juxtaposition of the two scenes presents an implicit comparison of Arjuna's skill in archery with Ekalavya's, a comparison made more apparent in the short episode immediately following the one in which Droṇa tests the concentration and aim of his disciples, in which Arjuna is said to fire five arrows in rapid succession into a crocodile that had gripped Droṇa's shin (*Mahābhārata* 1.123.68–78). For the narration of the capture of Drupada, see *Mahābhārata* 1.128.

[48] See *Mahābhārata* 1.122.38: *drupadenaivam ukto 'haṃ manyunābhipariplutaḥ | abhyāgacchaṃ kurūn bhīṣma śiṣyair arthī guṇānvitaiḥ ||*.

[49] See *Mahābhārata* 1.128.15–18.

[50] See *Mahābhārata* 7.165, esp. 7.165.51.

On Truthfulness and Caste: Karṇa

While Droṇa's demise is a major development of the *Mahābhārata*, the Ekalavya episode is a relatively minor one in the scope of the larger narrative, though it is appropriate that it generates a lot of attention and concerned interest to this day, notably but not only among Dalits, who rightfully tell the story as an exemplar of the cruelties and injustices of caste hegemony. The issues at play in the episode, moreover, are not isolated to it, and they reappear in relation to some of the epic's most important and significant characters who serve as teachers or prepare themselves as students in search of knowledge in the art of war.

Take Karṇa, for example. In an effort to gain knowledge of magical weapons, he approached the Brahmin sage Paraśurāma for instruction, who had vowed to kill all *kṣatriyas*.[51] Karṇa, however, whose mother Kuntī had abandoned him at birth, did not know his ancestry. To gain access to instruction, he was compelled to lie about his genealogy, claiming to be a Brahmin, certainly not a *kṣatriya*, who as a class stood as Paraśurāma's collective mortal enemy. The ruse paid off, temporarily—Karṇa acquired knowledge of superior, magical weapons—but not decisively. When one day his teacher fell asleep, his head on Karṇa's lap, an insect (sometimes said to be Indra, i.e., Arjuna's father) burrowed into the latter's thigh. In order not to disturb his teacher, Karṇa unflinchingly endured the pain. Eventually stirring, anyway, Paraśurāma noticed that his student was bleeding, queried its cause, and upon hearing Karṇa's explanation realized the latter could not be but a *kṣatriya*, since, he said, no Brahmin would endure such pain so steadfastly as only a warrior could.

It follows that Karṇa's fantastic display of devotion cannot compensate, in the eyes of his teacher, for his lie. To punish him, Paraśurāma promises that Karṇa will forget what he has been taught at the very moment he needs it most. This curse bears itself out on the battlefield, when the wheel of his chariot catches in the mud, and Arjuna, prodded by Kṛṣṇa's instant—and transgressive—counsel on the battlefield, unchivalrously kills him in his moment of vulnerable forgetfulness.[52] Like Ekalavya's, Karṇa's punishment is to lose the very teachings he so assiduously, but fleetingly, acquired.

[51] See *Mahābhārata* 8.29. On the narratives around Paraśurāma see Collins 2020.

[52] That the wheel catches is of course the result of a different curse. It is Karṇa's inability to defend himself that results from Paraśurāma's curse. See *Mahābhārata* 8.67.

Lying costs Karṇa, despite his unflinching loyalty to his teacher, and the epic again depicts a heroic act of virtue—there is no other way to interpret Karṇa's endurance for pain—forestalled by contravening shortcomings in virtue. And although *Manu* considers misrepresentation of one's caste to be the equivalent of killing a Brahmin,[53] in this instance one might expect that Karṇa's great forbearance would in some way have served to mitigate, or even outweigh, the severity of his transgression. Regardless of how one calculates the *dharmic* equation, however, it is clear that the power of the episode—in particular, the sympathy one feels for Karṇa, who is almost but not quite a tragic hero[54]—is derived from Karṇa's conflicting virtues and *dharmic* transgressions, along with the questionable cross-purposes of one of the characters involved.

The cross-purposes in question, of course, are Paraśurāma's, for the teacher had his own agenda to prosecute: his indiscriminate disdain for *kṣatriya*s is in service of a personal vendetta. Although he comes to be considered a god, the *Mahābhārata*'s contemporaneous audience probably did not yet acknowledge Paraśurāma's divinity,[55] and regardless, his hatred of *kṣatriya*s stemmed from his desire to avenge the murder of his father, Jamadagni, by a member of the warrior caste, Arjuna Kārtavīrya.[56] (It's worth noting that Paraśurāma himself faced an Abrahamic task, when his father demanded he kill his own mother to punish her singular lapse of self-restraint. The fifth of five sons, Paraśurāma faithfully complied with his father's wishes by severing her head with an axe, after his four older brothers refused to do so.[57]) Thus, what seems to be a simple moral tale, one exhorting the value of honesty, is not so simple as that. Not only does Karṇa's lie outweigh his heroic devotion, but also, like Droṇa with Ekalavya, Karṇa's teacher is motivated by an agenda that relates only in the most general of terms to the student who is

[53] See *Manu* 11.56: *anṛtaṃ ca samutkarṣe rājagāmi ca paiśunam | guroś cālīkanirbandhaḥ samāni brahmahatyayā ||*.

[54] Had Karṇa never learned his true ancestry, had he not been given the opportunity to join his Pāṇḍava brothers prior to the start of the civil war, and had he not consistently counseled Duryodhana to engage in treachery, one could rightly label him a tragic hero.

[55] See Brockington 1988: 284–286; see also van Buitenen 1975: 193. It is worth noting that Paraśurāma's repeated annihilation of the *kṣatriyas* is said to have taken place at the moment of transition from the Tretā- to the Dvāpara-yuga. See *Mahābhārata* 1.2.3.

[56] Arjuna Kārtavīrya was properly welcomed, but he did not accept the hospitality due to his own bent for war. Stealing what he liked and ransacking the house, he left, incurring the wrath of the family—and Rāma's in particular. Rāma responded by attacking him, whose kin later responded in turn, killing Rāma's defenseless father, who, being an ascetic, refused to resist and instead waited for his son's protection, which arrived too late. See *Mahābhārata* 3.115–117, esp. 3.116.19cd*ff.*

[57] See *Mahābhārata*, 3.116.1–19. Cf. Collins 2020: 79–148.

caught in its vortex, and here consists fundamentally in the breakdown of the *brāhmaṇa-kṣatriya* bond, which the epic narration, offered as counsel to Janamejaya, seeks to repair (as we shall see). Indeed, it is hardly the regular order of things when a Brahmin vows to exterminate the *kṣatriya* order, this to avenge his father's demise; and in the normal order of society, Karṇa, who in fact is a *kṣatriya* by birth, would make an ideal candidate for a Brahmin's instruction.

On Truthfulness and Caste: Satyakāma

Issues of caste—the abrogation of the laws of *varṇāśramadharma*—disqualify Ekalavya from Droṇa's martial arts studio, despite the fact that in all other respects he would have been the ideal student. In Karṇa's case, an otherwise appropriate caste identity disqualifies him in the eyes of his teacher, who has it against the warrior class. Both episodes stand in contrast to one in the *Chāndogya Upaniṣad*,[58] which recounts the intriguing story of a boy who wishes to learn the secret teaching concerning the identity of *ātman* and *brahman* and further highlights the severity of Karṇa's encounter with Paraśurāma.

The child in question, Satyakāma, approached his mother to learn the details of his heritage, in anticipation of the questions his prospective guru would ask him. His mother, Jabālā, was promiscuous in her youth and as such was uncertain of who precisely fathered the boy. Unable simply to identify his father, she instead instructed Satyakāma to tell his prospective teacher that his name is "Satyakāma Jābāla."[59] He presented himself in this manner, and his prospective guru, Hāridrumata Gautama, observed that only a Brahmin could speak as honestly as the boy had spoken, and he taught him the secrets of the Veda. Moreover, the text explicitly notes that the teaching he received was complete,[60] and he is later depicted

[58] See *Chāndogya Upaniṣad* 4.4.

[59] In other words, he is Satyakāma, the son of Jabālā.

[60] However, the text does perhaps hesitate in endorsing the validity of teaching someone of such an unknown heritage. We are told that, serving his teacher loyally for a number of years, Satyakāma was taught one-quarter of *brahman* each by a bull, by fire, by a wild goose, and by a water bird. When Hāridrumata saw him approaching with apparent knowing, he asked Satyakāma how he learned the nature of *brahman*. Hearing that "others, than men" taught him, but that his teacher should teach him again, Hāridrumata Gautama did so without leaving anything out. I prefer to think that the implication of this, however, is that the boy was bound to learn the Vedas. See *Chāndogya Upaniṣad* 4.5–9 and Radhakrishnan 1953: 408–412, esp. 411–412.

as a guru in his own right, teaching the nature of self and *brahman* to others.[61]

Thus, a child of uncertain birth could become learned in the Veda and knowledgeable in its greatest wisdom, and as such the episode stands in contrast to both the story of Ekalavya and that of Karṇa, in contrast to the latter because of Satyakāma's honesty and to both by virtue of the fact that Satyakāma's (obviously unknown) caste identity did not disqualify him in the eyes of his teacher. The moral of the story is that the truthfulness *Manu* expects of Brahmins was thought at one point to be not only prescriptive to but also descriptive of that *varṇa*, something patently not true of the Kali age.[62] (On this view, it is Satyakāma's Brahmin-hood that led to his honesty, not his honesty that qualified him for a Brahmin's education.) And yet, the story further speaks to Karṇa's fate, for he can equally be said not to know his heritage—all the more reason he must accept the consequences of his lie. The pristine virtue ethic exemplified by Satyakāma's truthfulness may scarcely be found in the *Mahābhārata* and at the dawn of the Kali age.

On Truthfulness and the Teacher: Yudhiṣṭhira

Nor is truthfulness, or more specifically its absence, uniformly regarded in the *Mahābhārata*. In one instance, at least, lying is sanctioned by Kṛṣṇa's counsel and materially rewarded on the battlefield. I am of course speaking of Yudhiṣṭhira's deception of his Brahmin teacher of the martial arts, Droṇa. Famous for being a truth-teller, the virtue so closely associated with the first *varṇa*, honesty so defines Yudhiṣṭhira's character that he is often referred to as the most Brahmin-like of the five Pāṇḍavas.[63] Yet, it is Yudhiṣṭhira,

[61] Satyakāma's learning is confirmed in the next passage, where we are told of his successful instruction of one Upakosala (see *Chāndogya Upaniṣad* 4.10; cf. *Bṛhadāraṇyaka Upaniṣad* 6.3.11–12), although he is associated with the wrong view that *brahman* is the mind (*manas*) at *Bṛhadāraṇyaka Upaniṣad* 4.1.6.

[62] Indeed, *Manu* suggests as much when mentioning the deterioration of *dharma* through the eons. See *Manu* 1.81–86. (Note, however, that both Olivelle and Bühler consider the passage in question to be a later addition. See Olivelle 2005: 52–54; Bühler 1886: lxvi.) The story in question, however, being narrated in an Upaniṣad and therefore a part of the Vedic canon, cannot by tradition be ascribed to *any* of the four eons, but rather is timeless. It nevertheless is more indicative of the state of affairs in the first eon, which is of course the most nearly perfect of the four. At the least, we can say there is a register of a difference of perspective in the narration of caste identity, comparing as we do the Upaniṣadic episode around Satyakāma with the epic episodes of the *Mahābhārata* around the advent of the Kali age.

[63] See, e.g., van Buitenen 1973: 15.

on the advice of Kṛṣṇa, who famously lies to Droṇa about the death of his son Aśvatthāman. Of course, it is a half-lie, but nevertheless it is a ruse: the wheels of Yudhiṣṭhira's chariot, which previously never touched the earth, sink to the ground shortly after he loudly uttered the words "Aśvatthāmā is slain," referring not to Droṇa's son but, in a deceitful verbal sleight, to an elephant of the same name.[64]

The full irony lies in the fact that Yudhiṣṭhira is lying to—misleading, if you like—his *teacher*, the one who instructed him in the arts of war, just as Karṇa had done his own. Unlike Karṇa, however, who showed his teacher nothing but respect, reverence, and stoical devotion in allowing the insect to burrow into his leg, Yudhiṣṭhira goes on to fight Droṇa in battle, hardly an act of loyalty to his guru.

The comparison does not end here. I do not think it is a coincidence that Karṇa is condemned for misidentifying himself as a Brahmin while Yudhiṣṭhira is successful in wearing the same guise during the year of hiding in Virāṭa's court.[65] After all, given Karṇa's true identity as the eldest of the Pāṇḍavas, with a legitimate claim to the throne—one that Kṛṣṇa emphasizes in the Udyoga Parvan while trying to win Karṇa over to the Pāṇḍava side prior to the war[66]—Yudhiṣṭhira is something of a substitute for Karṇa. Similarly, it is symbolic that Karṇa falls in battle after his chariot wheel sinks, just as the symbol of punishment for Yudhiṣṭhira's lie involves his chariot wheels sinking from the air above the ground merely to stand on it.

It is for Arjuna, however, that Karṇa saves the full force of his anger and hatred. In part this is sensible, for a warrior always measures his strength against other warriors, and Arjuna and Karṇa are two of the toughest. I would also like to think there is a further, underlying and implicit hatred in Karṇa, however, one stemming from the felicitous fate that ultimately falls to Arjuna: it is through the latter and not the former that the royal line ultimately passes, from Abhimanyu, Arjuna's son by Subhadrā, to Parikṣit to Janamejaya (for whom the entire *Mahābhārata* is narrated), a subtle rebuke perhaps unnoticed by all but the most attentive in the audience, but a matter of central concern for the characters in question.[67] Lying, in any event,

[64] See *Mahābhārata* 7.164.72c–73b: *aśvatthāmā hata iti śabdam uccaiś cakāra ha | aśvatthāmeti hi gajaḥ khyāto nāmnā hato 'bhavat ||*.

[65] There is, of course, also a difference in their guises: Karṇa deceives his teacher, while Yudhiṣṭhira's disguise is meant for general consumption.

[66] See *Mahābhārata* 5.138–141.

[67] See also Hiltebeitel 1985: 76.

utterly disqualifying in Karṇa's case, is encouraged in Yudhiṣṭhira by Kṛṣṇa, and though consequential—Yudhiṣṭhira's chariot wheels are weighted to the ground—it also is rewarded, for killing Droṇa furnished a major turn of the Pāṇḍava's fortunes in the course of the Bhārata war.

On Honesty and the Guru: Bhīṣma

The *Mahābhārata* also narrates a crucial instance of an honest guru killed, in part, by his honesty. I am of course speaking of the ever-truthful Bhīṣma, whose vow of celibacy gives him the power to choose the moment of his own death, his ferocious presence on the battlefield therefore presenting a serious obstacle to the Pāṇḍavas' prospects for victory.[68]

A promise to Duryodhana leads Bhīṣma to choose the Kauravas' side in the war,[69] though as the uncle, protector, and, indeed, teacher of both the Kauravas and Pāṇḍavas, Bhīṣma concerns himself with the welfare of both camps, promising to give Yudhiṣṭhira sound counsel despite his commitment to fight for the other side.[70] And while by no means perfect, Bhīṣma's respect for his role as mentor demands his honesty even at the expense of personal well-being. True to that ideal—living as he does admirably closely to the virtue ethic that defines dispassionate, righteous action—he freely answers Yudhiṣṭhira when the latter, counseled by Kṛṣṇa to ask,[71] inquires of him how he can be killed,[72] and it is on Bhīṣma's advice that Arjuna and the others attack him, using Śikhaṇḍī as cover. *Kṣatriya* counsel of *kṣatriyas* issues advice where *dharma* is in the breach, for it produces the most difficult instances imaginable of counsel taken and successfully engaged. Because he had promised never to harm a woman, Bhīṣma refuses to fight Śikhaṇḍī, who is Ambā reborn, and so his honest counsel costs him his own life. In addition, the men firing from behind Śikhaṇḍī win a battle but lose something of their *kṣatriya* valor and honor along the way, all of this, it must be added, again facilitated by Kṛṣṇa's guidance.

68 See Hiltebeitel 1976: 244–250.
69 See *Mahābhārata* 5.153.16–24.
70 See *Mahābhārata* 6.103.44–45; cf. 5.153.16.
71 See *Mahābhārata* 6.103.50–51.
72 See *Mahābhārata* 6.103, esp. 6.103.70–82.

On the Guru of the *Gītā*: Kṛṣṇa and Arjuna

Thus, Bhīṣma's counsel is both effective and pivotally important to the Pāṇḍavas in the war effort, but it is brought about by Kṛṣṇa's counsel, whose famously transgressive leadership shapes the course of the war. He is the teacher par excellence of the *Mahābhārata*, Viṣṇu incarnate, yes, but although he is God in a human form, he also is a *kṣatriya* offering *undharmic*—if effective—counsel, a warrior who has taken up the role of teacher, of guru, a role usually and normatively reserved for Brahmins. Here, then, is another instance of the confusion of *dharma* at the dawn of the cosmic eon—the Kali Yuga—marked by the very deterioration of *dharma*: the caste status of the one taking the role of teacher matches the nature of his advice. Kṛṣṇa is on the side of the righteous to be sure; but the means he recommends are morally hardly uncomplicated: as is well known, Kṛṣṇa not only convinces Yudhiṣṭhira to lie to Droṇa and induces Arjuna to kill a defenseless Karṇa but also encourages Bhīma to break the laws of combat and to strike Duryodhana below the waist in the mace fight,[73] all acts that contravene the laws of *dharma*.[74]

Now, a counselor (*mantṛ*) is *prima facie* something close to a teacher,[75] but the *Mahābhārata* is more explicit in assigning Kṛṣṇa the role: whether the "Song of God" is understood to be integral to the *Mahābhārata* or an essentially autonomous work[76]—I assent to van Buitenen's view that the *Bhagavadgītā* "was not an independent text that somehow wandered into the epic" but rather "was conceived and developed to bring to a climax

[73] Apropos of gurus in the epic, it is worth noting that Balarāma, who taught both Duryodhana and Bhīma how to fight with the mace, absents himself from the civil war because he is unable to bear the pending destruction of the Kurus. See *Mahābhārata* 5.154.23–34.

[74] See Hiltebeitel 1976: 244.

[75] See also Gonda 1965: 243–252 for a discussion of the guru's role as the royal priest and advisor, the *purohita*.

[76] Both views are commonly held. To give two representative examples, Edgerton argues that one must "think of the *Gītā* primarily as a unit, complete in itself, without reference to its surroundings," while van Buitenen suggests that the text is "a creation of the *Mahābhārata* itself." Edgerton goes on to suggest that the *Gītā*'s treatment of nonviolence is "disappointing," because the text is "hampered by the fact that it is supposed to justify Arjuna's participation in war." Van Buitenen argues that "whatever the further thrust of Kṛṣṇa's teaching and its elaborations, the *Gītā* addresses itself in the first place to a specific issue that the Bhārata war posed to a more reflective age, whose attitude toward violence was changing." The *Gītā*, he further suggests, "occurs where it does for excellent reasons." The principal reason, he suggests, that the redactors of the final version of the epic include it is to justify the pre-existent, violent narrative of the *Mahābhārata* to an increasingly "more reflective" audience, which no longer regarded the war as a "glorious event for celebration" but rather as a "horrendous, blood-curdling finale to an eon." See Edgerton 1944: 105–106 and 185–186; van Buitenen 1981: 1–6, esp. 3–4 and 5–6. See also Brockington 1988: 267–271, which provides a comprehensive review of the literature.

and solution the *dharmic* dilemma of a war which was both just and pernicious"[77]—the form in which the text presents itself, more than merely "a long dialog, which is almost a monolog," as Edgerton described it,[78] suggests a private and uncompromised bond between a teacher and his disciple.

Indeed, the *Gītā*'s didacticism and narrative style, put forth by intricately developed narrative characters and embedded in the context of the larger epic story, implicitly and explicitly evoke an instructional mode and with it the guru-disciple relationship and the counsel it promises. So too does Arjuna's predicament, which is typical of an epic dilemma for presenting him with two "irreconcilable obligations,"[79] reflect the *Mahābhārata*'s larger concerns regarding the integrity of the bond between teacher and student and the sanctity of effective counsel, wrapped as it is in the question of how to act in accordance with the law, with *dharma*. It is no coincidence that the teacher-student relationship is so thoroughly queried in a text concerned with the diminishment of adherence to *dharma*: the institution of the guru, cemented socially in the institutionalization of the *brāhmaṇa-kṣatriya* bond, is meant to perpetuate conformity to *dharma*.

The loyalty that is central to the guru-student dynamic, moreover, constitutes the very dilemma of the *Bhagavadgītā*, for there can be no doubt that the welfare of his teachers stands at the core of Arjuna's quandary:

> How can I fight Bhīṣma and Droṇa with arrows in battle, Madhusūdana? The two deserve [my] worship, Enemy Slayer. Indeed, it would be better not to kill [my] highly dignified gurus and to enjoy even begged food here in the world than to kill my greedy gurus and enjoy spoils dipped in [their] blood. Nor do we know which is better for us: either that we win or that they win against us. Having killed Dhṛtarāṣṭra's men, who are standing in front of us, we would have no desire to live.[80]

[77] See van Buitenen 1981: 5–6.

[78] See Edgerton 1944: 105. Nor, incidentally, do I fully agree with Edgerton's assertion, on the following page, that the "opinions" that the poem puts forth are "not so much 'opinions' in the intellectual sense as emotional—or, let us say if you like, intuitional—points of view."

[79] I here quote B. K. Matilal, who suggests that Arjuna's question at the beginning of the *Bhagavadgītā* is "typical" in that he "was faced with a choice between two irreconcilable obligations." See Matilal 1989: 7–9.

[80] See *Mahābhārata* 6.24.4–6: *kathaṃ bhīṣmam ahaṃ saṃkhye droṇaṃ ca madhusūdana | iṣubhiḥ pratiyotsyāmi pūjārhāv arisūdana || gurūn ahatvā hi mahānubhāvāñ śreyo bhoktuṃ bhaikṣam apīha loke | hatvārthakāmāṃs tu gurūn ihaiva bhuṃjīya bhogān rudhirapradigdhān || na caitad vidmaḥ kataran no garīyo yad vā jayema yadi vā no jayeyuḥ | yān eva hatvā na jijīviṣāmas te 'vasthitāḥ pramukhe dhārtarāṣṭrāḥ ||*. The translation is mine but is an adaptation of van Buitenen's.

It is the very exhortation to obey the guru, to honor him, to do what is pleasing to him, that gives Arjuna pause. The spirit of *Manu* is utterly present in and indeed fuels his dilemma, just as a concern for the integrity of the teacher-student bond not only constitutes the dilemma of the *Gītā* but also frequently occupies the attention of the epic poets in the larger narrative, for with the sanctity of the bond is delivered the sanctity of counseled action that preserves the order of the world and guarantees both prosperity and heavenly reward.

Nor is it a coincidence that Arjuna takes Kṛṣṇa as his teacher immediately after uttering the words just quoted, saying (as is partially cited also in the epigraph to the present chapter), "afflicted by the fault of being weak, I ask you, my mind stupefied by *dharma*, what would be better? Tell me for sure. I am your student. Teach me who supplicates you."[81] In a moment of confused despair, Arjuna resorts to the tuition of his friend-become-guru, who provides extensive metaphysical and soteriological teachings to convince him to pursue martial ends and, indeed, to kill. Nor again is it a coincidence that Kṛṣṇa begins the long discourse that comprises the teachings of the *Gītā* immediately following Arjuna's pleading, as a student (*śiṣya*), for guidance.[82] The *Gītā* is nothing if not an instruction—an act of royal counsel—and while the *bhakti* it ultimately espouses is certainly not the same as the loyalty demanded of a student by the institution of the guru, it is sufficiently similar to it to justify the comparison.

Whether to defend his kingdom or fight his teachers, Arjuna's dilemma is well known and has been subjected to a nearly exhaustive quantity of analysis. It nevertheless is worth noting that Kṛṣṇa's exhortation to fight is supported by *Manu*, for the law book suggests that a warrior's royal *dharma* trumps his duty to honor his guru: a king should punish even his teacher (*ācārya*) for deviating from the law.[83] Yet again, however, the moral of the story is not quite so simple, particularly when one considers the content of Kṛṣṇa's teachings in the *Gītā* in relation to his role in the larger narrative of the *Mahābhārata*. As noted already, Kṛṣṇa's counsel in the *Mahābhārata*

[81] See *Mahābhārata* 6.24.7: *kārpaṇyadoṣopahatasvabhāvaḥ pṛcchāmi tvā dharmasaṃmūḍhacetāḥ | yac chreyaḥ syān niścitaṃ brūhi tan me śiṣyas te 'haṃ śādhi māṃ tvāṃ prapannam* ||.

[82] It is worth noting that the fact that Kṛṣṇa offers such metaphysical instruction is doubly ironic: it is ironic that he offers a spiritual teaching to promote war, and it is ironic that Kṛṣṇa, a *kṣatriya*, offers such a teaching to a fellow warrior on the battlefield, the metaphysics regarding the nature of *brahman* being the natural concern of Brahmins in particular.

[83] See *Manu* 8.335: *pitācāryaḥ suhṛn mātā bhāryā putraḥ purohitaḥ | nādaṇḍyo nāma rājño 'sti yaḥ svadharme na tiṣṭhati* ||.

narrative is persistently transgressive of the law. Despite all of his insistence in the *Gītā* on the performance of *dharma* for its own sake and without consideration of the fruits—or personal preference or reward—Kṛṣṇa in the *Mahābhārata*'s wider narrative consistently counsels Arjuna and the Pāṇḍavas teleologically and with utterly practical ends in mind, even at the cost of obedience to *dharma* and all in the name of ensuring a very real reward: control of the kingdom. He argues, that is, that in the Kali age when the order of all of civilization is at stake, wise action consists in nothing more or less than the kind of ruthless consequentialism that the *Arthaśāstra* exhorts. Indeed, while counted as the very incarnation of Viṣṇu, come to earth to preserve *dharma*, Kṛṣṇa is perhaps the character most ready to counsel actions that transgress the law in the larger epic narrative—even if, again, his story ultimately serves the ultimate end of returning the political world to order, the epic being offered to Janamejaya as a counsel to virtue ethics.

Now, the contrast between the Kṛṣṇa-as-guru of the *Gītā* and the Machiavellian Kṛṣṇa of the larger epic cannot but be intentional. And while proponents of the view that the *Bhagavadgītā* is an autonomous work, incongruously and awkwardly added to the *Mahābhārata*, may never be convinced of the epic's overall narrative integrity, for which Hiltebeitel has persistently (and to my mind effectively) argued,[84] it might nevertheless be useful to consider the relationship between the two portrayals of Kṛṣṇa through the lens of the institution of the guru. While Kṛṣṇa's counsel in the epic recommends acts that contravene *dharma*, the laws recorded in *Manu* also account for his role in the epic, in part at least. As mentioned,[85] the law book condemns the teacher to suffer the fruits of his student's sins. With this dictum in mind, and given that Gāndhārī curses Kṛṣṇa's family line to extinction to punish his inaction in the face of total war,[86] it is perhaps no exaggeration to understand Kṛṣṇa to have suffered the *karmic* fruits of the *dharmic* transgressions he counseled the Pāṇḍavas to commit. After all, it is Kṛṣṇa's family that is extinguished, though the war is fought (and *dharma* transgressed) to preserve the integrity of the Pāṇḍavas' royal power and, indeed, the Kuru's royal lineage. On this reading, then, Kṛṣṇa counsels acts that transgress *dharma*, but the transgressions seem small in comparison with what they accomplish.

[84] See footnote 2. See also Hiltebeitel 2001: 1–3 and following.

[85] See the section in the present chapter that is entitled "Ideals and Norms: *Manu* on the Institution of the Guru."

[86] See *Mahābhārata* 11.25.36–41, esp. 11.25.38.

The ends justify the means, for the kingdom is retrieved from the Kaurava brothers' malevolent hands and restored to the rightful heirs of the Kuru throne, who will do right by their subjects. Counsel that breaks *dharma* ultimately serves to preserve *dharma*, what is perhaps the best one can do in a world of *kṣatriya*s counseling *kṣatriya*s, the "dog eat dog" world of the "law of the fishes" being all one can hope for from warrior kings unbridled by chastening Brahminical instruction. And yet, under Kṛṣṇa's guidance, the Pāṇḍavas transgress *dharma* in relatively small ways to protect the greater *dharmic* order, which can only be provided by a Kuru kingdom justly ruled. He is a god after all. And yet again, the *dharmic* transgressions do not go unpunished—only it is the teacher, and not his disciples, who suffers them. There is an efficiently benevolent method to Kṛṣṇa's transgressive counsel.

It is worth noting that the *Gītā* claims only Arjuna as Kṛṣṇa's student, while the latter counsels a number of the Pāṇḍavas to perform questionable acts.[87] And the *Mahābhārata* explains Gāndhārī's curse exclusively as a condemnation of Kṛṣṇa's inaction, his failure to stop the war, while overlooking his active influence as counselor. In light of these two facts, Kṛṣṇa's support of the Pāṇḍavas—as well as the curse endured as a result of it—is perhaps better interpreted in light of the *bhakti* of the *Gītā*, and not merely in relation to the institution of the guru. "Give up all duties (*sarvadharma*)," exhorts Kṛṣṇa, "and come to me, [your] only sanctuary. I will free you from every sin, [so] do not despair."[88] Perhaps such a role can be played only by a god and not a mere teacher. Nevertheless, one can say that both *bhakti* and the loyalty demanded by the institution of the guru are synchronized, if not identified, in the epic narrative and in the character of Kṛṣṇa. If the litany of failed teacher-student relationships narrated in the *Mahābhārata* suggests, contra what is implicit in *Manu*, that one cannot presume that one's teacher is honest, loyal, and truthful—all values normatively held by Brahmins and imparted as gospel to *kṣatriya* kings, queens, and princes—it is also true, in the case of Kṛṣṇa as a divinized guru, that it is the teacher's divinity that ensures his integrity, in turn demanding the same reciprocal loyalty from his students that is prescribed in *Manu*.

[87] Perhaps, however, this fact is mitigated by other references to Kṛṣṇa as guru, in the mouth of Yudhiṣṭhira, for example, at *Mahābhārata* 14.70.21.

[88] See *Mahābhārata* 6.40.66: *sarvadharmān parityajya mām ekaṃ śaraṇaṃ vraja | ahaṃ tvā sarvapāpebhyo mokṣayiṣyāmi mā śucaḥ* ||. Ruben, quoted by Hiltebeitel, also interprets Kṛṣṇa's actions in the larger narrative in terms of the doctrine of the *Gītā*, for which (along with the author's own interpretation of Kṛṣṇa's expiation) see Hiltebeitel 1976: 287–296, esp. 288.

The Father as Guru, the Limits of Loyalty

Kṛṣṇa's relationship with his student, while both extraordinary and eminently successful, is not the only instance in the *Mahābhārata* of an unbroken teacher-student bond, however. If, as mentioned earlier and as Gonda suggests,[89] the guru-disciple relationship evokes and parallels the father-son bond—whether through the similarity in ritual obligations vis-à-vis both father and guru, the metaphor of "rebirth" into the study of the Veda, or the fact that the student lives in the house of the guru under a set of rules that makes the teacher an analog of the father[90]—then it is worth exploring further the ways in which the epic depicts the latter.

Given the repeated call to virtue ethics in Sanskrit literary narratives, it is vital to know that while the *Mahābhārata* often tells of extraordinary problems stemming from the mismanaged father-son relationship, the problems normally do not derive from the disloyalty of father to son, or vice versa; no, it is not nefarious palace intrigue that mars the relationship, as a mutual loyalty is usually secure in the epic's narrative, meeting the ideals outlined in *Manu*. Instead, the problem is rather the opposite, a surfeit of loyalty to the detriment of the larger social order. In other words, the problem presented by these relationships is something of the opposite of the paradox presented by Kṛṣṇa's transgressive counsel: while Kṛṣṇa counsels transgressive acts meant to preserve the larger *dharmic* order, the disciples in the following examples virtuously pursue loyalty to extraordinary limits, disrupting the larger *dharmic* order in the process: they break the virtue ethic by acting under the stated ideals of that ethic, but to extremes, serving not the ethic itself with dispassion, but desired ends defined by personal wishes and preference.

It should be underscored that the bond between father and son provides for particularly emotionally evocative tests of loyalty, not just in India but universally. Thus, Paraśurāma's aforementioned Abrahamic test, administered by his father, is reminiscent of the Ekalavya episode insofar as both demand

[89] *Manu*'s explicit association of the two institutions, father and guru, has already been noted, for which see the section of the present chapter that is entitled "Ideals and Norms: *Manu* on the Institution of the Guru." See also *Manu* 2.144–148.

[90] Even the etymology of the term reveals a certain connection of the two. First occurring in the form of an adjective referring to an important person, used in particular with reference to members of one's family, the term "guru" later appears as a substantive referring to the teacher. (See Gonda 1965: 240*ff.*) As mentioned, it is quite likely that the institution of the guru as it is known in the Vedic period served in a social role analogous to that of the father, with the guru serving to train the child in the Veda when the father could not do so, or could not do so to the same effect.

that the disciple choose unwavering faith or loyalty over an apparently tragic course of action. Matters are resolved rather more favorably for Paraśurāma, however, whose father, though testing him, never exploits the relationship for personal gain. Indeed, while the virtue of unblinking trust in the teacher, expressed in acts of utter obedience, is exploited by Droṇa to steal Ekalavya's thumb, Paraśurāma ultimately negotiates his father's test unscathed. His obedience even wins him an unlimited number of boons, only three of which he uses: one to restore his four elder brothers, who were cursed to insanity for failing to obey their father's command; another to revive his mother; and a third to cleanse the sin—and his memory—of the entire episode.[91]

While Paraśurāma skillfully acquits himself of his father's absurd demand, along the way proving himself to be both abstemious and unselfish with an unlimited number of wishes, it does not always end so well in the epic. Indeed, though admirable, emotionally satisfying, and laudable in the abstract, filial loyalty is also shown to be tragically overdone in the *Mahābhārata*, with devastating consequences not only for father or son but also for society at large, the link of filial loyalty to the wider social order being a natural one in a political system defined by inherited political power and, often if not always, the rule of primogeniture in particular. Take Bhīṣma, a.k.a. Devavrata, for example.

Devavrata's vow of celibacy, like Paraśurāma's matricide, reflects a son's concern to remain above all a loyal servant to his father, although he, Śaṃtanu, neither tests his son nor taxes him with the burden of solving his problems, and, unlike the Paraśurāma episode, this father-son relationship is critical to the core narrative of the *Mahābhārata*. As is well known, Śaṃtanu was desperate to fulfill the demands of Satyavatī's father, who would not permit his daughter to marry him without foolproof assurances that the royal line would pass to her children and not to, or through the line of, Śaṃtanu's previous son, Bhīṣma. Faced with his father's amorous bind, Bhīṣma took a vow never to procreate, also promising with a second vow never to ascend the throne, both so that his father might win his beloved. The results, however, were disastrous, not (only) for Śaṃtanu but for the Kuru line, for they set in motion a series of events that made it difficult to establish an indisputable order of royal succession, ultimately leading to the civil war. Had Bhīṣma simply done what is normally required of an eldest son—to marry and produce children—neither Citrāṅgada's death in battle nor Vicitravīrya's

[91] See *Mahābhārata* 3.116.1–19. See also Collins 2020: 106–108 and 112–114.

early demise would have affected the order of succession: both were born to Śaṃtanu by Satyavatī and were therefore second to Bhīṣma in their claims to the throne.

Bhīṣma's filial loyalty comes at the cost of dynastic stability in the Kuru line, but this fact was caused, in part, by fate: there was no way to anticipate that the sons of Satyavatī and Śaṃtanu would die without producing a royal heir. And yet, Bhīṣma's vow, itself a self-disciplining form of truth-telling, traps him in a moral dilemma,[92] for he is asked to choose either to honor the *dharma* of truthfulness by maintaining his celibacy or to fulfill his princely duties by performing the act of levirate: both are required of him, and yet he cannot perform both actions. Had Bhīṣma chosen the latter course, there would have been no need to ask Vyāsa to do so. It is therefore not entirely accurate to suggest, as Dhand does, that Vyāsa is the "author of the entire *Mahābhārata* war," this insofar as "it is his condemnation of the elder Bhārata widow [i.e., of Ambikā] that gives birth to the entire conflict,"[93] for Vyāsa would have had no role in the levirate at all were it not for Bhīṣma's celibacy: it is Bhīṣma's enthusiastic filial loyalty, driven by his father's somewhat misplaced desire, that precipitated the crisis. (On the other hand, one can speculate with some certainty that the ambiguities surrounding the royal succession might have been better negotiated had the irascible Vyāsa not cursed Dhṛtarāṣṭra to blindness.) Simply put: Bhīṣma's vow, undertaken in an overwrought act of loyal devotion to his father, set in motion the demise of his father's kingdom.

It should come as no surprise that the private bond of son to father could create such widespread social unrest. After all, the *Mahābhārata* is concerned largely with the lives of kings and princes, and in the epic as with any work concerned with royalty—and to reiterate what has been noted already—filial loyalty carries significance beyond the familial bond it seals, for political sovereignty is so frequently passed from father to son. Loyalty, moreover, is demanded not only of a king's princes but also of his subjects, just as those loyalties are tested in (civil) war. More than a son's personal bond with his father is at stake, for the loyalties implicated by it shape the wider web of political loyalty and thus the destiny of an entire kingdom, and the very ideals

[92] As Matilal suggests, a moral dilemma arises "when the agent is committed to two or more moral obligations, but circumstances are such than an obligation to do *x* cannot be fulfilled without violating an obligation to do *y*." In my view, this serves as an utterly appropriate definition of a moral dilemma in the *Mahābhārata*. See Matilal 1989: 5–9. Cf. footnote 79.

[93] See Dhand 2004: 53.

that are expressed in *Manu*'s normative description of the institution of the guru are tested in the Bhārata civil war.

Put into this light, Ajuna's proposed (in the *Gītā*) course of action—to live an ascetical life to avoid fighting his teachers and elders—can be understood precisely as this sort of overreaching act of loyalty, chosen in the face of a moral dilemma. To give up his duty to protect the kingdom, assigned to him by the strictures of *varṇāśramadharma* and his privileged position as a Kuru prince, would spare him from the patently unpleasant and morally ambiguous duty of killing his mentors and relatives, but it would condemn the kingdom to the rule of wicked men. Even loyalty—and filial loyalty at that—has its limits in the morally corrupted Kali Yuga. And its limits are precisely those of the virtue ethic of the Sanskrit narratives, that loyalty to the wider social order sometimes *must* come at the cost of setting limits to one's personal loyalties. Not to indulge a righteous and selfless, but private and socially insensitive, loyalty and, thereby, to deny a private wish or privilege in preference for maintaining the wider social order—this is what is required of those who truly adhere to the virtue ethic of the Sanskrit narrative literatures.[94]

Conclusions: Social Control, *dharma*, and the Divinized Guru: A Return to the *brāhmaṇa-kṣatriya* Bond

Whether one is concerned with the relationship of father and son, a king and his princes, or a teacher and his student, the bond implied by the relationship in question is more than merely a private one. Like the union forged by marriage, such bonds are both private, shared exclusively by the two individuals bound by them, and public. They are public because they confer particular rights and license certain socially relevant, powerful acts—from hereditary rights to the right to access sacred scripture and other relevant forms of

[94] This is indeed the fundamental lesson of the *Mahābhārata*, taught in the examples of its breach but as counsel to Janamejaya to repair the same, and this in a manner quite uncharacteristic of the *Rāmāyaṇa*, as we argue in Chapter 2. This epic's narrative also is utterly instructive for reading the *Rājataraṅgiṇī*, as we argue in Chapter 3, given that Kalhaṇa's history of the kings of Kashmir is explicitly modeled on the *Mahābhārata*: if Arjuna is explicitly told not to pursue asceticism in avoidance of facing the destructive catastrophes of the Kali age, then one should be hard pressed to argue that the sentiment evoked in either the *Mahābhārata* or the *Rājataraṅgiṇī*, that of the *śānta rasa* or sentiment of "peace" or "resignation," is meant to inspire one to turn away from the world in an act of renunciation, though, as we illustrate in Chapter 3, this is precisely what the prevailing scholarly view offers in reading Kalhaṇa's chronicle of the kings of Kashmir.

learning such as the martial arts to the right to rule the kingdom. It should come as no surprise, therefore, that *Manu* so assiduously regulates the institution of the guru. In expressing a normative model for social behavior (thereby articulating a normative social order), the law book must delineate the parameters within which the institution of the guru, the primary vehicle for the perpetuation of useful and salvific learning and the normative model of the *brāhmaṇa-kṣatriya* bond, should function.

Nor should it surprise that the epic, in narrating the advent of the most corrupt of cosmic eons, should tell the stories of failed teacher-student relationships. Such failure was understood to be nearly inevitable in the increasingly immoral Kali age. There should be no surprise, then, that the *Mahābhārata* describes teachers pursuing personal agendas for private reasons (e.g., Droṇa, Paraśurāma) and narrates the exploitation of the institution of the guru to the detriment of either teacher (e.g., Bhīṣma counseling Yudhiṣṭhira) or student (e.g., Ekalavya). It is characteristic of the Kali Yuga that the students encountered in the epic are often uneven in character, possessing an overabundance of, in particular, the virtue most vociferously prescribed in *Manu*, faith in and loyalty to the teacher (e.g., Ekalavya, Karṇa), while simultaneously lacking in other essential qualities, such as truthfulness (e.g., Karṇa) or obedience to *varṇāśramadharma* (e.g., Ekalavya, Arjuna in the *Gītā* being a near miss).

In narrating what cannot but be described as failed teacher-student relationships, moreover, the *Mahābhārata* invokes the very social norms encapsulated in *Manu*'s treatment of the institution of the guru. Indeed, the narrative power of a number of the episodes recounted in the present chapter stems from the epic's deft evocation of the very social norms prescribed in Dharmaśāstra. While *Manu* catalogs social ideals, the *Mahābhārata* invokes them implicitly and explicitly to create narrative tension and to portray a decline in *dharma* that is characterized, in part, by the confrontation of conflicting *dharmic* values and norms. Thus, Ekalavya's fate is regrettable in light of his great loyalty but (reprehensibly) mandated by *varṇāśramadharma* and driven by his teacher's desire to prosecute a personal agenda. Karṇa attracts sympathy in part because his true identity suggests he should be king and largely because of his admirably unflinching loyalty not only to his guru, Paraśurāma, but also (however misplaced) to his patron, Duryodhana. His lie, however, is sinful, even if his teacher is motivated by a personal vendetta, and his loyalty to Duryodhana is knowingly misplaced, given Kṛṣṇa's overtures in the Udyoga Parvan. Devavrata, in turn, is admirable for his steadfast commitment both to his vow and to the truth more generally, which allows him to serve the Kauravas without blemish to his reputation and to counsel the means to his own death without appearing to be suicidal, or foolish. Indeed, so unblemished is his record of action that he can unironically and fruitfully issue forthwith counsel to Yudhiṣṭhira across the long pages of the Śantiparvan. Yet, it is his vow, inspired by the misdirected desire of his father, that sets in motion the disastrous string of events culminating in the devastating fratricidal war.

That *Manu* and the *Mahābhārata* are equally concerned with the social order is readily apparent. After all, as Olivelle has already argued, "the socio-political environment that prompted the composition of the great epic was not too different from that of [*Manu*]."[95] It was an environment marred by threatening foreign invasions and troubled by "the historical reality and especially the historical memory" of rule under the Buddhist Mauryas, a period that knew the rule of *śūdra* kings as well as a significant loss of influence among the Brahmins.[96] What I wish further to suggest is that the two texts also share a concern for the integrity of the institution of the guru, and with it and by implication the normative bond between Brahmins and kings, evidenced in *Manu*'s legalistic prescriptions and the epic's failed guru-student bonds. At the least, the texts attempt to evoke concern for social order and obedience to the laws of *dharma* governing them by invoking the institution of the guru and the problems that threaten it.

Thus, it is more than a coincidence that the authors of both *Manu* and the *Mahābhārata* present their works in the form of narratives put across by both teacher and disciple, the latter providing most of the narrative under supervision of the former,[97] for by framing the texts in this manner, the authors rhetorically claim a certain propriety and integrity for their works. This marks them with the authority of the institution of the guru while simultaneously rendering the very transmitting of the texts—the very work of narrating them—instances of bardic counsel, the teachers of the frame narratives guiding their disciples in the very storytelling that passes the wisdom of the texts along, in the very presence of the audiences of the stories who stand as witnesses to the fruits of the counsel. However, while *Manu* innovates on the "previous literature of the *dharma* tradition" in presenting "a narrative

[95] See Olivelle 2005: 38.
[96] See Olivelle 2005: 37–41.
[97] See *Manu* 1.58–60 and *Mahābhārata* 1.54.

structure that consists of a dialogue" between "a teacher and others desiring to learn from him,"[98] the frame story establishing this narrative structure is much less elaborate than that of the great epic. The *Mahābhārata*'s frame story[99] not only mentions the teacher passing the job of narration to his student but also provides extensive details of the context in which he does so, thereby emphasizing the nature of the social order promoted in the text.

The audience is told that Vyāsa, with the help of Vaiśaṃpāyana, his disciple, recounts the story of the epic to educate the current heir to the Kuru throne, Janamejaya, Arjuna's great-grandson (and, not incidentally, Vyāsa's great-great-great-grandson: teacher and student are here bound by both a familial and a guru lineage, one we see represented, *mutatis mutandis*, in the *Kathāsaritsāgara*, in Chapter 4). Thus, the epic itself is an instrument for a teacher's instruction of a young king; it is itself an instance of royal counsel, offered by Brahmin instruction: in the frame story, we are told that the young Janamejaya hears the epic to know not only his ancestry but also how to preserve and protect the kingdom.[100] That story too begins with yet another a curse.

The then Kuru king, Parikṣit, was once hunting deer, and in anger and frustration he wrapped a dead snake around the neck of a Brahmin sage who, under a vow of silence, did not answer him when asked whether he had spotted his recently shot and wounded prey.[101] The sage ignores the slight, but the Brahmin's son does not—another instance of filial loyalty—and the latter curses King Parikṣit to die by the bite of Takṣaka, the snake-king, within a period of seven days.[102] Parikṣit assiduously avoids this fate but then allows a strange insect to sting and kill him, anyhow, to ensure the truthfulness of the sage's vow, thereby saving the latter from having uttered an untruth.[103] (This is the kind of loyalty to the wider social order so often absent in the *Mahābhārata*—a *kṣatriya* king sacrificing his own interests for the sake of upholding in his Brahminical counterpart the *dharma*, in this instance of truthfulness.)

Upon his father's death, Janamejaya is anointed king,[104] and to avenge his father's untimely passing he organizes a sacrifice to rid the world of snakes[105]

[98] See Olivelle 2005: 25 and *Manu* 1.58–60.
[99] See *Mahābhārata* 1.53.
[100] Hiltebeitel has written an important book on the subject of the epic as an educational instrument, for which see Hiltebeitel 2001.
[101] See *Mahābhārata* 1.36.
[102] See *Mahābhārata* 1.37.
[103] See *Mahābhārata* 1.39.
[104] See *Mahābhārata* 1.40.
[105] See *Mahābhārata* 1.47.

(yet another act of filial loyalty—excessive loyalty, a son avenging the death of his father, even while his father accepted it readily). Soon after the sacrifice commenced, a Brahmin, Āstīka, came to visit King Janamejaya and, praising him,[106] was granted a boon. Just at the moment when the sacrifice would bring Takṣaka to his end, having sent many snakes to their demise already, Āstīka asks that his boon be granted in the form of a pardon for the snake-king.[107] Giving Janamejaya time to decide what to do, the Brahmin uses a spell to suspend the snake-king in midair, above the fire, awaiting his fate. Knowing the importance of kings serving Brahmins' wishes, Janamejaya in the end complies with Āstīka's request, having also secured a promise no longer to be bothered by the snake-king,[108] and it is at this point that the *Mahābhārata* story is recounted for Janamejaya's benefit, with Vyāsa turning the narrative over to Vaiśaṃpāyana.[109] All ends harmoniously in the frame story, in contrast to the terrible events of the Bhārata war, with the handover of the kingdom to Janamejaya's able hands. Virtue ethics, restraint in the form of Brahmins honored by kings, saves the social order from a *Mahābhārata*-like calamity; because kings can make the cosmic era in the liking of their practiced virtue, the Kali Yuga can be forestalled by individual rectitude.

The frame story thus is instructive in a number of ways. First, one should note that it presents the audience with a pair of moral dilemmas (though in these instances they are readily resolvable): one is faced by Parikṣit, who must choose between the *dharma* of maintaining his kingdom and his duty to protect the integrity (in the form of truthfulness, in this instance) of the Brahmins who live in it, the other by Janamejaya, who chooses to honor his promise to a Brahmin rather than indulge his prerogative to avenge his father's death. Second, both father and son resolve their dilemmas by honoring the Brahmins with whom they are occupied. Third, while Parikṣit's act is similar to Bhīṣma's in that both exhibit extraordinary self-sacrifice for the sake of another,[110] one nevertheless senses that, rather than foreboding, a new beginning is promised in the frame story. Indeed, Janamejaya's decision, far from calling to mind the feelings of excess that characterize Bhīṣma's

[106] See *Mahābhārata* 1.50.

[107] See *Mahābhārata* 1.51.

[108] See *Mahābhārata* 1.53.1–26.

[109] See *Mahābhārata* 1.53.27*ff.*

[110] It is worth noting that both figures in question are teachers of sorts, the father in Bhīṣma's case, a Brahmin in Parikṣit's.

extraordinary vow, suggests instead that he knows how to act with a sense of proportion and discretion.[111]

It is no coincidence that Janamejaya's action embodies the sort of respect for Brahmins that is so pervasively demanded by *Manu*.[112] Just as his father sacrificed himself for the sake of a Brahmin's truthfulness, Janamejaya surrenders his own personal vendetta to honor a Brahmin, in this case Āstīka, who, as noted, acts with rectitude as well, using the boon he is personally promised to secure the snake-king's pardon and with it the order of society at large. All rejoice for Janamejaya's compliance with Āstīka's wish, and one suspects that the deference and respect Janamejaya shows his Brahmin guest, as did his father the Brahmin sage living in his kingdom, embodies precisely the conformity to *dharma* so famously advocated by Kṛṣṇa in the *Gītā*, one that guarantees the social order despite the arrival of the moral uncertainty of the last eon. The bond between *kṣatriya* and Brahmin supersedes even the one between father and son.

With this in mind, it is perhaps not out of bounds to conclude that the concern evidently expressed in *Manu* and the *Mahābhārata* over the integrity of the institution of the guru points to the larger sociopolitical concerns contemporaneous with the final redaction of the epic, to conclude, as Olivelle does, that "the authors of both [*Manu* and the *Mahābhārata*] probably came from the class of educated and somewhat conservative Brahmins intent on protecting the rights and privileges of their class."[113] This endeavor requires the preservation of the tradition of learning controlled by the institution of the guru, the preservation of the bond between Brahmins and *kṣatriya*s, and assurance of the integrity of the latter's royal lineages, all in the context of a world in which one can often count on others acting improperly.

What, then, does this tell us about the history of the institution of the guru and by implication the institution of the *brāhmaṇa-kṣatriya* bond? In the context of the epic narrative, it is for Ekalavya and Karṇa, and Bhīṣma and Droṇa, that the *paramparā* breaks. Caught in a morally complicated and conflicted world at the dawn of Kali Yuga, when the laws of *dharma* are

[111] This interpretation of what the *Mahābhārata* promises, namely, a reprieve from the Kali age ushered in by renewed guru-student, renewed *brāhamaṇa-kṣatriya*, relations is, I argue, echoed in the *Rājataraṅgiṇī*, which models itself on the great epic and for which see Chapter 3.

[112] Olivelle suggests, convincingly in my view, that the author of *Manu* has two goals: "he wants to tell Brahmins how to behave as true Brahmins devoted to Vedic learning and virtue, and he wants to tell kings how to behave as true kings, devoted to Brahmins and ruling the people justly." See Olivelle 2005: 41.

[113] See Olivelle 2005: 38.

prescriptive but no longer descriptive of human action, both teacher and student are all too often shown to be all too human. But the institution of the guru, paradigmatically associated with a Brahmin teacher and *kṣatriya* student, occupied with the perpetuation of valuable and valued systems of learning, and enmeshed with the royal court, the king, and issues of royal succession, is too important to surrender to the *dharmic* transgressions of men, so common in the Kali age. Perhaps, then, it is more than coincidence that the long tradition of the perfect, divinized guru, which becomes the normative form of the institution. In the body of the extant textual corpus postdating the epic, has Kṛṣṇa as exemplar and precedent. So vital is the *brāhmaṇa-kṣatriya* bond that God intervenes in the cosmic eon of moral turpitude to guarantee the very social institution that is central to its preservation and perpetuation, for as the *Mahābhārata* so abundantly illustrates, a politics voided of the virtues embodied by the sacrosanct bond between the two highest *varṇas*—that of the sacerdotal priest who teaches *dharma* with the disciplined warrior who acts accordingly—ushers in nothing less than utter chaos. The epic that introduces Kṛṣṇa as the divinized guru thus has its place in the Kali age, which is nothing more or less than to offer the perennial counsel of the Sanskrit narrative literatures, that ensuring the sanctity of the *brāhmaṇa-kṣatriya* bond ensures the virtue ethic that promises social stability, prosperity, and material reward alike.

2
The Perfect King
Rāma's Suffering, and Why His Story Must Be Told Anew

Introduction

The *Mahābhārata* depicts the divinization of the figure of the guru in the person of Kṛṣṇa, an *avatāra* of Viṣṇu the Preserver. The *Rāmāyaṇa* in its eponymous story of a young prince seeking to rescue his kidnapped wife, Sītā, from the hands of the villainous kidnapper Rāvaṇa perfects Rāma; and while Rāma and Kṛṣṇa may be equally divine, a world of difference distinguishes divinization from perfection. The cause of the difference may be explained by the disparate moments in cosmic history that contour the two epics, because of which differences are seen in what each *avatāra* is required to do to keep order. Kṛṣṇa's *dharma* is an *āpaddharma*, a call for action in a time of crisis in the Kali Yuga. Rāma models self-critical self-perfection in, according to tradition, the less chaotic Tretā Yuga,[1] embodying as he does the very possibility of living a devotion to a strict and narrow path of righteousness. The *Rāmāyaṇa* calls those who read and are instructed by its story, including Rāma himself, to chart a path toward self-transformation, a self-transformation that is eminently achievable, and it is for this reason that the *Rāmāyaṇa* opens a window to view and contemplate Rāma's internal state of awareness, to a degree not offered, nor felt to be germane—worthy of extended contemplation—with Kṛṣṇa.

A difference is found also in the nature of the *brāhmaṇa-kṣatriya* bond envisioned in each story, the *Mahābhārata* depicting a return to a normative relationship after a catastrophic break from the same, the *Rāmāyaṇa* depicting a vital mode of implicitly maintaining the bond despite occasional difficulties in doing so. Kṛṣṇa openly breaks *dharma* to restore the *dharmic* order. Rāma suffers, often privately, to preserve *dharma*; his bond is with the

[1] See Goldman 1984: 14.

Brahmins and Kings. John Nemec, Oxford University Press. © Oxford University Press 2025.
DOI: 10.1093/oso/9780197791998.003.0003

law. Kṛṣṇa acts as the average mortal cannot, in an extraordinary moment, so order can prevail. Rāma models the restraint and discipline all may emulate, however imperfectly, in following the law. How he honors *dharma* and suffers and perhaps even errs in doing so defines the nature of the very path of *dharma*, as well as the *brāhmaṇa-kṣatriya* bond, in times and instances when maintenance of just that is eminently possible.

To understand the ways in which the *Rāmāyaṇa* offers itself as royal counsel, and to witness the text narrating instances of counsel around kingship, we must engage a somewhat imaginative but perhaps not so speculative line of inquiry, which can capture an essential concern of the *Rāmāyaṇa* of Vālmīki.[2] What did Rāma feel? How did he think? Or rather, and to cast the matter in closely related but rather different terms, what are we, the readers or hearers of Vālmīki's epic, left to ponder of how he could have thought and felt? The text explores the engagement with *dharma* in a context of general fidelity to the same. It charts the difficulties but clear possibility—the plain likelihood—of successfully conforming to the ethical and moral order. It is only that the struggle that sometimes emerges in doing so is an internal battle, a matter of lapses from one's innate commitment to *dharma*, to the virtue ethic recommended to royals in Sanskrit narratives. The *Rāmāyaṇa* looks inwardly to subjective states of awareness, to feelings, precisely where the *Mahābhārata* looked outwardly to fraught familial relations.

We must tend to the question of feeling by way of a close reading of several passages of the epic, including episodes in which Rāma presents himself either with unusual stoicism or, contrariwise, with real and unbridled emotion. In particular, we must ask what we are to understand of how Rāma might have felt on hearing narrated *to him* his own life's story—his story as counsel—as he did in the Uttarakāṇḍa when it is was sung by his two estranged sons whom he had theretofore never encountered. The presumption I hold in this chapter and wish to test with it is that the political—the interpersonal—struggles that are represented in Vālmīki's text are simultaneously and primarily understood to be internal, subjective matters. Emotion is eminently at play, and of eminent concern. With these internal struggles, moreover, we find the key to the religious discipline, the virtue ethic, that is offered by Rāma's example and furnished to the epic's audiences, with

[2] See Goldman 1980 for an approach to the epic similar to the one here to be undertaken, one of analyzing the psychology of Rāma and his brothers, in particular around the composite nature of their characters.

which, in turn, we find the liaison that this epic fashions between Brahmins and kings.

Perfect Rāma

The present line of questioning calls to it what I will label a riddle,[3] though it is a riddle that is answerable, one whose solution I will propose toward the end of the present chapter: why, precisely, is the *Rāmāyaṇa* so often narrated and retold?[4] The fact *that* the story of Rāma is repeatedly retold is well known,[5] but *why* this is so is open to question. I propose it is a question regarding the internal logic of Vālmīki's text, which justifies and demands the act of retelling. This is also to say that to inquire after Rāma's internal dispositions as one can discern them in Vālmīki's text consists in an effort to identify the reasons that Rāma's story is so susceptible to repeated narration.

Circling closely around this riddle is yet another concern that has long occupied scholars and excited a tradition of commentary and narrative retelling in Sanskrit and other languages, namely, the question of Rāma's nature as God. The traditional ascription of Rāma as an *avatāra* of Viṣṇu is of course so well known as hardly to necessitate repeating. The divinity of Rāma, moreover, is attested across Hindu tradition—be it in the commentarial works on Vālmīki's text; in many of the various narrative retellings of the *Rāmāyaṇa* of North and South India, whether in Sanskrit, Tamil, or other Indian languages; or *en passant* in the writings of Hindu theologians, poets, and

[3] I am not the first to speak this way of the *Rāmāyaṇa*. See also Ramaswami Sastri 1944, of which Part II is entitled "Riddles of the Ramayana."

[4] That the story is one to be found well beyond the confines of Vālmīki's text is the subject of the collection of essays found in Richman 1991, as is well known. (See also, e.g., the collection of essays in Bose 2004.) A distinction may be made, as well, between retelling Rāma's story and renarrating Vālmīki's *Rāmāyaṇa*. Pollock (1993: 263) suggests that the Vālmīki narrative is the model for all other retellings of the tale of Rāma's life, but this needn't be the case, and anyhow such a view minimizes the power of the narrative retellings and reworkings of the text. Neither Vālmīki's text nor, I venture to suggest (though they will not be the subject of the present chapter), the many retellings of the story of Rāma's life may be uniformly reduced to the binary and dichotomizing imaginative resources identified in the *Rāmāyaṇa* by Pollock (1993: 281), namely those that "can be categorized under the two broad headings of divinization and demonization." Indeed, while Rāma's story has often been deployed in a manner that underscores the demonization of those of a perceived out-group, and while this tendency is in part built into Vālmīki's narrative, the same text also works against this tendency, at least in part, and it is to recover the more inward-looking and humbling and therefore moderating message of the narrative that I write this chapter.

[5] Shulman 1991: 93 identifies the story as fundamentally one of anamnesis, of a "consciousness hidden from itself" or "an identity obscured and only occasionally, in brilliant and poignant flashes, revealed to its owner." This is the deepest reflection known to me on the quality of the Vālmīki *Rāmāyaṇa* that demands the story be retold.

philosophers too numerous to count here. Regarding Vālmīki's text in particular, Sheldon Pollock has suggested that the very questioning in Indological circles of the inclusion of Rāma's divine status in the earliest narrative form of Vālmīki's *Rāmāyaṇa* is plainly "illogical," such a purported absence being proposed, he suggests, "in the teeth of evidence" and this, he further suggests, to an unprecedented degree, for he argues that Rāma's divinity is not only present in all the manuscript witnesses we have of Vālmīki's text but also is so fundamental to the epic as to render it impossible reasonably to imagine any narrative coherence in its absence.[6] And yet, Pollock's argument has not failed to invite scholarly opposition,[7] for he works against a widely accepted position that claims precisely that Rāma's divinity was added to a core, original epic story in which he was figured only as a great hero, a special human being but one not (yet) understood to be a god.[8]

Answering definitively to this binary of scholarly opinion need not occupy us here, because the question it poses is in an instructive sense unimportant for the purposes of answering our riddle and exploring what Rāma's subjectivity might meaningfully convey to its audiences. Whether Vālmīki's text originally presented a divine Rāma or only came to express this vital feature of his character subsequently, there can be no doubt that the epic's eponymous hero is meant to be seen as *exemplary*, worthy not only of veneration but also, insofar as might be possible, of emulation. Rāma, whether perfect or merely heroic, whether God or human—or both—is incontrovertibly the example one must follow into *dharma*.

[6] See Pollock 1984a: 241, fn. 24 (also cited in González-Reimann 2006: 204, fn. 6): "If I may offer the observation without sounding too petulant, Indological scholarship has probably few parallel cases of such illogical denial in the teeth of evidence as has occurred in the interpretation of Rāma's divinity over the past 150 years. Even when every single manuscript—every possible source of our knowledge of the poem—testifies in its favor, the representation can still be banished to the outer reaches of authenticity, to this suppositious archetype, whose sole *raison d'être* seems to be to provide a ghetto for ideas believed to be alien to the 'original' *Rāmāyaṇa*." See also Pollock 1991: 15–21.

[7] The most direct objection to Pollock's central claim known to me is that of González-Reimann 2006. González-Reimann concludes (2006: 216) that while Pollock "is correct in saying that it cannot be proved on textual grounds that Vālmīki 'was ignorant of or indifferent to the equation of Rāma and Viṣṇu,' the opposite is equally true; it cannot be proven that he was aware of such an equation or that it was important to him. Overall, the notion that Vālmīki's Rāma was, primarily, an exceptional human hero and that his status increased gradually to that of an *avatāra* of Viṣṇu—a process clearly attested to in later versions—still seems to offer the more plausible explanation, even within Vālmīki's text."

[8] His divinity, this argument suggests, was interpolated into the Vālmīki *Rāmāyaṇa*'s five central books and was written in more comprehensively and inextricably at the moment of the composition of the first and last *kāṇḍa*s (the Bālakāṇḍa and the Uttarakāṇḍa), which, the argument suggests, are later additions to the epic's five core books. Goldman 1984: 42–45 succinctly presents this well-known, text-critical view of the Vālmīki *Rāmāyaṇa* and this layering in of Rāma's divinity.

So much suffices to establish the claim we wish to make, because Rāma's manner of being—as a human being, as a divinity—presents with inherent complications. This too is well known. Whether a god or not, he is embodied in human form, which requires him to be able to feel various facets of the human condition. Indeed, Rāma must be human if he is to conquer Rāvaṇa, whose nearly impregnable boon protects him from any physical harm possibly inflicted by any creature apart from humans. And yet, Rāma of the final redaction of the Vālmīki *Rāmāyaṇa* is no ordinary human; he is (also) God incarnate,[9] not least because only such a superhuman being could possibly conquer Rāvaṇa.

"Perfection" nevertheless is, as Shulman says, "a process, magical, unfinished, flawed."[10] Rāma is shown to us in occasional moments of suffering, and he occasionally breaks from his habitual, heroic stoicism and dispassion. One needn't but recall several of the most famous and vexing episodes of the epic: Rāma sarcastically teased and had his devoted brother Lakṣmaṇa mercilessly mutilate Rāvaṇa's sister, Śūrpaṇakhā, for attempting to seduce him;[11] he lamented uncontrollably at the loss of Sītā in a fit of "madness;"[12] he shot and killed the monkey king Vālin while hiding in the blind;[13] and on defeating Rāvaṇa, he refused to accept Sītā with such anger that she cast herself into a funerary pyre to prove her purity.[14] And even this did not suffice, for he again sent her away in the Uttarakāṇḍa out of fear of offending popular opinion, because others could doubt her purity even in the teeth of the incontrovertible and well-documented evidence of her fidelity.[15]

[9] On the dynamic of divine incarnation, see, e.g., Clooney 2001: 111–121.

[10] See Shulman 1991: 111.

[11] *Rāmāyaṇa* 3.16–17. On this episode, see Erndl 1991. On the Rāma-Lakṣmaṇa bond, see Goldman 1980.

[12] *Rāmāyaṇa* 3.58–62. This is Pollock's term for Rāma's state, for which see Pollock 1991: 55–67.

[13] *Rāmāyaṇa* 4.16–18, esp. 4.16.25 and 4.17.13. On this episode and the doubtfulness (as he sees it) of Sugrīva's story regarding his relationship to his brother Vālin, see Masson 1975.

[14] *Rāmāyaṇa* 6.103. The fire test is found in the immediately following *sarga* (6.104, esp. 6.104.23–27). Cf. *Rāmāyaṇa* 6.5.5: *na me duḥkhaṃ priyā dūre na me duḥkhaṃ hṛteti ca | etad evānuśocāmi vayo 'syā hy ativartate ||*. "I do not suffer because my beloved is so far away, nor even because she has been abducted. This alone is the source of all my grief: her youth is slipping away." Translation that of Goldman, Sutherland Goldman, and van Nooten.

[15] Sītā did, after all, survive the act of *satī* in public view, and anyhow Hanumān managed to spy on her in the Sundarakāṇḍa, coming to know (when no one could know he was present) that she had in no way succumbed to Rāvaṇa's advances. See *Rāmāyaṇa* 5.13–38, which conveys the long episode of Hanumān's discovery of and conversations with Sītā. See in particular *Rāmāyaṇa* 5.18, where Rāvaṇa expresses his desire for her, and promises, at 5.18.6, not to touch her without her assent. And it is clear that Sītā was pure, for she endured a test: Rāvaṇa gave her two months to succumb to his desires, or he would kill her by eating her (*Rāmāyaṇa* 5.20.8–9)! She contemplates suicide (see esp. *Rāmāyaṇa* 5.24.49). Hanumān, we are told explicitly, heard her discuss these events with Trijaṭā, the elderly *rākṣasī* who is the daughter of Vibhīṣana, while he was in hiding. See *Rāmāyaṇa* 5.25–28, esp. 5.28.1. The last point, not often noted to my knowledge in the scholarly literature, seems to me

Such flawed perfections, if we may by adopting Shulman so label them, are also well known and will be addressed in what follows, with the addition of one more item, hardly mentioned in the scholarly literature so far as I am aware: Rāma kills a Brahmin. Yes, that Brahmin is none other than Rāvaṇa himself, who is only a half-Brahmin and is both plainly not only imperfect but also—as the Vālmīki *Rāmāyaṇa* conveys—evil. And yet he is repeatedly identified as a Brahmin by caste, which is no insignificant detail given the penalties imagined for Brahminicide in the Dharmaśāstras. Keeping sympathy with the major line of inquiry of *Brahmins and Kings*, moreover, it can be of no little concern that the *Rāmāyaṇa* exhibits a righteous *kṣatriya* slaying a sinful Brahmin, guided in no small part by his own internal compass for *dharma*. In particular, I will argue that it is by holding in mind Rāvaṇa's very caste identity that one can set in clearest relief the source and seriousness of his moral transgressions, which present in a hard contrast to Rāma's occasional slip against *dharma*: Rāvaṇa, unlike Rāma, is steadfastly willful in breaking *dharma*; he is untroubled by internal concerns.

Many Tellings: The Vālmīki *Rāmāyaṇa*'s Recursive Frame

But of course the epic story is Rāma's above all, as we are so often and from the outset reminded. Tending to its beginnings and endings, we see that the Vālmīki *Rāmāyaṇa* is framed reflexively. It offers a story about Rāma in which Rāma's story is repeatedly told. Like two facing mirrors the text reflects itself into itself, asking itself—and its audiences—to reproduce it, repeatedly to imbibe it, to know it in repetition as an object of contemplation.

The first chapter (*sarga*) of the first book (*kāṇḍa*) of the epic presents our narrator and author asking another sage for wisdom: "Vālmīki, the ascetic, questioned the eloquent Nārada, bull among sages, always devoted to asceticism and the study of sacred texts, 'Who is there in the world today who is virtuous? Who is brave, knows *dharma*, correct in his conduct, truthful in speech, and firmly committed to his vows?'"[16] So the narrative begins: a

thus to be elaborately laid out in Vālmīki's text and set in such a way as to suggest itself as incontrovertible evidence of Sītā's purity.

[16] *Rāmāyaṇa* 1.1.1–2: *tapaḥsvādhyāyaniratam̩ tapasvī vāgvidām̩ varam | nāradam̩ paripapraccha vālmīkir munipum̩gavam || ko nv asmin sāmpratam̩ loke guṇavān kaś ca vīryavān | dharmajñaś ca kṛtajñaś ca satyavākyo dṛḍhavrataḥ ||*. Translation a slight modification of that of Goldman.

Brahmin asking a Brahmin after *dharma*. Nārada's reply, as is well known, is nothing other than a *précis* of Rāma's biography, the story of a *kṣatriya* who is the *daṇḍa*-administering instrument of Brahminical ends, whose story in brief answers the question as to who in the world is virtuous (*guṇavān*), who knows dharma (*dharmajña*). His narrative is said to be "purifying" of all sins when read, and members of all the four *varṇa*s are welcomed to read it[17] (though women, in particular, will find the ideal life imagined for them to be one explicitly set in relation to men).[18]

So much stands in clear contrast to the *Mahābhārata*, which, though it is like the *Rāmāyaṇa* in purporting to offer a historical account of the lives and acts of historical kings and princes, presents—as we have seen in Chapter 1—a cautionary story of the woes of the ancestors, not a guiding tale to be kept in meditation and close to one's heart.[19] Framed as it is by the events around the snake sacrifice, in which the memory of the deeds—the failures—of Janamejaya's ancestors are recounted, the *Mahābhārata* speaks emphatically of those who are, by the time of its narration, in an important and final sense *gone*. At the very least, those who act like them (or at least the worst among them) should be stopped. The *Rāmāyaṇa*, given without such located and specific framing—indeed, precisely because it is not told for a particular ancestor situated as is Janamejaya (close in time to his forefathers)—may correspondingly be held to offer what can be relevant to, and positively influential for, all the devout who will want to hear it.[20] The story in offering itself as its frame transcends the kind of historicality (however mythical it may be) that defines the *Mahābhārata*'s frame story; it suggests a story that may ever and again be told.

[17] *Rāmāyaṇa* 1.1.77; 1.1.79.

[18] *Rāmāyaṇa* 1.1.72: *na putramaraṇaṃ kecid drakṣyanti puruṣāḥ kva cit | nāryaś cāvidhavā nityaṃ bhaviṣyanti pativratāḥ ||*. "Nowhere in his realm do men experience the death of a son. Women are never widowed and remain always faithful to their husbands." Translation Goldman's.

[19] Thus, the *Rāmāyaṇa*'s call to repeated narration stands in direct contrast to the reading habits around the *Mahābhārata*, which is customarily thought to be so inauspicious as to lead many Hindus not to keep a copy of it at home. If it is kept, at least one section is always separated from the rest in order to check the power of the unbroken text. Some even maintain that the *Mahābhārata* should never be read in its entirety, for the same reasons of its inauspiciousness.

[20] We are not given a frame that suggests a genealogical lineage from some *Ur*-narrator of Rāma's story to Rāma himself. This we have in the *Mahābhārata* from Vyāsa down in the ancestral line to Janamejaya himself. The *Rāmāyaṇa*, however, *because* it is not a narrative grounded by a finite genealogy but a perennial narrative, a story that was ever available that explains the (human) perfectibility or near perfectibility of virtue, is open to all—not just the *kṣatriya* line who should heed the words of Brahmins, but also members of any *varṇa* who could cleave to the ideal embodied as Rāma.

A perennial tradition is handed down, then, and it is a tradition to hand this story down.[21] The *Rāmāyaṇa*'s past in the form of its ideals—"is there a man in the world today who is truly virtuous?"—may be brought to the reader's or listener's present in its retelling, and because one owns the retelling by imbibing it, one may be changed—purified—by it. This is so even while the *Rāmāyaṇa* means to offer a glimpse into a time further removed from Vālmīki's contemporaneous audiences than the *Mahābhārata*'s historical moment is held to be removed from its own audience at the time of its final composition: Rāma by one calculation lived in the Tretā Yuga at around the year 867,102 BCE,[22] while the Bhārata war is said to have taken place only a few generations prior to Janamejaya's hearing of it and much closer to its contemporaneous audiences than was the time of Rāma.

While both the *Rāmāyaṇa* and the *Mahābhārata* are concerned with *dharma*, they do not have the same story to tell about *dharma*. There is nowhere in the *Rāmāyaṇa* any instance of utter doubt in the minds of the protagonists regarding a question that dominates the *Mahābhārata*, namely, that of what, precisely, is the right thing to do. Only with the killing of Vālin does any character so much as ask this question, and even there Vālin is quick to concede, after objecting to Rāma's apparent *adharma*—the cowardice and unchivalrousness of firing while in hiding—that his actions were, in truth, just.[23] Certainty regarding proper action defines the *Rāmāyaṇa*; chaos in various forms but also in impossibly pondering what is right pervades the *Mahābhārata*.[24] The *Rāmāyaṇa* harkens from a long-distant but perennially recoverable past, when *dharma* functioned more effectively.

[21] Indeed, as Goldman and Sutherland Goldman 2017: 60 indicate, the *Rāmāyaṇa* explains the very mode of its narration: "These passages [in the Bālakāṇḍa and the Uttarakāṇḍa at *Rāmāyaṇa* 1.4.13–27 and 7.85.2–3] devote much energy to describing the technical aspects of the musical performance and especially to the powerful emotional response it produces in those who hear it."

[22] See Ramaswami Sastri 1944, pt. 1: 23–24, also cited in Goldman 1984: 14, fn. 2.

[23] Vālin's address is recited at *Rāmāyaṇa* 4.17; Rāma's reply is offered immediately following, in the eighteenth *sarga* of the Kiṣkindhākāṇḍa. See esp. *Rāmāyaṇa* 4.18.56–57: *sa tasya vākyaṃ madhuraṃ mahātmanaḥ samāhitaṃ dharmapathānuvartinaḥ* | *niśamya rāmasya raṇāvamardino vacaḥ suyuktaṃ nijagāda vānaraḥ* || *śarābhitaptena vicetasā mayā pradūṣitas tvaṃ yad ajānatā prabho* | *idaṃ mahendropamabhīmavikrama prasāditas tvaṃ kṣama me mahīśvara* ||. "When he heard the sweet, calm speech of great Rāma, who followed the path of righteousness and crushed his enemies in battle, the monkey said these very fitting words: 'If when I was half unconscious with the pain of the arrow, lord, I unwittingly censured you, whose fearful prowess is equal to great Indra's, please be gracious and forgive me, ruler of the earth.'" Translation Lefeber's.

[24] There is no clear certainty, even, as to who the main protagonist of the *Mahābhārata* should be taken to be (at least when compared with the *Rāmāyaṇa*). Is it Yudhiṣṭhira alone, or he with his five brothers, or Arjuna above all?

Parallel to this difference in perspective on *dharma* are the respective structures of the epics: The *Rāmāyaṇa* in its central five books offers a straight narrative, a chronological story of one man's life that is largely unbroken by inset stories, side episodes, or discursive interpolations. It is the easier of the two epic stories to follow, that is, just as following *dharma* is more straightforward in the *Rāmāyaṇa* than it is in Vyāsa's epic. Vālmīki's text calls one simply to stick with *dharma*; it is a reminder to *dharma*, because it recalls a moment when adherence to righteousness was not only possible but also normal—and largely habitual, as we shall see.

We may fruitfully say this, then—that if the one epic concerns the limits of *dharma*, the places where *dharma* can fail, the other concerns the very possibilities of *dharma*. If the *Mahābhārata* largely is concerned with the actions that none should properly take, the *Rāmāyaṇa* is concerned with the actions that all must and should instinctively embrace. The former beckons the Kali age; the latter harkens to a brighter time. Most significantly, while the *Mahābhārata* signals that *dharmic* action might sometimes no longer be fully efficacious or at the least that sometimes the inclination to perform *dharma* presents one with a moral dilemma, the *Rāmāyaṇa* signals that the right action, performed in the right manner, is invariably the well-chosen—the better—path. The *Rāmāyaṇa* suggests that *dharma* perdures intact and remains the ordered way of fruitful action, and the same may be accessed by those who take up the tradition of the *Rāmāyaṇa*, repeating its virtues in part by reciting it.

Simple, except when it is not, for even Rāma forgets. His is "a process, magical, unfinished, flawed." Rāma—again, as Shulman's analysis indicates—must be reminded of his very divinity, something of which we, the text's audience, need no reminding. In this important sense, the community around the text knows Rāma's story better than Rāma knows himself. As Shulman puts the matter: "We, the listeners, know Rāma as god, but he clearly lacks this knowledge, which comes to the surface only in exceptional moments of crisis and breakthrough. The basic *Rāmāyaṇa* disjunction between the text's internal and external audiences sustains this play with levels of self-awareness."[25]

And yet, *the internal audience is fused with the external audience*! In the final movement of the final book of the epic, Rāma hears his own story when his sons, disciples of Vālmīki, recite it for him. It includes everything of his

[25] Shulman 1991: 95.

life, including "the good and the bad" (*śubhāśubham*),[26] and Rāma hears not only the lessons of his own life, those of selfless service to *dharma*, but also the moments of difficulty, not only of his chastened acceptance of exile or his conquest of Rāvaṇa and alliance with Hanumān and the monkey armies and their king, Sugrīva, but also of his questionable slaying of Sugrīva's brother Vālin, his lament at the loss of Sītā in the forest, and the cold reception he gives her at the end of the Yuddhakāṇḍa, when he forced her to prove her purity. Rāma also hears of what at the time of the narration are the future events of his own life, which had yet to occur; by hearing the *Rāmāyaṇa*, Rāma and the external audience simultaneously come to know for the first time the events of his last years on earth. Simply and decisively, the text's recursive frame marries the *Rāmāyaṇa*'s audience to Rāma.

And thus, Rāma's example, his story, is a salve not only to others, Sītā included,[27] but also to himself. The narrative tells us that on hearing his own story, Rāma comes to recognize the two bards as his sons.[28] He then asks them to request that Vālmīki, their teacher, bring Sītā to him, so that he could rectify the past and allow her again to prove her purity. Being in the audience of his own story leads Rāma more virtuously and completely and comprehensively to tend to his family. Vālmīki on Rāma's request appears and assures him that Sītā is and always has been pure, for only this incontrovertible fact could have qualified her to be admitted to his *āśrama*.[29] What is more, he promises she can once again prove the same. And she does. And when she does, by asking the goddess of the earth to open for her only on the condition that she has ever and only loved Rāma and no other,[30] he is thrown into a rage and overcome by grief over her (final) disappearance,[31] and he threatens to destroy the earth who holds Sītā, or "let everything in this world be once more nothing but water."[32]

[26] *Rāmāyaṇa* 7.85.20.

[27] Indeed, Hanumān tells Rāma's story to Sītā when he finds her in captivity, in the Sundarakāṇḍa, at *Rāmāyaṇa* 5.29.1–9.

[28] See *Rāmāyaṇa* 7.85. Rāma's recognition of the two bards who sing his story as "Sītā's two sons" (*sītāputrau*) is explicitly announced at *Rāmāyaṇa* 7.86.2–3. By his reference here only to their mother, should we understand Vālmīki's poem to suggest that Rāma did not yet accept them as his own, but only saw them as a conduit to his long-absent wife? On the force of this passage, see also Hiltebeitel 2001: 285; cf. Hiltebeitel 2001: 317 for his comments on father-son tales in the epic.

[29] *Rāmāyaṇa* 7.87.19.

[30] *Rāmāyaṇa* 7.88, esp. 7.88.9–16.

[31] *Rāmāyaṇa* 7.88.3.

[32] *Rāmāyaṇa* 7.88.20, translation that of Goldman and Sutherland Goldman. Note that this is recorded in a passage that is relegated to Appendix I, no. 13, lines 1–51 of the critical edition. Goldman and Sutherland Goldman include it in the body of the narrative, however, for reasons explained at Goldman and Sutherland Goldman 2017: 216–218.

Rāma's threats of anarchy and destruction are immediately and explicitly addressed by the gods themselves, led by Brahmā, who intervenes to remind Rāma that he is Viṣṇu incarnate. With his exalted identity, they remind him, comes his obligation to preserve the world's order and righteousness. Kings are bound to protect the earth, to protect the law embodied by Brahminical norms—to act with the virtue of restraint, personal preferences notwithstanding. And with this, Rāma will begin to listen, again, to his own story.

Shulman's understanding of the epic as a story fundamentally of anamnesis, of a "consciousness hidden from itself," "an identity obscured and only occasionally, in brilliant and poignant flashes, revealed to its owner," here shines forth.[33] The significant fact, moreover, is that it here arrives, and by the framing and ordering of the epic may be seen perennially to arrive, in the form of a call to narrate Rāma's story—and this is so because the story here is told to its principal hero. Brahmā exhorts him (7.88.12–19):[34]

> Rāma! Rāma! You of excellent vows! You must not torment yourself. Remember your immemorial nature and our counsel, dragger of your foes. At this time, you must recall that you are an unassailable incarnation of Viṣṇu. You must heed what I say in the midst of this assembly. This very poem that you have heard is the foremost of poems. No doubt, it will explain everything in great detail, Rāma. Vālmīki has rendered everything, hero, starting from the time of your birth, including your experiences of joy and sorrow, and even what is yet to come. This, the first poem, is entirely devoted to you, Rāma Rāghava; for no one other than you deserves to enjoy such poetic fame. Moreover, I heard it in its entirety a long time ago together with the gods. It is divine and of marvelous form. It is utterly truthful, and it obscures nothing. Now, Kākutstha, tiger among men, your mind focused in keeping with righteousness, you must listen to the poem, the *Rāmāyaṇa*, including the remaining events that are yet to come.

By listening, Rāma is led to perform ten thousand years of the *aśvamedha* sacrifice and ten times as many *vājapeya* rites (*Rāmāyaṇa* 7.89.5). He similarly is inspired to perform the *agniṣṭoma* and the *atirātra* and the *gosava* rites "at which great wealth was distributed, and [he performed] other

[33] See Shulman 1991: 93.

[34] Translation that of Goldman and Sutherland Goldman. Note that this is recorded in a passage that is relegated to Appendix I, no. 13, lines 1–51 of the critical edition.

rites as well, accompanied by ample sacrificial fees."[35] Listening effects all *dharmic* acts, particularly these, which support the Brahmin officiants who performed them. He will not destroy the earth but protect it as a chastened king would.

He sacrificed, moreover, without the company of a sacrificial wife, because Sītā, his only love, was gone. He had and would only accept as his companion a "golden Jānakī" (*Rāmāyaṇa* 7.89.4), a statue that stood in for the ritual role of sacrificer's wife, a role indispensable to Vedic ritual.[36] Thus, the kingdom prospered:

> And in this way a very long time passed while great Rāghava ruled the kingdom, exerting himself in righteousness.[37]

And:

> While Rāma was ruling the kingdom, no one suffered an untimely death, nor at that time did illness afflict any living creature, nor was there any breach of righteousness.[38]

Rāma-*rājya*—divinely ordered political rule, perfected political rule—resulted, that is, from Rāma having been reminded of his true nature.

Why Rāma's poem has this power, a question we will answer momentarily, can be seen in a flashing glimpse by contemplating this moment of the epic's last *kāṇḍa*. The narrative structure of the passage tells us that the tradition that is passed down is in this instance quite explicitly passed back to the very one who embodies it, and necessarily so. Rāma, the paragon of *dharma*, remembers how to effect a *dharmic* reign only on hearing his own story, replete with the narration of the future he has yet to live. He can fulfill his destiny and live up to his divine identity only on remembering himself—his values and righteous habits, his honor and practice of *dharma*—and this only by way of the poem written in memory of him.

[35] See *Rāmāyaṇa* 7.89.6: *agniṣṭomātirātrābhyāṃ gosavaiś ca mahādhanaiḥ* | *īje kratubhir anyaiś ca sa śrīmān āptadakṣiṇaiḥ* ||. Translation that of Goldman and Sutherland Goldman.

[36] On the indispensability of the sacrificer's wife to the ritual see Jamison 1996. Is there a symbolism in the gold, one echoing Sītā's desire for the golden deer? Or is it that gold is a metal among whose qualities is purity, a metal often associated with the purifying element that is fire?

[37] *Rāmāyaṇa* 7.89.7: *evaṃ sa kālaḥ sumahān rājyasthasya mahātmanaḥ* | *dharme prayatamānasya vyatīyād rāghavasya tu* ||. Translation that of Goldman and Sutherland Goldman.

[38] *Rāmāyaṇa* 7.89.10: *nākāle mriyate kaścin na vyādhiḥ prāṇināṃ tadā* | *nādharmaś cābhavat kaścid rāme rājyaṃ praśāsati* ||. Translation that of Goldman and Sutherland Goldman.

It is no coincidence, then, that Rāma receives this teaching from his sons. In contrast to the narrative *paramparā* of the *Mahābhārata*, as well as that of the *Mānavadharmaśāstra* (and a host of other Sanskrit works), the *Rāmāyaṇa* reverses the flow of the paradigmatic teacher-student relationship. It is the sons who instruct the father; it is not the father—who as we have seen in Chapter 1 is a guru figure—who teaches. Rāma is their example and ideal but not their teacher, rather the opposite: he is rendered in this moment their student. The crowned prince, whose example sets the very standard of *dharma*, is led to a moment of anamnesis by his sons, his successors to the throne. A community guides its leader, who needs reminding of his very identity in a moment of grief, a momentary lapse from *dharmic* poise, from the quotidian ethic of personal virtue.

We must base our literary analysis of Vālmīki's epic, then, on the premise that the *Rāmāyaṇa* is precisely what many who adore it today say it is and this in close echo of Vālmīki's words: it is the story of the perfect, *dharmic* king. In doing so we cannot but see Rāma's (human) suffering, for he must be reminded of himself in order to live up to his own perfection. Hearing the story of Rāma's acts demands we recognize that his was a difficult path, this simply inasmuch as Rāma himself from time to time required a reminder to *dharma*.

Of *śoka* and *ślokas*: Emotion and the Epic

Regret? To feel contrition or a moment of conscience? Or at the least an impulse to repair a misdirection? Vālmīki leaves us certain that Rāma must have felt, as a human, or must have performed, as a god playing the part of an exemplary man, what anyone with a committed heart, intent on *dharma*, must feel when slipping from the path.[39]

Again we tend to beginnings, to the narrative framing that reveals the mode of the epic's self-presentation—and why Rāma's poem has the power to purify, and why his story must be told anew. We are told that Vālmīki did not in fact initially compose his poem for Rāma; he first wrote about Rāma but for another reason.

[39] Rāma's identity as human or as divine incarnation is in this sense adventitious to his anamnesic slips: he might as a god perform them for the sake of his devout audiences, and as a human being he would exemplify, though on the best possible terms, human action. Either way, Rāma's need for instruction is itself an instruction to those who hold the epic dear.

Emotion, we must remember, is the language of this epic, which we know from the opening story, in which Vālmīki, we are told, discovers his poetic inspiration and invents the *śloka* meter. It is to lament a transgression—an injustice—that Vālmīki first sings. In sympathy with a sweet-voiced *krauñca* bird, whose mate was mercilessly shot by a hunter "filled with malice and intent on mischief" (*Rāmāyaṇa* 1.2.10), Vālmīki's sorrow bears poetic form:

> Fixed in metrical quarters, each with a like number of syllables, and fit for the accompaniment of stringed and percussion instruments, the utterance that I produced in this access of *śoka*, grief, shall be called *śloka*, poetry, and nothing else.[40]

Yes, the sorrow is born from a deep disdain for the act of another who, it is significant to note, is an outsider—a member of the Niṣādas, a tribe not included in Brahmanical society. In this sense the origins of the poem are presented as an act of speaking against those whose values and moral qualities are seen to fail to suffice, and whose identities are foreign and probably even thought to be dangerous to the one who sings. In this sense the emotions of the epic may be said to be directed outwardly, *against* those who do not share in the ethos captured by Vālmīki's new poetic form, the *śloka*.[41]

And yet, Vālmīki's core inspiration is also explicitly one of sympathy, and the core emotion is one not of righteous anger but grief (*śoka*). The origin story in the form of the poem meets with what I wish to suggest is presented as the core (if not the exclusive) content of the poem: shared, sympathetic emotion, a sense of a common regret for the departure from righteousness and the harm it causes. The event, the death—the merciless murder by a malevolent outsider—causes Vālmīki to turn inward, to let his innermost sincerity sing in shared sorrow with the *krauñca* bird who lost her mate.

This is to restate plainly what Vālmīki plainly states. The force of the *Rāmāyaṇa* is located in its emotion—heartfelt emotion—more than it is merely in the events it narrates. Affectivity matters. After all, Rāma's story as Nārada told it was concise and on the whole complete; yet, it was void of any

[40] *Rāmāyaṇa* 1.2.17: *pādabaddho 'kṣarasamas tantrīlayasamanvitaḥ | śokārtasya pravṛtto me śloko bhavatu nānyathā ||*. Translation that of Goldman.

[41] Indeed, those who would find justification for exclusivist claims in Vālmīki's poem may prefer this reading to the internal mode of concentration that I am arguing makes up the fundamental and core (if not the exclusive) message of the text. I wish to argue that this outward-focused reading must be understood to be secondary to the internal-looking one, however, for the reasons explained in what follows.

power to move the listener. Vālmīki had to rewrite it. He had to invent a new poetic medium to express the feeling he had around an injustice, the feeling he had in sympathy for a sympathetic creature done harm. Those who share emotionally in a social reality and, ultimately, in the full expression of the poem itself—yes, those who imbibe a shared polity—also share in a desire to embrace common and conventional practices and shared rules of conduct by which to live, together. These are the ones for whom the poem is sung; these are the ones who find sympathy when errant acts mar them, whether slightly or profoundly. Like the epic's eponymous hero, those who imbibe his story are wont to cleave to *dharma* and generally speaking may be expected to do so instinctively: the virtue ethic is both internalized and shared in community, and from time to time one needs reminding of the ways of the path. The *Rāmāyaṇa* in Vālmīki's novel *śloka* form is a reminder to *dharma* for those who habitually, implicitly, willfully, and happily adhere to *dharma*. Except when they don't: even Rāma must be reminded of his divinity.

This, then, is the fundamental dynamic of the epic, one shared in spirit by its intended and actual audiences and by its internal and external audiences. It is a narrative for an in-group, who perceive themselves to share common values and laws and who wish to hold themselves to them. Like the epic hero, those who have dedicated themselves to the path might occasionally slip, but because they are dedicated to it already and implicitly, a reminder is all they should need to find their way back to *dharma*. The audiences, internal and external, past and present and future, are in this qualitative sense also the same.

It is no coincidence, then, that Vālmīki offers a moral tale wrapped in a love story.[42] Kingship and a good marriage are properly married in a single

[42] Whatever one thinks of his treatment of his long-suffering wife, Rāma never loves again after losing Sītā. Indeed, it is the sorrow of Sītā that is placed at the center of the tale, Leslie 1998: 477 concludes, on the basis of her painstakingly careful identification of the birds in the *krauñca* scene as the Indian sarus crane: "At the heart of the *Rāmāyaṇa*, therefore, lies not Rāma's adventure—nor indeed Rāma's own despair at Sītā's disappearance—but Sītā's pain and, woven into it, the insurmountable anguish of the Sarus Crane."

Here, then, the monogamy of the epic's central couple is significant. It signals an exclusive love, a private but firm sharing of trust and companionship. It is similarly important that there is no love story at the core of the *Mahābhārata* as there is in the *Rāmāyaṇa*, for in Vyāsa's text loyalty is engaged to a fault, as we saw in Chapter 2. Indeed, there generally is a grudging quality, or at least a plodding and certainly a fatalistic quality, to the personal relationships narrated in the *Mahābhārata* (Kṛṣṇa's devoted loyalty to Arjuna being exceptional, however). It is no coincidence that rather the opposite is presented in Vālmīki's text.

So much is exemplified, moreover, in instances in the *Rāmāyaṇa* beyond that of the romantic relationship of Rāma and Sītā. Contrast, for example, the steadfast loyalty of Lakṣmaṇa to Rāma, on the one hand, with that of Karṇa to Duryodhana in the *Mahābhārata*, on the other. Even the more favorable comparison of Rāma and Lakṣmaṇa with Kṛṣṇa and Arjuna suggests that the latter relationship,

narrative, because they are bound together by the emotions of shared sympathy, by a shared sense of belonging, by reciprocal compassion. If emotion is the language of the *Rāmāyaṇa*, it is because it speaks to those who would naturally care for one another (as would a husband and wife), who inhabit a society and a world in which such caring is generally supported in community, is possible and fruitful. Yes, the *Rāmāyaṇa* envisions this community as closed, distinguished from other cultural worlds (like that of the monkeys Vālin and Sugrīva), and in this sense the emotions evoked are exclusivist: the laws and emotions of the *Rāmāyaṇa* have a double edge. And yet, it is for and within the community that the *Rāmāyaṇa* speaks most clearly. To preach, as it were, to the already convinced is thus no wasted effort, for—here, at least—to be human is occasionally to err but not to be excluded thereby from the community, from the system of values and beliefs that one only accidentally would defy. *Dharma* is readily followed in those places where (also in that Yugic eon when) it is valued and honored, if only sometimes imperfectly. On the occasions of a failing, the community lifts those who err, nurtures them to a return to the values they hold dear.

Rāma's Questionable Acts

Rāma, like all on the path, surely regrets transgressions. We witness him stoically sustaining the suffering caused by other members of the community, when doing so upholds the values that those members of the community instinctively, habitually (if sometimes imperfectly) enact. Suffering, on the one hand, is stoically tolerated where one can hold in memory the fact that one's deepest values are shared values, held in common even by those of one's community who might occasionally do one harm.[43] Suffering is acted out, on the other hand, where one has forgotten the greater context of *dharma*,

given Kṛṣṇa's counsel to acts that transgress *dharmic* norms, is knotted with complications in ways that the personal relationships of the *Rāmāyaṇa* largely are not—and one also must remember that we are told (in the *Gītā*, at least) that Kṛṣṇa's association with Arjuna is extraordinary, is special, in the context of the *Mahābhārata*.

[43] Rāma's reluctance to denigrate Kaikeyī for her role in his suffering signals just this. See, e.g., Goldman and Sutherland Goldman 2009: 1170, note on *Rāmāyaṇa* 6.70.14, where they remark that "most of the commentators agree that Rāma's righteous character is demonstrated by his having obeyed his father's instructions, while his control of his senses is proven by the fact that he entertained no evil thoughts toward Kaikeyī and Daśaratha for having deprived him of his rightful inheritance."

namely, that *dharma* matters in no small part because it is valued by so many others who care for the one who suffers. We thus witness Rāma's expressed regret, in the Uttarakāṇḍa, for the manner in which he angrily and dismissively treated Sītā after he killed Rāvaṇa and rescued her from Laṅkā.[44]

Just these habits of disposition may be found toward the beginning of the tale, at what is close to the root cause of Rāma's plight: Mantharā's influence over Kaikeyī, the queen she serves, and Kaikeyī's response to that hunchback servant's mischief, because—to state the matter simply—Kaikeyī is instinctively inclined toward *dharma*, initially at least. Yes, she is more than once described or depicted as having a "wicked nature" (*duṣṭabhāvatā*);[45] and yet Bharata's mother, King Daśaratha's second wife, is initially innocent of any malevolence, on first hearing from her hunchbacked servant that Kausalyā's son, and not her own, would be consecrated king:[46]

> Consumed with rage, the malevolent Mantharā approached Kaikeyī as she lay upon her couch, and she said: "Get up, you foolish woman! How can you lie there when danger is threatening you? Don't you realize that a flood of misery is about to overwhelm you? Your beautiful face has lost its charm. You boast of the power of your beauty, but it has proved to be as fleeting as a river's current in the hot season."
>
> So she spoke, and Kaikeyī was deeply distraught at the bitter words of the angry, malevolent hunchback. "Mantharā," she replied, "is something wrong? I can tell by the distress in your face how sorely troubled you are." Hearing Kaikeyī's gentle words the wrathful Mantharā spoke—and a very

[44] See *Rāmāyaṇa* 7.88.2–3: *evam etan mahābhāga yathā vadasi dharmavit | pratyayo hi mama brahmaṃs tava vākyair akalmaṣaiḥ || pratyayo hi purā datto vaidehyā surasaṃnidhau | seyaṃ lokabhayād brahmann apāpety abhijānatā | parityaktā mayā sītā tad bhavān kṣantum arhati ||*. The context for his regret is that Vālmīki himself had just sworn to Sītā's purity, the reason he could accept her into his *āśrama*. Rāma's reply in particular is as follows: "But although I knew Sītā to be innocent, brahman, I nonetheless abandoned her out of fear of the people. Therefore, please, sir, forgive me." Translation that of Goldman and Sutherland Goldman.

[45] See *Rāmāyaṇa* 1.3.5d. Cf., e.g., Kaikeyī's fight with Daśaratha after she decides to press for Bharata to take the throne in Rāma's place, this when Daśaratha wishes to equip Rāma with the kingdom's wealth in order to ease the ordeal of his exile, at *Rāmāyaṇa* 2.32.9–12.

[46] *Rāmāyaṇa* 2.7.9–16: *sā dahyamānā kopena mantharā pāpadarśinī | śayānām etya kaikeyīm idaṃ vacanam abravīt || uttiṣṭha mūḍhe kiṃ śeṣe bhayaṃ tvām abhivartate | upaplutamahaughena kim ātmānaṃ na budhyase || aniṣṭe subhagākāre saubhāgyena vikatthase | calaṃ hi tava saubhāgyaṃ nadyaḥ srota ivoṣṇage || evam uktā tu kaikeyī ruṣṭayā paruṣaṃ vacaḥ | kubjayā pāpadarśinyā viṣādam agamat param || kaikeyī tv abravīt kubjāṃ kaccit kṣemaṃ na manthare | viṣaṇṇavadanāṃ hi tvāṃ lakṣaye bhṛśaduḥkhitām || mantharā tu vacaḥ śrutvā kaikeyyā madhurākṣaram | uvāca krodhasaṃyuktā vākyaṃ vākyaviśāradā || sā viṣaṇṇatarā bhūtvā kubjā tasyā hitaiṣiṇī | viṣādayantī provāca bhedayantī ca rāghavam || akṣemaṃ sumahad devi pravṛttaṃ tvadvināśanam | rāmaṃ daśaratho rājā yauvarājye 'bhiṣekṣyati ||*. Translation that of Pollock.

> clever speaker she was. The hunchback grew even more distraught, and with Kaikeyī's best interests at heart, spoke out, trying to sharpen her distress and turn her against Rāghava: "Something is very seriously wrong, my lady, something that threatens to ruin you. For King Daśaratha is going to consecrate Rāma as prince regent."

Kaikeyī's first and instinctive reply?[47]

> After listening to Mantharā's speech, the lovely woman rose from the couch and presented the hunchback with a lovely piece of jewelry. And, when she had given the hunchback the jewelry, Kaikeyī, most beautiful of women, said in delight to Mantharā, "What you have reported to me is the most wonderful news. How else may I reward you, Mantharā, for reporting such good news to me? I draw no distinction between Rāma and Bharata, and so I am perfectly content that the king should consecrate Rāma as king. You could not possibly tell me better news than this, or speak more welcome words, my well-deserving woman. For what you have told me I will give you yet another boon, something you might like more—just choose it."

Her first response is not one of caution or hesitation, certainly not of regret, but rather of total certainty regarding what is right—and therefore joy in Rāma's fortune. Kaikeyī begins by exhibiting an innate *in*ability even to consider breaching *dharma*: she has internalized the virtue ethic that promises prosperity for all. Rāma's virtues outweigh any personal interest of dynastic inheritance and instinctively so, and she simply cannot imagine preferring her son to her stepson, whom she intuitively accepts as her own. We are in a world, in short, where *dharma* works, where *dharma* is natural—it is most nearly perfectly integrated into human culture and habit.[48]

Rāma, of course, is thoroughly associated with this innate impulse toward *dharma*, and he sustains it in ways Kaikeyī cannot and that Mantharā never

[47] *Rāmāyaṇa* 2.7.27–31: *mantharāyā vacaḥ śrutvā śayanāt sa śubhānanā | evam ābharaṇaṃ tasyai kubjāyai pradadau śubham || dattvā tv ābharaṇaṃ tasyai kubjāyai pramadottamā | kaikeyī mantharāṃ hṛṣṭā punar evābravīd idam || idaṃ tu manthare mahyam ākhyāsi paramaṃ priyam | etan me priyam ākhyātuḥ kiṃ vā bhūyaḥ karomi te || rāme vā bharate vāhaṃ viśeṣaṃ nopalakṣaye | tasmāt tuṣṭāsmi yad rājā rāmaṃ rājye 'bhiṣekṣyati || na me paraṃ kiṃcid itas tvayā punaḥ priyaṃ priyārhe suvacaṃ vaco varam | tathā hy avocas tvam ataḥ priyottaraṃ varaṃ paraṃ te pradadāmi taṃ vṛṇu* ||. Translation Pollock's.

[48] Simply, *dharma* when it goes wrong does so by way of a lapse, and Kaikeyī is a perfect example of this: she would have been happy to have Rāma as king until Mantharā interceded . . . but it is only with the intercession that the sort of favoritism that plagues the *Mahābhārata* is eventuated.

tries. He after all accepts the exile to the forest that is sentenced upon him with a stoical patience that moves the people of Ayodhyā loyally to follow him from the city. Kaikeyī began in a similar vein, as we here see, with a fidelity to *dharma* innocent of guile; but soon—too soon—she was convinced to act otherwise.

Mantharā cajoles Kaikeyī—"you who out of folly don't have your eye on the prize are not sensible to your own needs"[49]—and Kaikeyī folds. So she inquires of Mantharā as to how she can secure the throne for her son,[50] and Mantharā in reply reminds her that she had once conveyed her husband out of harm's way on a now-distant battlefield, in reward for which Daśaratha granted her two boons. With this the well-known and fated moment: she further counsels Kaikeyī to use the boons, respectively, to install Bharata on the throne and to banish Rāma from Ayodhyā for fourteen years.[51]

This history, this explanation of the source of Rāma's troubles, is clouded by a narrative confusion: the boons are highly unusual inasmuch as no queen was ever likely to have seen a hot battlefield in person. The narrative element bears the hallmarks of interpolation. What is more, the text also offers a second rationale to explain Kaikeyī's power over Daśaratha, this also in the ninth and tenth *sarga*s of the Ayodhyākāṇḍa, where the boons are first put into the narrative: she is beautiful, and her beauty, though approaching the limits of its longevity, will persuade Daśaratha to her sympathy.[52]

The boons for their part must be understood to have placed Rāma in a (*Mahābhārata*-like) *dharmic* bind: he faces the dilemma either of supporting his father's vow and losing the kingdom or of refusing to support the transgression of *dharmic* norms that the boons would precipitate but only by precipitating another *adharma* in doing so. To refuse to comply with Kaikeyī's wishes would force Daśaratha to untruthfulness, to breaking his vow to grant Kaikeyī whatever she wishes, which is akin to speaking a lie.[53]

[49] *Rāmāyaṇa* 2.8.12ab: *anarthadarśinī maurkhyān nātmānam avabudhyase* |.

[50] *Rāmāyaṇa* 2.9.7.

[51] *Rāmāyaṇa* 2.9.9–15.

[52] Pollock 1986: 25–32 goes over these features of the narrative with clarity and purpose. Cf. Pollock 1986: 59: "Daśaratha, in fact, should be viewed as one of several studies in calamitous passion, along with Vālin and Rāvaṇa himself, and like them a figure designed as a foil to Rāma. He conspicuously lacks the emotional control of his son, the self-discipline, equanimity, and dignity. Rāma's strictly monogamous sexuality likewise stands in sharp contrast to the habits of his father."

[53] Rāma's steadfastness in the face of the wicked boons is exemplary, but how different is it from the acts of those in the *Mahābhārata* who in acting in such ways harm *dharma*? Is Rāma's devotion to his father worthy of reward because of the age in which they take place? Is it only the aging of *dharma*—of fate—that condemns Bhīṣma and the others to the difficulties they face? One difference between Śaṃtanu and Daśaratha is that while Daśaratha offered the promise of the boons before knowing how they would be deviously deployed, Śaṃtanu owed no such debt of promise to Satyavatī (or her

If the boons were interpolated into the text, then, one can see why this was so: they develop an occasion in which Rāma's dispassionate adherence to *dharma* resolves a problem that, left unchecked, would undermine *dharmic* strictures: by surrendering the throne he saves his father from lying while simultaneously endorsing the succession to the crown that is forced upon him.

More generally, adherence to truth is habitually practiced in the *Rāmāyaṇa*. Among the Ikṣvākus, the Brahmin sages, the monkey warriors—even among the subjects of Laṅkā—one finds no penchant for speaking untruths. There is simply no chance Rāma could have fallen to the *adharma* of untruthfulness by voluntary commission. Untruthfulness, in fact, is rather overwhelmed in the *Rāmāyaṇa* by a different transgression, another voluntary vice. Yes, the more fundamental problem—for Daśaratha, for the epic more generally—remains that of desire. Indeed, when it comes to Rāma's banishment and Bharata's promotion to the throne, it is Kaikeyī's evocative beauty that—on my view—counts above all.[54]

This key to the epic's turmoil is communicated, not incidentally, in the words of Sītā, the epic's object of (male) desire par excellence. In the Āraṇyakāṇḍa she identifies the possible voluntary vices "as for deliberate misdeeds." "There are," she says, "just three. Telling lies is bad enough, but the other two, sexual intercourse with another man's wife and unprovoked violence, are even worse ... [and] the third one, violence—the taking of life without provocation, and recklessly—to this you [Rāma] may be prone."[55]

father), but Bhīṣma nevertheless indulges his father's desire on the spot and in a surfeit of loyalty. Rāma's honoring of his father's desire, by contrast, is not gratuitous but rather necessary, for it fulfills a long-standing promise innocently made.

[54] Note that Pollock 1986: 60 suggests that Daśaratha is utterly uninterested in upholding *dharma*: "Although Rāma seems clearly to recognize the failings of his father, the latter is not once shown to possess any awareness of the need to uphold righteousness." But his character, as Pollock has also noted (1986: 58, 60, 62–63), is made more complex by Vālmīki. A curse—earned by his having inadvertently shot and killed a young ascetic—promises he will grieve at the end of his days for his own son. I would add that one must note that Daśaratha listens to the demands and advice of sages, particularly in the Bālakāṇḍa, offering Rāma to their service on their command. This is, of course, a fundamental component of adherence to *dharma* and the core theme of this book, namely, that of *kṣatriyas* honoring the will and word of Brahmins. Thus, Pollock (1986: 61) suggests that the core of the narrative, a story of an elderly king who was "overmastered by his passion for a beautiful young woman," is transmuted (through additions to the core narrative) into one of a king who (1986: 62–63) "is no longer a victim of his own choices ... he is instead a victim of chance. And thereby, again, his probity is preserved intact."

[55] See at *Rāmāyaṇa* 3.8.3–6: *trīṇy eva vyasanāny atra kāmajāni bhavanty uta | mithyāvākyaṃ paramakaṃ tasmād gurutarāv ubhau | paradārābhigamanaṃ vinā vairaṃ ca raudratā || mithyāvākyaṃ na te bhūtaṃ na bhaviṣyati rāghava | kuto 'bhilaṣaṇaṃ strīṇāṃ pareṣāṃ dharmanāśanam || tac ca sarvaṃ mahābāho śakyaṃ voḍhuṃ jitendriyaiḥ | tava vaśyendriyatvaṃ ca jānāmi śubhadarśana || tṛtīyaṃ yad idaṃ raudraṃ paraprāṇābhihiṃsanam | nirvairaṃ kriyate mohāt tac ca te samupasthitam ||*. Translation that of Pollock.

Lying, one notes, is simply and thoroughly beyond the pale. To violence we shall return below, but it may suffice here to say that Rāma indulges violence in at least two places where his actions are suspect: he sees Śūrpaṇakhā mutilated and kills Vālin under questionable circumstances. And there is a third one already mentioned above, but one that elicits no sense of *dharmic* puzzlement or rebuke in Vālmīki's text (or, to my knowledge, in the scholarly literature): Rāma kills a Brahmin—Rāvaṇa.

Desire that overspills the borders of *dharma* is precisely what fuels the narrative turns of the *Rāmāyaṇa*. It is a love story, after all, inspired by sympathy for a *krauñca* bird who lost her lover. The fundamental conflict of the epic, it can therefore be no coincidence, is met between Rāvaṇa, who lusts unrepentantly, and Rāma, who, though thoroughly chastened, sometimes swoons—even to the point of madness—for his sole beloved, Sītā.[56] Maintaining the virtue ethic recommended by the narrative literatures consists in nothing less than controlling one's desires and impulses, and so it is no coincidence that the problems of this epic begin because Daśaratha desired Kaikeyī. And however he wins her favor—the epic, as noted, is self-contradictory on this point[57]—there can be no question that her beauty and youth, as Mantharā counsels, can—and do—help her win Daśaratha's consent to her wishes. Indeed, with much consternation Daśaratha complies with her requests, rendered thereby a man true to his word. The "deliberate misdeed" of desire drives the demand for truthfulness at the cost of the loss of Daśaratha's son to exile.

What do we have in a text that shows a common fidelity to truth, desire that can spin out of order, and the presence of the fundamental misdeed of intentional violence? We generally are not met with the kinds of falls from *dharma* that we saw (in Chapter 1) in the *Mahābhārata*, transgressions of convenient and self-directed logic, where self-dealing or a surfeit of loyalty is performed in the name of *dharma* despite the dangerous transgressions of and damage to *dharmic* order that they precipitate. Indeed, we hardly see in the *Mahābhārata* any repentance (as opposed to regret), any sense that by contrition over an error one can come to amend the same.[58]

[56] See *Rāmāyaṇa* 3.58–62, where Vālmīki's text narrates what Pollock 1991: 55–67 describes as "Rāma's madness" over the loss of Sītā.

[57] Pollock 1986: 26–28 has gone over this matter in some detail. See also *Rāmāyaṇa* 2.9.9–13 and compare with *Rāmāyaṇa* 2.10, esp. 2.10.14–25.

[58] Arjuna's apology to Kṛṣṇa in the *Bhagavadgītā* perhaps presents in this vein, but there we have a private relationship of honored trust, something akin to what is, by contrast, not private but engendered in the wider ambit of general social relations in the *Rāmāyaṇa*, it being an epic of an earlier eon, when *dharma* could function better.

The *Rāmāyaṇa*'s principal actors, in fortuitous contrast, can be expected not to produce sentiments of overwrought and overconfident indignance—a self-righteousness—but rather acts precipitating remorse after the fact.

Deliberate misdeeds around desire, but in the context of a fidelity to truth—this is the nature of a mere slip from the path, not that of an intentional warping of *dharma* to suit one's preferences or needs. It is not a sentiment of righteousness to cover one's in fact indulgent choices, but a pattern of anamnesis—of remembering *dharma* again and re-enacting it with self-restraint, after having forgotten it in a moment along the righteous path of values shared in community with others. There can be no doubt: Rāma—as a human being or as a God performing that identity for those who follow him—would have regretted *dharmic* transgressions, just as those loyal members of the community he leads and models would—and do—as well.

One thus witnesses *dharma* broken in regrettable slips at the points that in fact turn the narrative. Even Sītā, who is across the epic so utterly innocent, chastened, loyal, and pure, performed this transgressive act of commission, however slightly (this, it seems, being her sole flaw or slip from virtue): she wished for the golden deer, the pursuit of which created the occasion for her kidnapping.[59] But overall her *rôle* is that of impeccable purity embodied, such purity that fire cannot burn her, for there is no impurity to burn. (Fire here plays a metaphorical role as well as a literal one, of course, just as Hanumān burned Laṅkā to purify it, the city being a place of lust, the site of Rāvaṇa's overindulgence, but one of absolutely no interest to Sītā.[60])

Sītā wanted the deer in a costly lapse of discipline, a lapse triggered by desire; and, as so often transpires in the *Mahābhārata* if all the more devastatingly so, her loved ones are near to hand to fulfill her (ill-advised) wish. A certain surfeit of loyalty to her desire is what causes Rāma to chase the deer; the desire to give a loved one what is desired leads to harm. Sītā is in this sense partially responsible for her own kidnapping, but *so is he*. And yet—and this is crucial—the voluntary transgressions are but lapses in discipline.

[59] The deer is, of course, the *rākṣasa* Mārīca in disguise. See *Rāmāyaṇa* 3.41, esp. 3.41.9. Goldman and Sutherland Goldman 2009: 51 characterizes the episode in terms of Sītā's "willfulness in wheedling Rāma to pursue the illusory deer."

[60] Goldman has suggested that the rationale for the naming of the Sundarakāṇḍa is indeterminate. (See Goldman 1984: 10–11, fn. 13. Cf. Goldman and Sutherland Goldman 1996: 75–78.) One possible explanation is that the *kāṇḍa* is so named, in Vālmīki's text at least, to emphasize the riches of Rāvaṇa's world, which to any weak-willed woman might have appealed but by which Sītā was never tempted. Indeed, Kampaṉ depicts Rāma accusing Sītā of enjoying the "feasts" supplied in Rāvaṇa's company. See Shulman 1991: 100. The *kāṇḍa*'s name therefore could also refer to the beauty of Sītā's purity and resistance to such temptations.

No habit of denial, of lying to oneself, of covering one's error with righteous indignation, permits these transgressions to perdure, to be defended perpetually as right, when they were wrong and, crucially, they quickly come to be recognized as such. There simply is no stubborn insistence on doing what is infelicitous in the name of what is virtuous in the *Rāmāyaṇa*, as there is in the *Mahābhārata* (though Rāvaṇa acts with impunity, as we shall explore in what follows.) Yes, it is desire—what can be defined as pursuing a personal wish against normative social rules or restraints—that defines all the problems of Vālmīki's epic, this in a context of general truthfulness, of an implicitly followed virtue ethic.

Perhaps, though, with one exception? It is somewhat surprising that one discussion is largely absent from the *Rāmāyaṇa*, particularly given its prevalence in the *Mahābhārata*. It is this, that deliberate misdeeds around violence are hardly explored in Vālmīki's text. Indeed, as Pollock has noted, the Ayodhyākāṇḍa "seeks to establish an innovative definition of the *dharma*, the code of conduct of *kṣatriyas*: Violence as far as possible is to be eschewed in the realm of sociopolitical action."[61] One major concern over violence is expressed in the *Rāmāyaṇa*, however, though not around Śūpanakhā's mutilation in the Āraṇyakāṇḍa,[62] in which "this new definition of *kṣatradharma* is not always applicable."[63] It rather involves—this is well known—the famed episode around Rāma's slaying of Vālin: he shot him from a place of hiding.[64]

The episode begins to unfold from the very first pages of the Kiṣkindhākāṇḍa, which closely follows after the narration of Rāma's "madness" over the loss of Sītā. Indeed, the quest to search every inch of the forest to find her is precisely what brings Rāma and Lakṣmaṇa to Kiṣkindhā in the first place. Also well known is the fact that the episode presents a certain moral ambiguity, with the epic suggesting three (somewhat dubious) reasons to justify Rāma's questionable manner of killing Vālin: first, Rāma defends his action by claiming he must, as a representative of the Ikṣvāku king (i.e., of Bharata, his brother), punish all who commit adultery; second, he promised his ally Sugrīva he would do so, and so had to honor his pledge; and third, Rāma says Vālin was but a forest creature, and could therefore be hunted like

[61] Pollock 1991: 55.

[62] This episode goes without serious self-reflection in Vālmīki's text. The penchant of the Vālmīki *Rāmāyaṇa* to set women at a comparative disadvantage to men, alluded to around footnote 18, thus again finds voice, through this silence, in this episode.

[63] Pollock 1991: 55.

[64] See *Rāmāyaṇa* 4.16–18, esp. 4.16.25 and 4.17.13.

prey—a royal prerogative—and he needn't have been fought on equal terms and according to the strictures of *kṣatriyadharma*.[65]

Lefeber, following Srinavasa Sastri, speculates as to another reason for Rāma's violence. It is that Rāma had to resort to treachery because he perhaps would not have been able to defeat the powerful monkey if he chose to fight with the weapons and in the mode of combat most familiar to Vālin.[66] She goes on to suggest that, regardless, the story clearly was included from an early stage in the epic and was retained in Vālmīki's text because "it was understood to be a true account of what had actually happened or at the very least, a faithful repetition of the traditional tale."[67]

This minimal explanation for the presence of this episode is indisputable, but there must be more to the moral ambiguities here presented than this. Masson has suggested the following of Sugrīva's narrative, which explains his circumstance and is meant to fortify a rationale for alliance with Rāma and Lakṣmaṇa: "To put it bluntly: the story stinks."[68] Masson understands Sugrīva not to be innocently victimized by his brother, who refuses to understand or accept the explanation Sugrīva offered for closing Vālin in the cave into which he descended to kill a demon, as well as his subsequent ascension to the throne on the understanding that Vālin was killed in that cave. On Masson's reading of the episode, Sugrīva was malicious, but he successfully spins a tale to win Rāma's support, because Rāma is hardly impartial in his hearing it.

Rāma hears of Sugrīva's banishment, and that his brother had stolen his wife, Rumā, along the way, before ever setting eyes on Vālin. Suffering still from his recent loss of Sītā, Rāma sees—and wants to see—in his new acquaintance's predicament a striking affinity with his own circumstance. Here, moreover, a confluence of all the three voluntary misdeeds identified by Sītā can be seen: Rāma's lament over the loss of his wife, which he sees mirrored in Sugrīva's loss at the hands of his brother, exposes the lust of his newfound opponent, Vālin, who steals Sugrīva's wife. Rāma's promise, his commitment to truthfulness, requires his loyalty to Sugrīva (which perhaps

[65] See *Rāmāyaṇa* 4.18. These are of course well known and have been cited by other scholars repeatedly, for example, Lefeber 1994: 45.

[66] See Lefeber 1994: 47. This is not entirely implausible in light of, for example, *Rāmāyaṇa* 4.11.48: *etad asyāsamaṃ vīryaṃ mayā rāma prakāśitam | kathaṃ taṃ vālinaṃ hantuṃ samare śakṣyase nṛpa* ||. "I have made clear to you his unequaled strength, Rāma. How then will you be able to kill Vālin in battle, king?" Translation Lefeber's.

[67] See Lefeber 1994: 49. In doing so she notes (1994: 49, fn. 168) that Bulcke (1960: 58) took this to indicate that Vālmīki understood the Rāma story to be historical.

[68] Masson 1975: 674.

explains his capacity to overlook the fact that Sugrīva himself committed adultery with Tārā, Vālin's wife, and was overinvolved with her even after Vālin's death). And, finally, Rāma's capacity to commit the voluntary misdeed of excessive violence, as Sītā predicted he could, emerged with his killing of Vālin.

Key to the episode is not only the fact that Rāma met Sugrīva first, before Vālin, but also that Sugrīva could give evidence that Sītā lived: Sugrīva saw her being carried off, and she dropped her shawl and some ornaments as evidence of the same, which he presents to Rāma and Lakṣmaṇa.[69] Along with this, his alliance with Sugrīva calms Rāma's grief,[70] which further explains his preference for him over Vālin. Thus his pledge to do whatever he must to aid Sugrīva, who will help him find his wife: "You must tell me without reservation what I am to do for you. Everything will succeed for you, like crops in a good field during the rains. And you must regard as the truth those words that I proudly spoke, tiger among monkeys. I have never spoken a falsehood before, nor shall I ever speak one. I promise you this, I swear it to you, by truth itself."[71] A desire to be reunited with his wife drives Rāma to alliance with Sugrīva; it is a legitimate desire but one the need for which was precipitated by indulging misplaced desire—Sītā's for the deer, Rāma's to satisfy hers.

If he could have clearly thought about it, Rāma had much to find in common with Vālin. Both are elder sons who had been wrongly deprived of their rightful place as king.[72] Both had their wives taken from them. In Vālin's case, moreover, both difficulties are considerably more serious: Vālin's wife was an adulteress, and with his brother no less, while Sītā remained pure; Vālin's brother ascended the throne, while Bharata refused to do so. Rāma, however—likely out of distress, as noted already—is hasty in forming his

[69] *Rāmāyaṇa* 4.6.7–15.

[70] See *Rāmāyaṇa* 4.7.14–21, esp. 4.7.17 (*eṣa ca prakṛtiṣṭho 'ham anunītas tvayā sakhe | durlabho hīdṛśo bandhur asmin kāle viśeṣataḥ* ||), where Rāma says: "Here I am, my friend, comforted by you and restored to my normal state. Such a friend is indeed hard to find, particularly at a time like this." Translation Lefeber's.

[71] *Rāmāyaṇa* 4.7.19–21: *mayā ca yad anuṣṭheyaṃ visrabdhena tad ucyatām | varṣāsv iva ca sukṣetre sarvaṃ saṃpadyate tava || mayā ca yad idaṃ vākyam abhimānāt samīritam | tat tvayā hariśārdūla tattvam ity upadhāryatām || anṛtaṃ noktapūrvaṃ me na ca vakṣye kadācana | etat te pratijānāmi satyenaiva śapāmi te* ||. Translation Lefeber's.

[72] But there is a complication here. If Sugrīva had intended to dethrone his brother, the rightful heir to the throne, then Rāma had every reason to sympathize with Vālin and not Sugrīva. But if Sugrīva had indeed behaved more nobly, in a manner in consonance with both his own side of the story and Bharata's refusal to take the throne in Rāma's place, then Rāma's vitriol toward Vālin could be explained by a sensitivity to the danger he himself, at least theoretically, as a human, would face: his emotions uncontrolled, he too could have chosen to act as Vālin did (on this interpretation of Sugrīva's intentions) and violently accost his own brother, Bharata.

alliance with Sugrīva, who nearly fails to take up his part of the bargain after being returned to rule Kiṣkindhā (he procrastinates, enjoying the luxuries of kingship, rather than promptly harnessing his kingdom's resources to help find Sītā as he promised to do).[73]

Alliance with a usurping adulterer. Violence (perhaps) beyond the bounds of propriety. Loyalty in the form of a committed promise to act on behalf of such a questionable ally.[74] All stem from seeking to indulge what was wrongly wished for—the golden deer, for casually disfiguring a demoness whose brother was called to action in response. Slips from *dharma*, however small, can precipitate compounding difficulties, partial compromises with one's deeply held values (alliance with Sugrīva). The better path is strict fidelity to *dharma*, because the path away from *dharma*, even when the first step onto it is inadvertently taken, can quickly tread a difficult terrain, even if, due to fidelity to truth, one can say the path is not a slippery slope: it does not lead to cascading slips from *dharma*, only cascading consequences of the isolated slip.

This lesson alone, I propose, may explain what is emotionally perhaps the most upsetting of all of Rāma's acts, his (temporary) abdication of Sītā on winning the battle against Rāvaṇa. I believe the epic here wishes to make a rather *favorable* claim for Rāma, one of expressed repentance and a wish not to self-deceive, nor to elect to pursue his own desires over the greater good. Rāma's treatment of Sītā upon freeing her from Rāvaṇa is stunning, no doubt. His primary emotion is pure anger: "As he gazed upon Maithilī, who stood so meekly beside him, Rāma began to speak, as rage simmered in his heart."[75] Why does Rāma *feel* such anger here? Wherefrom his rage?

It is clear that he blames her for this turn of events, for he rejects her outright:[76]

> "I have recovered my reputation [by rescuing you], and that is the purpose for which I have won you back. I do not love you anymore. Go hence wherever you like."

[73] *Rāmāyaṇa* 4.28–31, esp., e.g., 4.29.45 and 4.31.8.

[74] Indeed, perhaps this explains Rāma's literal inability to distinguish Vālin from Sugrīva when he witnesses their combat for the first time: they are, morally speaking, approaching a level of indistinguishability.

[75] *Rāmāyaṇa* 6.103.1: *tāṃ tu pārśve sthitāṃ prahvāṃ rāmaḥ saṃprekṣya maithilīm | hṛdayāntargatakrodho vyāhartum upacakrame* ||. Translation that of Goldman, Sutherland Goldman, and van Nooten.

[76] *Rāmāyaṇa* 6.103.21: *tadarthaṃ nirjitā me tvaṃ yaśaḥ pratyāhṛtaṃ mayā | nāsti me tvayy abhiṣvaṅgo yatheṣṭaṃ gamyatām itaḥ* ||. Translation that of Goldman, Sutherland Goldman, and van Nooten.

This is precisely what shocks the audience so profoundly, for it can hardly be the case that all blame may rightly be placed at her feet. Surely he shares the blame for her kidnapping, and surely he knows this. Nor is the audience so credulous as to believe Rāma does not love Sītā. His "madness," precipitated by losing Sītā, was not wrapped up in Rāma's concern over his reputation. Does he not miss her? Could he truly not love her?

The episode must be read in contrast with those involving not only the likes of Daśaratha, who indulges his love of Kaikeyī at a cost to his son, but also all the characters of the *Mahābhārata* who out of a surfeit of loyalty give in to the personal whims and preferences of their loved ones, doing so over and against what must be done for the public good. Simply put, Rāma angrily relinquishes Sītā *despite* his love for her, not due to any lack of interest in and care for her; he acts with a surfeit of loyalty to *dharma*, the mirror opposite of the *Mahābhārata*'s surfeit of loyalty to loved ones despite the demands of *dharma*. Even if it is the case, as Goldman and Sutherland Goldman note, that this is the episode in which "for the first time in the epic, the hero, so rightly admired for his emotional stability and moral certitude, is shown to be prey to seriously conflicting emotions,"[77] so too is it the case, I argue, that the lack of care for Sītā he expressed—even perhaps felt in the heat of the moment—was born not out of any self-indulgence or casual care only for the personal but rather, quite the opposite, out of a care for the wider community that he is to serve (as Goldman and Sutherland Goldman also indicate). Consider Rāma's explanation of his actions to Agni:[78]

> "Unquestionably Sītā needed to be proven innocent before the three worlds, since this auspicious woman had long dwelt in Rāvaṇa's inner apartments. For surely had I not put Jānakī to the test, the virtuous would have said of me, 'Daśaratha's son Rāma is a lustful fool.' I know full well that Janaka's daughter Maithilī could give her heart to no other, since she is devoted to me and obeys my every thought. But in order that the three worlds, too, should have faith in her, I, whose ultimate recourse is truth, simply stood by as Vaidehī entered the fire, eater of oblations."

[77] Goldman and Sutherland Goldman 2009: 48.

[78] *Rāmāyaṇa* 6.106.11–14 (cited also in Goldman and Sutherland Goldman 2009: 49): *avaśyaṃ triṣu lokeṣu sītā pāvanam arhati | dīrghakāloṣitā ceyaṃ rāvaṇāntaḥpure śubhā || bāliśaḥ khalu kāmātmā rāmo daśarathātmajaḥ | iti vakṣyanti māṃ santo jānakīm aviśodhya hi || ananyahṛdayāṃ bhaktāṃ maccittaparirakṣaṇīm | aham apy avagacchāmi maithilīṃ janakātmajām || pratyayārthaṃ tu lokānāṃ trayāṇāṃ satyasaṃśrayaḥ | upekṣe cāpi vaidehīṃ praviśantīṃ hutāśanam ||*. Translation that of Goldman, Sutherland Goldman, and van Nooten.

Thus, while there is no doubt a certain blind spot here to the travails of the woman placed under this test,[79] the narrative purport of the same is intended to present Rāma in the act of putting the needs of a *dharmic* society ahead of his own wishes. The greater good trumps his personal preferences. As Goldman and Sutherland Goldman put it, "This reunion, much as Rāma has longed for it and suffered to achieve it, presents him with one of those painful dilemmas that the epic poets like to thrust upon their exemplary heroes—crises where they are confronted with a seemingly irresoluble conflict between public duty, or *dharma*, and personal loyalty. In this case Rāma, determined not to compromise his reputation as a *dharmic* monarch, must place the political over the personal, although doing so will cause him and his innocent wife terrible anguish."[80]

Yes, this is so because Sītā slipped and pursued a desire for the golden deer that was ill-advised and misplaced. And this in turn is so because Rāma too slipped in indulging of his wife just that desire out of a surfeit of loyalty to and affection for her.[81] But yes—and finally—these slips, *their* slips, were not destined to be perpetuated by self-denial, by overwrought self-righteousness, by any sense of personal preference and loyalty pursued in the name of public virtue; they rather served as vehicles to drive Rāma to his fundamental purpose: punishing the evil demon Rāvaṇa.[82] *Dharma* reigns in the *Rāmāyaṇa* because it is fundamentally internalized. Rāma, Vālmīki wishes to convey, shuns Sītā out of a sense that *dharma* outweighs personal preference, convenience, or whim.

Rāma and Rāvaṇa

Desire in the Vālmīki *Rāmāyaṇa*, then, is the voluntary misdeed that prevails, ahead of any penchant for untruthfulness. But again we must ask, what about the violence? We cannot forget, after all, the double edge of the *dharmic* community: shared virtue and restraint is held closely but also

[79] A similar gender bias is found as well in the *Kathāsaritsāgara*, for example, about which see Davis and Nemec 2016.

[80] Goldman and Sutherland Goldman 2009: 48.

[81] And thus perhaps his anger at her is partially misplaced anger with himself.

[82] On this reading, then, Sītā's suffering is presented as *beneficial* to the audience of the epic, because it serves to remind one of the very difficulties of adhering to *dharma*. It is difficult; it involves sacrifice. Sītā's suffering is of benefit to the epic's audience, that is, because Rāma deeply wishes it could be otherwise.

knows an out-group, in practice sometimes viciously so. Vālmīki narrates an internal struggle, one generally met successfully by the protagonists, if sometimes with slips against *dharma*; but what of the external dimensions of the *Rāmāyaṇa*'s narrative around *dharma*? What of the antagonists? The epic, after all, is largely composed of a literal quest to kill an enemy—Rāvaṇa—an enemy who lusts unrepentantly, yes, but also an enemy who, like the Niṣāda who shot the *krauñca* bird, is not only an outsider, a *rākṣasa*, but also (girded by his boon[83]) gratuitously violent, both martially and sexually.[84] How can one unlock the message of the *Rāmāyaṇa* with a key defined by interest in how Rāma felt—in how we are to understand his feeling and follow him into it—when the entire narrative arc is also driven, in some sense is primarily driven, by his endeavor to eliminate an external foe?

It would be naïve not to recognize the power that Vālmīki's text grants to those who find themselves faced with an external foe, real or imagined, an external enemy understood to be a fundamental threat to *dharma*. Both the Niṣāda hunter at the heart of the origin story of both the *śloka* meter and the poem, on the one hand, and the *Rāmāyaṇa*'s antagonist par excellence—Rāvaṇa—on the other hand, not only symbolize but also present themselves palpably as malevolent forces who fundamentally threaten the social order from the outside. Rāvaṇa, specifically, is a devil in Vālmīki's text, as his sexual and martial exploits in the Uttarakāṇḍa illustrate.[85]

Yet, Rāvaṇa in fact is not depicted entirely, or at least not merely, as a wicked king. The "otherness" of Rāvaṇa and the *rākṣasas* more generally is at the least partially undermined by the depictions of Laṅkā, for example, which in its qualities and beauty may be said to be comparable with Ayodhyā itself, as Pollock has suggested.[86] In death, moreover, the gap between Rāvaṇa and his human counterparts also is narrowed: as Goldman and Sutherland Goldman note, on being slayed by Rāma he is given "the full honors appropriate to a noble adversary and a member of brahmanical society."[87] Of

[83] Brahmā grants Rāvaṇa the boon of being invincible to all but a human opponent, for which see *Rāmāyaṇa* 7.10.13–22.

[84] See Goldman and Sutherland Goldman 2017: 24.

[85] Just one citation might suffice for the multiple *sargas* of stories in the Uttarakāṇḍa: Rāvaṇa is cursed at *Rāmāyaṇa* 7.24.15 to meet his death on account of a woman, due to his evil-minded lusting after others' wives.

[86] See Pollock 1991: 75.

[87] See Goldman and Sutherland Goldman 2009: 74–75. See also *Rāmāyaṇa* 6.99.36–40, where Rāma recommends a proper funeral for Rāvaṇa, and 6.99.41–42, where it is recorded that Vibhīṣaṇa gives him the same.

particular remark is the narration of the wailing regret of his wives, who despondently lament his passing.[88] Rāvaṇa's wives, that is, are hardly mere victims of abduction. In fact, they also love him for his charms.[89] Goldman and Sutherland Goldman go so far as to suggest that Rāvaṇa, perhaps more than any character in the two epics apart perhaps from Karṇa,[90] is presented as a sort of tragic figure.[91] Taking into consideration the circumstances around his birth, one could even say, as Goldman and Sutherland Goldman do, that "if we follow the logic of the story [of his birth], Rāvaṇa is hardly to be held accountable for his evil nature."[92]

The circumstances of Rāvaṇa's birth are worth pondering further, for they both raise into high relief and help to explain the silence in the *Rāmāyaṇa* regarding the Brahminicide, the killing of a Brahmin such as Rāvaṇa was.[93] His place in the world came to be in the following manner. His mother-to-be, Kaikasī, was sent by her father, who wished her to have a husband, to a Brahmin who was caught in the midst of performing a sacrifice. This man who would become Rāvaṇa's father was working the sacrifice in its "fearsome hour" (*dāruṇā velā*), and so when on being interrupted by her he promised to wed Kaikasī, he also warned that the interruption would precipitate a curse: the fearsomeness of the moment of the sacrifice promised that her children would be ferocious by nature from birth. (A modification of the curse explains the redemption of Rāvaṇa's brother Vibhīṣaṇa.)

We must not forget Rāvaṇa's pedigree. He cannot be entirely or at the least simply an outsider to the *dharmic* community, because he was in fact the son not only of Kaikasī, the daughter of the accomplished *rākṣasa* ascetic Sumālin, but also of Viśravas, the son of Pulasya, the very ascetic whom

[88] *Rāmāyaṇa* 6.98–99.

[89] See *Rāmāyaṇa* 5.7.66, cited also in Pollock 1991: 81–82. What is similar is also expressed, for example, at *Rāmāyaṇa* 6.98.5 (*tā bāṣpaparipūrṇākṣyo bhartṛśokaparājitāḥ | kareṇva iva nardantyo vinedur hatayūthapāḥ ||*): "Overcome with grief for their lord, their eye filled with tears, they cried, shrieking like elephant cows when the leader of their herd is slain." Translation that of Goldman and Sutherland Goldman.

[90] On Karṇa's status as a possible tragic figure, see Chapter 2.

[91] See Goldman and Sutherland Goldman 2009: 71.

[92] See Goldman and Sutherland Goldman 2017: 26.

[93] References to Rāvaṇa's brahmanical heritage are numerous in the epic. See, e.g., *Rāmāyaṇa* 6.68.17: *durātmann ātmanāśāya keśapakṣe parāmṛśaḥ | brahmarṣīṇāṃ kule jāto rākṣasīṃ yonim āśritaḥ | dhik tvāṃ pāpasamācāraṃ yasya te matir īdṛśī ||*. "Evil wretch! By way of seizing [Sītā's] hair, it is your own destruction that has been seized. You are born in the family of Brahmin Seers, having resorted [for that birth] to a *rākṣasa* woman's womb. Damn you, whose conduct is sinful, your mind being disposed as it is."

Kaikasī had interrupted. Rāvaṇa, that is, is not only the half-brother of Kubera (who also was fathered by Viśravas) but also the great-grandson of Viśravas's grandfather: Brahmā himself. Rāvaṇa's very pedigree not only is that of a Brahmin, but also he is born in the family line of the creator god himself. He is an outsider, no doubt, but by birth is half-insider as well.

If he is a tragic hero of sorts, it is so not as the product of his innately evil nature or his licentiousness, but rather of his arrogance, which is pitiful: he could have known Rāma would best him in battle, because Rāma clearly did so in their first round of combat;[94] but Rāvaṇa returns for more. And it is an arrogance found also in his unyielding desire for Sītā and his relentless insistence on keeping her captive even when it is clear that doing so will bring great difficulties to his kingdom of Laṅkā. And so there can be no doubt that Rāvaṇa's principal transgression was lustfulness, a stubborn and unceasing lustfulness, unrepentantly and for another's wife. Vālmīki's text, as is well known, is quite explicit about this as well.[95]

Circumstances progressively deteriorate under Rāvaṇa's reign in Laṅkā, as Rāma and his allies steadily close their vice on his fortress kingdom, once believed to be impenetrable. He is shown progressively to fall apart as he, consumed by passion, *fails to take the good counsel of his advisors*, that of his brother Vibhīṣaṇa, for example, or of his great-uncle Mālyavān,[96] which is a sure sign of failure in a king. His lack of virtue tells, and for this he pays the price. And yet, he remains to the last simultaneously beloved of his wives (as noted already) and well served by his loyal lieutenants. His person is not the king of virtue ethics, but the king of desire: wanted by women, but unable to control his senses, and therefore unable to maintain his kingdom. Unlike the kings who travel with tantric wizards in the *Kathāsaritsāgara*, as we shall see in Chapter 4, he is unable to win wealth and power (*artha*) in the course of winning the pleasure (*kāma*) found by way of winning wives. Liberation too, which we shall see earned in the form of immortality by the hero of the *Kathāsaritsāgara*, is also beyond his reach. Desire indulged as a voluntary vice renders to kings a passing pleasure that is transitory, intoxicating, and devastating.

94 The same is noted in Goldman and Sutherland Goldman 2009: 74. See *Rāmāyaṇa* 6.47.127, 6.47.135, 6.48.1–7.

95 See, to offer but one example, *Rāmāyaṇa* 6.99.14.

96 The same was noted in Goldman and Sutherland Goldman 2009: 71–72. (See *Rāmāyaṇa* 6.10.1–11, 6.26.5–33.) As they go on to note, "Rāvaṇa's inability to benefit from sound counsel is demonstrated time and again in the Book [i.e., the Yuddhakāṇḍa]."

So the *Rāmāyaṇa*'s battle is an external one, between two imposing and opposing figures of great power and *dharmic* qualities. But the battle is also one, in a certain sense, fought by brethren—at least insofar as Rāvaṇa's pedigree marks him as begotten of Brahmā and the heir to a great tradition of religious austerity. The struggle is one between a king devoted to *dharma* and a Brahmin who has little interest in upholding the same.[97] Here, the relationship between Brahmin and *kṣatriya* is patterned on the model of the latter righteously holding the former to *dharmic* ideals. They should be shared ideals, though Rāvaṇa falls short; but they share in the same law of the natural order: the virtue ethic wins all prizes, and falling short of that mark yields tragic *karmic* consequences.

Other clues tip toward understanding Rāma's challenge—his hero's quest (at least in the Vālmīki *Rāmāyaṇa* in its final form)—to be ultimately if not exclusively an internal quest. Vālmīki hints at as much through the speech of the sage Agastya in the Uttarakāṇḍa, for example, when he says the slaying of Rāvaṇa was no great event, no "serious challenge."[98]

> "By no means did Rāvaṇa, the lord of the *rākṣasas*, present you with a serious challenge. For, armed with your bow, there is no doubt that you could conquer the three worlds."

And:[99]

> "The defeat of Rāvaṇa in battle was no great thing. But thank heavens you engaged in single combat with Indrajit Rāvaṇi and slew him."

The same is exemplified, I would further suggest, in the episode in question in the Yuddhakāṇḍa itself, when Rāma in fact slays the demon-king. We are told it is a "great battle," this is true;[100] and it is one that is said to

[97] As Pollock 1991: 68 notes, there also is a contrast in the ways in which women are offended in the two epics: while the *Mahābhārata* narrates a public outrage with Draupadī's humiliation in the Sabhāparvan, Rāvaṇa's kidnapping of Sītā, occurring away from the city and in the isolating forest, is a private event. I would add that the forest setting is symbolic of internal struggle, the forest being associable with world renunciation and the striving of ascetical seekers.

[98] *Rāmāyaṇa* 7.1.14: *na hi bhāraḥ sa te rāma rāvaṇo rākṣaseśvaraḥ | sadhanus tvaṃ hi lokāṃs trīn vijayethā na saṃśayaḥ ||*. Translation that of Goldman and Sutherland Goldman.

[99] *Rāmāyaṇa* 7.1.19: *saṃkhye tasya na kiṃcit tu rāvaṇasya parābhavaḥ | dvandvayuddham anuprāpto diṣṭyā te rāvaṇir hataḥ ||*. Translation that of Goldman and Sutherland Goldman.

[100] See *Rāmāyaṇa* 6.95.1.

have continued night and day without interruption.[101] The external threat is presented as real, that is, and one can understand how this battle justifiably takes on epic proportions in various retellings and enactments of the *Rāmāyaṇa*. Yet, the narrative in Vālmīki's Yuddhakāṇḍa quickly puts the battle to rest. The entire combat of Rāma and Rāvaṇa is conveyed, start to finish, in only three *sargas*, composed of a total of only ninety verses.[102] And the moment of Rāvaṇa's death is recorded anticlimactically, by indirect description:[103]

> Filled with fury toward Rāvaṇa and exerting himself to the utmost, he [Rāma] bent the bow fully and loosed that arrow [from the "divinely charged weapon of Grandfather Brahmā" (*Rāmāyaṇa* 6.97.2)], which struck at one's vital points. As unstoppable as the *vajra* hurled by Indra, the *vajra* wielder, and as inescapable as fate, it fell upon Rāvaṇa's chest. Loosed with tremendous force, that lethal arrow pierced evil-minded Rāvaṇa's heart. Drenched with blood, the lethal arrow swiftly entered the earth, carrying off the life breaths of Rāvaṇa. Once the arrow had accomplished its purpose in killing Rāvaṇa, it dutifully returned to its quiver, glistening with its still-wet blood.

It is as if the arrow killed Rāvaṇa of its own volition.

The balance of the *sarga*, also concise, is dedicated to reactions of those around Rāma and Rāvaṇa, the troops of the monkey and *rākṣasa* armies respectively jubilant and in rout. The gods praise Rāma; flowers fall from the sky, yes. But that's it. Rāma is lost, almost, in the sea of the community around him. That and the wailing of Rāvaṇa's loving wives . . .

At the level of allegory, the *rākṣasas* more generally may be said to embody the kinds of forces that would drive one from self-constraining adherence to *dharma*. They harass the ascetical Brahmins doing *tapasya* in the

[101] See *Rāmāyaṇa* 6.96.31: *naiva ratriṃ na divasaṃ na muhūrtaṃ na cakṣaṇam* | *rāmarāvaṇayor yuddhaṃ virāmam upagacchati* ||.

[102] *Rāmāyaṇa* 6.95-97.

[103] *Rāmāyaṇa* 6.97.15–19: *sa rāvaṇāya saṃkruddho bhṛśam āyamya kārmukam* | *cikṣepa param āyattas taṃ śaraṃ marmaghātinam* || *sa vajra iva durdharṣo vajrabāhuvisarjitaḥ* | *kṛtānta iva cāvāryo nyapatad rāvaṇorasi* || *sa visṛṣṭo mahāvegaḥ śarīrāntakaraḥ śaraḥ* | *bibheda hṛdayaṃ tasya rāvaṇasya durātmanaḥ* || *rudhirāktaḥ sa vegena jīvitāntakaraḥ śaraḥ* | *rāvaṇasya haran prāṇān viveśa dharaṇītalam* || *sa śaro rāvaṇaṃ hatvā rudhirārdrakṛtacchaviḥ* | *kṛtakarmā nibhṛtavat svatūṇīṃ punar āviśat* ||. Translation that of Goldman, Sutherland Goldman, and van Nooten.

forest; they are associated from their earliest incarnations in Indian literature with "intemperate and aggressive sexuality."[104] They are dangerous, to be sure, and they can and do represent an external threat. Yet, the external threat at minimum also may be understood to be an internal one, because what makes the *rākṣasas* dangerous in part also is precisely what made the Niṣāda hunter dangerous: each engages practices and indulges whims and emotions that members of the *dharmic* community very well could indulge as well. Addiction to hunting, one must recall, is a perennial danger to kings, as is the addiction of chasing amorous encounters.

Rāvaṇa's ultimate *dharmic* transgression is his utter insistence on his wayward path. He simply refuses, as anyone could and as many in the *Mahābhārata* do, to adjust his actions, even when they show themselves to be infelicitous and dangerous. This above all, this unrepenting arrogance and willful continuance with *adharma*, is what justifies the killing of Rāvaṇa, the killing of one of a Brahmin's pedigree—the grandson of Brahmā—without any pondering of any problem therewith. Rāvaṇa deserves to die, and his unrepentant posture is the reason why.

Thus, in fact, a fundamental danger lies in merely understanding these foes to be external, in denying the potential transgressions in oneself that one sees in the *rākṣasas*. Fanaticism is the product of externalization; a true fidelity to *dharma* requires one to see *oneself* as its greatest threat. The *Rāmāyaṇa* instructs its audiences that a failure to repent and to adjust to one's slips from *dharma* is the pattern of the less auspicious times of the *Mahābhārata*. It is the transgression indulged by a demon like Vālmīki's Rāvaṇa. Self-serving logics, denial of one's own implication in any slip from *dharma*, seeing only the other and not oneself as to blame—these are the falls from virtue ethics that are real dangers to one such as Rāvaṇa, to any and all who claim *dharma* as their guide. Vālmīki's epic must be understood to present this as the matter to hand, for otherwise Rāma would never have forgotten his true identity. Rāma the god, the incarnation of Viṣṇu in human form, would otherwise never have needed reminding of his true self—and nor would those of us who are members of the epic's external audience.

104 See Pollock 1991: 79. He there cites (1991: 79, fn. 170) *Śatapatha Brāhmaṇa* 3.2.1.40, as well as *Ṛg Veda* 10.162.5.

Conclusion

One needn't resort to allegory to permit an internalized reading of Rāma's quest. Rāma throughout the epic is depicted as a god, but also as human. He thinks and feels and is presented as one who errs at times in human ways. That this is so not only signals an internal concern, a concern to get the internal struggles around *dharma* right, but also offers a resource to those who share a deep devotion to the values and traditions that Rāma embodies. Rāma, embodying a perfection that is "a process, magical, unfinished, flawed," opens an avenue to a shared community, that supportive community that presses each who is a part of it toward perfection, this via the internal struggle, one with external manifestations to be sure, but one fundamentally involving self-control, an internal struggle for *dharma* in the context of a community that shares in valuing just that. The strictures and norms defined by Brahmanical order, that is, are internalized and must be so, which takes effort, self-reflective and emotional work. But it is work divinely sanctioned, and work by no means engaged in alone, because Rāma himself did the same.

Control of desire—restraint—is what forestalls and corrects any slip from *dharma*. The *Rāmāyaṇa* of Vālmīki presents a world where it is possible thus to restrain oneself precisely because the voluntary misdeed of untruthfulness is held (Rāvaṇa aside) under a hard cap. Transgressions occur, but they are acknowledged, and because they are acknowledged they can be repaired.[105] It is the epic of those who refuse to lie to themselves. *This* is why

[105] But how well are they acknowledged, or how soon? Among the various perspicacious comments Gregory M. Clines made in the course of reading and responding to this chapter is the following:

> This [passage of your chapter] deals with what I wrote above [concerning the degree to which Rāma, Sītā, and others recognize any slip from *dharma* they commit as just that]. I am not sure they ever *are* really acknowledged until the end of narrative. . . . [D]oes Sītā actually acknowledge that her desire for the golden deer was a *dharmic* slippage? Does Rāma ever acknowledge that fact with respect to disfiguring Śurpanakhā? There is certainly self-correction on the part of the characters, and you are right in pointing out that there is no self-denial or perpetuation of these slippages. As you demonstrate, they do not willfully go against *dharma* in the same way that Rāvaṇa does. But I am not sure that is the same thing as true acknowledgement of their *dharmic* slippages. What has always struck me about the *Rāmāyaṇa* is just how little self-reflection there is in the text. While *the reader* might recognize these as *dharmic* slippages, it seems like, at the very least, any acknowledgement on the part of the characters is a *delayed one*. I guess another way of putting this is: Is Rāma reminded of who he really is too late?

In response to this challenging and thoughtful response I can only say that while I agree that the *Rāmāyaṇa* does not frequently detail the inner thoughts of regret felt on the part of its principal ("good") characters, there can be no doubt that the characters in question exhibit a concern to chart

the *Rāmāyaṇa* must be told anew. It is a reminder to *dharma*, to repairing one's misdeeds when they occur, to containing misdeeds by rendering them ultimately as involuntary deeds—slips that are corrected by way of truthful acknowledgment of the same. And the emotions matter, because those who feel strongly about shared values, and about one another, can be forgiven when they err, can admit error and forgive themselves.

A community around *dharma*, moreover, is made or affirmed not merely by the narrative plot of the epic, which shows Rāma quite intently interested in the subjects of Ayodhyā and his closest of kin. It is also developed in a brilliant fashion by fusing the external and internal audiences of the text. This fusion is achieved in the person of Rāma, who as a human being or a god presents the ideal, a paradigm for proper action. He feels; he cares, as must—and as do—the members of the audiences of his story, who share his values and who, not coincidentally, share in hearing Rāma's story simultaneously with him.

There can be no denying, therefore, the articulation of an insider-outsider divide in the *Rāmāyaṇa* of Vālmīki.[106] It is no small matter that it is a social outsider, the Niṣāda hunter, who kills the *krauñca* bird after all. And Rāvaṇa was justifiably killed not only because he was willful in his transgressions of *dharma*, because he did not feel about *dharma* what the community around Rāma so habitually feels, but also because he was half-outsider as well. And yet—indeed, because one is at all costs to avoid the path presented by Rāvaṇa's negative example—an exclusively outwardly guided attention is not what the epic cultivates, for even Rāma feels, slips, and shows that perfection is sometimes incomplete. Those of the community who forget this therefore do so at their own peril.

The deeper dangers—to one's loved ones, to the community, and indeed to Rāma himself—lie on such a path of externalization and its easy self-deceit, lying to oneself to permit a sustained and self-righteous transgression of

more chastened courses of action. This is so in a manner sharply contrasted in the text with the acts and intentions of Rāvaṇa, who not only fails to show contrition for his *adharmic* acts but also willfully continues with them in the teeth of being confronted directly with the fact that they are transgressive, immoral. And this is explicitly stated in the text. The acts of Rāma, Sītā, and others, who show the capacity to self-correct after their slips from *dharma* (as I have described them), also contrast with the exemplars of the *Mahābhārata*, which cannot but have been an intentional narrative strategy. In short, my reply is that actions speak louder than words and cannot but indicate the intentions that guide them.

[106] As Pollock 1991: 69 indicates, Rāma's *rākṣasa* opponent, Rāvaṇa, is foreignized and "hardly belongs to the same biological order as the hero."

dharma. One's passions must be properly directed, one's emotions checked, one's virtuous ethics maintained. An exclusively outwardly looking Vālmīki *Rāmāyaṇa*, an exclusively outwardly looking Rāma of Vālmīki's text, would rather bring one to the *dharmic* circumstances—and tragic consequences—of the *Mahābhārata*.[107]

This, then, again tells us why the *Rāmāyaṇa* must be told anew. Emotions are of all human experiences the most subjective and intimately felt. The text, both a love story and a moral tale about a righteous king, speaks emotionally and in the language of shared values and truths to establish these truths and to share them. Thus, it is the first work of poetry, and thus, it is the foremost instrument for expressing and embodying what is truly shared among those of sympathetic hearts. *Śoka* effects *ślokas*: its function and meaning create its very poetic form. The poem may be told anew when it is needed in the epic narrative itself—to right Rāma's despair, to comfort Sītā in her captivity. It is sung to emote change, to right a wrong more gently with the music of poetry, in order to guide those in and who hear or read the *Rāmāyaṇa* story gently to return to their good intentions. This is why the *Rāmāyaṇa* must be told anew: it is an emotionally resonant counsel.

But Rāvaṇa *is* killed. While the poem prominently features an internal element that is subjective, figured around self-control, and an internal element that is social, figured around a community's heartfelt and shared commitment to *dharma*, the *Rāmāyaṇa* also polices action in the community and counsels its members to protects themselves against their enemies. It states that those who do not share the values around *dharma* are outsiders and are dangerous. This too is why the *Rāmāyaṇa* comes to be told anew, and retold, and reworked—because it *defines* the community on particular terms, with innate privileges granted to some (by gender, by caste, even by religious identity) more than others. The communities around the *Rāmāyaṇa* can seek—and have sought—to reiterate or recast those terms of inclusion (and exclusion) in various ways, in various parts of the subcontinent, in various moments of the history of the *Rāmāyaṇa*'s telling and retelling. So much is needed, in fact, if the quest for perfection has any hope ever to be met, marred as it is by any self-righteous externalization of fault, any scapegoating where a shared commitment to shared values requires self-correction and a community of care.

[107] Indeed, if Vālmīki intended such an outwardly looking text, one imagines he would not have had the narrative shift so quickly away from the death of Rāvaṇa and back to the most intimate of Rāma's concerns—his love for his rescued wife.

What, in turn, does this tell us about the relationship of Brahmins and kings, that fundamental social dynamic that shapes and maintains social rules and normative structures? The moral battle in Vālmīki's text is not one pitched between a prince-to-be-king and a wayward and villainous Brahmin—or it is not merely thus. Rāma is more than the *daṇḍa*-administering instrument that enforces Brahminical values and ends. Vālmīki's epic depicts too much, too often (in particular in its opening and closing) of the royal-Brahminical alliance, of sympathy between these two *varṇa*s. Thus, Daśaratha heeds the advice of the sages in the Bālakāṇḍa, and Rāma performs the sacrifices and patronizes Brahmins in the Uttarakāṇḍa. Vālmīki rather argues for the internalization of Brahmanical norms (among *kṣatriya*s, among all subjects of a righteous king, guided by righteous Brahmins), and this not at the cost of the presence or influence of Brahmins. In the *Rāmāyaṇa*, the community and all who compose it—the king and his subjects—are to elect intuitively and habitually to pursue Brahmanical norms around *dharma*.

The *Mahābhārata* brooks in uncertainty, difficulty, and moral compromise; the *Rāmāyaṇa* engages the confident agency of those who know that to do the right thing is to do well, to succeed, and they know as much not in theory but by the tests of repeated experience—success at being successful by having been righteous, honest, upright. The *Mahābhārata* with its repeated acts of the willful misdeed of untruthfulness (in the form of a surfeit of loyalty in the name of *dharma*) is first a book for the head, for thought, for deep reflection, for intellectual puzzles that self-servingly can justify questionable or dangerous acts. The *Rāmāyaṇa* is first of all a book of the heart, wherein all in a community share—they habitually want to share—the sort of committed friendship known in the *Mahābhārata* only privately and quietly, by Kṛṣṇa and Arjuna. The *Rāmāyaṇa* is the epic in which kings and their subjects have thoroughly imbibed and internalized the *dharmic* ideals articulated and—it is implicitly expected—embodied by Brahmins, and counseled by hearing Rāma's story told, just as it is told to Rāma to console and counsel him as well. In a word, the *Rāmāyaṇa* of Vālmīki embodies the shared feelings and acts of a *dharmic* community, a community whose members, like Rāma, need but the occasional reminder to the virtue ethic of the Sanskrit narrative literatures, a clearly *dharmic* virtue ethic, the reminder of which they receive on hearing Rāma's purifying story, which is why the *Rāmāyaṇa* must be told anew.

3

Kingship in Kashmir

Brahminical Norms in Kalhaṇa's *Rājataraṅgiṇī*

prāpuś ciram avasthānaṃ pārthivā na tadā kvacit |
dhārāsaṃpātasaṃbhūtā budbudā iva durdine || RT 5.279 ||

The kings at that time could in no way secure a long reign, and resembled the bubbles produced [in the water] by a downpour of rain on a dull day.

(Translation based on that of Stein)

Introduction

The *Mahābhārata* narrates a catastrophe; it narrates *dharma* in the breach, when *kṣatriya*s are no longer properly constrained by the practices of virtuous restraint that are cultivated, transmitted, and said to be embodied by Brahmins. Kṛṣṇa as a divinized guru of the *kṣatriya* rank must intervene; and the matter is so dire that he must break *dharmic* strictures to save *dharma* itself. The war's resolution, guided by Kṛṣṇa's counsel, effects a restoration of proper respect for Brahmins by the kings in charge, but it is a dirty business, an instance of counsel that transgresses *dharmic* strictures to save the *dharmic* order more generally, and perhaps only a (divinized) *kṣatriya*, not a Brahmin one, could have been set to such a Machiavellian task.

It is just this respect for Brahmins and, perhaps more importantly, the values they defend and embody that is presumed not just as normative but as implicitly and habitually felt and honored in the *Rāmāyaṇa*, which queries the nature of conforming flawlessly, or nearly so, to these moral-ethical strictures, in acts, spirit, and intent. Rāma honors the Brahmin sages of the epic's opening *kāṇḍa*, and he lives—he comes to embody—*dharmic* ideals, even at a tremendous personal cost. To do so is divine, and the king is thus both divinized and perfected in the person of Rāma, who is always with us

Brahmins and Kings. John Nemec, Oxford University Press. © Oxford University Press 2025.
DOI: 10.1093/oso/9780197791998.003.0004

both in potential and in his divinized person, an exemplar of Brahminical ideals embodied in the ideal royal sovereign, the ideal *kṣatriya*. His story perennially calls the devout back to virtue ethics, which they feel and imbibe on a deeply personal level, just as the counsel found in narrating the *Mahābhārata* engenders a return from the abyss of fratricidal civil war to that perennially prescribed social institution, the *brāhmaṇa-kṣatriya* alliance.

History, of course, inevitably was to know kings who erred, a fact not lost on the Brahmins, who fashioned themselves the protectors of proper conduct and the political order itself. So much is famously evident in that renowned Sanskrit-language historical poem, Kalhaṇa's *Rājataraṅgiṇī* (RT), which chronicles the real-to-life transgressions and successes of all the kings and queens of the Valley of Kashmir and this, Kalhaṇa suggests, across the span of the cosmic eon in which he lived, the Kali age that was ushered in at the end of the Bhārata war.

What the *Rājataraṅgiṇī* conveys regarding the relationship of Brahmins and kings is perhaps surprising given the work's narrative intent—to chronicle the lives and acts of the royal sovereigns of the Vale of Kashmir. I shall argue that the narrative, while it is *about* kings (and queens), is written *for* Brahmins (as well as sympathetic *kṣatriyas*), to reinforce their normative habits of maintaining *dharmic* virtues, this in turn precisely to effect efficacious rule in Kashmir. I argue, that is, that Kalhaṇa himself seeks to claim that good Brahmins produce good kings, and the telos of the *Rājataraṅgiṇī*, if it may be said to have one, is to guarantee the quality of the former in Kashmir so as to ensure the presence of the latter. But let us not get ahead of ourselves, for to make this case we must tend first to the extant scholarly views of the text, which have not interpreted Kalhaṇa's *magnum opus* on these terms.

History and Narrative

Once identified by scholars as the first historical work of Sanskrit literature and for a time thought to be the only text of its kind,[1] the *Rājataraṅgiṇī* of Kalhaṇa chronicles a relentless history in a highly articulated and syntactically artful poetic verse,[2] a parade of the kings—and queens—of the Kashmir Valley from, as noted, the time of the dawn of the Kali Yuga to

1 See, e.g., Wilson 1825: 1, cited in Zutshi 2013: 201. Cf. Ali 2013: 237–240.

2 Shulman 2013: 129 elegantly refers to Kalhaṇa's "highly atypical hypotaxis."

the author's day. As is well known, several authors followed Kalhaṇa in his project of recounting royal acts and misdeeds, extending an unbroken historical account into the Mughal period. Jonarāja commences with the reign of Jayasiṃha (r. 1128–1155) in 1148 AD/CE, beginning where Kalhaṇa's narrative left off, and reaches to the year 1459, during the reign of Zayn al-'bidīn.[3] His disciple Śrīvara continues the work in a composite text, the *Jainarājataraṅgiṇī*,[4] further extending the history to cover the years 1459 to 1486. Śuka, in turn, brings the narrative "into the reign of the Mughals after the annexation of Kashmir in 1589,"[5] noting too (though without access to it) the history of one Prājyabhaṭṭa, which covers a historical span from the end of Śrīvara's account to the Shah Mir dynasty. Finally, and as Chitralekha Zutshi has illustrated, the tradition carries even further, into Persian-language, Kashmiri historical compositions.[6] In this way, the culture of writing historical memory in Sanskrit finds its mature expression in Kashmir with the *Rājataraṅgiṇī*s,[7] even if it is executed in a manner not perfectly comparable with the mores of a Western, "objective" historiography.[8]

Scholars have demonstrated renewed interest in Kalhaṇa's *magnum opus* in recent years. Zutshi, for one, examined its utility for nationalist and colonialist authors in the British period.[9] Kaul, in turn, devoted a monograph to identifying the "landscapes" articulated by Kalhaṇa, which, she argues, defined Kashmir as a unique—and cherished[10]—region that nevertheless was imaginatively tied to the Indian subcontinent.[11] And Narayana Rao, Shulman, and Subrahmanyam concisely measured Kalhaṇa's narrative habits in their landmark study of the literary "texture" of a range of South Asian works that record history.[12]

[3] See Slaje 2014; cf. Nemec 2017a.

[4] On the composition of this work and the title thereof, see Obrock 2013a: 225–226.

[5] See Obrock 2015: 142.

[6] See Zutshi 2013.

[7] Indeed, the works in question were anticipated by important Sanskrit-language textual antecedents. See Witzel 1990, which traces the influence of *vaṃśāvalī*s in the production of the *Rājataraṅgiṇī*.

[8] On this matter see, e.g., Slaje 2008, which suggests Kalhaṇa endeavored to narrate events as they happened (*yathābhūta*) but not without both expression in his own poetic voice and his own purposes—in particular that of evoking the sentiment of *śānta* or "equanimity" (as Slaje has rendered the term).

[9] See Zutshi 2011.

[10] This Kaul 2018 does in contrast to the subsequently published view of Slaje 2019. See also my own review of the latter in Nemec 2020b.

[11] Kaul 2018. Cf. the review essay of Obrock 2020, esp. at p. 164, which questions this thesis and suggests Kaul has a contemporary, nationalist concern in mind in reading the *Rājataraṅgiṇī*, one by which she claims Kashmir is rightly to be incorporated into the contemporary Indian state.

[12] Narayana Rao, Shulman, and Subrahmanyam 2001.

In particular, Narayana Rao, Shulman, and Subrahmanyam famously argued that the *Rājataraṅgiṇī* is poetic and not historical in nature,[13] a position not only challenged by Pollock and others[14] but one that Shulman revisited and ultimately partially revised by allowing that Kalhaṇa, if "'cynical' or 'skeptical,'" expresses a "philosophical attitude very much his own" that recognizes that "life offers an illusion of stability" but with his task being to "see through such ephemera."[15] It is to this and related views of the disposition of Kalhaṇa and the historical message of his *magnum opus* that I wish to draw attention in order to support a more hopeful interpretation of Kalhaṇa's historical narrative.

Shulman's partially revised view of Kalhaṇa's masterwork is expressed in his introduction to a special issue of the *Indian Economic and Social History Review*, which comprises a series of six essays that question the nature and purpose of the *Rājataraṅgiṇīs* and related literatures. All the essays in the issue also present Kalhaṇa's view of the world as dour, cynical, and resigned to the inevitability of chaos and disorder. Cox, for example, suggests that a particular style of writing defines the *Rājataraṅgiṇī*, which he labels the Kashmiri *ślokakathā*. It is born, he argues, from particular habits of syntactic, metric, and morphological expression and shaped by a perennial Kashmiri habit of rewriting extant literary works in a condensed form.[16] Echoing Auerbach, he further claims that Kalhaṇa's style reflects his very psychology or consciousness, defining his mode of representing reality poetically. We may leave aside for the moment the fact that the essential features of and the scope envisioned for Cox's "*ślokakathā* style" are robustly anticipated by what

[13] Narayana Rao, Shulman, and Subrahmanyam 2001: 254–260.

[14] See Pollock 2007. Cf., e.g., Slaje 2008.

[15] Answering the question in the title of his introduction to the special issue on the *Rājataraṅgiṇī* published in the *Indian Economic and Social History Review*—"what is it?"—Shulman 2013: 128 says the following of Kalhaṇa's text: "We can say on the basis of many of his summing up conclusions that he is often poised on the edge of a philosophical attitude very much his own. Words like 'cynical' or 'skeptical' come readily to mind. Evanescence is built into political ventures, and power has a way of devouring the once-powerful. There are moments of respite, usually relatively short, under the aegis of a temporarily good king. Life offers an illusion of stability, useful above all to courtiers. The poet sees through such ephemera—indeed, this is his primary task." McCrea 2013: 191 offers a similar assessment of the text: "In adopting this decidedly dark vision of politics and its principal actors, Kalhaṇa is not entirely out of step with his times or his contemporaries. Several other Kashmiri poets of the tenth and eleventh centuries manifest a similarly dispirited view of the moral and aesthetic potential of kings and their courts. Several recent studies have highlighted this theme in Kashmiri literature of the early second millennium, to the extent that I think one may fairly speak of an emerging consensus view that Kashmir in this period witnessed the emergence of a culture of political cynicism."

[16] See Cox 2013: 131–135.

Luther Obrock conceptualized before Cox as the "Kashmiri *kathā*."[17] What is of immediate concern in Cox's analysis is his sense that the *Rājataraṅgiṇī* "with its uneven, rough rhythms and its luxuriant overabundance of verbal matter—of one action spilling over into the next—can be seen . . . as a means by which [Kalhaṇa] used language to enact something of the chaos that he understood the last two generations of Kashmirian public life to present."[18] He argues in other words that a troubled world effected a turbulent style, one born from the author's deep awareness of Kashmir's political and other societal difficulties.

McCrea similarly identifies in the *Rājataraṅgiṇī* a quality akin both to Cox's "chaos" and Shulman's "cynicism" or "skepticism," arguing as he does that Kalhaṇa's identification of the *śānta rasa* as the text's primary emotional mood ties it to the *Mahābhārata*, what was the only literary work expressly associated with that poetic sentiment in Kalhaṇa's day. Noting Kalhaṇa's explicitly articulated self-understanding of his work as poetic in form (*kāvya*), McCrea, like Cox and others,[19] fruitfully eschews the genric dichotomization of history from literature and in doing so suggests that no characters *in* the *Rājataraṅgiṇī* exhibit the dispassion of the *rasa* or sentiment in question. The significance of his observation is this, that "it seems that for Kalhaṇa the emotional experience of 'pleasure that comes from the

[17] Compare Cox 2013: 131–135, and *passim* with the introductory paragraph to Obrock 2012: 107 (noting also that in an otherwise excellent review article, Silk 2020: 284, without referencing Obrock 2012, suggests that Obrock follows Cox, rather than the other way around): "In the last centuries of the first millennium, Kashmiri intellectual culture experienced an efflorescence that dramatically changed the literary landscape of the subcontinent. The innovations of Ānandavardhana in aesthetic theory and Jayantabhaṭṭa in Nyāya philosophy, to take just two examples, have been celebrated; here I will concentrate instead on the literary output of Jayantabhaṭṭa's son, Abhinanda. Obscured by other luminaries in the Kashmir valley, Abhinanda nevertheless merits a contextualization within this period of intellectual ferment. The work that appears at this moment in Kashmiri history is perhaps surprising; Abhinanda chose to rewrite the classic prose romance of Bāṇa, the *Kādambarīkathāsāra*, 'The Essence of the Story of Princess Kādambarī.' This understudied work is the first to show certain formal and stylistic categories that will come to mark a whole range of texts produced in Kashmir from the 9th century until well into the second millennium. Beginning with Abhinanda, these texts come to form a specifically Kashmiri literary genre including works such as the *Kathāsaritsāgara* of Somadeva, the epitomes of Kṣemendra, the *Rājataraṅgiṇī*s of Kalhaṇa and his followers, and even Śrīvara's Sanskrit translation of Jāmī's Persian romance Yusuf-o-Zuleikha. This diverse body of texts—which I will call Kashmiri *kathā*—was founded by Abhinanda in his *śloka*-based retelling of the Kādambarī story, the *Kādambarīkathāsāra*. These works are characterized by a predilection towards the use of the *śloka* meter, a terse yet graceful style, and a 'translational' logic."

[18] Cox 2013: 153.

[19] Indeed, as Ali 2013: 237 notes, doing just this constitutes the central ambition of the special issue of the *Indian Economic and Social History Review*. His thoughtful contribution to the same tests this proposition in light of reading Jain *prabandha* literature of Western India.

cessation of desire' is not one displayed by his characters, but rather one recommended for his readers."[20] The text, McCrea further suggests, fundamentally grapples with human failure, with "moral decay—the way even 'good' kings regularly go bad and the most promising political endeavours lead only to decay, loss and despair."[21] Kalhaṇa on this view wrote to guide those who read the *Rājataraṅgiṇī* to face up to the inevitability of these human failures and to the decay, loss, and despair they in turn were certain to effect.

Needless to say, the text as McCrea describes it is understood to offer a thoroughly negative assessment of worldly hopes and pursuits, for on his view Kalhaṇa understands the works of *kāvya* preceding his own erroneously to offer their audiences a false sense of security:

> The dominant forms of both political and literary discourse are actually designed, as the Kashmiri critics themselves seem clearly to show us, precisely to keep us from such unpleasant thoughts as this. They are the lies we tell to encourage ourselves: that virtue will be rewarded, that hard work and perseverance will pay off, that our end, at least, will be something other than bitter. They are the illusions we need to strip away if we are ever truly to have peace as Kalhaṇa understands it.[22]

The *Rājataraṅgiṇī* narrative on this reading is ever driving its readers to a heightened awareness of the chaos that Cox deems central to the author's narrative style, the only logical implication of this view being the one McCrea himself identifies:

> To tell the real story, the whole story—of a life, a reign, a dynasty, or a kingdom—is, almost inevitably, to tell a tragic story; one that, if we see it clearly, will fill us with a conviction of the futility of all human endeavour and lead us to turn away in despair. If we had any sense, we would see this for ourselves and retreat from worldly hopes and worldly pursuits.[23]

[20] McCrea 2013: 185. Slaje 2008 shows concurrence with this view.
[21] McCrea 2013: 179. Cf. McCrea 2013: 191: "His survey of Kashmiri royal history is very far from panegyric and seems often to veer into a scathing critique not only of individually bad kings (a handful of 'rotten apples'), but of kings and kingship in general."
[22] McCrea 2013: 198.
[23] McCrea 2013: 198.

On Kalhaṇa's Narrative Intent

Given the historical realities with which he dealt, there can be little doubt that Kalhaṇa was a clear-eyed realist, as the analyses of Cox, Shulman, and McCrea indicate. One would similarly stand on tenuous grounds in claiming any unbridled optimism in the narrative tone or contents of the *Rājataraṅgiṇī*. Kalhaṇa was no Pollyanna, as the facts of both history and contemporaneous life that were readily available to him were very often depressing to know. And yet one finds an alternative—and likelier—interpretation of the *Rājataraṅgiṇī* to the ones reviewed above by way of remembering the sociological realities "on the ground" in Kalhaṇa's day. One may disambiguate the contents of the text from the author's judgment regarding the same if one only recalls both the author's vaunted social position and that of those similarly situated as was he, who would have read or heard his poem.[24]

Rather than deduce from the admittedly recursive narration of calamities in the *Rājataraṅgiṇī* an unequivocal world weariness, simple disillusionment, and a recommendation to world resignation, one may—and should—find in the text a this-worldly prescription for action, Kalhaṇa's counsel to his readers as to how they could and should meet the all-too-real social and political challenges that were all too familiar to the inhabitants of the Kashmir Valley in their day. Kalhaṇa in fact recommends not world resignation but a constructive place in society for the fundamentally conservative, elite, and literary tradition of householder Brahmanism of which he was a part. Even despite the often-tragic turns of events of the day, he imagined that the cadre of socially privileged Brahmins who were attached to the court, who advised kings and won gifts of patronage there for their ritual and literary lives, could influence events, if not invariably or perfectly so. At the least, he argues, they must try.

On this conviction, namely, that Kalhaṇa did not write a poem that vitiates the very social position he shared with many of his fellow Brahmins, I therefore propose an interpretation of the *Rājataraṅgiṇī* that echoes the one I offered of the *Mahābhārata* in Chapter 1, which in turn is consonant

[24] Pollock 2001: 395–400 figures the moment when "the lady" vanishes, when he claims that Sanskrit literary culture died—in a salon in Kashmir, with Kalhaṇa present. What is evident in the description in question is that Kalhaṇa's colleagues, who would have read and heard his poem, were fellow high-caste, literary Brahmins who often were connected to the royal court.

with the message Kṛṣṇa shares with Arjuna in the *Bhagavadgītā*.[25] The *Rājataraṅgiṇī*, I argue, elaborates a perennial narrative call to social restoration. It beckons a return to the normative order of things, if under a certain duress (as so often is the case in the Kali age). It is a call to seek to produce in kings a fidelity to *dharma*, an embracing of the virtue ethic of self-chastening, to cultivate kings who hear out their equally chastened and therefore wise Brahminical ministers. Kalhaṇa on this reading must be understood often to write about chaos but with the intent of cultivating a Brahminical culture that elicits and supports a social order that could prevail over such chaos, sometimes even for great lengths of time.

Thus, the poem's accurate memorialization of tragic historical events may be understood not to serve to shatter illusions that were cultivated or reinforced by panegyrical poems, which were said to lull Kalhaṇa's countrymen into an idyllic and sentimental faith in the natures of Kashmir's kings and queens, for why would his audiences have succumbed to such lulling at all? Real-world calamities—awful kings—would have been far too easily known first-hand, or else by first-hand reports of the same from elder kin.[26] Kalhaṇa's contemporaneous audiences were likelier to have greeted the contents of his poem with a somber understanding than with any stunned surprise or sobering reflection. It is precisely for this reason that he placed a demand on those whose station in life it was to influence kings, a call not to surrender cynically to fate and the maelstrom, not simply to renounce worldly affairs, not cynically to view political power as merely and inevitably corrupting. Brahmins could always shun (*parihāra*) corrupted kings, but, although mentioned as a possible course of action in the *Rājataraṅgiṇī*, it is only occasionally recommended or elaborated in story,[27] and anyhow so much defined a manner of influencing the political order, not a method of abandoning it altogether. In a word, the dismal facts of political and social life were put into poetic verse not to recommend a mode of conduct so rarely invoked in the narrative—the turning away from the world of politics—but to allow for the analysis of their causes and to recommend remedies thereto.

The proposed course of action is to perdure in *dharma* as possible in a broken, difficult world. It is to act dispassionately, without regard for the fruits

[25] I thus follow McCrea in understanding the *Rājataraṅgiṇī* to parallel and follow the model of the *Mahābhārata*, what was intended by Kalhaṇa himself.

[26] As Slaje 2019: 20 notes, not a single generation of Kashmiris could escape the ravages of warfare. Misery was all too easily known in the Kashmir Valley.

[27] On shunning see Nemec 2017b: 57.

of the effort, with equanimity but not a surrendering disillusion. Tenuous as it surely was, Kalhaṇa viewed virtuous action as possible, certainly desirable, despite the nearly inevitable difficulties of the Kali age.[28] The path of virtue in action could only be made evident and viable when chastened Brahmins properly directed kings and queens who, chastened in turn and in no small part by way of the counsel of Brahmins, elected to do the right things for their subjects. Kalhaṇa's readers might have had to surrender to the fact that many—perhaps even most—who were charged with upholding *dharma* often failed to do so. Even so, the *Rājataraṅgiṇī* argues, Brahmins like Kalhaṇa could not comprehensively surrender their own *dharma*—that of cultivating *dharma*—along the way.

In what follows I thus read the *Rājataraṅgiṇī* as an integrated work, meaning that I understand Kalhaṇa's to be a sophisticated historiography that also operates in consonance with the "old traditions," as Philips labels them,[29] the normative views around *dharma* that are there described and to which Kalhaṇa would have adhered.[30] Replicating the narrative arc of the *Mahābhārata*, Kalhaṇa implicitly argues for the indispensability of the learned literary Brahmin to the success of the king and with him the greater polity, and he narrates stories of the former counseling the latter to effect the same. Success, moreover, was measured by the degree to which the royal sovereign could guarantee what cannot but be labeled good government, exemplified in particular by his, or her,[31] generosity, the offering of material assistance to religious institutions and the religious and intellectual agents of the day, as well as a liberal generosity with all royal subjects across the spectrum of caste statuses. Indeed, and as Kaul suggests (and as did Slaje

[28] Here, then, I wish to argue in consonance with Kaul 2014: 199, who suggests that "*karma* and fate serve as an opportunity for Kalhaṇa to ethicize and add a moral accent [to his narrative of events in Kashmir], which is . . . his chief interest."

[29] See Philips 1961: 22.

[30] This is to say I here proceed in a manner sympathetic in approach with Kaul's understanding of Kalhaṇa's work as a poetic presentation of historicity, one engaging precedent works (of myth, literature, law, etc.) as "intertexts" and not (merely dispassionately viewed) historical "sources." Set in emic terms, I wish to suggest that the text and the (verifiable) history it offers perennially articulate and implicitly reinforce the king's mandate to uphold *dharma* and lead his kingdom to prosperity thereby. See Kaul 2014: 203. As will presently be made clear, I understand that Slaje would agree with this assessment of Kalhaṇa's use of dispassionate historical reporting.

[31] At least two queens are mentioned in the *Rājataraṅgiṇī*: Sugandhā (at RT 5.243*ff.*), the wife of the Utpala king Śaṅkaravarman (r. 883–902) who reigned briefly (904–906) after the demise of her husband's lineage, and the famed Queen Diddā (r. 980/981–1003), whose (awful) reign is described at RT 6.332*ff.*

in a similar if distinguishable manner), the *Rājataraṅgiṇī* is a teaching or *upadeśa* of a kind: Kalhaṇa had an "educative" intent in composing his work, and a normative one at that.[32]

The Historiography of the *Rājataraṅgiṇī*: The Prolegomenon

Yet again we must tend to beginnings,[33] because Kalhaṇa there explains his reasons for and methods in writing the text. Rather extraordinary for a premodern Sanskrit work, the introduction is well known explicitly to asseverate its author's wish to produce historically accurate information. As also is well known, Kalhaṇa names his sources explicitly (RT 1.8–21), extolling the virtues of dispassionate historical analysis in doing so (RT 1.7), even if he abstains, as Stein noted,[34] from explaining how he weighs the relative merits of his various sources.[35] More germane to the question of the author's judgment regarding the significance of the historical realities about which he writes is the fact that the prolegomenon indicates Kalhaṇa's wish to evoke the sentiment (*rasa*) of *śānta* and with it a particular disposition vis-à-vis worldly affairs.[36] What he meant by referring to the *śānta rasa* must therefore be weighed—as McCrea rightly calls us to do—if one is to understand the nature of Kalhaṇa's concern.

As already noted, McCrea finds evidence of world weariness in the opening passages of the *Rājataraṅgiṇī*, translating the key verse as follows:[37]

kṣaṇabhaṅgini jantūnāṃ sphurite paricintite |
mūrdhābhiṣekaḥ śāntasya rasasyātra vicāryatām || RT 1.23 ||

[32] See Kaul 2014: 204–205; Slaje 2008.

[33] In the instance of the *Rājataraṅgiṇī* we are aided in doing so by Slaje 2008, which is that author's contribution to a volume (edited by Slaje himself) that is dedicated to an examination of the beginnings of *śāstric* works.

[34] Stein [1900] 1989 (vol. 1): 27.

[35] Note too that Kalhaṇa criticizes a previous work—Kṣemendra's *Nṛpāvali*—for proliferating historical inaccuracies, for which see RT 1.13.

[36] So much is perhaps to be expected of one who saw himself primarily as a poet (*kavi*) and not an historian, as numerous others have noted already. RT 1.23, where the *śānta rasa* is evoked, is read here below. See also RT 1.3–5, 1.45–47, and Stein [1900] 1989 (vol. 1): 10.

[37] See McCrea 2013: 181.

> Reflecting that the flickering existence of living beings passes away in mere moments, one should regard the *rasa* of "peace" (*śānta rasa*) as having prime importance in this [work].

McCrea also suggests that we should understand the sentiment here evoked to be precisely the one cultivated in the *Mahābhārata*, as understood by Ānandavardhana.[38]

While the *Rājataraṅgiṇī* compellingly may be said to be associated with the *Mahābhārata*—in this I follow McCrea's analysis[39]—Kalhaṇa in no way explicitly evokes Ānandavardhana's interpretation of the sentiment nor his reading of it as a call to the pursuit of liberation.[40] An important alternative understanding of the sentiment was available to Kalhaṇa, moreover, which is significant in that it may be taken to support an alternative course of action than that of world renunciation. As Slaje has noted, the *Nāṭyaśāstra* (NŚ) presents the *śānta rasa* as one composed of "equanimity." So much, moreover, calls not for world renunciation but only a habit of dispassion vis-à-vis worldly concerns, this on terms that cite and echo the eighteenth chapter of the *Bhagavadgītā* (NŚ 6c = *Bhagavadgītā* 18.54c):[41]

> *na yatra duḥkhaṃ na sukhaṃ na dveṣo nāpi matsaraḥ* |
> *samaḥ sarveṣu bhūteṣu śāntaḥ prathito rasaḥ* || NŚ 6 ||

> Where there is no pain and no pleasure, no hatred, nor even selfishness there is an equanimity toward all beings. The sentiment of "peace" is [thereby] displayed.

Emergent in this reading is the suggestion that Kalhaṇa argued for disinterestedness and not world renunciation, just what Kṛṣṇa recommended to Arjuna in the *Bhagavadgītā*, which presents a conception of the *rasa* in

38 McCrea 2013: 188: "The didactic purpose of the *Mahābhārata*, on Ānandavardhana's reading, is to promote despair with the possibilities of worldly endeavour, thereby prompting one to turn to the pursuit of liberation from rebirth by spiritual means."

39 Slaje 2008: 228 also makes this association explicit.

40 See Tubb 1985, esp. 144.

41 Slaje 2008: 226. On the authenticity of this verse—probably not in the original text but present in the one received by Abhinavagupta—see Slaje 2008: 226, fn. 68. Slaje also there notes the consonance with the *Bhagavadgītā*.

question that is consonant with another metaphor of the prolegomenon—that of the *Rājataraṅgiṇī* as a medicinal salve:[42]

tadamandarasasyandasundarīyaṃ nipīyatām |
śrotraśuktipuṭaiḥ spaṣṭam aṅga rājataraṅgiṇī || RT 1.24 ||

Now let this *Stream* of Kings *be drunk in* (*/experienced*) distinctly through your shell-shaped ears, where the unimpeded *flow* of the dominant *sap* (/ *sentiment*) of [equanimity lends its] beauty.

Slaje in reading this metaphorical conception of the *Rājataraṅgiṇī* as elixir elegantly emphasizes its metaphor of liquidity: the poem in its hearing is a cure for the disease plaguing Kashmiris in Kalhaṇa's day. For some kings, the poem is deployed in praise (*ullāse*); for others it is to put them in their place (*hrāse vā*). Let the elixir suit the patient:

iyaṃ nṛpāṇām ullāse hrāse vā deśakālayoḥ |
bhaiṣajyabhūtasaṃvādikathā yuktopayujyate || RT 1.21 ||

This medicinal narrative story, which discusses past events, tied as it is to [a particular] time and place, is employed for the giving of prominence or the diminution of kings.[43]

If what flows heals, moreover, it is also worth noting that the sentiment in question is itself said to be poured upon: as cited already, Kalhaṇa when first mentioning the *śānta rasa* at RT 1.23 literally refers to it as what is used in the rite of coronation, the *mūrdhābhiṣeka* that is performed by way of sprinkling water on the head of the man who is to become king. And as Slaje notes

[42] It is Slaje 2008: 231 that calls our attention to just this with the citation of a key verse of the prolegomenon. The translation here recorded is Slaje's. Cf. also Salomon's note on the same (1987: 153), which also records Stein's translation: "Imbibe, therefore, straight with the folds of your ear-shells this 'River of Kings' (*Rājataraṅgiṇī*), which is rendered pleasant by undercurrents of powerful sentiments." Note also that the present passage follows the reading offered by Hultzsch 1915: 271.

[43] The present, somewhat tentative, rendering is my own and is based on those of Slaje, who cites also Salomon, about which see Slaje 2008: 232–233, esp. fns. 88 and 89. See also Salomon 1987: 152–153, which includes a long note of interpretation and also records Pandit's translation, as follows: "This saga which is properly made up should be useful for kings as a stimulant or as a sedative, like a physic, according to time and place." Salomon translates, "This medicine-like tale is fit to be prescribed when kings grow (too) great, or when their reigns or realms are shrinking."

by citing Gerow, the term *rasa* itself evokes a liquid metaphor "inasmuch as both the sap, the 'essence' of plants, etc., is liquid, and the capacity to taste takes that peculiar form of 'liquidity' as its object."[44]

Who pours the elixir of poetry but a Brahmin? And none can pour the waters of consecration but a Brahmin. And for what reason is the pouring done but to set matters right in the world, to cure the ills in this world, and to install a *dharmic* king? Simply put, all of these "liquid" metaphors point to a life lived *in* the world. One is beckoned to consecrate, not to renounce the social world that is governed by rituals and norms of purity and the good conduct associated therewith. One drinks and pours the medicine—poetry, written by a court poet—not to escape the world where medicine is fashioned and dispensed but to recover one's health therein.

The Brahmin offers the cure—a poem of equanimity in worldly affairs; the problem is the errant king, and each is tied to the other, the latter healed by the elixir offered by the former. Not only is the poet a "creator" (*kaviprajāpati*)[45] but also—as Slaje indicates—kings depend on poets even to be remembered:[46]

> *bhujataruvanacchāyāṃ yeṣāṃ niṣevya mahaujasāṃ*
> *jaladhiraśanā mediny āsīd asāv akutobhayā* |
> *smṛtim api na te yānti kṣmāpā vinā yadanugrahaṃ*
> *prakṛtimahate kurmas tasmai namaḥ kavikarmaṇe* || RT 1.46 ||

> We venerate the poet, [who is] distinguished by his nature. Without whose favor the mighty rulers would not even be remembered, in the shade of whose forest tree-like arms the earth here rested fearlessly, girded with the ocean.

Poets moreover are simply bound to the world, inasmuch as their very poetic ability is tied to their capacity to see it and share their interpretive awareness of the same.[47]

[44] Slaje 2008: 215, citing Gerow 1977: 245.

[45] See RT 1.4: *ko 'nyaḥ kālam atikrāntaṃ netum pratyakṣatāṃ kṣamaḥ | kaviprajāpatīṃs tyaktvā ramyanirmāṇaśālinaḥ* ||. "Who else is able to lead a passed moment in time into view apart from those poet-creators who are amply furnished with delightful compositions?" On this verse see Slaje 2008: 217–219.

[46] Slaje 2008: 216–217. Translation that of Slaje.

[47] Slaje 2008: 221. Translation his. See also Slaje 2008: 221, fn. 56 for his understanding of the bivalence of the term *bhāva* in this verse.

na pasyet sarvasaṃvedyān bhāvān pratibhayā yadi |
tad anyad divyadṛṣṭitve kim iva jñāpakaṃ kaveḥ || RT 1.5 ||

If he did not see the entities (*bhāva*) [he wants] to convey [as transformed into emotions (*bhāva*)] to all [of his audience] by [his] powers of imagination, what else would then indicate, as it were, that the poet's eye is divine?

Is it possible to read these passages otherwise? Can the poet sing of kings while his poem is set to dispose those who hear it to abandon the social world and courtly life in preference for renunciation? Is it possible to read the *śānta rasa* as a replacement for royal consecration, an instrument of a final ritual act ushering one out of the this-worldly realms of ritual and politics? Is it possible the medicine is drunk not as a cure or a salve, but again as a final act, leading the world-worn householder not to health at home but to a cure found apart from the sickness of society? Possible, yes. But the more likely interpretation? I submit, no. All the metaphors and images that open the *Rājataraṅgiṇī* are of transformation, and of a ritually made, structured social order, one that is to be cured and corrected rather than abandoned, to be rectified by an equanimity that calms.

To surrender the world out of hopelessness presupposes a hopeless world; but while Kalhaṇa's discerning eye records events that evince frequent, even overwhelmingly regular, tragic turns, there are exceptions to this tendency, important ones, which are also noted sometimes at great length in the *Rājataraṅgiṇī*. It is to key episodes of the text and, following this, its narrative arc that we shall now turn, marked as they are by the repeated, if exceptional, appearance of successful kings who inevitably are guided to virtue by way of the company and good counsel of properly chastened Brahmins.

Brahmins and Kings, and Brahmins *as* Kings, in the *Rājataraṅgiṇī*

One can say that Brahminical company makes for good kings, because Kalhaṇa's comments on the privileged place of the learned poet-Brahmin amount to much more than a *non sequitur* that opens the *Rājataraṅgiṇī*. Viewed in the context of the bulk of the narrative, the attention he gives to and the role he imagines for the literary Brahmin can hardly be overemphasized. Indeed, while the text mentions no fewer than eight of what we could describe as types of social roles for Brahmins in his day,[48] it furnishes the reader with a tilted vision of Kashmiri intellectual history and with it the social history of Brahminical intellectual culture. It is in particular to Brahmins with access to the court that he pays the most attention, for the vast majority of authors whom Kalhaṇa cites or to whom he refers worked in proximity to the royal sovereign, among them poets, literary theorists, and grammarians. Conversely, the intellectual history Kalhaṇa offers is less forthcoming in recording the contributions not only of tantric authors, as Sanderson has noted already,[49] but also of philosophers, whether Buddhist or Brahminical, as well as the many Tibetan intellectual pilgrims who came to the Kashmir Valley in the period in which Kalhaṇa's chronicle is most detailed in its historiographical account.[50] (See the appendix to this chapter for a list of authors mentioned in the *Rājataraṅgiṇī*.[51])

While Kalhaṇa's emphasis on literary Brahmins and works over and against their tantric or philosophical counterparts might betray nothing other than his own predilections or the company he preferred to keep, he

[48] By my count, the *Rājataraṅgiṇī* suggests that kings (and/or queens, ministers, and other wealthy members of the court) created sinecures for Brahmins by (1) endowing *agrahāras*; (2) endowing temple foundations; (3) endowing religious monasteries (Maṭhas), often with land grants; (4) creating employment for Brahmins in the court, not on a lifetime basis, but certainly with what apparently was a comfortable compensation (whether as a court poet, an advisor to the king, or an officer of the royal bureaucracy); (5) employing some Brahmins, at least, as *kāyastha*s; and (6) employing Brahmins as ministers of the government. (7) Brahmins also of course could make a living by performing rites for patrons, though ideally they would not need to do so to sustain themselves; those who did were often associated permanently with a particular religious institution, such as a temple. (8) Finally, some Brahmins charged a tax at particular *tīrtha*s in order to sustain themselves (for which see, e.g., RT 6.254–255). One can imagine that Brahmins ensconced in most any of these institutions theoretically could find themselves reasonably secure financially and could have used their places in society to write literary or other works in Sanskrit.

[49] Sanderson 2009: 119–120.

[50] One particularly prominent name that is notable for its absence is that of Abhinavagupta. This Śaiva polymath was of course a commentator on Ānandavardhana's *Dhvanyāloka*, a fact that should have placed him in the neighborhood of authors of intrinsic interest to Kalhaṇa. Is there something particular about the *Locana*, in its contents or in the circulation of the work, that distinguished it from other works of *alaṃkāraśāstra*, rendering it of less prominence or significance in Kalhaṇa's view? (I am grateful to Deven Patel for his comments on this matter, offered November 1, 2012, at the South Asia Colloquium of the University of Pennsylvania, in the question-and-answer session following my presentation of an earlier version of this book chapter.)

[51] One reason for such an emphasis on those who had contact with the court and who clearly wrote for kings and his cohort (as this was the raison d'être of many poetic and literary works) may be traced to Kalhaṇa's use of sources: he famously accessed temple and royal inscriptions (see RT 1.15), which would have furnished the types of information he offers. Brahmins of course wrote such inscriptions and regularly did so in a poetic style. Conversely, tantric (and perhaps to a lesser degree philosophical) authors were generally less forthcoming in recording any evidence of their historicality, leaving Kalhaṇa with narrowed avenues for accurately placing them in time. (On this phenomenon see Nemec 2020a: 295, fn. 25.) This is to say that the issue to hand could be in part a methodological one, for Kalhaṇa nowhere attempts to develop relative chronologies of undated texts.

simultaneously narrates a key role for literature—and the literary Brahmin—in the royal court. He suggests that close familiarity with letters and association with those who speak and write well and, therefore, think well cultivates the production of a well-run and prosperous kingdom. Consider, for example, the following metaphor found in a verse that is recorded early in the fourth chapter (literally the fourth *taraṅga* or "wave") of the *Rājataraṅgiṇī*:[52]

> *ekapādākṛtir dharmaḥ samasyevojjhito nṛpaiḥ* |
> *śuddhaślokakṛtā yena pādaiḥ saṃyojitas tribhiḥ* || RT 4.46 ||

> He [i.e., the king Candrāpīḍa] completed the *dharma* that had been abandoned by [other] kings, just as a part of a stanza proposed by one to be completed by another (*samasyā*)—the first quarter-verse—is made a full *śloka* verse by way of being completed with the three [remaining] quarters.

The king who completes *dharma* is a poet of sorts!

A brief story exemplifying Candrāpīḍa's *dharmic* sensibilities follows this verse. The king had commissioned the construction of a Vaiṣṇava temple to Tribhuvanasvāmin at a site owned by an outcaste tanner (*carmakāra*), who agreed in principle to sell his land for this cause but hesitated in practice to let the surveyors take measure of the site. When asked why, he requested an audience with the king in his capacity as the one who ultimately adjudicates legal procedures, and they met the next day outside the court's audience hall. (Lamentably, as an outcaste the tanner was not permitted inside.) The landholder touchingly explained his attachment to his familial home but nevertheless promised that if properly approached by the purchaser, who in fact was to be the king himself, then he would duly sell.

The following day, Candrāpīḍa himself visited the tanner's home and properly inquired after the sale, subsequently securing the site. His chastened attitude, his modesty, then, is exemplified in this story by his respect for the property rights of an "untouchable" (*aspṛśya*, RT 4.76d), his willingness *dharmically* to follow the proper procedures for securing the land and this despite the caste status of the seller. The story signals the virtue of the king, which mirrors that of the virtuous Brahman, for Kalhaṇa compares the

[52] See also Salomon 1987: 169–170, which notes that the present makes an oblique reference to *Mānavadharmaśāstra* 1.81–82, which states that *dharma* begins in the Satya Yuga on four feet but decreases by one foot each age, leaving it like a cow, wobbling on one foot at the time of the Kali age.

event to that famous episode of the *Mahābhārata* in which the lowly dog who is in fact the god Dharma in disguise tested the famously Brahmin-like Yudhiṣṭhira's loyalty.[53] And while this comparison is on the one hand strikingly inelegant for setting the tanner in analogy with a dog—albeit Dharma in disguise—it is also nevertheless the case, on the other hand, that the author meant by it to compliment the king for his fair treatment of a less than socially privileged subject of his kingdom, which justified his comparison with the Brahmin-like Pāṇḍava prince.

Just as RT 4.46 metaphorically entwines the respective virtues of the Brahmin poet with those of a good king, so the entire poem is similarly peppered with gnomic verses and narrative vignettes extolling the virtues derived from the cooperation of *brāhmaṇa* advisors and *kṣatriya* sovereigns, the former counseling the latter. The reader is told that to raise doubts in the king's mind regarding his ministers is a sure way to lead him to folly, for example,[54] while, contrariwise, the mutual, trusting bond between *kṣatriya* and *brāhmaṇa* guarantees success in the kingdom.[55] Similarly, the minister who tends to the king's word assists the latter in his success, as did the Śaiva counselor Śūra, who served King Avantivarman, for example:

[53] RT 4.76: *śvavigraheṇa dharmeṇa pāṇḍusūnoḥ purā yathā* | *dhārmikatvaṃ tathā te 'dya mayāspṛśyena vīkṣitam* ||. "Just as of yore the *dharmic* nature of the son of Pāṇḍu was seen by way of [the God] Dharma in the form of a dog, so also your *dharmic* nature has been seen today by way of me, an untouchable."

[54] See RT 2.65–67: *tasyābhūd adbhutodantabhavabhaktivibhūṣitaḥ* | *rājñaḥ saṃdhimatir nāma mantrī matimatāṃ varaḥ* || 2.65 || *nasty upāyaḥ sa saṃsāre ko 'pi yo 'pohituṃ kṣamaḥ* | *bhūpālamattakariṇām eṣāṃ capalakarṇatām* || 2.66 || *atyadbhutamatiḥ śaṅkyaḥ so 'yam uktveti yad viṭaiḥ* | *tasmin dhīsacive dveṣas tenāgrāhyata bhūbhujā* || 2.67 ||. "The king had a minister called Saṃdhimati, the greatest of sages, who was distinguished by his wonderful life and devotion to Śiva. There is no device in the world which could stop the ears of kings and of rutting elephants from moving unsteadily. Thus [it came about that] wicked men raised the king's hatred against that trusted adviser, by telling him to beware of a person of such wonderful mental power." Translation Stein's. Note, however, that Hultzsch 1915: 274 suggests one should read with the Pune manuscript (P), *adbhutodanto* for *adbhutodanta-*.

The story goes on (RT 2.68–143): The king has Saṃdhimati imprisoned, then executed at the cremation ground. But a hoard of *yoginī*s comes to the skeleton of Saṃdhimati, all donating a part of their respective bodies to reconstitute his own, after which they enjoy his physical company and leave him to remain on earth "reborn." Saṃdhimati's guru sees him and brings him back to the kingdom that had since been left bereft of a royal sovereign (the implication being the king died as a *karmic* consequence of punishing his wise and innocent minister). And Saṃdhimati assumes the throne in fulfillment of a prophecy. He rules Kashmir for some forty-seven years, consecrating multiple *liṅga*s and other Śaiva sites of worship during his reign. Ultimately, however, he neglects his royal duties in preference for a wanton enjoyment of the company of Śaiva ascetics and devotees, this at a material cost for his subjects. (Presumably, had he himself taken in a good royal minister—none is mentioned in the narrative—he could have better served his subjects.)

[55] See, e.g., RT 5.47*ff.* Cf. RT 3.153*ff.* for an example of how to choose a good minister. See also RT 5.63 for a concise summary of the virtues of a well-ordered *brāhmaṇa-kṣatriya* bond. Good counsel is elsewhere said to advance a king, for which see RT 4.502. It similarly rescues one from danger, for which see, e.g., RT 4.530.

parasparam anutpannamanyukāluṣyadūṣaṇau |
na dṛṣṭau na śrutau vānyau tādṛśau rājamantriṇau || RT 5.63 ||

No other pair was seen or heard of, which was equal to the two, the king and [his] minister, who were uncorrupted by [any] emergent anger or disagreement between them.

Not incidentally, Śūra funded a Śaiva temple (named Śūreśvara) (RT 5.37), with a monastery, the Śūramaṭha, attached thereto (RT 5.38).[56] These gifts mirrored Avantivarman's, who also funded a Śaiva temple (named Avantīśvara) after having had built a Vaiṣṇava one that was duly named Avantisvāmin (RT 5.45). With Śūra's donation, we are told, the Śaiva master Bhaṭṭa Kallaṭa, who is likely to be the same person as the famed author of the Śaiva Spanda school, crossed down to earth along with other accomplished ones (*siddhas*) in order to grace the people of the Kashmir Valley.[57] Minister and king, acting in mutual harmony and generously supporting religious institutions (which were populated and run by Brahmins), thus found a way to facilitate the Kashmir Valley's blessing at the hands of perfected saints.

Elsewhere we are told that those who are engaged in the arts and letters are the most likely to possess the wisdom to discern good from wicked counsel.[58] And the best of kings are independent thinkers,[59] for real danger threatened the royal sovereign who succumbed to the ill influences—the wicked counsel—of others. This was the fate of Yudhiṣṭhira I, for example, also called "Blind Yudhiṣṭhira" for his small eyes (RT 1.350), who in his vice and unwisdom alienated the wise and righteous of his kingdom: "By parasites who turned faults into virtues and virtues into faults, he was gradually deprived of his intellect, and rendered like a slave of women."[60] His wicked ministers

[56] See Hultzsch 1915: 280 for his conjecture of *svarveśmeva* for Stein's *svaveśmeva*. (I prefer Stein's reading.)

[57] See RT 5.66: *anugrahāya lokānāṃ bhaṭṭaśrīkallaṭādayaḥ* | *avantivarmaṇaḥ kāle siddhā bhuvam avātaran* ||.

[58] Learning is also said to be something of a double-edged sword: it gives the virtuous a tranquil mind, the wicked a passion for harm, about which see, e.g., RT 4.625.

[59] See RT. 4.51: *vyanīyata na yo 'mātyair vinayaṃ tān svaśikṣayat* | *vajraṃ na bhidyate kaiścid bhinatty anyān maṇīṃs tu tat* ||. "He was not instructed by his ministers, but gave them instructions. The diamond is not cut by any other precious stones, but [on the contrary] it cuts them." Translation Stein's.

[60] RT 1.356: *nayadbhir guṇatāṃ doṣān doṣatāṃ ca guṇān vitaiḥ* | *sa luptapratibhaś cakre śanakaiḥ strījitopamaḥ* ||. Translation recorded is that of Stein. See also Hultzsch 1915: 274, who notes that if the P (Pune) manuscript is correct in reading *strījitopamām* for *strījitopamaḥ*, then one must also read *jagme* for *cakre*.

then exploited the occasion to reduce his authority and eventually banished him from the Kashmir Valley.[61]

Good governance, simply put, involves the royal sovereign in the act of cultivating learning:

> *dhatte śriyaṃ sṛjati kīrtim aghaṃ lunīte mitratvam ānayati hanta virodhino 'pi* |
> *yāty adhvabhiḥ pratipadaṃ sumano 'nukūlair gauḥ kāmadhuk kam iva nāpaharaty anartham* || RT 7.789 ||

> Speech (*go*) brings wealth, creates fame, removes sin, and indeed procures friendship from an enemy; with every word (*pratipadam*) it follows paths which are agreeable to the wise. Resembling the cow of plenty, what misfortune can it not put right? (Translation Stein's)

Wisdom in turn is forged by the forming of alliances with wise and trustworthy Brahminical advisors:

> *āsatāṃ*[62] *kṣitipāmātyau tau dvāv api parasparam* |
> *ājñādāne parivṛḍhau bhṛtyāv ājñāparigrahe* || RT 5.3 ||
> *kṛtajñaḥ kṣāntimān kṣamābhṛn mantrī bhaktaḥ smayojjhitaḥ* |
> *abhaṅguro 'yaṃ saṃyogaḥ sukṛtair jātu dṛśyate* || RT 5.4 ||
> *vikektā prāptarājyaḥ sa kṣamābhṛd vīkṣya nṛpaśriyam* |
> *aviluptasmṛtir dhīmān antar evam acintayat* || RT 5.5 ||
> *gobhujāṃ vallabhā lakṣmīr mātaṅgotsaṅgalālitā* |
> *seyaṃ spṛhāṃ samutpādya dūṣayaty unnatātmanaḥ* || RT 5.6 ||
> *sa nāsti kaścit prathamaṃ yaḥ pradarśyānukūlatām* |
> *saṃtāpyate na*[63] *caramaṃ nīcaprītyeva nānayā* || RT 5.7 ||

> The king and his minister were towards each other both [equally] masters in respect of giving orders, and servants in respect of receiving them. If the king is grateful and of mild disposition, and the minister devoted and free of arrogance, such a connection may at times be found to be lasting, owing to merits [from previous births]. The king, who was full of judgment and

[61] See RT 1.360–373.

[62] On this form see Hultzsch 1915: 280 (under his note on RT 5.3), which refers readers to Hultzsch 1915: 279, under RT 4.558, which suggests reading *āsātāṃ* or *āsatuḥ*.

[63] Hultzsch 1915: 280 conjectures *saṃtāpyate [']tha* for *saṃtāpyate na*.

> wisdom, did not lose his memory when he obtained the throne and saw regal splendor, but inwardly reflected as follows: "Lakṣmī, the mistress of kings, who dallies on the back of her elephant, creates violent desires and spoils the high-minded. For whomsoever she has first shown fondness, he is [sure to be] brought into distress by her in the end, just as by a low attachment." (Translation Stein's)

Tied in this way to his minister, seeing him as an equal, Avantivarman therefore chose to give his wealth to Brahmins and facilitated the endowment of *agrahāra* lands, all of which was praised by Kalhaṇa.[64] Most notably, Avantivarman avoided the temptations of wealth *through all his years* and because of it he ruled in a manner that "made the Kṛta [Yuga] appear again" in Kashmir (i.e., he was *pravartitakṛtodaya*). There are happy lives and happy endings to be found in the *Rājataraṅgiṇī* after all.

Nearing the moment of death, Avantivarman revealed a hidden affection for Viṣṇu over Śiva, listened to the *Bhagavadgītā* recited to him, and passed away on the third day of the bright half of Āṣādha in the Laukika year 3959 (883 CE/AD), a king who fulfilled his duties to the letter and to the last.[65] The generosity and dispassion toward wealth displayed by him are said to have been key to his successful reign, the habit of generosity or liberality being repeatedly praised in the *Rājataraṅgiṇī*,[66] notably including in particular instances of gifting to the very institutions that guaranteed Brahmins their livelihood. To repeat, as Kalhaṇa so often does: engagement in the arts and letters, coupled with appropriate religious devotion, sets one on the narrow path of good governance, and this goes for ministers as well as kings.[67]

This was perhaps nowhere more the case than with the famed Kārkoṭa king, Jayāpīḍa, as Bronner has illustrated in detail. He argues that Jayāpīḍa's reign stands as a turning point of the narrative, for being depicted by Kalhaṇa as a turning point in Kashmiri history, one by which kingship moved from a model of securing political authority via military hegemony to cultivating cultural learning as the fundamental ethic and value of the royal court.[68] Jayāpīḍa was, after all, the patron of no lesser figures than Bhaṭṭa Udbhaṭa,

[64] See esp. RT 5.16–18, 5.21, 5.22–25.

[65] RT 5.122 and 5.123–127.

[66] Among many possible examples are RT 5.189*ff*., 7.259, 7.512, and 7.515.

[67] Thus, Avantivarman's minister, Śūra, also supported learning and the work of literary Brahmins (see RT 5.32–33), including among others the work of Ānandavardhana and Ratnākara (RT 5.34).

[68] See Bronner 2013.

Dāmodaragupta, Vāmana, and four other (admittedly lesser-known) poets, Manoratha, Śaṅkhadanta, Caṭaka, and Saṃdhimat, among others; and he himself was a poet of some renown. Jayāpīḍa is heroic in his virtuous reign, we are told, because he governs with all the enlightenment one could imagine of a sovereign, and—and because—his generosity to Brahmins was epic.[69] Yes, he turns to evil in the end, and famously so, by subjugating his own people, violently taking the wealth of the very subjects and institutions he had so generously supported before: Kalhaṇa says of him *svamaṇḍalam adaṇḍayat*: he punished his own realm.[70] And yet, even in his demise, Kalhaṇa emphasizes the significance of the *brāhmaṇa-kṣatriya* bond, if in regretting its breach, and does so with literary flair: Jayāpīḍa is condemned with brilliant *śleṣa* verses, the paronomasia offering three meanings in each of two verses comparing Jayāpīḍa to Pāṇini, but also condemning him, and not merely for his rapaciousness.[71] In particular, he is damned for ignoring the pleadings—the counsel—of Brahmins, allowing them to fast unto death (*prāya*) before honoring their petitions. In the end, he is cursed by a Brahmin to die by the blow of a Brahmin's staff (RT 4.651cd): *mayi kruddhe kṣaṇād eva brahmadaṇḍaḥ paten na kim*? "Why, when I have been (thus) provoked, should the staff of Brahman not fall (upon you) at this very moment?" Immediately afterward a pole that held up the canopy above him crashed down upon Jayāpīḍa's head, leaving him with injuries that soon after, in complication, caused his death. The symbolism of course is clear: Brahmins wield a disciplinary stick (*daṇḍa*) that trumps even the

[69] See RT 4.491–502.

[70] On this passage see also Nemec 2017b: 55–57.

[71] Stein was first to identify these as *śleṣa* verses and examined them in some detail; my translations reflect, in part, his. (See Stein [1900] 1989: 177–178.)

> *nitāntaṃ kṛtakṛtyasya guṇavṛddhividhāyinaḥ | śrījayāpīḍadevasya pāṇineś ca kim antaram* || RT 4.635 ||. "What difference is there between Pāṇini, who prescribed rules for *guṇa* and *vṛddhi* (*guṇavṛddhi-vidhāyin*) and completely (*nitāntam*) dealt with *kṛtya* suffixes (*kṛtakṛtya*), *and the venerable king Jayāpīḍa, who completely* (*nitāntam*) accomplished that which is to be done (*kṛtakṛtya*), [and] occasioned (*-vidhāyin*) the increase of virtues (*guṇavṛddhi-*)?::: *OR* is one whose wickedness (*-kṛtyasya*) has been completely (*nitāntam*) cultivated (*kṛta-*) [and] who has dispensed with (*-vidhāyin*) the increase of virtue (*guṇavṛddhi-*)?"

And:

> *kṛtavipropasargasya bhūtaniṣṭhāvidhāyinaḥ | śrījayāpīḍadevasya pāṇineś ca kim antaram* || RT 4.637 ||. "What difference is there between Pāṇini, who dealt with the preverbs *vi* and *pra* (*kṛta-vi-pra-upasarga*) and prescribed rules for the *niṣṭhā* terminations for the past [tense] (*bhūta-niṣṭhā-vidhāyin*), and the venerable king Jayāpīḍa, who suborned [himself] to the Brahmins (*kṛta-vipra-upasarga*) and brought about the perfection of beings (*bhūtaniṣṭhāvidhāyin*)?::: *OR* who has produced calamities for Brahmins (*kṛta-vipra-upasarga*) and has accomplished the destruction of beings *(bhūtaniṣṭhāvidhāyin)*?"

These translations are also offered and interpreted in Nemec 2017b: 55–56.

king's—need we recall that the *daṇḍa* is the very symbol of discipline and punishment in the royal context?—and they are to use it when the latter strays from his obligations. Kings need Brahmins and Brahmins need to discipline errant kings.

In fact, Brahmins and kings are so thoroughly mutually bound that sometimes Brahmins *become* kings in the *Rājataraṅgiṇī*, this in instances that redound, if not inevitably,[72] to the benefit of the subjects of Kashmir.[73] Take Mātṛgupta, for example. He was, we are told (RT 3.125–129), a poet who worked for the famed king Vikramāditya of Ujjayinī.[74] He is further said to have been willing to praise the qualities of others and by self-restraint and a display of his own learning gained the confidence of the king's courtiers (RT 3.158). In Vikramāditya he recognized several qualities of particular note: Brahmins didn't need to beg to receive honor or distinction from this king (RT 3.132); one could speak frankly with him (RT 3.133);[75] those of good character (*mahāśaya*) received his gifts (*prītidāya*) without hesitation and with gratitude, because they were properly given (RT 3.136); he maintained no counselors of false merits (*mithyākhyātaguṇa*) or who were querulous (*kalahapriya*), who were thieving, or who broke their promises (RT 3.139);[76] and those who served him did not speak of him harshly or abuse one another (RT 3.140). Indeed, he was by these qualities rendered "faultless" (*sarvadoṣojjhita*) (RT 3.143).

Vikramāditya, seeing in turn the virtue of his loyal, honest, and chastened minister, sent Mātṛgupta to Kashmir with a message that he should be anointed as king (RT 3.182*ff.*). Accordingly, he is installed on the throne soon after reaching the Kashmir Valley (RT 3.239–242).[77]

Mātṛgupta's rule in Kashmir was thoroughly measured and fruitful. Extolling the virtues of his patron, we are told he instinctively governed in a manner that mirrored Vikramāditya's virtues:

[72] See above at footnote 54: Saṃdhimati is a minister who becomes king but ultimately neglects his office by way of a surfeit of interest in (tantric) religious practice.

[73] This stands in contrast to the troubles of the complex Brahminical identity described both in Collins 2020 (in analyzing Paraśurāma stories) and, before him, in Shulman 1985.

[74] See Stein [1900] 1989, vol 1: 83–84, fn. at verse 129 for reference to citations of Mātṛgupta's poetry in the *Aucityavicāracarcā* of Kṣemendra and the *Subhāṣitāvali* of Vallabhadeva.

[75] On RT 3.133, see Salomon 1987: 165, which compares Stein's translation to Pandit's.

[76] See Salomon 1987: 165, where he notes an error in Stein's translation, which renders *stheya* as referring to theft and not as a term of art meaning a "judge."

[77] One may incidentally mention that this episode points to the need for a more thorough examination of forms of royal succession in premodern South Asia, as primogeniture was hardly the only mechanism for the same. (I have made this point before, for which see Nemec 2017b: 58–59.)

nākāram udvahasi naiva vikatthase tvaṃ ditsāṃ na sūcayasi muñjasi satphalāni |
niḥśabdavarṣaṇam ivāmbudharasya rājan saṃlakṣyate phalata eva tava prasādaḥ || RT 3.252 ||

You show no sign of emotion and do, indeed, not boast; you do not indicate your liberal disposition, but yield your good fruits [like a tree]. Your favour is perceived only when you grant your rewards, just as [that] of the cloud which pours down silently its rain. (Translation Stein's)

His good actions speak louder than words. And indeed, Mātṛgupta governs Kashmir without incident for the duration of his reign. Despite his proximity to power, he remains ever attached to a religious ambition, such that when his benefactor leaves the world, Mātṛgupta willingly abdicates the throne, taking up a life of asceticism in Vārāṇasī in an effort to honor Vikramāditya himself (RT 3.289–320).[78] To the end he followed *dharma*.

Thus, while one might be tempted to read a sentiment of despair in Mātṛgupta given the last turn of events in his life, as McCrea suggests one must,[79] what are rather the more evident in both the abdication and renunciation are the implacable bond of minister and king and the unqualified virtues of each, furnished in no small part by the quality of their mutual relation. Mātṛgupta is explicit in claiming that his political role in Kashmir must expire with the demise of his patron: as a vassal king his time in office had by definition come to term. And we are in fact told that he entered his religious asceticism with a heart filled with regard for Vikramāditya, not at all out of a despair for the ills of the world or those who oversee it. Good Brahmins could be made kings by a king, because kings were good when their counsel was sound.[80]

Such stories may be multiplied exponentially in their retelling, for Kalhaṇa sprinkles across all the eight *taraṅgas* of the *Rājataraṅgiṇī* narrative episodes that model the fruitful collaboration of counselors and kings. To offer but one additional example, and as I have argued elsewhere, Kalhaṇa suggests that Brahmins chastened the king not just by their counsel but by

[78] See Hultzsch 1915: 276 for a pair of variant readings found in the passage in question.
[79] McCrea 2013: 192–193.
[80] There are other examples as well of wise counselors or those who speak and think well being anointed king. See, e.g., the example of Yaśaskara, discussed in Nemec 2017b: 49–51.

their acts, including notably that of the supremely coercive undertaking of the fast unto death (*prāya*/*prāyopaveśa*), which they sometimes deployed to force the king to enact policies that supported not only their fellow Brahmins but also other, lower-caste subjects of the crown.[81] The objective ever and always was to restrain the king in his desires and to guide him to cleave to a disciplined virtue ethic. As we have already been told and repeatedly so in the *Rājataraṅgiṇī*, it is selfishness that regularly endangers good government, avarice pure and simple, to which, alas, the royal sovereign frequently succumbed.

The Chronicle's Pattern of Narrative Emplotment

It is not just a sprinkling of gnomic wisdom or snippets of happy stories of kings behaving well that suggest the *Rājataraṅgiṇī* presents a call to the virtues of *dharma*, for the very narrative order of the text does the same. Indeed, the directional flow of the long poem is rather toward a more hopeful possibility. While it is perhaps banal to cite Hayden White in reading the *Rājataraṅgiṇī*, and although Slaje warns against it,[82] one must minimally understand Kalhaṇa to offer his historical account in a narrative emplotment, what is defined by White as "the way by which a sequence of events fashioned into a story is gradually revealed to be a story of a particular kind."[83] Here one must visit the types of narrative as identified by White, not to affirm any universal applicability thereof but rather to illustrate how none precisely captures the flow of this poem's long narrative arc, so too that adopting to the *Rājataraṅgiṇī* the narrative mode among White's that is admittedly closest to Kalhaṇa's text—that of Tragedy—misleadingly could induce one to discover in it only a dour, cynical, forlorn narrative mood and purpose.

White's emplotments are four: Romance, Tragedy, Comedy, and Satire. Tragedy, as noted, comes closest to what is found in the *Rājataraṅgiṇī*. White suggests it offers not a diachronic but a synchronic view of history, a narrative in which "the sense of structural continuity . . . or stasis . . . predominates."[84]

[81] Nemec 2017b.
[82] Slaje 2008: 209, citing Schnellenbach in doing so.
[83] See White 1987: 7.
[84] White 1987: 10.

In such narratives it is the work of a historian to "perceive behind or within the welter of events contained in the chronicle an ongoing structure of relationships or an eternal return of the Same in the Different."[85]

So far, so good, but it is the very tragic quality of White's Tragedy that both guides and misleads when interpreting the *Rājataraṅgiṇī*. For "in Tragedy," he further suggests,[86]

> there are no festive occasions, except false or illusory ones; rather there are intimations of states of division among men more terrible than that which incited the tragic agon at the beginning of the drama. Still, the fall of the protagonist and the shaking of the world he inhabits which occur at the end of the Tragic play are not regarded as totally threatening to those who survive the agonic test. There has been a gain in consciousness for the spectators of the contest. And this gain is thought to consist in the epiphany of the law governing human existence which the protagonist's exertions against the world have brought to pass.

This expression both illuminates and misleads in any faithful reading of Kalhaṇa's text. The *Rājataraṅgiṇī*'s audiences are frequently presented with "the fall" of major characters in the drama, also "the shaking of the world," and they are offered an "agonic test" that is perennial and cyclical in nature, one in which many, but not all, "protagonist[s]"—good kings and the good Brahmins who counsel them—must struggle against the vices that lead monarchal rule to ruin. The "fall" occurs, however, not "at the end of the Tragic play" but continually, perennially—excepting if it does not. It is not a singular, shattering event but a perennial danger that defined and continued in Kalhaṇa's contemporaneous day to define human action in the Kali age. The *Rājataraṅgiṇī*, however, also allows for the kind of hope found in White's "Comedy," which for him is like Tragedy in suggesting "the possibility of at least partial liberation from the condition of the Fall and provisional release from the divided state in which men find themselves in this world."[87] For in White's Comedy "hope is held out for the temporary triumph of man over his world by the prospect of occasional *reconciliations* of the forces at play in the social and natural worlds,"[88] which is precisely what Kalhaṇa occasionally

[85] White 1987: 11.
[86] White 1987: 9.
[87] White 1987: 9.
[88] White 1987: 9.

chronicles, though in a milieu of no comic relief, only a relief of the kind White classes as "Comic," emergent occasionally in the context of "Tragedy."

One may agree that "a gain in consciousness for the spectators of the contest[s]" described in the Kashmiri chronicle is offered by suffering tragedy, but not one consisting in an "epiphany of the law governing human existence," only a confirmation of the same, since the dangers of the Kali Yuga were universally known. And it is precisely because it is not the case that "there are no festive occasions, except false or illusory ones," that the *Rājataraṅgiṇī* can and must be read as a work of occasional redemption and not a tragedy *tout court*. The "epiphany" offered is less novel discovery than a perennial reminder to *dharma* of continuous relevance in the Kali age.

Similarly, it is also not the case that the *Rājataraṅgiṇī* offers "intimations of states of division among men more terrible than that which incited the tragic agon at the beginning of the drama," for the tragic agon—played out as moral decay, the decay of *dharma*—is perennial by definition given the text's cosmic timeframe. It similarly is not the case in Kalhaṇa, as it is in White's Tragedy, that the reconciliations of the text are "much more somber" than those of Comedy. Kalhaṇa's reconciliations are not merely moments characterized by the "resignations of men to the conditions under which they must labor in the world," whereby "these conditions, in turn, are asserted to be inalterable and eternal," the implication being "that man cannot change them but must work within them. They set the limits on what may be aspired to and what may be legitimately aimed at in the quest for security and sanity in the world."[89] While this does capture what one must see in the *Rājataraṅgiṇī* in order to read it as a cynical or dour work, doing so belies a fundamental claim of the Arthaśāstras and the *Rājataraṅgiṇī* itself, that a king can *make* the Kṛta age in the world by his actions. Reprieves are to be found in Kashmiri history, and they occasioned true breaks from the limits of the Kali age.

Such are the explicitly signaled historical parameters of the narrative, and with them is presented not only a particular kind of narrative emplotment but also one that echoes the great Indian epic with which is ushered in the Kali Yuga. Not only is the *Mahābhārata* a text that Kalhaṇa knew well, as Stein,[90] among others, has already suggested, and not only are the two works similar for their common association with both the *śānta rasa* and the Kali Yuga, as McCrea indicated, but also the great epic served as the model for

[89] White 1987: 9.
[90] Stein [1900] 1989 (vol. 1): 11.

the narrative structure of Kalhaṇa's work. The *Rājataraṅgiṇī* in a manner echoing the core narrative structure of the *Mahābhārata* may be understood to chronicle three broad narrative phases.

First, after outlining the hoary origins of the Kashmir Valley, the text describes a relatively near past that was witness to prosperity, order, and simple good government, one analogous perhaps to the time of peaceful rule under the guidance of the wise caretaker, Bhīṣma. The height of this phase may be found in the fourth book of the *Rājataraṅgiṇī* in the description of the kings of the Kārkoṭa dynasty, where giving to religious institutions and patronage of higher learning is at its height. Narayana Rao, Shulman, and Subrahmanyam describe this book as "Kalhaṇa's real masterpiece,"[91] and it is indeed a high point of Kalhaṇa's history of Kashmir. Kings are said to be wise, generous, and powerful—most notably Jayāpīḍa's generous patronage, as reviewed by Bronner—and this is so much the case that, as Meister has noted, the *Rājataraṅgiṇī* even exaggerates the military successes of the Kashmiri king Lalitāditya.[92] Their reigns are not perfect—of this there can be no doubt—but this narrative period presents more instances of kings acting wisely, as we saw with Avantivarman and Mātṛgupta, for example, than the period that follows it.

Succeeding this moment of relative calm, of a relative inclination to virtue ethics, is what the *Rājataraṅgiṇī* narrates as a fundamental rupture in the order of the Kashmir Valley, one analogous to the occurrence of the Bhārata war in the *Mahābhārata*. From the time of the abdication in 1063 of Ananta (a king of the first Lohara dynasty) to his son Kalaśa (r. 1063–1089) and up to but not including the reign of Jayasiṃha, who ruled Kashmir from 1128 to the end of the period covered by the chronicle in 1149/1150, the Kashmir Valley was consumed by incessant civil war, struggles for power, and palace intrigue. All told the narration of these episodes occupies close to half the entire *Rājataraṅgiṇī*. It is a narrative punctuated by the portrayal of the actions of the single most dastardly of all the sovereigns of Kashmir, the hardened iconoclast Harṣa (r. 1089–1101), who is said not only to have plundered the very religious and Brahminical institutions that were endowed by those who came before him but also to have sent men to defile the images in the temples whose wealth he pilfered for personal gain.[93]

[91] Narayana Rao, Shulman, and Subrahmanyam 2001: 259.
[92] Meister 2006: 29.
[93] About this see Basham 1948; Slaje 2019.

The fulcrum of the narrative of the *Rājataraṅgiṇī*, then, pivots on the descriptions of the extreme and reportedly unprecedented transgressions of this terrible king, just as the narration of the civil war stands as the central event around which all the episodes of the *Mahābhārata* are organized. That Kalhaṇa is explicit in comparing Harṣa to Duryodhana, moreover (and as McCrea has noted already[94]), renders the connection in question explicit.

Finally, the *Rājataraṅgiṇī* culminates in the articulation of hopes for a peaceful restoration of *dharmic* order, which is full of promise of what might come—a moment that I propose is analogous to the closing frame narrative of the *Mahābhārata*, when, as we saw in Chapter 1, Janamejaya is shown to end the retributive cycle of war by pardoning the snake-king and his ilk for any implication in the death of his father, Parikṣit, in order to honor a boon given by him to the Brahmin Āstīka, restoring thereby the proper bond between *brāhmaṇa* and *kṣatriya*. The *Rājataraṅgiṇī* closes with Jayasiṃha having regained control of his kingdom and with reports that renewed patronage of religious institutions and institutions of learning in the Kashmir Valley again issued regularly from the hands of that king and those of members of his court.[95] As the penultimate verse of the narrative of his reign suggests, this king, Jayasiṃha, is mature in wisdom:

iyad dṛṣṭam ananyatra prajāpuṇyair mahībhujaḥ |
paripākamanojñatvaṃ stheyāḥ kalpātigā samāḥ || RT 8.3405 ||

May the matured wisdom of this king [which has been produced] by the subjects' merits and which has not been seen to such an extent in any other [ruler], last for years exceeding this Kalpa. (Translation Stein's)

Hope springs eternal, in this case with some good reason, for this sanguine look at Jayasiṃha is confirmed by Jonarāja's continuation of the history: his *Rājataraṅgiṇī* records the completion of Jayasiṃha's reign in peace and good governance, which redounds to the benefit of the Kashmir Valley's royal

94 McCrea 2013: 195.

95 See, e.g., RT 8.3316*ff.* Cf. RT 8.2391–2450. Note also that Jayasiṃha was also said to go on expeditions abroad to conquer his proximate foes and enrich the kingdom, about which see RT 8.2452*ff.*

subjects.[96] But as the final verse of the historical poem notes, vigilance is ever needed, for fate takes its toll in the Kali age:

> *ambho 'pi pravahatsvabhāvam aśanair āśyānam aśmāyate grāvāmbhaḥ sravati dravatvam uditodrekeṣu cāveyuṣaḥ |*
> *kālasyāskhalitaprabhāvarabhasaṃ bhāti prabhutve 'dbhute kasyāmutra vidhātṛśaktighaṭite mārge nisargaḥ sthiraḥ* || RT 8.3406 ||

> Even the water, which is liquid by nature, freezes and turns in time hard as stone, [while] the stone may dissolve into water. Under that wonderful dominion of Time, which has witnessed, even in beings of exceptional greatness, the rapid change of unlimited might, whose nature can remain unchanged on the road laid out by the power of fate? (Translation Stein's)

Solid entities liquify and waters turn to ice. Time, the waves of kings, the waters of consecration, the elixirs of *rasa* and medicine—they flow, or freeze. Hope springs eternal, but dark winters ever threaten to harden with cold turns of fate the nurturing flow of kings and the medical salves of Brahminical counsel. *Dharma* in the Kali age is ever in play.

A Yugic Theory of Action in the *Rājataraṅgiṇī*: Fate and *Dharma*

If the *brāhmaṇa-kṣatriya* relationship is central to the *Rājataraṅgiṇī* narrative, it is further supported by the cosmic periodization of the text. It is worth considering more closely the meaning imbued by invoking the Kali Yuga, which Kalhaṇa does in the first verses of the poem by referring explicitly to the *Mahābhārata* war (RT 1.51) and indexing it temporally to his narrative both by incorporating the reign of Yudhiṣṭhira into these opening passages (at RT 1.56) and by identifying the Kashmiri king, Gonanda II, who reigned in the time of the epic (RT 1.74–82).[97] Such recognition of the emergence of the Kali age announces a theological view of action and its consequences,

[96] See Jonarāja's *Rājataraṅgiṇī*, verses 27–38, esp. 27, 28, and 32, edited and translated in Slaje 2014: 58–59. The historical truth of this depiction may of course be called into question. It is nevertheless the case that the narrative end that Jonarāja offers squares with the arc of the *Rājataraṅgiṇī* narrative here outlined.

[97] Gonanda II, we are told, was an infant at the time of the war and so remained neutral throughout.

which stands at the center of the author's vision of the world. The progressive degeneration of the eons is implicated in the entirety of Kalhaṇa's narrative and this by the very fact that Kashmir perennially faces a host of political and other problems. While by no means inerrantly fatalistic, as I have argued already at length, Kalhaṇa's poem does repeatedly invoke the notion that events in the Kashmir Valley frequently turn for the worse. "Fortunes," we are thus told in the *Rājataraṅgiṇī*, "are the passing flashes of lightning from the cloud of fate, and exceptional greatness finds a disgusting end. Notwithstanding this, the pride of imaginary greatness does not cease in those whose souls are struck by delusion."[98]

More directly stated, the narrative conveys a *yugic* theory of subjectivity and action. Time and space are not neutral locations in Kalhaṇa's narrative, unchanging for all ages and equally impinging on all agents (as Kant, for example, would have them). A cosmic time shapes one's *karmic* trajectory, affects and effects both one's actions and the results they may render. The cosmic timeframe, moreover, contours not only the circumstances of those about whom the book is written but also those of its audiences. Those who read or heard the *Rājataraṅgiṇī* and those whose acts it narrates share in the fact of inhabiting the same eon of *dharmic* decline. The reader is bound on firm theological grounds to the lives and activities of the characters in this chronicle, not just by their shared geography (many who engaged the text being Kashmiris), but also because those who can accept and adopt Kalhaṇa's wisdom in its narration would naturally find common ground with those in the text who had themselves held up, lived up to, the standards of *dharma*.

All this of course begs the very question with which this chapter opened. Is Kalhaṇa's text fundamentally fatalistic, because the age it chronicles is congenitally doomed to harm? Or can those living in a broken world find certain respite by acting productively to repair it and stave off the worst of the Kali age? I've indicated already my own view, that Kalhaṇa holds the latter position, for the narrative emplotment rises in its final phase, kings do sometimes rule justly for all their days, and the stories suggest, on too many occasions to ignore them, that the discerning action of disciplined kings and queens, guided by learned Brahminical counsel, reliably can tip favor in a calamitous world. Kings can make, for a time, the Kṛta age anew. While the Kali is no

[98] See RT 7.1729: *bhāgyāmbuvāhataḍitastaralāḥ śriyas tās tac cāvasānavirasaṃ prasabhonnatatvam* | *tatrāpi naiṣa vata mohahatāśayānāṃ śāntiṃ prayāti vibhavānubhavābhimānaḥ* ||. The translation is Stein's.

golden age for *dharma*, neither is it an eon in which social life must of necessity be quit, in which only world renunciation can offer any escape from the serial and progressive degradation of the moral order.

Still, another, theological interpretation presents in considering the narratives to hand when read in mutual relation. If the *Rājataraṅgiṇī* echoes the *Mahābhārata* in offering its lessons for the age and is composed and engaged in the Kali Yuga, and if the *Rāmāyaṇa* teaches self-chastening in a deeply devotional and inspiring mode by narrating a divine history from an earlier eon, then one may rightly ask after the position of the audiences not only of the latter epic but also of the two narratives engaged as a pair. If both stories are to be of guiding value and available in the Kali Yuga, then both the ethic of the *Mahābhārata* and that of the *Rāmāyaṇa* must have occasion to have purchase on devout Hindus who follow their stories in that single eon of cosmic time. The *Mahābhārata* might predominate inasmuch as any hearer or reader of that narrative lives in the eon it ushers into history; yet because the *Rāmāyaṇa* continues fruitfully to be read and heard even after the *Mahābhārata*'s great war, it must offer guidance on the occasions when its strictures are applicable even "out of its cosmic moment."

With the two epics are furnished a complementary pair of modes for action. The *Rāmāyaṇa*, on the one hand, articulates a hopeful view of human discretion and motivation: repeatedly we see agents regularly inclined toward *dharma*, toward virtue, in the absence of aberrant and anomalous choices that lead one (temporarily) astray. The *Mahābhārata*, on the other hand, anticipates a world in which one can expect others to fail to uphold *dharma*, or worse—even to serve what they count as *dharma* with a surfeit of loyalty but for personal ends.

It is clearly the *Mahābhārata* mode that stands in the foreground of Kalhaṇa's thought and narrative, for the various places where he invokes fate and fatalism show sharp turns for the worse among those who had once intended better but turn to folly (although the motivations in the *Rājataraṅgiṇī* are depicted as reflexive and feel almost mechanical, while the *Mahābhārta* excavates deep emotion behind the misconduct of Duryodhana and many others). It is without question that although replete with the careful narration of the negative (and I would add positive) influences of historical agents, the *Rājataraṅgiṇī* closes (at RT 8.3406, cited earlier) with a recognition of the vicissitudes of fate (*vidhātṛ*). What Stein labeled a superstition[99]—belief in

[99] Stein [1900] 1989 (vol. 1): 35–37.

karmic and other forms of causality—and what cannot be supported by the "positive evidence" of an objective historical account nevertheless stands at the heart of Kalhaṇa's historical poem, and, I suggest, his philosophy of history. This is not to say a sort of "*Rāmāyaṇa* mindset" nowhere is present in the text—rather the opposite. We see this disposition in the happy moments of the text, when king and minister work hand in glove and with deep mutual trust. It is only that these instances of virtuous human action in relation to *dharma* are like "bubbles produced [in the water] by a downpour of rain on a dull day," to refer to the epigraph cited at the beginning of this chapter. The *Rāmāyaṇa* contexts known in the Kali age might be comparatively isolated islands of refuge in the choppy seas of the Kali Yuga, dominated therefore by a "*Mahābhārata* mindset," but they are possible, necessary, and vital, even in this decrepit age.

Conclusion

The narrative arc of the *Rājataraṅgiṇī* thus ushers in a return to, a sort of tenuous but hopeful reinvigoration of, the normative political order, one defined by the trusting bond between king and counsel—the sovereign and the Brahminical men of letters who advise him. One may swim against fate in the Kali age, and with some luck and by cultivated virtue one can beat the adverse currents. Significantly, Kalhaṇa portrays the succession of kings (and queens) as an *inevitable* flow, however disrupted or frozen it might become—not without moments of tumult and calm, but a perpetual cycle that, along with normative social divisions such as those related to caste and gender inequities,[100] is offered simply as part and parcel of the natural order. No evolution of political forms of governance is imagined or sought in the work, and one suspects that Kalhaṇa gave little if any thought to alternative political structures. Kingship, its parameters marked by the strictures of *dharma*, is measured in the currency of prosperity; it is guaranteed by both the capacity of the sovereign to protect the Kashmir Valley and, perhaps more importantly, his or her willingness to share its wealth. So much, Kalhaṇa narrates, is possible with the right royal sovereign and by that sovereign honoring the right values and cultivating the best of influences. The narration of a perennial and seemingly incessant cycle of royal sovereigns

[100] About this see, e.g., Davis and Nemec 2016.

thus emphatically conveys a pronounced homeostasis in the political order: good or bad, a king (or queen) shall come to power, with any luck advised by a learned Brahmin, as they always could be. Whatever break with king and court is evinced in Kalhaṇa's willingness to speak a realism in lieu of a royally sponsored panegyric, then, is balanced by the overarching support his narrative offers to the very institution of kingship as conceived in the classical *śāstras*.

Kalhaṇa thus offers a distinct philosophy of history, one that might appropriately be described as imputing what might be termed a yugic historiography. What distinguishes this historiographic mode from a modern, positivist historiography is that Kalhaṇa clearly distinguishes fact from error without simultaneously dichotomizing, as Thucydides did, "history" and "myth." In doing so he reinforces normative Brahminical claims regarding the nature of political power, cultural authority, time, human action, a "mythic" past, and individual agency, claims that communicate the indispensability of good government, which is prescribed by the laws of *dharma* and which secured and is securing of a privileged place for Brahmins—for the lettered Brahminical advisor to the king—in the social order. History and myth are fused in this narrative, which nevertheless seeks to sift out errors and report facts, though it is a narrative that simultaneously and implicitly supports the normative truth claims to which the author subscribes. The political *history* of the *Rājataraṅgiṇī*, imbued as it is with these normative claims, consequently set Brahmanism at the core of the social order, the Brahmin advisor at the side of the king, and the institution of royal sovereignty beyond political reform, allowing the "myths," "beliefs," and normative truth claims that are expressed in the work implicitly and explicitly to support precisely the same social vision and ideals.

The *Rājataraṅgiṇī* thus may be said to offer a kind of modified vision of the seer, expressed in the voice of the court poet. Not from *śoka* comes *śloka*, as in the *Rāmāyaṇa*, for the Kali age with which Kalhaṇa contends needs no revelation from sorrow, which ever invaded Kashmiri political and social life. The sorrow of a *Rāmāyaṇa* mindset is substituted for, as Kaul notes,[101] a discursive, rational insight that produces poetry: "[Kalhaṇa's] ethicized commentary runs through the text, *unifying his account in a moral logic*."[102] It is the moral logic of the fight against a perennially rising tide of immorality

[101] See Kaul 2014: 205–206.
[102] Kaul 2014: 207. Emphasis Kaul's.

and wrong action fated by the Kali age; but it is a moral logic that suggests that even *dharmic* castles built in sand may withstand the rising waters for a time, and so try one must—for where else is there to go in an age where so many are of a kind? Thus—and as Kaul again correctly indicates—Kalhaṇa's *kāvya* has a normative purpose and intent, one that suggests not only that he teaches morals in the *Rājataraṅgiṇī* but also that there is purpose to doing so: the *karmans* of the Kashmiri people, Kalhaṇa suggests, determine the nature of the Kashmir Valley's political rule.[103] It is not just to read the text but to incite his audiences to do something about the state of the world, as possible in the cosmic eon in question and using what his text has to offer, that Kalhaṇa wrote. Thus the stories of kings heeding the counsel of Brahmins; thus the stories of Brahmins counseling kings in word and by the example of their own virtuous restraint.

In this *Mahābhārata*-like age, the perennial hope that comes like spring must ever be reinforced, even if a winter of despair is inevitable or nearly so. Bubbles of peace in an ocean of torment, perhaps, but the *Rājataraṅgiṇī* argues that with a disinterested application of *varṇāśramadharma*—in the right time, in the right way—the literary Brahmins who advised the royal sovereign had recourse to acts that could produce positive turns of events, islands of a *Rāmāyaṇa* mindset in the ocean of decaying *dharma*, defined in the *Mahābhārata* narrative. For Kalhaṇa and his sympathetic readers, they should have wanted, would ever have wanted, to effect just this—precisely what the *Rājataraṅgiṇī* counsels them to do.

[103] See RT 1.187–189, also cited in Kaul 2014: 207.

Appendix to Chapter 3

List of Literary and Other Authors Mentioned in the *Rājataraṅgiṇī*

Author	*Reference in Rājataraṅgiṇī (RT)*	*Selected Literary Contributions*
Suvrata	RT 1.11	A literary history of Kashmir
Kṣemendra	RT 1.13	His *Nṛpāvali*
Helārāja	RT 1.17–18	His *Pārthivāvali*
Padmamihira	RT 1.17–18	
Candrācārya	RT 1.176	Brought the *Mahābhāṣya* to Kashmir on command of King Abhimanyu
Nāgārjuna	RT 1.177	
Vasunanda	RT 1.337	Author of a work of *ars amatoria* (*smaraśāstra*)
Candaka[a]	RT 2.16	Author of a play "worthy of attention of the people"
Mātṛgupta	RT 3.129	Quoted by Kṣemendra in *Aucityavicāracarcā* and by Vallabhadeva in *Subhāṣitāvali*, and listed in Catologus Catologorum as author of commentaries on *Alaṃkāra*- and *Nāṭya-śāstra* (see Stein [1900] 1989 [vol. 1]: 83–84, fn. 129)
Bhartṛmeṇṭha (a.k.a. Meṇṭha)	RT 3.260*ff.*	Author of *Hayagrīvavadha*, mentioned by Kṣemendra and by Maṅkha, and quoted by Śrīvara in the *Subhāṣitāvali* (see Stein [1900] 1989 [vol. 1]: 93, fn. 260)
Vākpatirāja	RT 4.144	
Bhavabhūti	RT 4.144	
Bhappaṭa	RT 4.214	
Kṣīra	RT 4.489	Author of a commentary on the *Amarakośa*
Bhaṭṭa Udbhaṭa	RT 4.495	Author of the *Alaṃkāraśāstra*

Author	*Reference in Rājataraṅgiṇī (RT)*	*Selected Literary Contributions*
Dāmodaragupta	RT 4.496	Minister to Jayāpīḍa and author of the *Kuṭṭanīmata*
Manoratha	RT 4.497	Verses quoted in Vallabha-deva's *Subhāṣitāvali*
Śaṅkhadanta[b]	RT 4.497	A poet
Caṭaka	RT 4.497	A poet
Saṃdhimat	RT 4.497	A poet
Vāmana	RT 4.497	A coauthor of *Kāśikāvṛtti*(?); also associated with author of one *Kāvyālaṃkāravṛtti*
Dharmottara[c]	RT 4.498	A Buddhist philosopher
King Jayāpīḍa	RT 4.550	Wrote poems during his capture by the king of Nepāl. Stein says some among them are recorded in Vallabhadeva's *Subhāṣitāvali* (Stein [1900] 1989 [vol. 1]: 171, fn. 550)
Pāṇini	RT 4.635	
Śaṅkuka	RT 4.705	Wrote the *Bhuvanābhyudaya* about the civil war between two uncles, Mamma and Utpalaka
Rāmaṭa	RT 5.28–29	Said to be an expert in grammar, assigned to recite (as a *vyākhyātṛ*) at a Viṣṇu temple funded by Mahodaya, a "door keeper" of the brother to the king
Muktākaṇa	RT 5.34	Quoted by Kṣemendra (see Stein [1900] 1989 [vol. 1]: 189, fn. 34)
Śivasvāmin	RT 5.34	Quoted by Kṣemendra (see Stein [1900] 1989 [vol. 1]: 189, fn. 34)
Ānandavardhana	RT 5.34	
Ratnākara	RT 5.34	According to Stein he composed his *Haravijaya* under king Bṛhaspati (=Cippaṭa-Jayāpīḍa) (see Stein [1900] 1989 [vol. 1]: 189, fn. 34)

Author	*Reference in Rājataraṅgiṇī (RT)*	*Selected Literary Contributions*
Kṛtamandāra	RT 5.35	A bard who recited a verse in the hall of the minister Śūra, which is quoted in RT 5.36
Bhaṭṭa Kallaṭa	RT 5.66	A (tantric) Siddha and author
Nāyaka	RT 5.159	Said to be installed in charge of Śaiva temples by Śaṃkaravarman. Abhinavagupta; quotes Bhaṭṭa Nāyaka as an author on Alaṃkāra (see Stein [1900] 1989 [vol. 1]: 207, fn. 159)
Bhallaṭa	RT 5.204	Author of *Bhallaṭaśataka* and a dictionary titled the *Padamañjarī*; oft quoted by Kṣemendra
Bhoja	RT 7.190–193	
Kalaśa	RT 7.606	A king said to have introduced "choral songs" (*upāṅgagīta*) and carefully selected female dancers to Kashmir, importing traditions from outside Kashmir
Bilhaṇa	RT 7.937	
Harṣa	RT 7.942	The king as author of emotionally resonant songs!

[a]Candaka is said to be descended from or an incarnation of Vyāsa.
[b]Consider also the variant reading offered in Hultzsch 1915: 278, of Śaṅkhadatta for Śaṅkhadanta.
[c]I am grateful to Dominic Goodall for this reference, offered in a personal communication dated January 18, 2013. See also the note on the same verse at Hultzsch 1915: 278–279.

4

Wizards and Kings, or "Tantra beyond the Tantras"

The Śaiva-Brahminical Narrative of the *Kathāsaritsāgara*

Introduction

A matter of vital but underexamined intellectual, religious, and cultural-historical concern may somewhat colloquially be labeled with the moniker "tantra beyond the tantras." By this I refer to instances when doctrinal, ritual, or other religious elements of the Śaiva esotericism are found in what are understood to be nontantric contexts. The presence of tantric influences in nontantric traditions, while widely known to exist—in temple ritual, for example—is by and large insufficiently documented or studied, and that this is so is the product of the combination of two circumstances.

First, contemporary tantric studies scholarship is largely inward looking and therefore insular in its articulation, this not unjustifiably so given the fact that tantric traditions had been left largely unexamined in the scholarly literature in India and Asia, Europe, and the Western Hemisphere until recent decades. This circumstance demanded remedy by way of a close examination of the relevant tantric source materials, which are themselves rather sophisticated and complex. Second, scholars working in nontantric fields of research are often insufficiently conversant with the latest discoveries of tantric studies scholarship. This is so, one suspects, not only due to the specialized nature of the work but also due to the fact that its greatest advances are relatively new. Translational work is required of tantric studies scholars, therefore, from subspecialty to scholarly conversations that may more readily reach non-subspecialists. Nontantric studies scholars similarly must work more deeply to familiarize themselves with the cutting edge of this area of study, given the extensive influences of tantra on South Asian religions, history, and society.

Brahmins and Kings. John Nemec, Oxford University Press. © Oxford University Press 2025.
DOI: 10.1093/oso/9780197791998.003.0005

One particular concern worthy of further interrogation—what is the subject of the present chapter—lies with the representation, as opposed to the transmission or appropriation, of tantric motifs, habits, and concerns not as found in the scriptural works of Śaiva, Vaiṣṇava, Buddhist, or Jain tantric practitioners, the Tantras, Āgamas, Saṃhitās, and other works explicitly associated with these tantric traditions, but in what are known today, as they were in their own day, to be nontantric textual sources. Among the possible works in which to find such representations, the *Kathāsaritsāgara* (KSS) recommends itself unreservedly. In reading the tantric elements evoked in this famed fictive narrative, moreover, one will find witness to modes of imagining the mutually beneficial relationship of Brahmins and kings not primarily to the end of serving *dharma*, the major concern of the two epics and the *Rājataraṅgiṇī*, as we have seen, but more directly in service of the other normatively recognized human ends (*puruṣārthas*), in particular pleasure (*kāma*) and wealth (*artha*) and, after a fashion, the fourth goal, spiritual emancipation.[1]

The *Kathāsaritsāgara* is a magisterial narrative, so large as to begin to constitute an encyclopedia of Indian story literature, even as it is likely to convey only a fraction of the original text of which it is a retelling.[2] Composed in the Kashmir Valley sometime around 1070 CE by a Brahmin named Somadeva, it is self-consciously and explicitly based on Guṇāḍhya's perhaps sixth-century, Paiśācī-language narrative, the *Bṛhatkathā*, though probably by way of a now-lost intermediary, also composed in Paiśācī, which influenced both the *Kathāsaritsāgara* and the other of two Kashmirian versions of the story, Kṣemendra's *Bṛhatkathāmañjarī*.[3] The text marries the narratives of a pair of kings, those of both Udayana and his son Naravāhanadatta, in the course of elaborating eighteen books that are referred to as *lambakas*. Each of the two kings of the *Kathāsaritsāgara* sets out on adventures and "attains" and marries wives along the way, gaining suzerainty over vast territories by doing so, each of them advised by key Brahminical ministers in the course of their endeavors. As Nelson, following Lacôte, has noted, the narrative structure—the Udayana story preceding the Naravāhanadatta story—allows the *Kathāsaritsāgara* to compile what were originally two distinct city

[1] Nelson 1974: 266–268 similarly notes how *artha*, *dharma*, and *kāma* (in that order) shape the reasons given for Udayana to wish to have a son in the *Ur-Bṛhatkathā* narrative as he seeks to reconstruct it.

[2] See Lacôte 1908: 208 for his calculation of the probable length of the original, now-lost text.

[3] See Nelson 1974: 5–6. Cf. Lacôte 1908: 61, 110, and 122–145. See also Um 2014: 20–24 (section 2.3 of her MA thesis).

epics, those of Ujjayinī and Kauśāmbī, a conceit inherited from the original *Bṛhatkathā* narrative.[4] Naravāhanadatta is the principal character, however, as he is destined to become the emperor of the semidivine class of beings, the *vidyādharas*. The *Kathāsaritsāgara* elaborates with endless substories and side stories his epic journey to this end, which, despite its roots in the early, pretantric history of Indian religions and despite the "undeniability of a latent Buddhism"[5] in the *Bṛhatkathā*, could be described as a kind of quasi-tantric endeavor that comes to be associated with early Śaiva tantric literature.[6]

The *Kathāsaritsāgara* further has been shown to have transformed this quest, which is common to all the *Bṛhatkathā* narratives, into a rather more *yoginī*-centric tale. This much was rather clearly established in particular by Shaman Hatley, who has charted the various stories of the text that evoke the culture of the cult of *yoginīs* and the rituals and deities characteristic of the Vidyāpīṭha Bhairavatantras,[7] including but not limited to the presence in the narrative of skull-bearing ascetics, the selling of human flesh in the cremation ground, the capacity of *yoginīs* to fly through the air, and an emphasis on the control of powerful and dangerous forces that congregate in cremation grounds, all of which are hallmark features of a stratum of Śaiva tantric scriptural literature that was well represented in Kashmir in Somadeva's day.[8] Hatley also notes the number of tales that refer specifically to *yoginīs*, *ḍākinīs*, and *śākinīs* in manners that correspond to tantric sources in their terminology and ritual references, or even by going so far as to make reference by name to the famed Kālasaṃkarśinī *mantra*.[9]

[4] Lacôte 1908: 36 concludes that it is likely that Guṇāḍhya's text probably originally was composed somewhere along the line from Ujjayinī to Kauśāmbī, matching Nelson's discussion of the work, which as noted follows Lacôte's. See Nelson 1974: 61 and Lacôte 1908: 234, 246, and 247.

[5] This is Lacote's estimation of the influences on the *Bṛhatkathā*, for which see, e.g., Lacôte 1908: 231–236, esp. 233 where he says "un bouddhisme latent est indéniable" in the work.

[6] Hatley 2007: 99 notes: "Attainment of *vidyādharapada*, the status of a *vidyādhara*, was in fact the aim of much of the non-soteriologically oriented ritual outlined in early tantric literature, from the Śaiva Niśvāsa corpus to early Tantric Buddhist texts." Lacôte 1908: 37 in turn notes the association of *vidyādhara* stories with Śaivism and locates the literary Paiśācī language used by Guṇāḍhya in the northwest of the subcontinent, on the basis of the sound changes common to both the literary language in question and the spoken languages of that region, which both have a habit of deploying voiceless consonants where their voiced counterparts are found in Sanskrit (Lacôte 1908: 50–59). Finally, Lacôte 1908: 59 further suggests that Paiśācī eventually lost favor in Brahminical circles but did so more slowly in Kashmir due to linguistic similarities between it and Kashmiri itself.

[7] See Hatley 2007: 95*ff.*

[8] Indeed, all are particular characteristics of the Vidyāpīṭha Bhairavatantras. Also mentioned in such works is human sacrifice (as in the *Brahmayāmalatantra*), about which see Hatley 2007: 89.

[9] The spectrum of *yoginīs* present in the *Kathāsaritsāgara* accords with taxonomies in tantric literature: "In the KSS, *yoginīs* are classified, variously, as *ḍākinīs* or *śākinīs*—lowly and cruel

There can be little to question of the fruitfulness of an approach that seeks to mine the text for historical information, as Hatley does so aptly in tracing a historical awareness of *yoginī* traditions in the text. I myself have engaged the *Kathāsaritsāgara* on similar terms.[10] And while studies that trace the relationships of both Somadeva's text and other retellings of the now-lost *Bṛhatkathā* to that source work[11] or which develop the "*microanalysis* of particular stories from a comparativist point of view"[12] have proven to be of substance and consequence, I here wish, in keeping with the overarching structure and focus of the present book, to dwell on what has surprisingly slipped all too often from the purview of contemporary scholarship: the text's narrative dimensions, the force and effectiveness of the stories of the *Kathāsaritsāgara*, which are arrayed and told in particular ways for particular reasons and with particular narrative consequences.

We must pay close attention to the structure and contents of the text, which, despite the pedigree of the work in the *Bṛhatkathā*, are unique: Somadeva

varieties—while *yoginīs* without such qualifiers are frequently benevolent" (Hatley 2007: 102). Hatley enumerates a handful of *yoginī* stories, as follows (all references to the *Kathāsaritsāgara* here and in this chapter are by *lambaka*, *taraṅga*, and, where applicable, verse number): (1) The story of the *yoginī* Citralekhā. There is a woman named Uṣā, who is given the boon of winning the husband of her dreams. She is united with him in the Gāndharva form of marriage quite literally in a dream, but when she awakens she does not know where to find him. Consulting Citralekhā, the latter offers to draw all the creatures of the universe until Uṣā spots him, which she does. She subsequently carries Uṣā through the air to her beloved. (See KSS 6.5.) (2) The story of Somasvāmin. A man, Somasvāmin, who is a Brahmin and the son of one Candrasvāmin, had a lover named Bandhudattā, who is the daughter of a great merchant and the wife of another. They met to make love regularly, but then her husband returns from his trade mission. She was to be taken by him back to Mathurā, where he was trading and otherwise engaged in business. Not wishing to go, her friend, the *yoginī* Sukhaśayā, gave her two spells, one to turn her lover into a monkey, another to turn him back into a man. She took her lover along as a pet to Mathurā and lived happily ever after. (See KSS 7.3.) (3) The story of Kālarātri, the grotesque wife of an orthodox Brahmin. She secretly acts as a guru to a coven of *ḍākinīs*. (See KSS 3.6.) (4) The story of a weary traveler who accepts the hospitality of a *śākinī*. (See KSS 12.4.) He is almost turned into a goat by her, but then is caught by the butcher's wife, a wicked *yoginī*, who turns him into a peacock. (5) "A jealous queen, a greedy female renunciant, and a clever barber conspire to make the king think his newest bride is secretly a *ḍākinī* who sucks out his vitals while he sleeps." This is the description of Hatley 2007: 102. (See also KSS 6.6.) (6) Finally, there is the story of the witch Śarabhānanā, for which see KSS 8.5. See also Hatley 2007: 103*ff.* for reference to yet other relevant tales, and, finally, note that the reference to the Kālasaṃkarṣinī *mantra* is to be found at KSS 12.1.65.

[10] Don Davis and I sought to furnish evidence of legal consciousness extant in the historical period when the *Kathāsaritsāgara* (among other works) was composed, for which see Davis and Nemec 2016.

[11] I have here in mind Nelson 1974 and Lacôte 1908, both cited repeatedly in these footnotes. See also the useful, concise overview of extant scholarship on *kathā* literatures to be found in Um 2014: 6–10 (section 1.3).

[12] See Nelson 1978: 669, emphasis his.

includes numerous tales excluded from other retellings of the *Bṛhatkathā* and orders them in a distinctive sequence (as is well known).[13] This is to say that I here seek to identify the "particular set of effects [that both the subject matter and the form of the work have] upon our opinions and emotions by virtue of [the] particular structuring of those materials."[14] More simply put, the present chapter will offer a close reading of the *Kathāsaritsāgara* that asks what the text, as a literary work, may tell us about the representation and understanding in the time when it was composed of the relation of tantric practices to the *brāhmaṇa-kṣatriya* alliance. With that one can see not only the ways in which the *Kathāsaritsāgara* narrates instances of royal counsel but also that it elucidates another dimension of the dynamic relationship of Brahmins and kings in premodern South Asia: it offers as counsel to kings the idea that the work of kingship is not merely obligatory and rule bound but also can be quite pleasant, personally fulfilling, and powerful; the work of the royal sovereign can be a world-embracing endeavor and not merely a dutiful one, if the royal sovereign is aided by the proper counsel of powerful, tantric Brahminical advisors.

The Double Narrative of the *Kathāsaritsāgara*

My argument *in nuce* is this, that the *Kathāsaritsāgara* advances a double narrative. Brahminicized and tantricized, Somadeva's storybook spins a web of tales that reiterates and reifies orthodox norms regarding the position of the king in society while simultaneously offering its audience a popularized vision of the tantric path, one that emphasizes the quest for the kinds of magical powers associated with tantric initiation while warning of the potential dangers of the same, those involving *ḍākinīs* and *śākinīs* in particular. The text emphasizes the king's role in society, even while preserving some of the "popular" elements that are often associated with traders and the Vaiśya *varṇa* and that are probably original to the antecedent *Bṛhatkathā* narrative.[15] While Somadeva frames his story with an emphasis on the

[13] On the organization of the books (*lambakas*), see Lacôte 1908: 123–131, esp. 131: "L'étude de la *Mañjarī* nous avait fait présumer qu'elle reproduisait la composition de l'original. Le *Kathāsaritsāgara* nous le confirme en nous fournissant, pour ainsi dire, la contre-épreuve."

[14] See Nelson 1978: 670.

[15] Note that Nelson 1974: 116–117 (cf. 1974: 194) agrees with Lacôte that "the *Bṛhatkathāślokasaṃgraha* of Buddhasvāmin is the most accurate version of the *Bṛhatkathā*"

brāhmaṇa-kṣatriya bond, he further adds to this orthodox model what may be described as tantric or quasi-tantric contexts, and he renders them central to the very progression of the *Kathāsaritsāgara* narrative itself. The quests in the narrative are aided by what is found only in such (quasi-)tantric contexts: the *vetāla* stories, so famously recorded in the *Kathāsaritsāgara*, are presented as the apotheosis of the narrative arc, offering the key that allows the hero of the story to achieve his ends, this because a prince seeks the *vetāla*'s aid and counsel on the advice of his Brahminical minister. What is good for the royals is aided by what is made available in a typically tantric context—the cremation grounds—presented largely stripped of sectarian particularities but nevertheless identifiable with tantra as it might have been received in a wider social context, namely, the noninitiate's imagination. To trace these royal and tantric elements as they appear in parallel in the narrative is precisely the prospectus for the balance of this chapter.[16] With this parallelism is shown a way in which princes and kings could simultaneously secure pleasure, power, and wealth—and even spiritual emancipation—by the aid of the good counsel of a wise Brahminical advisor, versed in what could be found at the margins of proper society, in the haunting charnel grounds.

inasmuch as it is not nearly so "aristocratic" as are the two Kashmiri versions of the text, this in turn because it emphasizes the "popular" elements of the story.

[16] This reforming of the text is fascinating given the structure of the original narrative of the *Bṛhatkathā* as Nelson recovers it. There, a core theme is birth: Madanamañjukā is the daughter of a prostitute and is low caste; Naravāhanadatta is not a *vidyādhara* but interlopes in their numbers on the way to becoming their emperor. Across the text, it is gaining powers, *vidyās*, through gaining wives who give access to them that makes the narrative. It is to overcome an insufficient birth (given by destiny) through heroic acts—and gaining thereby magic—that the narrative is structured. In the *Kathāsaritsāgara* the same theme of overcoming with magic is emphasized, but in this case without the implicitly anti-*varṇa* (as I read them) themes of the core *Bṛhatkathā* narrative (as Nelson recovered it). For his recovery of the narrative structure, see Nelson 1974: 245–323, esp. p. 306: "Therefore, in a culture in which birth and the consequences of birth—*jāti, kula*, etcetera—are the central symbols, the Vidyādhara takes on a special importance. He or she is to a great extent self-made; what powers he possesses are in no way the result of his birth(right) but come only from his actions in *this* life. He may learn *vidyās* from another Vidyādhara, acquire them as the legacy of another, or even 'subdue' them entirely on his own with the appropriate rituals. This is why the *Bṛhatkathā* (and the *Bṛhatkath āślokasaṃgraha*, Maten stresses) is the literature of *puruṣakāra*, human or individual effort, and why the *Bṛhatkathā* is so easily associated with (if not originated from) Jainism and urban culture (with its powerful, old merchant corporate bodies and their wide experience of distant places, risk, and self-reliance). The possibilities for metaphorical expression here are quite broad: at its broadest the successive adventures and marriages not only produce but are symbolic of Naravāhanadatta's change from human (*mānuṣa*) to 'super' human (*divyamānuṣa*). This part of the *Bṛhatkathā* is rich, detailed, multileveled, and concerned with the possibilities of individual human effort: from making money to conquering higher worlds."

The Preamble Story

A Śaiva context, if not an explicitly tantric one, is clearly intimated in the narrative that precedes the *Kathāsaritsāgara*'s concentrically framed mass of stories. The text begins with a preamble story, referred to as the Kathāpīṭha, which explains how the *Bṛhatkathā* came down to humanity in the first place. After the *maṅgala*s and a recitation of a table of contents that names the eighteen books of the tale, the story begins in the abode of Śiva.[17] Pārvatī is there with him, and she wishes to hear a story.[18] Śiva seeks to oblige her request but begins rather feebly, offering only well-known and therefore uninteresting tales, such as those of the *liṅga* of fire and of Dakṣa's sacrifice.[19] Unamused, she asks for something special, and here Śiva must begin in earnest.[20] Nandin is then set to guard the door so that she alone would hear her husband's narrative, and Śiva recounts a splendid tale, which includes the contents of the *Bṛhatkathā*.[21]

While he does so, however, one Puṣpadanta stealthily manages to enter the hall and to catch the stories. Having done so he returns home, elated, and enthusiastically relates them to his wife, Jayā, in order to please her.[22] Herewith emerges a problem: Jayā knows Śiva's wife and having enjoyed the stories so well turns around and relates them right back to her, wishing to please her and ignorant of the stories' origin with Śiva. This enrages Pārvatī, who infers they are nothing special, nothing like the tales presented to her by her husband as unique.[23]

Śiva immediately comes to understand just how Jayā could have heard his novel tales and explains everything to his wife.[24] And so Pārvatī summons

[17] See KSS 1.1.13–17.

[18] This she requests at KSS 1.1.23: *tataḥ provāca girijā prasanno 'si yadi prabho | ramyāṃ kāṃcit kathāṃ brūhi devādya mama nūtanām ||*. "After that, the daughter of the mountain said, 'if you are kindly disposed [toward me], Lord, narrate for me some delightful story today, your majesty, which is new to me.'" Translation a modification of Tawney's.

[19] See KSS 1.1.27–43.

[20] KSS 1.1.44–45.

[21] See KSS 1.1.46: *neha kaiścit praveṣṭavyam ity uktena tayā svayaṃ | niruddhe nandinā dvāre haro vaktuṃ pracakrame ||*. "Upon her declaration that no one at all should be allowed to enter there, Nandin barred the door, after which Hara began to speak." Translation a modification of Tawney's.

[22] See KSS 1.1.52: *śrutvātha gatvā bhāryāyai jayāyai so 'py avarṇayat | ko hi vittaṃ rahasyaṃ vā strīṣu śaknoti gūhitum ||*. "Now, having heard [Śiva's stories] he left and then himself narrated [those stories] to his wife Jayā; for who is able to conceal wealth or a secret from women?" Translation a modification of Tawney's.

[23] See KSS 1.1.53–54.

[24] KSS 1.1.55–56ab: *praṇidhānād atha jñātvā jagādaivam umāpatiḥ | yogī bhūtvā praviśyedaṃ puṣpadantas tadāśṛṇot || jayāyai varṇitaṃ tena ko 'nyo jānāti hi priye |*. "Thereupon Śiva the lord of Umā came to know [what had happened] by meditating on the matter and related as much as

Puṣpadanta to punish him, but his aide Mālyavān tries to intercede, leading Pārvatī to curse both to be reborn on earth and to suffer there until a time when, first of all, Puṣpadanta can tell the tale he overheard in full to one Kāṇabhūti—a *yakṣa* who also is cursed to live a life on earth, as a *piśāca* ghost—and, secondly, Mālyavān can hear it in turn from Kāṇabhūti and then publish it for the sake of others.[25] In hearing and transmitting the story thus, all three are promised release from their earthly forms, meaning the tales are quite literally liberating for their narration.

And so it goes.[26] Puṣpadanta is born as Vararuci, a.k.a. Kātyāyana,[27] what is of course also the name of the famed grammarian whose *vārttika*s annotate Pāṇini's grammatical *sūtra*s. Quickly, he finds Kāṇabhūti trapped in an unexalted existence, as a *piśāca* ghost.[28] When he asks him how he became so aggrieved, Kāṇabhūti replies that he does not know, but that Śiva in Ujjain had told a tale that sheds light on the matter.[29] This indeed it does, as follows.[30]

"Why, O Lord, are you enamored with the skull-bone (*kapāla*) cremation grounds?" Upon being questioned by the Goddess in this way, the

follows: 'Puṣpadanta engaged yogic power and entered this place, at which time he heard [the stories]. It is by him that they were conveyed to Jayā; for who else knows them, my dear?'" Translation a modification of Tawney's.

[25] KSS 1.1.56cd–61.

[26] See KSS 1.1.62–66.

[27] The alternative name is given at KSS 1.2.1.

[28] He spots him at KSS 1.2.5.

[29] See KSS 1.2.7cd–8: *tac chrutvā kṛtasauhārdaṃ kāṇabhūtis tam abravīt* || *svato me nāsti vijñānaṃ kiṃ tu śarvān mayā śrutam* | *ujjayinyāṃ śmaśāne yac chṛṇu tat kathayāmi te* ||. "Having heard that [i.e., what Puṣpadanta as Vararuci/Kātyāyana said to him, namely asking him how he arrived at the awful state of being a Piśāca despite his good nature] Kāṇabhūti replied to him, who had shown his care for him[, as follows]: I have no knowledge myself [in this], but I heard [about it] from Śiva (*śarvāt*) in the cremation ground (*śmaśāna*) in Ujjayinī. Listen to that [which he said], which I shall narrate to you." Translation a modification of Tawney's.

[30] See KSS 1.2.9–20: *kapāleṣu śmaśāneṣu kasmād deva ratis tava* | *iti pṛṣṭas tato devyā bhagavān idam abravīt* || 9 || *purā kalpakṣaye vṛtte jātaṃ jalamayaṃ jagat* | *mayā tato vibhidyoruṃ raktabindur nipātitaḥ* || 10 || *jalāntas tad abhūd aṇḍaṃ tasmād dvedhākṛtāt pumān* | *niragacchat tataḥ sṛṣṭā sargāya prakṛtir mayā* || 11 || *tau ca prajāpaīn anyān sṛṣṭavantau prajāś ca te* | *ataḥ pitāmahaḥ proktaḥ sa pumāñ jagati priye* || 12 || *evaṃ carācaraṃ sṛṣṭvā viśvaṃ darpam agād asau* | *puruṣas tena mūrdhānam athaitasyāham acchidam* || 13 || *tato 'nutāpena mayā mahāvratam agṛhyata* | *ataḥ kapālapāṇitvaṃ śmaśānapriyatā ca me* || 14 || *kiṃ caitan me kapālātma jagad devi kare sthitam* | *pūrvoktāṇḍakapāle dve rodasī kīrtite yataḥ* || 15 || *ity ukte śaṃbhunā tatra śroṣyāmīti sakautike* | *sthite mayi tato bhūyaḥ pārvatī patim abhyadhāt* || 16 || *sa puṣpadantaḥ kiyatā kālenāsmān upaiṣyati* | *tad ākarṇyābravīd devīṃ mām uddiśya maheśvaraḥ* || 17 || *piśāco dṛśyate yo 'yam eṣa vaiśravaṇānugaḥ* | *yakṣo mitram abhūc cāsya rakṣaḥ sthūlaśirā iti* || 18 || *saṃgataṃ tena pāpena nirīkṣyainaṃ dhanādhipaḥ* | *vindhyāṭavyāṃ piśācatvam ādiśad dhanadeśvaraḥ* || 19 || *bhrātrāsya dīrghajaṅghena patitvā pādayos tataḥ* | *śāpāntaṃ prati vijñapto vadati sma dhanādhipaḥ* || 20 ||.

> Lord [Śiva] said the following. "Long ago when the destruction of the cosmic eon was set in motion the world came to be reduced to water. After that, I pierced my thigh, [and] let a drop of blood fall [therefrom], which reached the waters [covering the world]. It[, in turn,] became an egg; by its being broken in two, the Supreme Soul (*puṃs*) came forth; from that I manifested materiality (*prakṛti*) in order to effect the creation of the world. And those two [i.e., Spirit and Materiality] manifested the other lords of creatures, and they [too] had their descendants. Hence, that Spirit is referred to in the world as the Grandfather, my dear. [Then:] Having manifested the universe of animate and inanimate entities in this way, that Man [i.e., the Spirit called Grandfather, i.e., Brahmā himself] became arrogant, because of which I proceeded to cut off his head. Then I undertook a great vow (*mahāvrata*) in repentance [for my sin of Brahminicide], after which I came to hold a skull in my hand and to love the cremation grounds. What is more, O Goddess, the world that is held in my hand is itself a skull inasmuch as the two skull-bone pieces of the egg I mentioned earlier are celebrated as heaven and earth [themselves] (*rodas*)." This being uttered by Śaṃbhu, I set my thoughts to listening [further], staying on there in curiosity, whereupon Pārvatī once more addressed the Lord. "How long until that Puṣpadanta comes back to us?" Hearing this, Maheśvara replied to the Goddess, having first pointed me out to her. "The Piśāca seen here is that very one who was once a *yakṣa* who served Kubera; he had a friend who was a demon (*rakṣa*) named Sthūlaśiras. The lord of Wealth [i.e., Kubera] saw him to be associated with that sinful one; [so] that Lord of Wealth banished him to a state of being a ghost in the Vindhyā forest. But after that his brother Dīrghajaṅgha fell at his two feet; [thus] beseeched, the Lord of Wealth told of the end of the curse." (Translation a modification of Tawney's)

The story goes on to recount precisely the terms of Puṣpadanta's own curse, and on hearing this story narrated to him by Kāṇabhūti, Vararuci/Kātyāyana recalls his past exploits in Śiva's abode. Realizing thus that it is he who was Puṣpadanta in his previous life, he narrates the great tale of the seven *vidyādhara*s to Kāṇabhūti.

Puṣpadanta is thus freed from Pārvatī's curse as promised, though he lingers long enough to relate to Kāṇabhūti his life's story as a human and this at some length. We need not go into the narrative details here except to mention that he meets a Brahmin named Vyāḍi and one who was "exceedingly stupid" (*jaḍabuddhitara*) named Pāṇini,[31] who was bad at his work until he went on a pilgrimage to the Himālaya and obtained a boon from Śiva, which rendered Pāṇini able to produce a grammar that superseded all the others.[32] With this opening narrative, then, we find an invocation of storytelling as a means for both freeing individuals from suffering and entertaining their audiences. It also features prominently the kind of tangle of stories that characterizes the *Kathāsaritsāgara* itself, which enclose stories within stories in often intricate ways.

The opening narrative is particularly complex. Here we have a story told by Śiva to Pārvatī for her pleasure, which is passed by way of one who overheard it (Puṣpadanta) to Pārvatī's friend, who again recounts the same back to her. After this, the one who overheard and filched the story—Puṣpadanta, now in human form—must tell the same story to another who is trapped as a ghost, one Kāṇabhūti. But to remind Puṣpadanta that he must recount the story in question to him, Kāṇabhūti first himself must recount a story of Śiva's, in which Śiva and Pārvatī discuss the very curse she placed on Puṣpadanta. Thus, the story that was told to Pārvatī and retold to her after being overheard is one about which a story is told by the one whose story was stolen, which is told to one to whom the one who stole the story must retell it after hearing of his own act of stealing the story from the very one to whom he will retell the stolen story, that story about his theft having first been told by the one from whom he stole the story. The narrative structure is built into a staggering forest of mirrors, with stories swirling around themselves and in doing so effecting the emancipation of various characters in the stories and delighting their audiences.

So much sets the tone for the entire massive "Ocean of Rivers of Stories,"[33] but the opening does so not merely by evoking the powerful flows of narratives. The tale that opens the *Kathāsaritsāgara* also evokes Śaiva esoteric traditions in its motifs, vocabulary, and contents. The narrative that Kāṇabhūti tells Puṣpadanta as Vararuci/Kātyāyana is first heard in the cremation ground of Ujjain, to begin, a perfect setting for engaging daring, esoteric Śaiva ritual. Next, the sin of cutting off Brahmā's head, while itself a Purāṇic and widely circulated tale, causes Śiva to engage a "great vow"

[31] See KSS 1.4.20cd: *tatraikaḥ pāṇinir nāma jaḍabuddhitaro 'bhavat* ||.

[32] KSS 1.4.21–22.

[33] On the meaning of the title of Somadeva's text, see Lacôte 1908: 63, where he proposes that *Kathāsaritsāgara* means "La (Bṛhat) Kathā, Océan formé par les rivières (des contes)" (The [great] story, an Ocean formed by the rivers [of tales]).

(*mahāvrata*) that has connotations of Śaiva esotericism as well.[34] Finally, reference to Śiva piercing his own thigh (*ūru*) to allow a being to emerge therefrom recounts a mode of narrative common to esoteric tantric works, the story of which involves Śiva entering the cremation grounds with the goddess hidden in his thigh.[35] This opening narrative, then, evokes both Śaivism and the power of the stories themselves in narration and renarration,[36] setting the stage for the massive and winding story that is about to begin and to which we shall turn momentarily.

First, however, to finish the frame story, for the fate of Mālyavān, Puṣpadanta's attendant, remains to be resolved. We are told in the preamble that he is reborn as one Guṇāḍhya,[37] who of course is the author of the *Bṛhatkathā*; and he is said to have served a king, Sātavāhana, until the time when he meets Kāṇabhūti,[38] who, after having Guṇāḍhya tell him a host of tales,[39] narrates for him the story told to him by Puṣpadanta in his human form, reborn as Vararuci, a.k.a. Kātyāyana.[40] Mālyavān-as-Guṇāḍhya records the tale in blood, which comes to seven hundred thousand verses;[41] but after offering it to the king Sātavāhana he is forced to modify it, reducing it by six hundred thousand verses. When his two helpers offered the story to that king on the notion that only he is worthy of such a great narrative, he turned it away for the fact that it was written in an undesirable language

[34] Engagement with and the nature of the *mahāvrata* were the subject of the monograph of Christian Wedemeyer (2013), about which see also the review of the present author (Nemec 2014). See also Goodall 2020.

[35] See, e.g., Nemec 2013: 307–308. Also discussed briefly there is a parallel story found in the *Haracaritacintāmaṇi*.

[36] Indeed, stories are repeatedly said themselves to have power in the *Kathāsaritsāgara*. For example, the *vetāla* stories are said at KSS 12.32.29 to negate the power of various nefarious creatures wherever they are celebrated (this being noted as well in Dezső 2010: 406): *yakṣavetālakūṣmāṇḍa-ḍākinīrākṣasādayaḥ | na tatra prabhaviṣyanti yatraiṣā kīrtayiṣyate ||*. "*Yakṣa*s, *vetāla*s, *kūṣmāṇḍa*s, *ḍākini*s, *rākṣasa*s and others will not be powerful in that place where this [series of *vetāla* stories] comes to be celebrated."

[37] KSS 1.1.63–65: *atha jātu yāti kale gaurī papraccha śaṅkaraṃ sadayā | deva mayā tau śaptau pramathavarau kutra bhuvi jātau || avadac ca candramauliḥ kauśāmbīty asti yā mahānagarī | tasyāṃ sa puṣpadanto vararucināmā priye jātaḥ || anyac ca mālyavān api nagaravare supratiṣṭhitākhye saḥ | jāto guṇāḍhyanāmā devi tayor eṣa vṛttāntaḥ ||*. "Now Gaurī at some point reached the moment in time when, [having become] merciful, she asked Śaṅkara the following: Lord, where on earth were those two choice attendants of yours born, who were cursed by me. And the moon-crested one [= Śiva] said [in reply]: There is a great city called Kauśāmbī; Puṣpadanta, my dear, was born there, having Vararuci as his name; and what is else, Mālyavān for his part was born in a choice city named Supratiṣṭhita under the name Guṇāḍhya. This [following] is their story, O Goddess." Translation a modification of Tawney's.

[38] See KSS 1.6.1–6.

[39] These begin at KSS 1.6.7 and continue up to the end of KSS 1.7, constituting approximately 270 verses in all.

[40] KSS 1.8.1.

[41] KSS 1.8.2–3.

(i.e., *Piṣācabhāṣā*), was delivered by those who themselves appeared to be *piśācas*, and was written in blood.[42]

This led Mālyavān-as-Guṇāḍhya to burn the leaves of the text one by one in the presence of his two disciples; having read aloud that which he burns for the benefit of those around him at that moment; but he spares one portion of the text, the aforementioned fragment of one hundred thousand verses.[43] Finally, Mālyavān/Guṇāḍhya gives the truncated story to that king, who came to that place where he was burning the leaves. Sātavāhana accepts it and with the help of Guṇāḍhya's two disciples comes to understand it in full, and it becomes well known across the world. Having conveyed the story thusly, Mālyavān is liberated.[44]

The Narrative Frames of the *Kathāsaritsāgara*

The narrative that was preserved in this way, we are told, is what is now presented in the balance of Somadeva's text. The tale unfolds, as is well known, by way of a set of nested narratives, and although there are numerous detours in the *Kathāsaritsāgara*—substories and stories within substories of various lengths and patterns of nested intricacy—the basic structure involves an ordering in only three major frames, four if the framing of the *vetāla* stories that are about to be discussed is included. Notably, this nesting is more pronounced than what is found in several of the other *Bṛhatkathā* retellings, suggesting that the flow of substories and the structure of their nesting are vital to Somadeva's narrative.[45] While it has oft been noted, moreover, that the core narrative of the *Bṛhatkathā* involves the quest of the prince Naravāhanadatta to win wives and endure the trials and adventures on the path to becoming a *vidyādhara* (and, as a result, a world-conquering king),[46] it has nowhere to my knowledge been observed that all the three major

[42] See KSS 1.8.14–16.

[43] KSS 1.8.17–20.

[44] All this is narrated at KSS 1.8.21–38.

[45] Nelson 1974: 119 notes on the one hand that the *Bṛhatkathāślokasaṃgraha* and the *Peruṅkatai* contain few substories, very much unlike the *Kathāsaritsāgara*. "The *Vasudevahiṃdi*," on the other hand (Nelson 1974: 200), "presents the most complicated set of frame stories of any of the versions of the *Bṛhatkathā*."

[46] See, e.g., Nelson 1974: 245: "The weight of the evidence seems very much in favor of those premises—that the *Bṛhatkathā* is the story of how Naravāhanadatta, son of Udayana, became emperor of the Viyādharas and husband of twenty-six wives." Cf. Nelson 1974: 217: "Hints like these [i.e., Naravāhanadatta's capacity to fall slowly, lightly like a leaf (*parṇalaghu*)] suggest the *Bṛhatkathā* was concerned with Naravāhanadatta's acquisition of *vidyās* on his path to the station of Vidyādhara."

concentric frames of the *Kathāsaritsāgara* in particular prominently feature the *brahmaṇa-kṣatriya* relationship, deploying it to advance the narratives' plots. Moving through these major concentric frames from the inside out, we may observe the following.

First, the innermost frame encloses the narrative cycle of *vetāla* stories. Here, the narrative suggests that the ghoulish and delightful tales of these undead creatures are told to one Vikramakeśarin, who is himself one of ten ministers who serve a prince named Mṛgāṅkadatta. The minister was by happenstance separated from the prince he is meant to counsel, the remedy for which lies with the stories he is told: a Brahmin advises Vikramakeśarin to get hold of a *vetāla*, for such a creature, he suggests, would be able quickly to help him return safely to the prince he serves. The cycle of twenty-five *vetāla* stories are offered, the *Kathāsaritsāgara* states, to convince him to do just that. Here, then, is a prime example in the *Kathāsaritsāgara* of stories told *as counsel* and this to a Brahmin minister who serves a *kṣatriya* prince.

Outside this framing is the second one. The tale of Mṛgāṅkadatta and his ten ministers is related to Prince Naravāhanadatta, who, resting by a lake, seeks encouragement in the course of his quest for his far-off bride-to-be, Madanamañcukā. Naravāhanadatta is despondent over the difficulty of winning his beloved, and so a sage named Piśaṅgajaṭa tells him the Mṛgāṅkadatta story in which the *vetāla* stories are embedded. (Here again, a Brahmin sage counsels a *kṣatriya* hero.) Mṛgāṅkadatta's ten ministers at one point are turned into fruits on a tree and suffer other difficulties, all of them endured in the quest to help him win his beloved. Piśaṅgajaṭa thus encourages Naravāhanadatta to carry on with his quest: if Mṛgāṅkadatta could face such challenges and nevertheless win his beloved, then so could he. In this frame too, we find both an instance of story deployed as counsel and a narrative of a prince who is accompanied on his journey by a Brahmanical advisor: Naravāhanadatta is aided by his minister Gomukha, who is ever alongside to aid him in his quest.

Third and finally,[47] the Naravāhanadatta story is also framed by story, this time that of Naravāhanadatta's own father, the king Udayana, who with the help of *his* minister, Yaugandharāyaṇa, wins wives on the way to global conquest, with the winning of Vāsavadattā, Naravāhanadatta's mother,

[47] Finally, that is, if we exclude the famed Kathāpīṭha, the introductory story reviewed already, by which the audience hears of the genesis of the story in Śiva's abode. For another review of this opening section of the text and for what distinguishes it from the beginning of the nested narratives proper, the chapter entitled the Kathāmukha, see Lacôte 1908: 68–72.

being of particular note.[48] Interestingly enough, continuity in the lineage of king to prince is matched by a parallel familial lineage in the minister-advisors: Yaugandharāyaṇa is the father of Gomukha, who, as noted, serves as the advisor to Naravāhanadatta, Udayana's son.

Thus, reciting the same again but this time from the widest frame to the narrowest: (1) Udayana's story frames that of (2) his son, Naravāhanadatta, which encapsulates, in turn, the story of (3) Mṛgāṅkadatta, which itself encapsulates (4) the *vetāla* cycle of stories, told as they are to Mṛgāṅkadatta minister. This telescoping of concentric frames thus finds its deepest reach at the level of the cycle of *vetāla* stories, narrated as they are as a story within a story within a story within a story.

The force on the reader of this narrative telescoping is felt most palpably when one reads (or listens) all the way through the text in an unbroken manner. Doing so, the reader or listener is presented with something of an apex in the narrative at the point when one encounters the cycle of *vetāla* stories, specifically when one emerges from this story-cycle back to its encapsulating frame. This is so because one finds a resolution to a major framing narrative with this cycle of stories, signaling clearly a decisive move in the direction of "closing doors" to the concentric frames and thus moving from the depth of the frames of the ocean of stories upward, toward the end of the *Kathāsaritsāgara* itself, which otherwise can leave one feeling as if adrift, flowing in an apparent infinitude from story to digressive story in endless streams and currents.[49] This flow toward an exit is felt precisely inasmuch as the *vetāla* stories facilitate the resolution to the narrative that frames them, that of Mṛgāṅkadatta, which allows a return to the story of Naravāhanadatta and, with it, the promise of a return to the opening frame of the entire ocean of story. There is a causal link, that is, because hearing the *vetāla* stories aids in the resolution of the problem of the Mṛgāṅkadatta story that frames them. It is all an upward movement from there, with one emerging successively

[48] All extant narrations of the *Bṛhatkathā* excepting the *Vasudevahiṃḍi* also contain the stories about Udayana. (See Nelson 1978: 665.) Yet, he also argues (Nelson 1974: 152) that "the *Bṛhatkathā* was not Udayana's story." Nelson 1974: 133–134 further notes that the *Peruṅkatai* offers the most detailed Udayana story of all, which he infers is original to the *Bṛhatkathā*. The Naravāhanadatta story, he elsewhere suggests, is only preserved (Nelson 1974: 25) "in any completeness" by the "sectarian writers—the Kashmiri Śaiva authors and the Jainas."

See Nelson 1974: 58–117 for a detailed account of the narrative in the *Bṛhatkathāślokasaṃgraha*, which emphasizes the motifs of Naravāhanadatta's marriages and the conquest of the Vidyādhara kingdom.

[49] Consonant with this interpretation is Lacôte's observation (1908: 104) that Naravāhanadatta's quest for Madanamañcukā is central to the *Kathāsaritsāgara tout court*.

from the deepest fathom of the ocean of nested stories to rise quickly to the upper frames from there: the Mṛgāṅkadatta frame closes immediately following the closing of the *vetāla* frame, once the *vetāla* stories convince Mṛgāṅkadatta's minister, Vikramakeśarin, that he needs a *vetāla*'s help to accomplish his ends (which of course also serve his prince).[50]

So much leaves the reader with the clear understanding that appeal to creatures of the charnel ground has a salutary effect, because just this message is both literally stated and affectively conveyed by the force of the narrative flow itself. If the *vetāla* stories are the fulcrum that turns the entire narrative arc of the text, as I here wish to argue, it is similarly of no coincidence that they are explicitly presented as proof of the indispensability of *vetālas* to a minister's and a king's ambitions. It is also no coincidence that such creatures are understood to be of use in other Sanskrit works of *belles lettres* and, more significantly, in the Śaiva esoteric literatures themselves, as Csaba Dezső has shown.[51] One needs such creatures and their dark world, which stands at the edge of polite company, as one cannot doubt that it would have been well-known in nontantric circles in the time of the composition of the *Kathāsaritsāgara* that the world of the cremation ground was familiar to, and often thoroughly mastered by, tantric adepts. At hand is more than merely a matter of stories, moreover.[52] As Dezső further notes, there is some evidence that "perhaps the most famous historical figure who bore the name Vikramāditya also seems to have been involved in a *vetālasādhana* at an early stage in his career (end of the 4th century CE)."[53] Art perhaps imitates reality

[50] See KSS 12.33.2–5: *tataḥ kathāvasāne sa mārgamadhyāt samutthitaḥ | mṛgāṅkadatto muditaḥ prāptavikramakesarī || guṇākareṇa sahitas tathā vimalabuddhinā | savicitrakatho bhīmaparākramasamanvitaḥ || pracaṇḍaśaktiyuktaś ca śrutadhidvijasaṃgataḥ | prāptaśeṣān vicinvānaḥ śāpaviśleṣitān sakhīn || śaśāṅkavatyāḥ saṃprāptyai prāg evojjayinīṃ prati | gantuṃ pravṛttaḥ punar apy uccacālātmanāṣṭamaḥ ||.*

[51] See Dezső 2010. He there identifies three types of *vetālasādhana*, attested in particular in the early tantric Śaiva scriptures of the Niśvāsa corpus, and charts the prevalence of such creatures in the story literatures as well. The commonalities in the representations of these creatures in the two bodies of literature is plainly evident. Dezső further notes (2010: 404–405) that the *bhairavācārya* of Bāṇa's *Harṣacarita* engages in a *vetālasādhana*, which ends with the *sādhaka* flying in the sky as a *vidyādhara*, having been assisted by the king Puṣyabhūti in the ritual. His essay concludes with an effort to reconstruct a chronology of types of *vetālas*, which, however (p. 417), "is of course not rigid: various kinds of *vetālas* may well have existed at the same time." Earliest in the order are *vetālas* of the type that are reanimated dead bodies, followed by a type that is a spirit of sorts that inhabits a corpse, "a being with [its] own willpower, whose favour could be won by the performance of dangerous rituals, or by otherwise demonstrating one's courage and other merits." Finally, there are *vetālas* existing independently of any corpse, which "had their own characteristic features." It was even possible for Bhairava, "Śiva's manifestation as a skull-bearing ascetic associated with the cremation ground," to "appear as a *vetāla*."

[52] For a useful summary of the place for *vetālas* in tantrism, see Huang 2009.

[53] Dezső 2010: 402.

in this case, not only with the echo of Vikramāditya's name in both that of the protagonist of the *Kathāsaritsāgara*'s *vetāla* stories, Trivikramasena, and that of the minister for which the stories are told, Vikramakeśarin, but also because the historical Vikramāditya's acts were explicitly memorialized in Viśākhadatta's play, *Devīcandragupta*, "Candragupta and the Queen," inasmuch as Vikramāditya was crowned as Candragupta II.[54]

The *Kathāsaritsāgara* thus prominently locates a narrative concerning what is often associated with tantric religion, namely, the practice of harnessing powers found only in the cremation grounds. But it is not just the narrative placement that distinguishes the cycle of *vetāla* stories in the text, for they in their very contents marry the charnel grounds to the royal court and emphasize the vital relationship of Brahmins and kings. It is to the details of these stories that we therefore must now turn our attention.

Stories upon Stories

There once was a fearless king named Trivikramasena,[55] who came to be visited daily at the royal court by a Brahmin mendicant name Kṣāntiśīla. On each occasion, he would offer the king a piece of fruit as a gift, which the king always kept but regarded with the triviality fitting an item of such modest value,[56] a course of events that transpires for ten years.[57] Soon, though, he comes to see the fruit, and the Brahmin, in a new light, for one day he offered the day's gift to a monkey who happened to escape captivity and come into the audience hall, and while eating it the monkey exposed a lustrous jewel that had been encased therein.[58] The king thus comes to know that hidden in each and every piece of fruit offered to him was a precious jewel,[59] the wonder and tremendous value of which inspire Trivikramasena to render himself of service to the unknown visitor.[60]

[54] Dezső 2010: 402. Dezső further notes that it is in Raghavan 1978: 843*ff.* that the plot of this lost play is reconstructed (see in particular Raghavan 1978: 843–865 and esp. 849–852). He also cites Bakker 2006, which interrogates the contents of the play to determine the nature of the political relations between the Gupta and the Vākāṭaka dynasties.

[55] This is the opening frame of the cycle of *vetāla* stories, the narration of which begins at KSS 12.8.21d.

[56] KSS 12.8.23–24.

[57] KSS 12.8.25.

[58] KSS 12.8.26–27.

[59] KSS 12.8.28–32.

[60] KSS 12.8.33–35.

The Brahmin asks of him a surprising favor: he tasks him with fetching from the cremation ground a corpse that is inhabited by a *vetāla*, which he wishes delivered to him so he can gain control over that undead creature and perform a desired ritual.[61] Like the fruit the Brahmin offered the king, the impure detritus that is a human corpse holds something of value much greater than its vessel would suggest, and this Brahmin sage asks for the king's help in securing the same.

Trivikramasena, fearless as he is, assents to the request. But the task is not so simple because the *vetāla* does not wish to be handled so easily. In attempting to fulfill his mandate, the king thus finds himself repeatedly tested by the *vetāla*, who scouts the limits of both his intellect and his courage and persistence. Each time Trivikramasena lifts up that corpse to his shoulder to carry it to the Brahmin, the *vetāla* challenges him with a story that is in fact a riddle, which the king must answer at the penalty of his head exploding should he withhold any insight. Each time he does answer and correctly so, and each time until the last time the *vetāla* teleports himself back to the cremation ground, requiring Trivikramasena to begin the endeavor anew. Thus the cycle of twenty-five *vetāla* stories, and with this narrative device are married tantric knowledge of a sort—the use of a corpse in a powerful ritual[62]—with the notion that stories hold knowledge, as well as with what is more exoteric and mundane, namely, the discerning habits of the royal sovereign, who must be brave but above all wise in judging individuals and circumstances that persistently if unpredictably can threaten his well-being and that of his subjects.

The *vetāla* stories themselves not only are delightful but also prove to be interpretable in ways that are significant for understanding the culture of the royal court and the relationship of Brahmins and kings. Consider, to begin, the twelfth occasion when the king goes to fetch the *vetāla*. Thrown onto his shoulder as he is each round, the *vetāla* begins to distract and, he hopes, redirect the impetus of the king by relating the following tale, introducing it by way of praising the king for his persistence in chasing the *vetāla* down.[63] It goes like this.

[61] KSS 12.8.36–48. Included is a colorful description of the cremation ground and the banyan tree under which the king is instructed to meet the mendicant.

[62] As is well known, the carrying of a corpse is common in tantric rituals involving *vetālas*, for which see Dezső 2010.

[63] See KSS 12.19.1–3: *sa trivikramaseno 'tha punas taṃ śiṃśapātarum | gatvā prāpya ca vetālaṃ rājā skandhe cakāra tam || pratasthe ca tam ādāya tūṣṇīm eva sa pūrvavat | tato bhūyas tam āha sma vetālaḥ so 'ṃsapṛṣṭhataḥ || rājann evamanudvignaḥ paryāptam asi me priyaḥ | tad etāṃ śṛṇv akhedāya hṛdyām ākhyāmi te kathām ||*. "Then that king, Trivikramasena, again went to that

There once was a young king named Yaśaḥketu who valiantly conquered all of his enemies. Subsequently, he entrusted the kingdom to his minister, this "out of an infatuation with his own youth and beauty" (*vayorūpamada*), and "became devoted to pleasure only" (*sukhaikasakta*).[64] Indeed, "he remained continually in the harem instead of the judgment hall; he listened to delightful songs in the women's apartments, instead of hearkening to the voice of his well-wishers; in his thoughtlessness, he was devoted to latticed windows and not to the affairs of the kingdom, though the latter were full of holes."[65]

Yaśaḥketu's minister, one Dīrghadarśin, did what he could and kept the order of the kingdom, performing all the duties necessary for the same and not only for quite some time but also unimpeachably so—until, that is, a rumor began to spread, to the effect that he had usurped the king's power to pursue his own ends. Trapped between a desire to maintain order in the kingdom and the need to keep his good name and avoid scandal, Dīrghadarśin turned to his wife for advice: what, he asked, could he do to counter the malevolent rumors?[66] (Note the more positive model of gender, here, with the minister's wife serving fruitfully to counsel her husband, whose life is devoted to proffering and executing wise political counsel.)

The answer she furnished and the solution it offered were elegantly simple: he must elect to go on pilgrimage, to visit holy sites situated far from the kingdom, only to return after sufficient time had passed for the rumors to die out. How could he be said to wish to usurp the throne once it is known that he voluntarily left the kingdom to pursue a wholesome religious agenda, safely away from the levers of power?[67] And so, he departs.

Along the way, he endures a great adventure, one that brought him onto the ocean in a trading expedition. With this is conveyed that recurring

Śiṃśapā tree, took hold of the *vetāla* and put him on his shoulder. And with him [thus] taken he set out silently, as before. After that, the *vetāla* again said the following to him from his place on his shoulder. 'O king, you are dear to me for being so steadfast. So listen to this delightful story which I will tell you to ease your suffering.'" Translation a modification of Tawney's.

[64] KSS 12.19.6: *tasmin mantriṇi vinyasya rājyaṃ sa hatakaṇṭakam | śanaiḥ sukhaikasakto 'bhūd vayorūpamadān nṛpaḥ ||*.

[65] KSS 12.19.7–8: *tasthāv antaḥpure śaśvan nāsthāne pramadāspade | śuśrāva raktimadgītaṃ vacanaṃ na hitaiṣiṇām || rajyati sma ca niścinto jālavātāyaneṣu saḥ | na punā rājakāryeṣu bahucchidreṣu jātv api ||*. Translation Tawney's.

[66] KSS 12.19.12–14ab.

[67] KSS 12.19.14cd–17.

element of the *Kathāsaritsāgara*, the "merchant's" quality of the stories, as van Buitenen described it, the trader's quest for riches and status in society.[68] In the ocean, Dīrghadarśin witnesses a wave rise up, and out of it a wishing tree emerges, adorned with gold. Sitting in it is a beautiful and well-adorned maiden, who with a lyre in hand sings an entrancing hymn and then disappears into the water. Needless to say, Dīrghadarśin, the minister, was delighted and astonished.[69]

Returning to his home after some time, he tells the story of his adventures to the king, who promptly falls irredeemably in love with the maiden of the sea, only from hearing her described.[70] His reputation having been rehabilitated, Dīrghadarśin again safely associates with the king, and he brings him to the place where the maiden was seen. As luck has it, they catch sight of her, and again she sinks into the sea after singing her song. The king bravely but brashly refuses to countenance her disappearance and leaps into the ocean in a reckless attempt to reach her. We are told, in fact, that the king's past *karmans* brought him to seek this maiden, to whom he was married in a past life, so the attraction is in fact fated to be.[71]

Once in the water, King Yaśaḥketu discovers a beautiful city,[72] finds the maiden there, and enjoys his time with her. He kills a demon that tormented her and, after convincing her to stay with him in the city's gardens for seven days to amuse themselves, tricks her out of returning to her father and her celestial kingdom—we discover she is divine, no mere human—this by bringing her home to his kingdom, a kidnapping of sorts for which Yaśaḥketu shows no evident regret.[73] Upon witnessing the king's return, that faithful minister Dīrghadarśin, who had returned home to the kingdom of Aṅga again to protect the land and his patron's subjects, immediately dies of heartbreak.

Now the riddle imposed by this story. "Why," the *vetāla* asks King Trivikramasena, "did Dīrghadarśin's heart break?" Is it that he wished he had

[68] Various cities found on known trade routes are frequently mentioned in the tale, and merchants marry kings and have status in the courts in the *Kathāsaritsāgara*. Here, the minister goes to sea on a trading expedition or, more specifically, travels with traders on a great adventure. And the name Naravāhanadatta, van Buitenen suggests, refers to one "given by the god of riches [=Kubera]." See van Buitenen 1959: 3. Cf. Penzer 1968 (vol. 9): 119, where he indicates that it is Kuvera who is the presiding deity of the *Bṛhatkathāślokasaṃgraha*.

[69] The voyage at sea begins at KSS 12.19.37; he sees the tree at KSS 12.19.41.

[70] The king, missing his minister, leaves the city limits to greet him at KSS 12.19.57; he is said to fall in love with the maiden at 12.19.64ab: *sa tāṃ śrutvaiva ca nṛpas tathā smaravaśo 'bhavat* |.

[71] KSS 12.19.79–80.

[72] KSS 12.19.90cd.

[73] He takes her through a tank that is a magical portal to his home kingdom at KSS 12.19.150–151.

won the nymph for himself? Or is it rather that, because he longed for power, he was disappointed to see the king's return?[74]

The answer in fact is neither of the two reasons. Trivikramasena replied, the *Kathāsaritsāgara* tells us, that the minister's thinking must have been as follows: "'This king neglected his kingdom out of devotion to mere human females, much more will he do so now that he is attached to a heavenly nymph. So, though I have gone through much suffering, the disease has been aggravated by it instead of being cured, as I had hoped.' It is under the influence of such reflections," Trivikramasena replies to the Vetāla, "that the minister's heart broke."[75]

Kings can only be led so far by wise counsel and aid, for no counsel can be kept if the one counseled has failed to cultivate the very virtue ethic meant to be guaranteed by the *brāhmaṇa-kṣatriya* bond. This is true, moreover, both of the kings of fiction—in the *kathā*s—and in historical narrative, if one considers, that is, the presence of a parallel story to be found in the *Rājataraṅgiṇī*. There we hear of one Ananta, the king, and his advisor Haladhara, the son of Bhūti, a Vaiśya watchman at the temple of Gaurīśa (*Rājataraṅgiṇī* [RT] 7.207). Haladhara, we are told, rises to the level of prime minister (*sarvādhikāritā*; see RT 7.208) and is credited with skill such that he made "smaller chiefs" submit to the king (RT 7.209), efficiently ran the Pādāgra office (according to Stein this is a high office connected to the finance ministry[76]), reconfigured the tax system (RT 7.211–212), executed some dishonest horse trainers who were bilking their customers (RT 7.213), and helped Ananta conquer his enemies, both the *ḍāmara*s (RT 7.217) and rival kings (RT 7.218*ff.*), saving him from danger along the way (RT 7.220).

Yet, for all his successes, and like the minister of the twelfth *vetāla* story, Haladhara became the object of slander "on account of his continual attendance upon the queen" (RT 7.225). He consequently was thrown into prison and deprived of his property by the king (RT 7.226). Eventually set free from his confinement, Haladhara and the king made amends (RT 7.227–8), but Ananta fell "in the course of time . . . under his wife's domination, which was the harbinger of evil issues" (RT 7.229, translation Stein's). In particular, and despite Haladhara's efforts to dissuade him, the queen convinced the king

[74] KSS 12.19.164–166.

[75] See KSS 12.19.168cd-170: *naitat tasmin dvayam api śubhacarite yujyate hi mantrivare* || *kiṃtu strīmātrarasād upekṣitaṃ yena bhūbhujā rājyam* | *tasyādhunā tu divyastrīraktasyātra kā vārtā* || *tan me kaṣṭe 'pi kṛte pratyuta doṣo batādhikībhūtaḥ* | *iti tasya vibhāvayato hṛdayaṃ tanmantriṇaḥ sphuṭitam* ||. The translation of elements of this passage is that of Tawney.

[76] See Stein [1900] 1989 (vol. 1): 286, note on RT 7.210.

to abdicate to his son Kalaśa, who on the sixth day of the bright fortnight of Kārttikeya in the year 4039 (AD 1063) became king, and a truly horrific one at that. A stronger alliance of the king with his minister (not a Brahmin, it must be noted, but a Vaiśya playing the ministerial role of one) could have forestalled such misdirection, the implication is clear. It should also be noted, if as an aside, that Ananta is the king whose wife, Sūryamatī, is told the tales of the *Kathāsaritsāgara* to cheer her in a time of difficulty, though one cannot be entirely sure that the similarity of motifs here with the *Rājataraṅgiṇī*—the loyal minister wrongly shunned by the king he serves; troubles in the kingdom resulting therefrom—involves art imitating reality, assuming, that is, that the *Rājataraṅgiṇī* here faithfully records historical events.

Sometimes we are told of ministers' success in forestalling the king's excesses. Take the story of Yaśodhana, for example, told to Trivikramasena by the powerful *vetāla* in the seventeenth episode of the cycle. He was virtuous, learned, capable of managing military affairs—a good king with a safe and prosperous kingdom.[77] One day, a merchant approached him and described the beauty of his daughter, offering her to him in marriage.[78] Hearing the offer and clearly tempted by her beauty, Yaśodhana sent his Brahmins to verify that she matched her father's description.[79] On seeing for themselves her incredible beauty, however, the ministers quickly divined that should she be won the kingdom would be wrecked, this for the danger of a reckless wont of sensual pleasure to the neglect of royal duties. The ministers therefore choose to lie to the king and report that she in no way resembled the qualities attributed to her.[80]

One day by chance, however, the king ventures near her place, and the maiden, Unmādinī, who was wedded to the head of the army in lieu of the king's flagging interest, appears on the roof of their palatial home, intentionally so to taunt her would-be suitor.[81] Yaśodhana of course falls immediately and desperately in love with her on seeing Unmādinī for himself. Coming to know this turn of events, the head of the army suggests that she should again be sent to the king—that, he suggests, or he will give her over to the temple

[77] See KSS 12.24.4–7.

[78] See KSS 12.24.8–12.

[79] See KSS 12.24.13: *ity ākarṇya vaṇigvākyaṃ sa rājā brāhmaṇān nijān* | *sādaraṃ vyasṛjat tasyāḥ saulakṣaṇyam avekṣitum* ||. "Having heard this discussion of the merchant, the king dispatched his own Brahmins with due politeness to see [about] her good qualities." Translation a slight modification of Tawney's.

[80] KSS 12.24.14–15.

[81] She shows herself to him at KSS 12.24.24.

to be a dancing girl.[82] Such was his loyalty that he could not keep to himself the one for whom his patron professed such burning love (though the gendered quality of the story is betrayed by the fact that her feelings and wishes regarding her own fate are nowhere addressed). And yet, somehow the king's virtue prevails, and he refuses to take the wife of his general, but at a cost: he dies of heartache. The master of the army, in turn, commits suicide in grief for his passing.[83]

Here is the *vetāla*'s riddle: who was superior in virtue (*kaḥ . . . sattvenābhyadhikaḥ*, KSS 12.24.47), the army chief or the king? Answer: the king, presumably (though we are not told why) because he avoided certain debilitating distraction in preference for honoring his royal obligations, and, presumably, because he chose not to use his social standing to trump that of his army chief.[84] But, the *vetāla* retorts, didn't the minister go far beyond any typical call to duty by surrendering Unmādinī, his wife, so freely to the king? Didn't his suicide in sorrow for the king's passing further illustrate his remarkable virtue?[85]

Trivikramasena replies by noting that it is the job of ministers to be loyal, whereas kings are regularly infatuated with their own self-importance:[86]

> When the *vetāla* said this to the king, the latter laughed, and said, "Admitting the truth of this, what is there astonishing in the fact, that the commander-in-chief, a man of good family, acted thus for his master's sake, out of regard for him? For servants are bound to preserve their masters even by the sacrifice of their lives. But kings are inflated with arrogance, uncontrollable as elephants, and when bent on enjoyment, they

[82] KSS 12.24.35–37.

[83] KSS 12.24.44–45: *tataḥ krameṇa tenaiva smarajvarabharoṣmaṇā | prakṣīṇadehaḥ prayayau sa yaśaḥśeṣatāṃ nṛpaḥ || senāpatiś cāsahiṣṇus taṃ tathā pramayaṃ prabhoḥ | so 'gniṃ viveśa bhaktānām anirvācyaṃ hi ceṣṭitam ||*.

[84] KSS 12.24.46.

[85] See KSS 12.24.49–51.

[86] See KSS 12.24.52–60. *vetālenaivam uktas tu vihasya sa nṛpo 'bravīt | yady apy evaṃ tathāpy etat kiṃ citraṃ kulaputrakaḥ || 52 || senāpatiḥ sa bhaktyā yat svāmyarthe tat tathākarot | prāṇair api hi bhṛtyānāṃ svāmisaṃrakṣaṇaṃ vratam || 53 || rājānas tu madādhmātā gajā iva niraṅkuśāḥ | chindanti dharmamaryādāśṛṅkhalāṃ viṣayonmukhāḥ || 54 || teṣāṃ hy udriktacittānām abhiṣekāmbubhiḥ samam | viveko vigalaty oghenohyamāna ivākhilaḥ || 55 || kṣipyanta iva coddhūya calaccāmaramārutaiḥ | vṛddhopadiṣṭaśāstrārtharajomaśakamakṣikāḥ || 56 || ātapatreṇa satyaṃ ca sūryāloko nivāryate | vibhūtivātyopahatā dṛṣṭir mārgaṃ ca nekṣate || 57 || te te ca vipadaṃ prāptā māramohitacetasaḥ | jagadvijayino 'pīha rājāno nahuṣādayaḥ || 58 || eṣo rājā punaḥ pṛthvyām ekacchatro 'pi yat tayā | unmādinyā capalayā lakṣmyeva na vimohitaḥ || 59 || prāṇān api sa dharmātmā tatyāja na punaḥ padam | amārge nidadhe dhīras tenāsau me 'dhiko mataḥ || 60 ||*. The translation is Tawney's.

> snap asunder the chain of moral law. For their minds are overweening, and all discernment is washed out of them, and is, as it were, swept away by the flood. And the breeze of the waving chowries fans away the atoms of the sense of scripture taught them by old men, as it fans away flies and mosquitoes. And the royal umbrella keeps off from them the rays of truth, as well as the rays of the sun; and their eyes, smitten by the gale of prosperity, do not see the right path. And so even kings, that have conquered the world, like Nahuṣa and others, have had their minds bewildered by Māra, and have been brought into calamity. But this king, though his umbrella was paramount in the earth, was not fascinated by Unmādinī, fickle as the goddess of Fortune; indeed, sooner than set his foot on the wrong path, he renounced life altogether; therefore him I consider the more self-controlled of the two."

Thus, we are told, with language that plays on the very symbols of royal power (the chowries, the umbrella), that a king is ever the more heroic for refusing what can so easily be attained by them, it being so rare that they would do so, fed as they are in their position of power by ego and opportunity to be deprived of no wished-for pleasures at all.[87]

It is worth noting that a version of the same story is again related in the *Rājataraṅgiṇī* as true-to-life history, as Winternitz noticed some time ago.[88] There, we are told of the passion of one Durlabhakaratāpāditya II, who spotted the wife of a merchant, one Narendraprabhā (RT 4.16*ff.*), and on doing so falls irredeemably in love, lamenting the "poison-tree" called passion (RT 4.26). Yet, here there is a different resolution: the merchant suggests to the king that he is above the law, essentially, and offers his wife to him. And she goes to him, sponsors the construction of temples, and bears him a son. Historical narrative, the plainly realist narration of how events (supposedly) transpired in real life, excludes what is found in the decidedly fictional *kathā*: it is in fiction and not Kashmir's historical chronicle that a king's admirable, if heartbreaking, restraint is to be narrated. Kings in the "real world" fail in the virtue ethic, despite their ministers' efforts.

[87] One might also interpose on the narrative the following, alternative question: who is in fact to blame for the king's heartache? Can one not call into question the actions of the ministers? This is, however, something that never transpires in this Sanskrit, and "Brahminicized," text: the Brahminical ministers are never shown to err in any fundamental way in the *Kathāsaritsāgara*.

[88] See Winternitz [1963] 1986 (vol. 3, part 1): 361, fn. 5. Winternitz cites Vetāla 16, however, whereas the story is found in Vetāla 17 of the Tawney translation.

Stories upon Stories, Again: The King's Good Judgment

If the relationship between the king and his minister is central to the *vetāla* stories, so too is the king's good judgment, for this is precisely what is at stake not only in answering their riddles but also in particular in the first of the *vetāla* stories, with which begins the entire cycle of twenty-five. There we are told of the existence of a king of Vārāṇasī, Pratāpamukuṭa by name.[89] His son, Prince Vajramukuṭa, was in the habit of frolicking in the kingdom with his friend Buddhiśarīra, the son of one of his father's ministers. The two one day happened to set eyes on a beautiful maiden, though only at a distance, and it is love at first sight. Noticing them, she gestured as follows: taking a lotus from her garland she placed it on her ear; twisting for some time a *danta-patra,* literally a "tooth-leaf," in her hand, she placed another lotus on her head; and finally, she placed her hand upon her heart.[90]

The prince, Vajramukuṭa, was despondent from the moment she departed from sight. Luckily, the minister's son, Buddhiśarīra, understood the signs. He explained that the placing of the lotus on her ear signaled she lives in the kingdom of Karṇotpala (Lotus of the Ear); twisting the tooth-leaf signaled she was the daughter of a dentist; lifting the other lotus signaled her name: Padmāvatī. Finally, by placing her hand on her heart, she signaled that she was his.[91]

And so the *kṣatriya* prince and his Brahminical advisor travel to Karṇotpala's kingdom, whose favorite courtier is a dentist named Saṃgrāmavardhana, whose daughter of course is named Padmāvatī. They recruit an elderly woman to visit Padmāvatī as a go-between, who calls on the maiden and conveys to her the good words of the prince who sent her, to which Padmāvatī bluntly replies with a scold, slapping the elderly lady on both cheeks with her two hands, which were smeared with camphor. Again the prince despairs. But his friend the minister's son replies by suggesting that what has transpired offers another sign to be interpreted: Padmāvatī has signaled that they must wait for the remaining ten nights of the moonlit, white fortnight to pass, because they can offer only unfavorable occasions for meeting.[92]

[89] KSS 12.8.59–61.
[90] KSS 12.8.73–74ab.
[91] KSS 12.8.80–86.
[92] This occurs around KSS 12.8.103–106.

Ten days later they again send the elderly lady to Padmāvatī, who is greeted by being struck on the breast with three fingers dipped in red dye (KSS 12.8.110–111). Again it is a sign, of course, and again it is the minister who is able to interpret its meaning. By marking the elderly woman's heart with red dye, Padmāvatī signaled her wish to see the prince, but the strike and the triple mark also indicated that she could not be available before three additional nights had passed (KSS 12.8.113).

They wait the three nights and again sent the old woman to the maiden; after visiting with Padmāvatī for some time, pleasantly on this occasion, she expressed her wish to return home. At just that moment, though, a calamity arises: a wild elephant is loose in the palace, threatening to trample its inhabitants. To allow the elderly lady to escape unharmed, Padmāvatī offers her a seat on a saddle that is attached to a rope, by which she lowers the prince's go-between down from outside the palace walls. This too offers a sign that is entirely clear to Vajramukuṭa's minister, who knows it to illustrate the very method for bringing Vajramukuṭa to Padmāvatī undetected. Finally, the two may find occasion for their amorous *rendez-vous*.

After their encounter, the prince eventually comes to wish to leave her company, but before he sets out she asks him who of the two of them interpreted her signals: was it he himself or his companion the minister's son (KSS 12.8.134–135ab)? When Vajramukuṭa answers honestly, she suggests that she must do something to honor the prince's friend, because he had made their relations possible. Buddhiśarīra, however, greets this news with tremendous caution. And so new events transpire. Padmāvatī's confidante soon comes to visit Vajramukuṭa and Buddhiśarīra with a gift, a specially prepared meal, and she simultaneously asks for Prince Vajramukuṭa again to visit Padmāvatī. This is so, it emerges, because his hastened visit would ensure he had no occasion to eat any of the food (KSS 12.8.143–144), which it turns out is poisoned, which in turn is divined by the clever minister and proven when he feeds the meal to a dog, who dies on the spot after eating. Why such a malicious act? Again, Buddhiśarīra interprets: she knows he is wise, and she wants to rid herself of him so she alone would control the destiny of her relationship with Vajramukuṭa—and, perhaps, with his wise minister out of the way, the kingdom whose throne he was to inherit.[93]

Buddhiśarīra and Vajramukuṭa therefore hatch a plan, devised of course by the former: they will get her drunk and then brand her on the hip with a

[93] See KSS 12.8.135cd–151.

hot iron spike while she is unconscious! After that, they will steal her jewelry and depart (KSS 12.8.153–156). This will allow them to enact a ruse that will work to their favor.

The prince obediently obliges in the scheme and manages to do just as instructed. On doing so he rejoins his companion, the minister's son, who takes on the guise of an ascetic and places the prince in disguise as his disciple, and they enter the cremation ground. From there he instructs his disciple (who of course is none other than the disguised Vajramukuṭa) to go to market with a pearl necklace that had been stolen from Padmāvatī, in an effort to sell it at a highly inflated price. Doing so, of course, draws the attention of many, including the authorities (KSS 12.8.162–167).

The powers that be inquire of the disciple as to where he managed to acquire such a lovely necklace. He, in turn, responds as he was instructed to do, saying that his spiritual preceptor gave it to him to make the sale (KSS 12.8.169–170). And so the authorities visit the cremation ground, seeking to confront that renunciant preceptor—Buddhiśarīra, Vajramukuṭa's advisor in disguise. Questioned by the authorities, he explains the matter as follows:[94]

> I am an ascetic, in the habit of wandering perpetually backwards and forwards in the forests. As chance would have it, I arrived here, and as I was in the cemetery at night, I saw a band of witches (*yoginīcakra*) collected from different quarters. And one of them brought the prince, with the lotus of his heart laid bare, and offered him to Bhairava. And the witch, who possessed great powers of delusion, being drunk, tried to take away my rosary, while I was reciting my prayers, making horrible contortions with her face. And as she carried the attempt too far, I got angry, and heating with a charm the prongs of my trident, I marked her on the loins. And then I took this necklace from her neck. And now I must sell this necklace, as it does not suit an ascetic.

The magistrate who heard this story informed the king. The king confirmed that the pearl necklace was that of Padmāvatī, and so he had then

[94] See KSS 12.8.172cd–177. *ahaṃ tapasvī bhrāmyāmi sadāraṇyeṣv itas tataḥ || so 'haṃ daivād iha prāptaḥ śmaśāne 'tra sthito niśi | apaśyaṃ yoginīcakraṃ samāgatam itas tataḥ || tanmadhye caikayānīya yoginyā rājaputrakaḥ | udghāṭitahṛdambhojo bhairavāya niveditaḥ || pānamattā ca sā hartuṃ japato me 'kṣamālikām | prāvartata mahāmāyā vikārān kurvatī mukhe || atipravṛttā ca mayā kruddhena jaghanasthale | aṅkitā sā triśūlena mantraprajvālitāśriṇā || hṛtā muktāvalī ceyaṃ tasyāḥ kaṇṭhān mayā tadā | saiṣādya tāpasānarhā vikreyā mama vartate ||*. Translation Tawney's.

only to verify that she could be the "witch" who had had the altercation in the cremation ground. He set an elderly woman to check for the branded mark, and surely enough Padmāvatī was found to bear a brand that matched the ascetic's description.

The king, credulous, decided it was she who was wicked, that she was not really the daughter—or merely the daughter—of his courtier the dentist. He went to the minister's son and asked how he should punish Padmāvatī, who responded by advising the king that she should be banished from his kingdom. The king complies and sends her into the wilderness. But she's no fool and figured it was all an artifice, and simply awaited her beloved (though she would have to join him not on the terms she had envisioned, for she did not manage to rid herself of his clever minister). Vajramukuṭa and Buddhiśarīra then took her to their kingdom to live happily ever after; but Padmāvatī's father the dentist, assuming her banishment had led her to be killed by wild beasts in the forest, died of grief and was followed by his wife—her mother—to the same fate.[95]

The *vetāla*, having narrated this, the first story of the *vetāla* cycle, then asks Trivikramasena who is to blame for the death of Padmāvatī's parents. Is it the minister's son, Buddhiśarīra; the prince, Vajramukuṭa, who fell in love with her; or Padmāvatī herself?[96] The answer given is none of the three, for the guilt, Trivikramasena suggests, rather lies with the duped king, Karṇotpala.

The answer is correct, but the *vetāla* asks for further explanation as to why this is so. Trivikramasena's answer is this, that the minister's son served his master and therefore is blameless, and Padmāvatī and Vajramukuṭa were in love and blinded by it and excused for this reason. The king, on the other hand, can be afforded no allowance for his failure to meet the obligations of his office:[97]

[95] KSS 12.8.185: *dantaghāṭas tv araṇye tāṃ kravyādair bhakṣitāṃ sutām* | *matvā vyapādi śokena bhāryā cānujagāma tam* ||.

[96] See KSS 12.8.187: *mantriputrasya kiṃ pāpaṃ rājaputrasya kiṃ nu vā* | *padmāvatyāḥ kim athavā tvaṃ hi buddhimatāṃ varaḥ* ||. "Is the minister's son sinful, or is it the son of the king? Or, alternatively, does it [the sin] belong to Padmāvatī? [Tell me, for:] You are the best of the wise."

[97] See KSS 12.8.194–195: *karṇotpalas tu rājā sa nītiśāstreṣv aśikṣitaḥ* | *caraiḥ prajāsv ananviṣyaṃs tattvaśuddhiṃ nijāsv api* || *ajānan dhūrtacaritānīṅgitādyavicakṣaṇaḥ* | *tathā tan nirvicāraṃ yac cakre tena sa pāpabhāk* ||. Translation a modification of Tawney's.

It is worth further noting that the narrative here recounted is also found, *mutatis mutandis*, elsewhere in Sanskrit literature, for example, in Daṇḍin's *Daśakumāracarita*. See Onians 2005: 440–449. Cf. Hatley 2007: 83–84. See also Penzer 1968 (vol. 6): 259. Penzer's note on the tale makes clear that the motif in question does not in its earlier versions include the detail of the minister interpreting the signs (as is shown by the absence of the same in Daṇḍin's text). This, then, is an example of how a focus only on *motifs* can direct the analysis of narrative, for this very story is markedly different when told with the minister involved.

> King Karṇotpala, on the other hand—he is unlearned in the sciences of statecraft (*nītiśāstra*) and is not interested in clarifying with [the aid of his] spies the state of affairs among even his own subjects; he does not comprehend the tricks of rogues and is inexperienced in interpreting gestures and other external indications; that [king] is to be considered guilty, [therefore,] this for the lack of consideration in his action.

Kings cannot afford to be lax, or naïve, for they are to be blamed for the adverse consequences of the acts of others in their kingdom, whenever their own effort could have forestalled the same.

Brahmins, Kings, and Tantric Powers

The narratives furnished above suffice to represent what is replicated in innumerable stories and side stories in the *Kathāsaritsāgara*, which reinforce the key Brahmanical values of encouraging the mutual loyalty and respect of minister and king, the need for the king to cultivate and deploy good judgment and practice restraint in his desires, and the king's obligation to honor the proper counsel of his wise ministers along the way. These values—these ways of living up to the virtue ethic of the Sanskrit narratives—are repeatedly represented and reinforced in the *Kathāsaritsāgara*, just as they are not only in the *Rājataraṅgiṇī* but also in the literatures on statecraft, among other Sanskrit narrative works, and as we have seen. One may in fact go so far as to suggest that there is a certain underlying didactic quality to the *Kathāsaritsāgara*, not only in the sense of wishing to teach something to its audiences, but also in the sense that the narrative builds the idea of didacticism into the stories themselves. Although the collection, as noted, is said in its preamble to have been composed to entertain and distract Sūryamatī, the troubled queen and wife of King Ananta,[98] the *Kathāsaritsāgara* also frequently presents its stories as vehicles for the characters in the stories to acquire learning, which would be of practical use in the world of affairs. The *Kathāsaritsāgara*, that is, tells its audiences that it aims to please its intended (external) audience while simultaneously narrating stories that are tools for teaching their (internal) audiences, which of course serve the

[98] On this see also Slaje 2019: 6–7 and Nemec 2020b: 975.

external audience as well.[99] Pleasure (*kāma*) and worldly successes (*artha*) are thus married in the text's own explanation of the purpose and power of its stories: they delight while they educate; they narrate stories the contents of which marry pleasure and success by intimating that the attainment of lovers-as-wives coincides with (and eventuates) world conquest and *dharmic* order therein and, ultimately, the attainment of immortality as a *vidyādhara* as well.

Yes, wisdom and good judgment are foundational for the success of a king. Understanding the motivations and inclinations—the agendas—of others, in turn, is the key to executing good judgment. But what is at stake must be stated not only positively but also negatively, for there is also a danger lurking in all of this, and the danger is more potent and more immediate than many of our stories' protagonists—or audiences—might know.

A prime example is found in the very story of Padmāvatī the "witch," for it invokes the notion that tantric practitioners—particularly female practitioners—are dangerous and merit banishment from the kingdom. One exposes oneself to the gravest of dangers, however, not by keeping the company of *yoginīs* but by failing to cultivate that Brahmanical virtue so highly valued in the *Kathāsaritsāgara* and all the narrative literatures on Brahmins and kings: good judgment. In the *Kathāsaritsāgara* we find narrated a phenomenon of human relations that has been present in all historical epochs, cultures, and places of the world but has so often been and is so often left undetected until it is too late. It is this, that one often wagers one's own well-being, sometimes even one's very existence, in the course of dealing with others. But it is also more than this (for there are many occasions when one knows one's own welfare is at risk, in entering combat, for instance, or in negotiating a difficult financial transaction): what is rarely understood until it is too late is that one often makes the mortal wager *unawares* (and I think it no coincidence that this lesson is conveyed in a narrative context marked by tantric themes and concerns, the esoteric traditions being famously both powerful and dangerous).

This, indeed, is what we discover had transpired for that brave king Trivikramasena, the hero of the *vetāla* cycle of stories. As so often is the case with human cunning, the danger lurked where he would least have expected

[99] In this the *Kathāsaritsāgara* is similar to the *Pañcatantra*, as we shall see in Chapter 7. Perhaps it is no coincidence, then, that the *Kathāsaritsāgara* includes a narration of the *Pañcatantra* stories, though Penzer is convinced that the tale as Guṇāḍhya told it could never have originally included the animal fables. See his "Terminal Essay" in Penzer 1968 (vol. 9): 95.

it, just as help was offered from the most unlikely of sources. The *vetāla* was no enemy, and the sage who seemed so friendly, who gave the king the treasury of jewels in pieces of fruit, was sinister and cynical.

In the twenty-fourth story, the *vetāla* accedes to the will of the king and informs him of the following:[100]

> "King, though you have been worried with so many journeys to and fro in this cemetery terrible with black night, you seem quite happy, and you do not show the least irresolution. I am pleased with this wonderful courage that you show. So now carry off this body, for I am going out of it; and listen to this advice which I give you for your welfare, and act on it. That wicked mendicant, for whom you have fetched this human corpse, will immediately summon me into it, and honor me. And wishing to offer you up as a victim, the rascal will say to you, 'King, prostrate yourself on the ground in such a way that eight limbs will touch it.' Then, great king, you must say to that ascetic, 'Show me first how to do it and then I will do exactly as you do.' Then he will fling himself on the ground, and show you how to perform the prostration, and that moment you must cut off his head with the sword. Then you will obtain that prize which he desires, the sovereignty of the *vidyādharas*; enjoy this earth by sacrificing him! But otherwise that mendicant will offer you up as a victim; it was to prevent this that I threw obstacles in your way for such a long time here. So depart; may you prosper!"

Thus, and although he did not know it, Trivikramasena himself was to be the subject—and the victim—of the twenty-fifth and last *vetāla* story; but he did exactly as instructed and won the prize that was promised him, which the wicked Brahmin mendicant had sought for himself. Indeed, he is promised a life as a *vidyādhara* after enjoying his life on earth, and is offered a boon as well from the *vetāla*. Trivikramasena asks and is given that final wish, which is for the twenty-five *vetāla* stories to become famous and honored

[100] KSS 12.31.65cd–74ab: *rājan kṛṣṇaniśāghore smaśāne 'smin gatāgataiḥ || etaiḥ kliṣṭaḥ sukhārhas tvaṃ na vikalpaś ca ko 'pi te | tad āścaryeṇa dhairyeṇa tuṣṭo 'ham amunā tava || śavam etaṃ nayedānīṃ nirgacchāmy amuto hy aham | idaṃ tu śṛṇu yad vacmi hitaṃ tava kuruṣva ca || ānītam etad bhavatā yasyārthe nṛkalevaram | kubhikṣuḥ so 'dya mām asmin samāhūyārcayiṣyati || upahārīcikīrṣuś ca tvām eva sa śaṭhas tataḥ | bhūmau praṇāmam aṣṭābhir aṅgaiḥ kurv iti vakṣyati || tvaṃ prāg darśaya tāvan me kariṣye 'haṃ tathaiva tat | iti so 'pi mahārāja vaktavyaḥ śramaṇas tvayā || tato nipatya bhūtau sa praṇāmaṃ yāvad eva te | darśayiṣyati tāvat tvaṃ chindyās tasyāsinā śiraḥ || tato vidyādharaiśvaryasiddhir yā tasya vāñchitā | tāṃ tvaṃ prāpsyasi bhuṅkṣvemaṃ bhuvaṃ tadupahārataḥ || anyathā tu sa bhikṣus tvām upahārīkariṣyati | etadarthaṃ kṛto vighnas tavātreyac ciraṃ mayā || tat siddhir astu te gaccha.* Translation Tawney's.

on earth.[101] Their lessons, then, are destined to be shared together with the pleasure of hearing these entertaining tales.

In this instance, Brahmin and king are not allies but enemies. Tantric power can cut both ways, as, evidently, can the Brahmins who engage it. In the face of their mutual confrontation, however, it is the power of the *vetāla*, born from that milieu so commonly associated with tantric religion—the cremation ground—that makes all the difference. Trivikramasena was to be the sacrificial victim, the Brahminical sage his sacrificial executioner, all unbeknownst to him. With the counsel of the *vetāla*, however, won by his strenuous effort, determination, and wisdom—tantric power won by the virtues of a virtuous king—it is instead the wicked Brahmin who is made the victim, and the king the victor, and the one to achieve immortality at that.

We are similarly told immediately following the close of this narrative that the minister Mṛgāṅkadatta also achieved his success, quickly closing in turn the narrative frame in which he appears, for he managed, also by way of the aid of a *vetāla*, to reunite himself with Vikramakeśarin, the prince he served, upon taking the advice furnished to him by hearing the narration of the twenty-five *vetāla* stories.[102] In his case, the *vetāla* that was in possession of a human corpse carried him on its back and through the air to be by the side of his prince. The powers of the charnel grounds are deeply influential, and deeply to be desired, if properly harnessed.

Conclusion: The Far Shore of the Ocean of Stories

We do, then, finally find conclusion to the narratives of the *Kathāsaritsāgara*, first quickly and then slowly. Quickly because it is, relatively speaking, a short distance from the end of the *vetāla* stories to the happy ending we would want, with Naravāhanadatta married to his beloved Madanamañcukā, and others, ruling unopposed and with great confidence with his reliable advisor, Gomukha, by his side.[103] His parents, Udayana and Vāsavadattā, at this point decide to take leave of him, to depart the Ṛṣabha mountain where he reigns as a *vidyādhara* king, lord of that world of demigods, to return to their

[101] See KSS 12.32.26–27.

[102] See KSS 12.32.42–58.

[103] On Gomukha's instrumentality to Naravāhanadatta's success as narrated in the *Bṛhatkathāślokasaṃgraha* see Nelson 1974: 108–109. Note, however, that Nelson emphasizes the dynamic between destiny and action in their relationship, which he sees narrated in the version of the story he there examines.

mother-country, Vatsa, out of a fondness for home. They secure a promise that their son will call on them from time to time, and a tearful separation marks the happy ending, a temporary separation of parents and son, each successful and comfortable and living harmoniously. The story is finished and happily so, for Naravāhanadatta has won his brides and immortality.

But the *Kathāsaritsāgara* is not finished with its audience, and the slowness of the close of the text is the result of the presence of an addendum of considerable length, which ensues from just after this happy ending.[104] The addendum extols Naravāhanadatta's virtue and relays stories of his adventures, in particular those around his separation from Madanamañcukā, which he recounts in the hermitage of the sage Kaśyapa over the weeks of the rainy season. Only after working through this long cycle of appended stories does one reach the true end of the *Kathāsaritsāgara*. Too much is conveyed in them to summarize fruitfully, but it is worth noting, first, that the stories of the addendum include a large substory around the exploits of King Vikramāditya of Ujjayinī, in which interesting side stories are also embedded.[105]

In addition, several stories toward the very end of the narrative describe the dangers of trusting women, thus a contrast with the overall thrust of the narrative, which marries the pursuit of marriage with the attainment of immortality as a *vidyādhara* and wealthy and powerful king of the world, as we have seen. Yes, pleasure and power meet, furnishing also a liberation of sorts, along with the security of the kingdom under just rule, but only if the immortal king-to-be ensures not to allow himself to overindulge, or unsuspectingly to be targeted, to become the victim of the cleverness of another.

Other interesting things also happen in the massive addendum. For example, a story is told explaining how a young Brahmin could retrieve his wife from death. All had to do with a wicked Śaiva Kāpālika, who gave her the evil eye, which brought a fever upon her that killed her, this when he

[104] Lacôte 1908: 118 suggests that the order of stories is remarkable in Somadeva for having these stories included as addenda. I argue this structure allows the *vetāla* stories, and the tantric control thereof, to take a central place in the narrative flow of the *Kathāsaritsāgara*: they are rendered the fulcrum of the narrative structure of the work.

[105] There is use, moreover—and this according to Daud Ali—in thinking of the work of *kathā* in consonance with more "realist" or "historical" accounts of kingship in Kashmir and elsewhere in South Asia. As Ali 2013: 251 put the matter: "So if Vikramāditya's entry into the *kathā* tradition placed him in a 'once upon a time' temporality removed from the present, the Vikrama Saṃvat reckoning, as an inauguration of continuous quantifiable time, served to bridge the time of ideal kingship with the present. Vikramāditya's heroic time was thus connected to the present, a connection amply demonstrated by the naming practices of the royal houses of medieval India. The concatenation of Vikramāditya as a narrative figure, a royal title and a time reckoner, served to link story time with historical time."

came near their home to beg for alms. She was placed on a funeral pyre that was set alight, but the Kāpālika put out the fire with ashes and caused her to arise unharmed. He then kept her with him in a cave, along with two other women, but the Brahmin husband, who had trailed him carrying bow and arrow, stole his staff (*khatvāṅga*) and threw it in the river. Being deprived of what was the source of his magical power, the Brahmin killed him with a poisoned arrow (to be found at KSS 18.5). Yet again, then, the reader is regaled with stories of the powers and dangers of Śaiva ascetics, adepts associated with tantric learning and powers.

The text finally concludes. Naravāhanadatta completes his story of his separation from his beloved, which in turn was aided by the encouraging narrative of a hermit named Kaṇva. It all ends like this:[106]

> When the hermit Kaṇva had told during the night this story of Viśamaśīla, dealing with separations and reunions, he went on to say to me who was cut off from the society of Madanamañcukā, "Thus do unexpected separations and unions of beings take place, and so you Naravāhanadatta shall soon be reunited to your beloved. Have recourse to patience, and you shall enjoy for a long time, son of the king of Vatsa, surrounded by your wives and ministers, the position of a beloved emperor of the *vidyādharas*." This admonition of the hermit Kaṇva enabled me to recover patience; and so I got through my time of separation, and I gradually obtained wives, magic science, and the sovereignty over the *vidyādharas*. And I told you before, great hermits, how I obtained all these by the favor of Śiva, the giver of boons.

These (nearly) final words from the *Kathāsaritsāgara*—only five verses and the *praśasti*s follow—offer what we could not more succinctly state in this chapter's conclusion. Somadeva's text gives us, on the one hand, a tale that is typical for featuring the king and discussing his proper place in the world. He is to conquer his enemies, marry well and happily, judge wisely, protect the kingdom, and enjoy its proper rewards. Guided by wise ministers, his aims are explicitly and regularly shown to be those of the *dharmarāja*, the righteous

[106] KSS 18.5.241–245: *iti saṃyogaviyogair nicitām ākhyāya viṣamaśīlakathām | kaṇvamuniḥ punar avadat tasmin māṃ madanamañcukāvirahe* || 241 || *evaṃ bhavanty acintyā virahāś ca samāgamāś ca jantūnām | tat syāt tavāpi nacirān naravāhanadatta saṃgamaḥ priyayā* || 242 || *avalambasva dhṛtiṃ tat suciraṃ bhoktāsi vatsarājasuta | bhāryāsacivasameto vidyādharacārucakravartipadam* || 243 || *evaṃ kaṇvarṣigirā labdhadhṛtiḥ kṣapitavirahakālo 'tha | bhāryā vidyāḥ khecarasāmrājyaṃ ca kramād ahaṃ prāptaḥ* || 244 || *tac ca yathā saṃprāptaṃ varadasyānugrahān mayā śaṃbhoḥ | ādāv eva tadakhilaṃ varṇitavān eva vo mahāmunayaḥ* || 245 ||. Translation Tawney's.

king, patient, wise, measured in action. The outmost of the three frame stories even embeds within it the natural inclination of king and queen to ensure the birth of a son, a successor to the throne. And that prince is destined too to be courageous and adventuresome, to be a young hero successfully seeking his beloved. To do so ensures the fulfillment of a desire, to have his beloved, and with it his ascension to the status of a *vidyādhara*, a "semidivine" status,[107] liberation, but not just this: together with such pleasures and material reward, together with *kāma* and *artha*, and liberation to boot, is the cultivation of a successful, fruitful kingdom—*dharma*—happiness and success all to be found in a single, *dharmic* path, the magic of the virtue ethic.

Thus, the faithful king and prince, first. But there is a second, Śaiva Tantric dimension to the narrative as well. The *Kathāsaritsāgara* regularly brings the hero to the cremation ground, in contact with Pāśupata ascetics, into covens of *yoginī*s and crossing the paths of *vetāla*s who crave the consumption of human flesh, all in search of an empowered woman who can in being obtained bring him to the status of *vidyādhara*. Unlike the *Rājataraṅgiṇī*,[108] the *Kathāsaritsāgara* is not overtly hostile to tantrism, though it warns in various places of the existence of dangerous tantrics.[109] Indeed, the very narrative structure of the work demands that we read the hero's adventure as just such a double path, one that leads him to engage successfully and in a measured way with the rights and obligations of kingship while simultaneously engaging him in a tantricized quest for his beloved, by the winning of whom he will gain power and a powerful state beyond death.

If it is true, then, as van Buitenen and others have argued, that the *Kathāsaritsāgara* "Brahminizes" the work of Guṇāḍhya, taking its origins in a merchant's tale and rendering it friendly to Brahminical norms and concerns, then it does so by establishing a Brahmin's vision of the king—valiant and guided by the wisdom of his ministers who are, of course,

[107] See van Buitenen 1958: 311.

[108] For example, the text tells us that a wise king, Yaśaskara, was so effective a king that tantric rituals did not take place in his day in the land. See RT 6.11–12: *na mūrkhaguravo matsyāpūpayāgavidhāyinaḥ | cakrire svakṛtair granthais tarkāgamaparīkṣaṇam || nādṛśyanta ca gehinyo gurudīkṣotthadevatāḥ | kurvāṇā bhartṛśīlaśrīniṣedhaṃ mūrdhadhūnanaiḥ ||*. Stein [1900] 1989 (vol. 1): 237 translates as follows: "11. Ignorant Gurus did not perform Matsyāpūpa sacrifices, and did not by texts of their own composition revise traditional doctrines. 12. There were not seen house-wives figuring as divinities at the Guru-consecration (*gurudīkṣā*), and by shakes of their heads detracting from the distinguished character of their husbands."

[109] For example, the text warns that women possess three faults: "being fickle, recklessness, and a love for the congregation of witches." See KSS 7.3.170: *cāpalaṃ sāhasikatā śākinīśambarādayaḥ | doṣāḥ strīṇāṃ trayaḥ prāyo lokatrayabhayāvahāḥ ||*.

Brahmins. The path, however, is not just orthodox but is a tantric one of sorts as well. The *Kathāsaritsāgara* deeply imbibes tantric mores, lauding as it does the fruits of the charnel grounds at the margins of society, so commonly associated with Śaiva esotericism, for the acts of the faithful royal sovereign are coupled with a cultivated dependence on the magic of tantrics. The one path ultimately is the other. This double path similarly effects both pleasure in its proper place *and* prosperity and felicity, what stands in line with the narrative's account of itself (told as it is to entertain a despondent queen, but by way of didactic stories that pave the way to success in worldly affairs), which in turn mirrors the double ends of tantra, which simultaneously can promise both worldly enjoyment and the transcendence of liberation.[110] Stories serve as counsel, both in the narrative and in the form of this narrative, for both the *Kathāsaritsāgara*'s internal and external audiences. Tantra has entered the *imaginaire* of the mainstream, and we are told there is much to gain from it: not only is it compatible with the virtue ethic of the Sanskrit narratives, but also—by way in particular of the *vetāla*'s coaxing—it is conducive to the same. The didactic *and entertaining* narration of a web of stories evokes tantric mores, figures, and sentiments, and in doing so facilitates the cultivation of tantra's double fruits, wise counsel in an entertaining mode, the double ends of tantra now to be met—by Brahmins and kings and princes and queens—even beyond the canonical ambit of the Śaiva esoteric scriptures.

110 This double focus of Śaiva tantra is well understood, embodied as it is in the *bubhukṣu* and *mumukṣu*, the one desiring enjoyments and the one desiring liberation, both of whom can be served by tantric initiation and who can also be one and the same. What is more, this doubled narrative is matched by the very figure of the *vidyādhara*, which, as Lacôte 1908: 23, fn. 2 noted, is a sort of "moral" figure who is "généralement ami de l'opprimé," but also, of course, exists in an exalted state beyond the mere world of humanity.

5

The King in the Garden

Pleasure in Dramatic Imagination

Introduction

Pleasure and success may find mutual company under good counsel. The former may in fact serve to support the latter, as the *Kathāsaritsāgara* suggests, just as the pleasure of reading or hearing an "ocean of stories" can cultivate the development of the virtues modeled, explained, and supported in Brahminical circles. Acting the right way, acting in accordance with *dharma*—this by the counsel of wise Brahmins sometimes said to be magically powerful—allows the possibility of doing well and doing good, simultaneously.

A similar compatibility of the human ends of pleasure (*kāma*) and success (*artha*) is to be found in the dramatic literatures of Sanskrit, as I shall argue in the present chapter. Here, however, the relationship of the two is conceived differently inasmuch as the king is left to pursue pleasure with reckless abandon. It is precisely this dynamic, I argue, that facilitates the pleasure of the dramas in their performances, which, while sharing with the *Kathāsaritsāgara* the literary ambition of entertaining their audiences, do so without elaborating the kind of pedagogic metanarrative concerning the didactic virtues of stories, which is a feature of Somadeva's text.

The plays—these plays[1]—are for fun and are beautiful, which is precisely why they depict the relationship of Brahmins and kings as they do: the king is freed *exclusively* to enjoy the privileges of kingship, doing so even fulfills his obligations as the head of state, but the king may frolic only for having the implicit support and aid of his Brahminical ministers. In this genre too can be conveyed a certain counsel, but a counsel the meaning of which must

[1] Sanskrit dramas historically have served a host of purposes. Some, for example, are quite philosophical in orientation or even serve soteriological ends. See, e.g., Wulff 1984, Dezső 2005, and Allen 2016.

Brahmins and Kings. John Nemec, Oxford University Press. © Oxford University Press 2025.
DOI: 10.1093/oso/9780197791998.003.0006

be discerned—after the dramatic performance, on further reflection—by seeing through to the hidden suggestions of the dramatic spectacle, which emphasizes the direct presentation of what is not quite real. In placing fictive narratives in palpable form—a performance on the stage—a certain play in the dramas between illusion and reality helps to define both the genre and the counsel the works in question implicitly offer to kings and those who surround them: there is an easy freedom in reliance on Brahminical counsel and culture.

Dramatic Sensibilities: Plays and Emotions

Sanskrit dramatic works sought in their performance to awaken in their audiences the sentiments, the *rasas*, depicted therein, as is well known.[2] Indeed, among all the genres of narrative literature, we find the emotions perhaps most explicitly and directly evoked and exemplified in drama, which is intimately and extensively associated with royal acts of recreation, most of all wooing women. This freedom, this privilege to play—to imbibe feelings and pursue passions for pleasure—is particularly the prerogative of the king, who is the character type par excellence of the dramas.[3] This is so, moreover, because his responsible Brahminical advisors are offered no holiday from their social obligations.

The dramas thus reflect implicit assumptions about kingship and its opportunities and challenges, the emotional force of which we must recapture by imagining how their audiences could have received them. Here we may identify the presence of an emotional relief in their narration, because the typical, true dangers perpetually and implicitly confronted by the king and his courtiers—the murderous double-cross, the threat of assassination, the very possibility that it is oneself, one's very life, that one has inadvertently put at stake in taking or failing to take an action—these mortal concerns are set off the table by the dramas. Their absence is unspoken, though these concerns are fully present elsewhere in the narrative literatures, and this unspoken but palpable absence is precisely what renders the dramas, with their

[2] "The function of literature," as Coulson 1981: 23, for example, said of the dramas, "is to generalize emotion so that it can be tasted in this way."

[3] Coulson 1981: 18–19 rightly suggests that the dramas present characters as types more than individuals, types with which members of their intended audiences would naturally have identified: "the characters in these dramas are types rather than individuals. The method of the Indian poet was not to elevate particular people to universal status but to take universal types and then infuse them with individual human life."

perennial happy endings, playful in their performance. If the surprise in the *Kathāsaritsāgara* is that a king had inadvertently risked his life and well-being in his acts, as we argued in Chapter 4, in the dramas one can find surprise only in how *little* kings put at risk in the course of recklessly pursuing personal pleasure.

Two plays are here elected for close reading.[4] The first is the famed *Abhijñānaśākuntala* of Kālidāsa.[5] It is classed a *nāṭaka*, the first of ten types of dramas as enumerated in the *Nāṭyaśāstra*.[6] In works of such form the hero "should always be an honorable or highly placed personality, a king, a demi-god or a god."[7] The second play, the *Ratnāvalī* by Harṣa, in turn, is traditionally classed a *nāṭikā*, which is a subsidiary type (*uparūpaka*) of dramatic work, the first of eighteen such types that are distinguished from the ten principal types of dramas (*rūpaka*s) traditionally enumerated in the later treatises on poetics. It is said to be a combination of the first and second principal types of dramas, namely, the aforementioned *nāṭaka* and, secondly, the *prakaraṇa*.[8] *Nāṭikā*s are set in four acts, give prominence to the sentiment of love, and feature strong female roles, among other qualities.[9]

Harṣa (r. 606–647), there can be no doubt, was a historical figure, a king who also was a poet who reigned in Kanauj, near modern-day Kanpur.[10] Kālidāsa too is a historical person, though his dating is famously disputed: scholars alternatively place him in the fifth century and perhaps near the time of Chandragupta II (r. 380–415 CE) or, alternatively and in a theory less likely, in the first century before the Common Era.[11] Both plays narrate delightful tales of the king in the garden, not on the battlefield, nor in the audience hall to adjudicate legal or other disputes. Both were known

[4] It would not be possible to review all the dramatic works available to us, nor do I wish to claim that Sanskrit dramatic works invariably represent the theme here identified. The motif of the Brahmin ably serving the royal sovereign from behind the scenes is none too difficult to find, however, and the works here selected for close reading may be said to exemplify what is regularly found, in one form or another, in the dramas: safety in indulging the emotions.

[5] On the various recensions, or versions, of the play, see, e.g., Vasudeva 2006: 27–40 and Bansat-Boudon 1994.

[6] On this classification see, e.g., Konow 1969: 42–43 and Marasinghe 1989: 422–429.

[7] See Winternitz [1963, 1965] 1985: 185.

[8] The *prakaraṇa* is distinguished from the *nāṭaka* on the basis of the fact that the plot is invented by the author of the play, and the hero is often of inferior status. "He is a Brāhmaṇa, a minister, a grosser, etc., but never a king or a god. Slaves, epicurean, prostitutes, etc., may appear in a *prakaraṇa*. It should have five to ten acts, but otherwise its requirements should be same [*sic*] as those of a *nāṭaka*." See Winternitz [1963, 1965] 1985: 185.

[9] See, e.g., Konow 1969: 51; Marasinghe 1989: 435–437.

[10] See Doniger 2006: 15.

[11] See D. Smith 2005: 15; Mallinson 2005: 15; Vasudeva 2006: 15–20; Bakker 2006; and Balogh and Somogyi 2009: xxii–xxiv.

in Kashmir and circulated widely in the subcontinent. Both plays, moreover, signal what their audiences would have known and expected of the emotions around pleasure in their day. With them we can recognize something vital of the relationship of Brahmins and kings in premodern South Asia: the former could guarantee that the latter could do well by being good, being good consisting here in the king delegating affairs of the state to his able Brahminical counselors, or implicitly accepting Brahminical norms around caste and related social norms and restrictions, despite wielding his free hand in the pursuit of pleasure.

Kings Just Want to Have Fun

The dramatic celebration of pleasure (*kāma*), not without drama or emotional twists but in a general context of play, is reinforced by what we know of life in the royal courts of premodern South Asia. This we can appreciate most directly by way of Daud Ali's thoughtful analysis of court culture, in which he depicts in vivid detail how those privileged to live in that world were endlessly tempted to abuse their privilege.[12] Excessive pursuit of pleasure and in particular the addictions of gambling, hunting, drinking, and the pursuit of women presented themselves regularly and ominously as fundamentally dangerous, as we have seen in the *Kathāsaritsāgara* and *Rājataraṅgiṇī*, for their capacity to draw the king away from his duties at the cost of the welfare of those under his charge and, ultimately, his own as well.

The cultural world of the court had its own gravitational pull, as Ali has further shown, and while Brahminical culture made up a part of it, the contours of court culture were not always determined thereby. There was, in fact, something of a tension to be found between Brahminical norms and royal prerogatives, with the dramatic character type of the *vidūṣaka* or "clown" in my view best embodying this tension on the stage. The humor to be found in this character type, who is always classed as a Brahmin, is his uncharacteristic disinterest—uncharacteristic for his *varṇa*, that is—in the austere and controlled life of the chastened Brahmin, this or the implicit mocking of the foolishness of the same character, particularly when sensual and other pleasures—good food—are readily to be had. Brahmins were paradigmatically said to be learned and chastened, embodiments of *dharma*, and

[12] Ali 2004.

the *vidūṣaka* regularly is not. The humor is in this incongruity, a mismatch in the dynamic between Brahmin and king, between the chastened life of control and the prerogatives, the freewheeling inclinations, of one with access to the powers of sovereignty. The *vidūṣaka* recasts the "conservative" Brahmin type not as the keeper of moral strictures and a cultured knowledge of the law that secures it, but as one who is uninterested in or ignorant or incapable of the same—but always and ever in the dramas without any real consequences to be paid for being thus.

Abhijñānaśākuntala: The Pleasures of Illusory Troubles

The pleasures of kingship in mind, and turning to the first of the two dramas we wish to engage closely in the present chapter, we note that there is no coincidence in the fact that Kālidāsa opens his most celebrated drama with its protagonist, the king Duṣyanta, on the hunt. The first lines of the narrative have our *nāṭaka*'s hero closing in on his mark—a deer—when work, as it were, intervenes with play: an ascetic from off the stage calls a warning, suggesting the hunted deer belongs to his hermitage and therefore could not be shot. The hero heeds the warning and surrenders his pursuit, and he receives for doing so a blessing from the Brahmin ascetic: "You are a true scion of Puru's race, a true light among kings. May you gain a son to be emperor of heaven and earth."[13] The king's honorable reply? "I accept a Brahmin's blessing."[14]

Seeking the blessing of the head of the hermitage whose *āśrama* it was his duty to protect, the king is ushered instead to see his daughter: on her father's absence for an errand that took him to Somatīrtha (in fact on her behalf), she was deputized as acting head of the retreat. The virtues of the place, the products of successful asceticism, are immediately evident. Deer fear not the visitors for happy familiarity with the anchorites in their midst; the area's *darbha* grass is visibly trimmed, their shoots being of use in Vedic sacrifices; discarded ascetics' clothes, made of bark, are strewn all about in the area. The peace of renunciation abides in the grove.

[13] Kāle [1898] 1980: 18: *sadṛśam etat puruvaṃśapradīpasya bhavataḥ | janma yasya purovaṃśe yuktarūpam idaṃ tava | putram evaṃguṇopetaṃ cakravartinam āśnuhi* || 12 ||. Translation that of Coulson 1981: 45.

[14] *pratigṛhītaṃ brāhmaṇavacanam* |. See Kāle [1898] 1980: 18. Translation that of Coulson 1981: 45.

But not for long, or at least not so simply. Love at first sight evokes a stir of emotion. The women there, watering the young trees, prove themselves of their beauty, and the king quickly shifts his attention from hunting to another royal prerogative—not gambling or drinking, the other oft-wished-for dangers, but chasing the fairer sex. Duṣyanta observes:

> When looks so rare in palace women
> Can be found in hermitage-dwellers,
> Then our cultivated vines, it seems,
> Must yield in excellence to the wild woodland kind.[15]

The civilized world of the householder, the wild world of the ascetical retreat, the city and the jungle: the former regularly offers finer things, but not here, where ceding to nature and not a studied and urbane cultivation seems to offer the greatest possibility for pleasure.

Duṣyanta loves the young woman, Śakuntalā, at first sight, but is she eligible? After all, her father is a Brahmin ascetic, meaning the opening act immediately and directly raises the question of caste identity:

> Without question she is a proper wife for a warrior,
> For my heart is noble and yet desires her.
> The virtuous, on those matters which admit of doubt,
> Are rightly guided by their own inner inclination.[16]

Instinct and the fruits of virtuous conduct (in his role as king) nourish in him a certainty that his intentions cannot miss the mark. He may frolic in nature, because his goodness is intrinsic: the virtue ethic of the Sanskrit narratives is inherent, not earned. Thus, we have entered the dramatic and playful world of play without consequence: the king's very impulses prove to be pure, and his desire is true—precisely not what we find in, for example, the *Rājataraṅgiṇī*, and precisely what makes this drama a pleasurable exception that proves the rule of *dharmic*, Brahminical conduct. But what of her connection with him? That too is quickly made evident.

[15] *Abhijñānaśākuntala* 1.16: *śuddhāntadurlabham idaṃ vapur āśramavāsino yadi janasya | dūrīkṛtāḥ khalu guṇair udyānalatā vanalatābhiḥ* ||. See Kāle [1898] 1980: 24. Translation that of Coulson 1981: 47 (though counted there as verse 1.15).

[16] *Abhijñānaśākuntala* 1.20: *asaṃśayaṃ kṣatraparigrahakṣamā yadāryam asyām abhilāṣi me manaḥ | satāṃ hi saṃdehapadeṣu vastuṣu pramāṇam antaḥkaraṇapravṛttayaḥ* ||. See Kāle [1898] 1980: 30. Translation that of Coulson 1981: 50 (though counted there as verse 1.21).

After Duṣyanta set the question of caste aside, the play immediately turns playfully to the good he can do as king, above all in his role as protector. A bee (a symbol of the amorous season) mars Śakuntalā, who asks her two friends, Anusūyā and Priyaṃvadā, to help her escape it. They impishly reply: "*We* can't help you. You'd better try king Duṣyanta—the hermitage is under royal protection."[17] Sensing the moment, the king presents himself to them, but he does so in the guise of an anonymous, if honored, guest. Thus occasion for his love to be reciprocated: from the first moment Śakuntalā wonders, "Oh dear, why does the sight of this man fill me with feelings so much at odds with my religious life?"[18]

We here see the very tensions of society stretched by the desires of the principal characters of the plot, and this in the play's initial movement. Duṣyanta and Śakuntalā find one another immediately in a mutual attraction, but their mutual feelings must confront the strictures of society and the obligations of their roles therein, which stand implicitly in their way. The *dharma* of both *varṇa* and *āśrama* is called into question. Each is given reason to doubt the significance of the obstacles, however: the king in trusting the virtue of his desires assumes he could never be drawn to misdeed by love. The maiden has her mind set at ease, as well, when Duṣyanta presents himself not as king but a scholar who, charged with the spiritual welfare of the cities, was touring holy places, this identity explaining his evident sophistication. When Anusūyā shrieks with enthusiasm—"Holy people have a champion!" (*saṇāhā dāṇiṃ dhammaāriṇo*)[19]—Śakuntalā shows with her body language her love's affection. Duṣyanta, presenting himself as a Brahmin, is *prima facie* qualified for her love. Mistaken identity and disguise thus playfully permit a flirtation with caste transgression, for Duṣyanta is in fact no Brahmin but really a *kṣatriya*; and as we shall see Śakuntalā both is caste eligible and is not bound to the renunciant's stage of life.

Flirting quickly ensues. Śakuntalā's girlfriends tease her, saying that her father, Kaṇva, would gift to their guest anything he asked for—even her, his "dearest treasure" (*jīvidasavvassa*).[20] Then Duṣyanta utters a vital

[17] See Kāle [1898] 1980: 32: *kāo vaaṃ parittāduṃ* | *dussandaṃ akkanda* | *rāarakkhidavvāiṃ tavovaṇāiṃ* |. (*Chāyā: ke āvāṃ paritrātum* | *duṣyantam ākranda* | *rājarakṣitavyāni tapovanāni nāma* |). Translation that of Coulson 1981: 51.

[18] See Kāle [1898] 1980: 36: *kiṃ ṇu kkhu imaṃ pekhkhia tavovaṇavirohiṇo viārassa gamaṇīahmi samvuttā* |. (*Chāyā: kiṃ nu khalv imaṃ prekṣya tapovanavirodhino vikārasya gamanīyāsmi saṃvṛttā* |). Translation that of Coulson 1981: 52.

[19] See Kāle [1898] 1980: 38. (*Chāyā: sanāthā idānīṃ dharmacārinaḥ.*)

[20] See Kāle [1898] 1980: 38. (*Chāyā: jīvitasarvasva.*) The translation is Coulson's.

question: how, if Kaṇva "lives in perpetual chastity" (*śāsvate brahmaṇi sthitaḥ*), is he possessed of a daughter at all?[21] As it turns out, another royal sage whose family name is Kauśika was challenged by the gods, who feared his success in austerity and sent a beautiful nymph to tempt him, with whom he bore this child. Kaṇva subsequently became the foster-father.

The identity of this royal sage is of particular note. His family name is associated with that of Viśvāmitra, who famously was born a *kṣatriya*, meaning the question of caste identity is here quickly resolved, because Śakuntalā's biological father shares Duṣyanta's caste status and her mother is a nymph and thus not bound by any limited caste identity. And Duṣyanta finds out on his query that she is indeed to be betrothed, if and when the right suitor appears. Śakuntalā thus having been shown to be free to consort with the king, Kālidāsa closes the first act.

Yet the tensions of the play are not resolved; indeed, they have barely begun. The mutual admiration must come to its resolution, and mistaken identities or missed identifications must be clarified. The tension that is present will be found not in a profound and irresolvable problem of social status or identity, however, but in the lighter whimsies of misapprehension, of forgetting and remembering one's beloved.

The second act consists principally of a dialogue between king and *vidūṣaka*, and it sets the stage for the ensuing drama in which Duṣyanta must win Śakuntalā, which is a personal matter, not one of social role or standing. The dialogue, of course, is humorous: the *vidūṣaka* wishes not to be inconvenienced by the hunt that had brought them to the *āśrama* in the first place, for he misses the comforts of the city and palace, and he is focused only on finding a comfortable bed and a hearty meal. It also clearly sets the terms of the encounter. The possibility of any caste incompatibility already ruled out, the clownish minister teases the king, suggesting he only loves Śakuntalā for the reason of being bored with the ladies of his seraglio. He likewise suggests there is no difficulty in developing a pretext for meeting her, because as king he can simply tax the hermitage and turn up to collect the fee in person.

The king implicitly accepts that love here releases his driving passion, but he rejects the *vidūṣaka*'s proposed approach to his beloved. The reason explicitly given is telling for its implicit virtue. The proposed action, Duṣyanta

[21] See Kāle [1898] 1980: 40.

says, conflicts with his innate respect for ascetical virtues, which offer "an imperishable tithe from their austerities:"

> The wealth kings get from the [four] social classes (*varṇa*)
> Is a transitory thing.
> But the ascetics of the forest
> Yield to us one-sixth [of the merit] of their *tapas*, an imperishable tithe from their austerities.[22]

But what to do? Will Duṣyanta continue the hunt, and how will he win the beautiful girl to his side?

A second attendant to the king enters the scene, a general named Bhadrasena. He and Mādhavya, the *vidūṣaka*, quickly confer, the latter explaining to the former that he is trying to cut the hunt short, so they could return home to their urban comforts. Bhadrasena instead humors the king, suggesting nothing is more worthy of royal pleasure than hunting. The play's spell is here being cast, for the legitimacy of the pleasures of kingship are shown. *Both* the foolish *vidūṣaka* and the presumably capable general counsel the king not to duty but to pleasure, but only by different means: Mādhavya longs for his comfortable bed and a good meal; Bhadrasena prefers the soldierly joy of the hunt. The place for pleasure is opened in this ultimately inconsequential debate, away from civic duty, caste obligation, or other related strictures. Ministers argue recreation, not the safety and future of the kingdom.

And yet the king's proper obligations are promptly brought again to his attention: two seers turn up to request his services, which the king readily promises.[23] The absence of Kaṇva, the abbot, has opened a door to evil spirits, which have turned up to mar the anchorites' austerities, the king therefore beckoned to protect the hermitage. A clear echo of Rāma's call to duty, then, is sounded: Duṣyanta is summoned to the forest by sages to protect and serve his ascetical, Brahminical counterparts. Also like Rāma, Duṣyanta will be with his beloved in the wilderness, though the circumstances here are entirely different. Far from an inconvenience, far from an unwanted disruption

[22] *Abhijñānaśākuntala* 2.13: *yad uttiṣṭhati varṇebhyo nṛpāṇāṃ kṣayi tat phalam | tapaḥṣaḍbhāgam akṣayyaṃ dadaty āraṇyakā hi naḥ* ||. Translation a modification of that of Coulson 1981: 66 (though counted as verse 2.14 there). See also the rendering of Kāle [1898] 1980: 77.

[23] The king says the following (Kāle [1898] 1980: 80): *ājñāpayitum icchāmi* |.

of a peaceful city life, and far from the thorny question of royal succession and the dangers of usurpation, this call to duty offers precisely what the king wished for: a *reason* to stay in the hermitage and chase a beautiful woman, and this by no mere pretext but to fill a royal obligation by the by. No conflict transpires between the goals of pleasure and duty, *kāma* and *dharma*, nor between city and the jungle, for here in the drama no such existential difficulties enter. No suffering in the forest is to be found, as there is in the *Rāmāyaṇa*; no betrayal of one's duties is at play, as in the *Rājataraṅgiṇī*; no fundamental conflict of *dharma* is evoked, as in the *Mahābhārata*. The emotional milieu is of a lightness in recreation; and while there is present here a similarity with the *Kathāsaritsāgara* in that the pursuit of *kāma* can conduce to the more fundamental aims of kingship, there is no present sense of danger, which so frequently confronts the adventurous kings and princes of the ocean of stories.

Another problem is nevertheless introduced—which delights the spectator, since problems are hardly serious in the dramas. Kālidāsa presents the king with simultaneous news from his queen, just as he is to step into the chariot that would take him to the ascetics' grove. She requests that he accompany her in a fast she must incur.[24] The king is thus conflicted:

> With two duties in different places,
> My mind is split down the middle —
> Like the stream of a river
> Divided against a rock.[25]

He is presented with a moral dilemma—defined as we saw in Chapter 1 as the pairing of equally valid and required, but mutually contradictory, obligations that cannot be performed simultaneously[26]—one echoing playfully the same kind of trap as found in the *Mahābhārata* but in this case with the resolution easily found to hand. Duṣyanta sends the *vidūṣaka* Mādhavya to the queen in his place, who, like a son, joyfully departs for the city life he prefers and

[24] See Kāle [1898] 1980: 82: *devī āṇavedi* | *āāmiṇi cautthadiahe pauttapārāṇo me uvavāso bhavissadi* | *tahiṃ dīhāuṇā avassaṃ saṃbhāvidavva tti* |. (*Chāyā*: *devyājñāpayati* | *āgāmini caturthadivase pravṛttapāraṇo me upavāso bhaviṣyati* | *tatra dīrghāyuṣāvaśyaṃ saṃbhāvanīyeti* |.)

[25] See *Abhijñānaśākuntala* 2.17 (Kāle [1898] 1980: 84): *kṛtyayor bhinnadeśatvād dvaithībhavati me manaḥ* | *puraḥ pratihataṃ śaile srotaḥ srotovaho yathā* ||. It is verse 2.18 in Coulson. Translation his.

[26] The precision of this formulation is the work of B. K. Matilal, for which see Chapter 1, footnote 93.

happily avoids any danger of evil spirits. The pretense for the substitution, moreover, is that his royal obligations to the ascetics require him to delay his return to her side.

Thus, then, will be the tensions of the play: false, illusory, and temporary—therefore entertaining. Tensions in echoes. While real grief is to be felt in the play—the pangs of separation, the pain of betrayal, the suffering of the loss of a beloved and the lack of offspring—nothing of the perduring and truly dangerous constraints and difficulties depicted in the epics (for example) are here ultimately to be felt. The tensions and difficulties are ultimately of no consequence; they are but mere moments of the drama. Duṣyanta does not in his intentions betray his newfound beloved, though a curse will cause him to forget her identity for a time. And the king in the end will not be deprived of his one deepest desire, which his previous wife could not give him—the birth of a son.

Yet Śakuntalā *is* to be forsaken, forgotten, by the father of her yet-to-be-born son; and Duṣyanta *is* to be left to live with the sorrow of believing there is no heir to be born to succeed him to the throne, this in the space of the drama that indulges attention to hurtful emotions under the comfort of knowing they will ultimately resolve. (One readily senses, however, that Śakuntalā bears the larger burden of the suffering, and she, the female lead, is left to do so off the stage and alone, away from the dramatic performance, which rather brooks in good feeling, by setting the female lead to the wings.) The dramas let courtiers imbibe feelings that in the audience hall and the royal palace could cloud their judgment. It is safe to *feel* in the course of the spectacle, which is hardly always the case. And so love ensues, and the ultimately illusory consequences emerge.

> On one horizon the Lord of Plants [the Moon] nears the
>   western mountain,
> On the other the Sun has sent the dawn to herald its arrival.
> That one great light should fail as the other grows in splendor
> Shows how inexorable is the wheel of this world's fortune.[27]

Śakuntalā, we come to know, is pregnant, but her husband will not remember her for a time. And the advice that her father gives is that of any father to any

[27] *Abhijñānaśākuntala* 4.2 (Kāle [1898] 1980: 128): *yāty ekato 'staśikharaṃ patiroṣadhīnām āviṣkṛtāruṇapuraḥsara ekato 'rkaḥ* | *tejodvayasya yugapadvyasanodayābhyāṃ loko niyamyata ivātmadaśāntareṣu* ||. Translation Coulson's.

daughter on her departure for the house of her husband's family (in the gendered world of betrothal in India's premodernity); he speaks to real-world sorrows and fears, though in the drama the pains prove to be ephemeral:

> Obey your elders, treat your fellow wives as your friends,
> Though your husband should treat you poorly, do not cross him
> in anger.
> Be generally considerate to your servants and not made
> vain by luxury.
> This is how girls become wives: if they are otherwise, they are
> a grief to their family.[28]

With trepidation Śakuntalā is dispatched to her husband, her father's blessing in her ears—"may you have that which I desire for you."[29]

What is real, and what is a fantasy? The reality is that such departures were a regular part of life in India's premodern cultural world.

> A daughter is a possession belonging to someone else:
> And so by sending her now to her husband
> I [the father, Kaṇva,] have become more tranquil in my mind,
> As if I had at last handed over what was given me for safekeeping.[30]

The echo with real life renders the pain palpable; but the pleasure of the play is in the joy of the happy ending, the certain knowledge that what ideally would be will come to pass, for nothing but a curse of the sage Durvāsas, a temporary impediment, can cause the pain that outside the illusion of the play is all too common. The lovemaking that occurred between scenes, as convention suggests it must, took place prior to this, the fourth act; and it leaves the audience with the heartfelt tropes of real loss and separation, but they are losses sublimated by their ultimate illusion in the drama. Neither

[28] *Abhijñānaśākuntala* 4.18 (Kāle [1898] 1980: 152): *śuśrūṣasva gurūn kuru priyasakhīvṛttiṃ sapatnījane / bhartṛviprakṛtāpi roṣaṇatayā mā sma pratīpaṃ gamaḥ | bhūyiṣṭhaṃ bhava dakṣiṇā parijane bhāgyeṣv anutsekinī / yānty evaṃ gṛhiṇīpadaṃ yuvatayo vāmāḥ kulasyādhayaḥ ||* (4.20 in Coulson). Translation a modification of Coulson's.

[29] See Kāle [1898] 1980: 154: *yad icchāmi te tad astu |*. Note, however, that Kāle identifies the speaker of this line as Kāśyapa, which cannot be possible given the context: it must be Kaṇva, the stepfather, who speaks.

[30] *Abhijñānaśākuntala* 4.22 (Kāle [1898] 1980: 158): *artho hi kanyā parakīya eva tām adya saṃpreṣya parigrahītuḥ | jāto mamāyaṃ viśadaḥ prakāmaṃ pratyārpitanyāsa ivāntarātmā ||* (4.24 in Coulson). Translation Coulson's.

maiden nor king will fall to the fates of Ambā or Bhīṣma; no Śikhaṇḍī will rise from the failure of betrothal. The play of reality and fantasy again favors the king, as we, the audience, surely shall soon enough see.

Act 5. The fated twist bites. A group of ascetics comes with Śakuntalā to see Duṣyanta, who cannot imagine why they would have made the journey. Had he not done all he was to do on the obligation of his royal *dharma* to serve and protect their *āśrama*?

> Have the austerities of devoted sages been spoiled
> by hinderances?
> Or has someone done wrong to the creatures that
> roam the holy grove?
> Can it be that my own misdeeds have stopped
> flowering their plants?
> With so many possible conjectures, my mind is
> sorely puzzled.[31]

His transgression, however, ultimately *is* illusion, for he is not the author of his forgetfulness, and all his other duties he had faithfully fulfilled. It was his wife's neglect of Durvāsas and not his own that caused his error, his inability to remember her identity and their love (this being yet another instance of a narrative placing blame on the woman). Not only his intentions but also even his actions are ultimately pure.

The context of the play, moreover, is ultimately the happier of the ones defined in the epics: it is a "*Rāmāyaṇa* world" more than that of the *Mahābhārata*. This is so not only in the general sense that the sage-renunciants whose guidance should be followed are so thoroughly represented both here in the drama and in the *Rāmāyaṇa*, though this is true, but also because one may generally expect the right actions of king, maiden, and subjects, barring the occasional slip-up, both here and in the *Rāmāyaṇa*. His—the king's—reign is righteous and effective; his follies are temporary slips. And Śakuntalā too is pure, her neglect of Durvāsas having been a momentary and unintended error.

[31] *Abhijñānaśākuntala* 5.9 (Kāle [1898] 1980: 168): *kiṃ tāvad vratinām upoḍhatapasāṃ vighnais tapo dūṣitam / dharmāraṇyacareṣu kenacid uta prāṇiṣv asacceṣṭitam | āhosvit prasavo mamāpacaritair viṣṭambhito vīrudhām / ity ārūḍhabahupratarkam aparicchedākulaṃ me manaḥ* ||. This verse is listed as 5.10 in Coulson. The translation is a slight modification of his.

So much more the force of Śakuntalā's lament, then, when Duṣyanta fails her. Her ring finger bare, a signet lost, she woefully laments, "Oh holy mother earth, give me to a chasm!," asking the earth to swallow her whole, just as Sītā did—and was.[32] Had she not lost the ring, after all, Duṣyanta would have recognized it, for it was his gift to her; and by recognizing it he would have remembered her for who she was and ever would be to him. The curse would have been immediately broken.

Without it, Duṣyanta will not welcome her as he should, despite being one who "fears to do wrong"; and he under the influence of the curse is beset with a moral dilemma: he must either accept what is presented as his duty and mercilessly send her off or accept into his palace the (pregnant) wife of another,[33] defiling her purity for her proper husband (since he believed that he was not him). But in the happy play of the drama a divine intervention can solve the dilemma:

> Śakuntalā bewailing her wretched fate,
> Had just flung up her arms and begun to weep—
> When all at once, from near the Nymphs' Pool, a flash of light
> shaped like a woman
> Seized hold of the girl and immediately vanished with her.[34]

The ramifications of Duṣyanta's (illusory) shortcomings are, it is true, real within the context of the play. He loses his beloved and his son for a time. But that time is short, as the sixth act quickly introduces a fisherman who found the ring. He is arrested, "caught" for the impossible coincidence of locating the lost signet in the belly of a fish, there having been no theft involved in Śakuntalā's loss of the ring, after all. Yes, even a transgression of this kind—that of petty crime—is illusory, and again the virtue of the king is guaranteed, he being responsible for the acts of his subjects.[35] The recovered ring restores

[32] Kāle [1898] 1980: 194: *bhaavadi vasuhe dehi me vivaraṃ* |. (*Chāyā*: *bhagavati vasudhe dehi me vivaram* |.)

[33] See *Abhijñānaśākuntala* 5.29 (Kāle [1898] 1980: 192): *mūdhaḥ syām aham eṣā vā vaden mithyeti saṃśaye* | *dāratyāgī bhavāmy āho parastrīsparśapāṃsulaḥ* ||.

[34] *Abhijñānaśākuntala* 5.30 (5.32 in Coulson) (Kāle [1898] 1980: 194): *sā nindantī svāni bhāgyāni bālā bāhūtkṣepaṃ kranditum ca pravṛttā* | *strīsaṃsthānaṃ cāpsaras tīrtham ārād utkṣipyaināṃ jyotir ekaṃ jagāma* ||. Translation that of Coulson.

[35] On the king's responsibility for his subjects' transgressions, see also Coulṣon's note, recorded in his footnote 33.

Duṣyanta's memory, as it was promised to do and as is a trope of Indian and Western narratives around jewelry more generally.[36]

It is here that a telling remark is let loose. Duṣyanta expresses his regret for forgetting the identity of his beloved, whom he remembers now but whose person he is yet to recover, and the *vidūṣaka* offers him an ironic recourse for his suffering: he suggests he will destroy "Love's arrow" by wrecking with a stick the mango blossom they see in front of them, which had evoked Duṣyanta's memory of Śakuntalā.[37] The king's reply is directed by the playwright to be delivered with a smile: "All right, I've seen your Brahmin power. But friend, where can I sit and rest my eyes among the vines that remind me of her beauty?"[38]

A trio of ironies distinguishes this passage, which evokes the habits of court life in the playwright's day, as well as those of the intended audience of the text. First, there is humor in the idiocy of the *vidūṣaka*, and this is the core of the dramatic effectiveness of the exchange: it is silly for Mādhavya to imagine he could set the king's mind at ease by attacking a plant, both because the act itself is ridiculous and because Duṣyanta wishes not to forget his beloved but to recover her, immediately in memory and ultimately in the flesh. The contrast between the type—the wise Brahmin—and the foolishness of the character on the stage explains the very humor of the *rôle* of the *vidūṣaka*, here exemplified perfectly. Second, there is irony in the fact that this Brahmin, explicitly addressed as such, here as ever in the play speaks the vernacular and not Sanskrit, a reversal of sorts that also plays on the contrast of the character type of the *vidūṣaka* against the normative understanding of Brahmins as wise, Sanskrit being the language of the learned elite.

Third and finally—and most importantly—the exchange quite literally evokes a notion that would have been familiar to all in the court and in the audience of the drama, and is precisely what induces the stage instruction, for the actor playing Duṣyanta to deliver his reply with a smile: as one sees in the *Rājataraṅgiṇī* and elsewhere, it was Brahmins who set themselves to drawing kings away from overindulgence in love, pleasure, gambling, the hunt—the good life that kings often lived at the cost of tending to their

[36] See Doniger 2017.

[37] See Kāle [1898] 1980: 216, where the *vidūṣaka* says the following: *ciṭhṭhadāva* | *imiṇā daṇḍakaṭhṭheṇa kandappabāṇaṃ nāsaissaṃ* |. (*Chāyā: tiṣṭha tāvat* | *anena daṇḍakāṣṭhena kandarpabāṇaṃ nāśayiṣyāmi* |.)

[38] Kāle [1898] 1980: 216: *bhavatu* | *dṛṣṭaṃ brahmavarcasam* | *sakhe kvopaviṣṭaḥ priyāyāḥ kiṃcid anukāriṇīṣu latāsu dṛṣṭiṃ vilobhayāmi* |.

responsibilities. This passage nods to this contemporaneous sociological fact, but it makes a mockery of it—what above all explains the humor of the exchange. The third irony, then, is that the play depicts the Brahmin's destruction of the pleasures that distract the king as a ridiculous act, because the drama promises pleasure without raising into question the possibility of success in the world. The idea of destroying the plant is funny because it is as unwanted and unnecessary as ending the drama midperformance would have been, because pleasure in this context is of no danger at all.

The Brahmins and sages here issue but illusory, only temporary, hinderances or adjustment to the king's whimsical will: the *vidūṣaka* seeks comfort, not the king's conformity to *dharma*. The challenge faced by Sītā is not burdened upon Śakuntalā, who lives with sages in her exile from her husband and not forcibly with another (demonic) king. (There is an ironic reversal to be found, then, in the dilemma Duṣyanta faces while pondering the choice to turn her away: Rāvaṇa kidnaps Sītā, but Duṣyanta harmlessly ponders sheltering *his own beloved*.) Most of all, Śakuntalā and Duṣyanta are destined to achieve a happy and lasting reunion. Śakuntalā, unlike Sītā, is not swallowed into the earth. *This* is precisely what protects her and guarantees her ultimate reunion with Duṣyanta: she is deemed in the seventh and last act to be unquestionably pure.

In the Sanskrit drama, the king's dreams are his realities, and his troubles are illusions. The impediments are ultimately insubstantial; the love that seems ephemeral is actually real. Before their ultimate reunion, Duṣyanta pines so deeply for his missing wife that he paints her portrait in such exquisite detail that a bee takes it for reality and harasses the painted Śakuntalā, just as another bee did the same in the flesh on Duṣyanta's first sight of her. The king, however, notices no hopeful echo of first encounters but merely fears the worst:

> Whether it was a dream, an illusion, a mental aberration,
> Or whether it simply exhausted all that was due me for past good
> deeds,
> I am quite certain all hope is gone—
> Over the precipice and beyond recall.[39]

[39] *Abhijñānaśākuntala* 6.10 (Kāle [1898] 1980: 220): *svapno nu māyā nu matibhramo nu kliṣṭaṃ nu tāvat phalam eva puṇyam | asaṃnivṛttyai tad atītam ete manorathā nāma taṭaprapātāḥ ||*. Translation Coulson's, though it is recorded there as verse 6.11.

The association Duṣyanta here makes with his past merits in action is apt, for the play ties both king and action in an inextricable and ultimately entirely fortuitous knot: Duṣyanta's lament is witnessed by Miśrakeśī, a nymph who is friends with Menakā, Śakuntalā's mother. She sees the portrait he painted of his beloved and thus can attest to Duṣyanta's sincerity in his love, as Hanumān could of Sītā's.

And next, business is again mixed with pleasure, but easily so: news of a shipwreck reaches the king. So too does news of a yet-to-be-born but already half-orphaned child, who is to inherit the estate of a merchant, one Dhanavṛddhi, his father, who drowned in the wreck. The king guarantees the inheritance will be transferred, as it is *dharmic* for a king to do, so the matter will soon be closed; but in the course of doing so he is reminded of his own loss, and he laments the fact that he himself has no heir, no son of his own—or so he thinks.

Miśrakeśī promises reward, however, and again love and pleasure, *kāma*, are to produce a productive result, *artha*, the ultimate fruit of love being a son to inherit the earth. The king will come to know as much, soon enough; but first the work of kingship again interferes, if ephemerally so: a spirit of a kind has kidnapped his Brahmin minister, the *vidūṣaka* Mādhavya, and it is the king's royal duty to guard against any transgression his subjects might enact. Duṣyanta's reputation and his *karma* as king are both suddenly again on the line: he must catch the criminal who acts with impunity in his kingdom. But again we watch the play happily combine work and pleasure, for to remedy the immediate crisis will also bring the king to his love. The pursuit of *dharma* directly results in the fruits of a desire, in *kāma*, and in the *Abhijñānaśākuntala* (as most everywhere in the Sanskrit narrative literatures) it is never the case that serving the needs of a Brahmin leads to sorrow.

The abductor, in the end, was none other than Mātali, the charioteer of Indra, who is there to bring Duṣyanta to a task, just as Rāma is induced by urgent circumstances to the job he is sent to earth to do, to kill the demon Rāvaṇa: Duṣyanta must slay demons whom Indra cannot kill. And the ruse with Mādhavya, who is well and safe? It was meant to anger Duṣyanta, to stir him out of his sorrows with fresh emotion. Like Rāma, Duṣyanta is called to protect against demons, but here his passions are called to the fore, precisely what Rāma is determined to control, in order to fulfill his royal duties. The drama lets the emotions flow; *dharma* and the happy rewards of human existence all are won by unchastened feeling, for, again, the

danger of an enemy marring a close member of the court, which he had not anticipated or guarded against—this slip, which normally would call into question his capacities as royal sovereign[40]—was in the end an illusion. We say it again: in the drama the king's dreams are his realities, and his troubles are illusions.

In the seventh and last act, our king flies on Indra's chariot over the countryside, having in the interval just slayed the demons. From this height he surveys the estates his heir would control, if only he had a son. At some point they land, though not quite: the chariot's wheels do not touch the ground, as Yudhiṣṭhira's did not, before he lied (a turn of events that Duṣyanta is destined never to suffer). They find a sage, Kaśyapa, who is buried, like Vālmīki, in an anthill. Waiting for an audience with him, they catch sight of a boy playing with a lion cub, a magnificent boy the king wishes were his own (as he will be: the king's dreams are realities). "He bears the birthmark of a universal emperor," the king, stunned, remarks.[41]

If the boy has all the qualities of the king, the king shares too in those of the child. First, his family name is Paurava, a patronymic of Duṣyanta's Puru clan. Of that clan relation Duṣyanta says this in the presence of the hermitage boy:

> "The Pauravas do, it is true, have just such a religious dedication:
> 'They choose as guardians of the world to spend
> Their earlier life in white-stuccoed palaces.
> But later the roots of trees become their home,
> Where only the vows of ascetics are observed.' "[42]

Also, his mother is related to a nymph—another good sign. Then the boy fawns when an attendant mentions the beauty of a *śakunta* bird, misunderstanding the Prakrit "*saunda-lāvaṇṇaṃ*" or "beauty of the bird" for

[40] Of the abduction, Duṣyanta laments: "No one can recognize from day to day / Even the errors committed through his own oversights. / Could a king therefore ever know in full / Who is behaving in what way among his subjects?" *Abhijñānaśākuntala* 6.26 (6.31 in Coulson): *ahany ahany ātmana eva tāvaj jñātuṃ pramādaskhalitaṃ na śakyam* | *prajāsu kaḥ ke pathā prayāti ity aśeṣato veditum asti śaktiḥ* ||. Translation Coulson's. N.B.: Of this passage Coulson 1981: 140 says the following: "In the strict Indian theory, a king was responsible for (and therefore liable to divine punishment for) all the misdeeds in his realm which he did not recognize and redress."

[41] See Kāle [1898] 1980: 268: *kathaṃ cakravartilakṣaṇam apy anena dhāryate* |.

[42] *Abhijñānaśākuntala* 7.20 (Kāle [1898] 1980: 272): *bhavaneṣu rasādhikeṣu pūrvaṃ kṣitirakṣārtham uśanti ye nivāsam* | *niyataikavratāni paścāt tarumūlāni gṛhībhavanti teṣām* ||. Translation Coulson's.

"*Saundalā-vaṇṇam*," "the color of Śakuntalā."[43] The pleasure of the imminent recognition gathers, as the certainty of the audience is affirmed in happily accumulating repetitions of proof.

The boy drops his amulet, which the king retrieves for him. Proof again—this time definitive!—for the amulet is designed to turn to a snake and bite any who touches it, save the boy's relatives; that this did not transpire proves they are kin. When he tells the boy they will go together to his mother, he replies defiantly, "Duṣyanta's my daddy, not you."[44]

Thus, all is clear. The certainty of progeny promises Duṣyanta's line will inherit the earth.

Finally, Duṣyanta sees his wife, and all remaining doubts are eliminated: it is her, and he recognizes her, no question. Most importantly, he *knows* she has been chaste:

> Dressed in grey garments,
> Face gaunt with fasting, hair worn in a single braid,
> Steadfastly true though I have been so cruel,
> She still observes the long vow of separation from me.[45]

She questions his identity, and he begs her to recognize him. But there can be no doubt in her, either, for the amulet clarifies he can only be who he is supposed to be. He falls at her feet—the happy ending the *Rāmāyaṇa* wants. She sees his ring and understands that he was caused to remember as it was promised he would. Kaśyapa declares that he knew of Durvāsas's curse, discovered in his meditations, and Śakuntalā is assured that her husband's wrongdoing was in fact an illusion. And Kaśyapa looks at each of them, husband, wife, and son, declaring:

> Here is Śakuntalā the virtuous wife,
> Here the fine son, and here Your Majesty;
> Faith, Wealth, and Performance—
> The three are most happily met together.[46]

[43] See Kāle [1898] 1980: 272 and 274. See also the note in Coulson 1981: 152.

[44] See Kāle [1898] 1980: 276: *mama kkhu tādo dussando* | *ṇa tumaṃ* |. (*Chāyā: mama khalu tāto duṣyantaḥ* | *na tvam* |.)

[45] *Abhijñānaśākuntala* 7.21 (Kāle [1898] 1980: 278): *vasane paridhūsare vasānā niyamakṣāmamukhī dhṛtaikaveṇiḥ* | *atiniṣkaruṇasya śuddhaśīlā mama dīrghaṃ virahavrataṃ bibharti* ||. Translation Coulson's.

[46] *Abhijñānaśākuntala* 7.29 (Kāle [1898] 1980: 288): *diṣṭyā śakuntalā sādhvī sadapatyam idaṃ bhavān* | *śraddhā vittaṃ vidhiś ceti tritayaṃ tat samāgatam* ||. Translation Coulson's.

Śraddhā, *vitta*, and *vidhi*; faith, wealth, and the proper performance of acts. Dreams come true in a Brahminical worldview; but here there's nothing of burden, only a happy reunion.

After the blessing by Kaśyapa the play closes with that Brahmin asking how else he could help the king, who declines further assistance, only wishing well on all, as follows:

> Let the monarch work for the good of his people.
> Let the utterance of those [Brahmins who are] mighty in their
>   learning be esteemed.
> And let Śiva the self-existent, in his infinite power,
> Extinguish forever the cycle of birth and death.[47]

King and Brahmin are again asked to stand together, for the sake of the kingdom, for the sake of salvation, with the aid of the gods.

All the error and illusion of the play were caused by a simple act, for blame is placed, again without marking the incident, on the *kṣatriya* woman, who, it must be said, is otherwise proven to be blameless: she made a Brahmin sage, Durvāsas, wait for her, though this was only a *Rāmāyaṇa*-like slip in her otherwise faultless conduct. And the illusions of the play that mar the principal characters are only temporary problems; they are ultimately unreal, resolvable and not intractable as real infidelity would have been, or real caste incompatibility, or the real consequence of infertility, namely, the loss of dynastic succession—or yet, real separation from one's beloved, as Rāma from Sītā at the end of the epic.

Wealth and royal prosperity—the prosperity of the kingdom—are produced as the fruits of pleasure, the pursuit of a beautiful maiden who impossibly was eligible for the king's pursuit. Pleasure, the king's frolicking in the garden, is aligned in the playful world of the drama with his pursuit of royal obligations, guarded as they are by Brahminical norms, but only in pleasant echoes in this dramatic work, to soften the hard edges that define *dharma* in the *Rāmāyaṇa*. Passion is here *unleashed* to the good, for the king's very wishes fulfill the needs of the kingdom and serve his royal obligations.

[47] *Abhijñānaśākuntala* 7.35 (Kāle [1898] 1980: 296): *pravartatāṃ prakṛtihitāya pārthivaḥ / sarasvatī śrutamahatāṃ mahīyatām* | *mamāpi ca kṣapayatu nīlalohitaḥ / punarbhavaṃ parigataśaktir ātmabhūḥ* ||. Translation a modification of Coulson's.

The parallels with the *Rāmāyaṇa*, then, are pervasive. We are witness here to a successful king who does the right things—he protects the sages in the forest,[48] kills demons who mar the countryside,[49] listens to the Brahmins he serves, and tends lovingly to the needs of his kingdom and subjects—but the utter dispassion Rāma showed Sītā in Vālmīki's text proves to be transient and illusory in the drama. Kingship is easier on Duṣyanta than it was on Rāma, ultimately easier too on Śakuntalā than it was on Sītā. This escape from the difficulties of living *dharma*, represented so palpably and emotionally through *śoka*, sorrow and seriousness, in the *Rāmāyaṇa*, is transmuted into illusory sorrow and lasting joy in Kālidāsa's *Abhijñānaśākuntala*. And all this without the play questioning the implicit Brahminical values maintained in both works—those of honoring a Brahmin, a god, or a sage, that of living up to one's royal obligations. The king is set to have his fun and live in emotion, because fun is to the good, for him, his subjects, and the kingdom—Brahminical values, but in the context of cavorting with a Brahmin uninterested in maintaining Brahminical mores. The king can "have his cake and eat it too," for the virtue ethic of the Sanskrit narrative literatures requires no noticeable restraint on the part of the king. The world of the drama is a happy illusion, indeed.

Ratnāvalī

The dramas can offer escapist delight in other ways as well. Here in the second of the two dramatic works examined in the present chapter, for example, we again find sympathy for the same alliance of Brahminical and royal interests, but this time embodied in the covert actions of a clever chief minister of the king, who serves his patron behind the scenes, such that all his desires can be fulfilled in the course of leading his kingdom to prosper—and all while he plays carefree with foolish friends, chasing a beautiful woman.

After a string of benedictory verses read out in Kauśāmbī, the capital city of the empire of King Udayana, the stage director (*sūtradhāra*) appears to declare that it was the king himself, Harṣa, who composed the play in question and fashioned for it a unique plot,[50] which will be performed around the

[48] At the least at act 2, around verse 16.

[49] Duṣyanta does this, in particular, at the interval between the sixth and seventh acts.

[50] Doniger 2006: 74: . . . *asmatsvāminā śrīharṣadevenāpūrvavasturacanālaṃkṛtā ratnāvalī nāma nāṭikā kṛtā* |.

time of the Spring Festival (*vasantotsava*), today's Holi. The cause of the occasion is in part one of audience: various vassal kings had heard of the drama but had yet to see it performed. The play's preamble, then, presents the work and the event of its performance in realistic terms: the *sūtradhāra*'s introduction suggests the spectacle will draw a court audience to a drama written by a king. Reality frames a play that, as we shall soon see, is deeply engrossed with the mirrors of illusion: all of kingship can be made akin to the fleeting joy of the amorous Spring Festival.

Echoing (among other texts) the *Kathāsaritsāgara*, where elements of the plot of this *nāṭikā* have also appeared,[51] the interlude before the first act expresses a familiar theme: Yaugandharāyaṇa, King Udayana's minister, delights in events as they are about to transpire. He discovers that the princess of Siṃhala, named Ratnāvalī, was shipwrecked and is to be brought to Udayana's kingdom by a friendly merchant, who had recognized her royal identity by the qualities of her necklace. Yaugandharāyaṇa has her in mind for a strategic marriage with the king he serves. The outer frame of the play's narrative thus explicitly depicts a faithful minister working in harmony with the king's interests, the former guiding the latter to dominion over the earth by engineering a fortuitous marriage. Pleasure yet again can bring with it material gain (*artha*), the ultimate concern of a king who properly serves *dharma*; and yet again the minister will aid in that quest.

At the beginning of act 1, the performance of the play is justified as a happy interlude, an escape from regular work. The spectacle affords well-earned pleasure and delight, because the kingdom is safely controlled, this in turn because the king has upheld his *dharmic* obligations.

> The kingdom has conquered all its enemies;
> the entire burden of the country
> has been placed on a worthy minister;
> my subjects are well protected
> to the point of indulgence,
> and their troubles, without exception,
> have been remedied.
> I have Pradyota's daughter, the season of Spring,
> and you.

[51] See Doniger 2006: 23–28. A similar story is also told, for example, in Bhāsa's *Svapnavāsavadatta*, about which see Doniger 2006: 29–33.

Therefore let Kāma have just the name
as much as he desires,
but I rather think that this great festival is mine.[52]

The success of the kingdom is paramount and is guaranteed by the king's close connection with his minister—with royal assent to his aid, as is witnessed by the king's own testimony.

The connection is humorously reinforced by the *vidūṣaka*'s response to the king's righteous verse, and he was surely to be taken in jest given that he, the foolish, Prakrit-speaking clown, could never have had a constructive hand in governing the kingdom: "You're right, my friend. But I know that this Festival of Passion is neither yours nor the god Kāma's, but belongs to me, the one Brahmin [minister] whom my dear friend has spoken of in this way."[53] The *real* minister, Yaugandharāyaṇa, shall work from behind the scenes and off the stage, while the dramatic performance dwells on the display that is the king in the garden—like scenes from Versailles—at play with his lackadaisical Brahminical friend.

He, the *vidūṣaka*, carries on: "Look at the glory of the Festival of Passion, which has excited the desire of the men of the city; they're dancing, while passionate women, intoxicated by wine, spray water on them from the syringes made of horn that they've taken up in their hands."[54] And a powder that flies through the air, as the king's next verse suggests, "makes Kauśāmbī seem solid yellow, / as if its people were plated with liquid gold."[55] And "when vermilion powder falls into it [i.e., the courtyard where people play] / from the cheeks of passionate, / unrestrained women, / peoples' footprints make red as rouge the paved and inlaid floor before us."[56]

Hearing the queen will go there to worship Kāma, and that she needs her husband to join her in order to do so, the king and the *vidūṣaka* head to the

[52] *Ratnāvalī* 1.9 (Doniger 2006: 88): *rājyaṃ nirjitaśatru yogyasacive nyastaḥ samasto bharaḥ / samyakpālanalālitāḥ praśamitāśeṣopasargāḥ prajāḥ | pradyotasya sutā vasantasamayas tvaṃ ceti nāmrā dhṛtiṃ / kāmaḥ kāmam upaitv ayaṃ punar mama manye mahān utsavaḥ ||*. Translation Doniger's.

[53] *Ratnāvalī* 1.40 (Doniger 2006: 88): *bho vaassa evvaṃ ṇṇedam | ahaṃ puṇa jāṇāmi ṇa bhavado ṇa kāmadeassa, mama jjeva ekassa bamhaṇassa aaṃ maaṇamahūsavo jassa piavaasseṇa evaṃ mantīadi |*. (*Chāyā: bho vayasya | evaṃ nv idam | ahaṃ punar jānāmi | na bhavato na kāmadevasya mamaivaikasya brāhmaṇasyāyaṃ madanamahotsavaḥ yasya priyavayasyenaivaṃ mantryate |*.) Translation Doniger's.

[54] *Ratnāvalī* 1.40 (translation of Doniger 2006: 89).

[55] *Ratnāvalī*, 1.10d (Doniger 2006: 90): *kauśāmbī śātakumbhadravakhacitajanevaikapītā vibhāti ||*. Translation Doniger's.

[56] *Ratnāvalī* 1.11cd (Doniger 2006: 90): *uddāmapramadākapolanipatatsindūrarāgāruṇaiḥ / saindūrīkriyate janena caraṇanyāsaiḥ puraḥ kuṭṭimam ||*. Translation Doniger's.

Garden of Nectar (*makarandodyāna*). In come the women, Vāsavadattā, Kāñcanamālā, and Sāgarikā (who was rescued from the shipwreck), the sounding of their anklet bells mistaken by the king for the humming of bees. In the bacchanal of the Spring Festival, in the Garden of Nectar, we anticipate what is live in the air: love in the prosperous kingdom is palpably present in their mutual company.

The queen quickly recognizes that her husband is bound to notice Sāgarikā—her beauty, that is—and so she sends her away on a pretense, then watches her in hiding to see how she worships the God of Love. She is curious as to whether Sāgarikā's devotions will match the practices of her native land. The king too turns up but also remains hiding, watching the queen to see what she will do. To this point Sāgarikā and Udayana have yet to set eyes on one another, but of course they will. Spies abound in this playful court intrigue.

She sees him first, when he joins the queen to complete the worship of Kāma at the foot of an *aśoka* tree. Sāgarikā in fact mistakes Udayana for Kāma himself![57] And then she laments the loss of occasion, prior to the moment, to have set eyes on the man to whom her father had promised her.[58] Needless to say, it is love at first sight. By sunset, however, her love is yet to be reciprocated: the king and queen depart before he glimpses the young maiden of the seas.

Act 2 opens, after the interlude, onto Sāgarikā swooning in a loving despair. She has seen but cannot reach her beloved. To have him after a fashion, she paints his portrait, but to disguise her love she depicts him as she first saw him: in the image of Kāma himself. Susaṃgatā, her companion and the queen's lady in waiting, sees her painting and adds next to him a portrait of Rati, Kāma's wife; and like Sāgarikā's of Kāma, she paints Rati in the likeness of a real person—Sāgarikā herself. The lover's fantasy is made as if real, would-be lovers depicted as a well-known couple, Kāma and Rati, husband and wife.

Each of the two girlfriends sees through the other's ruse, of course, and Sāgarikā swears Susaṃgatā to secrecy. But a mynah bird hears her confessions of love, and they fear he will repeat them by rote. The parroted words, though meaningless to the mynah bird, threaten to convey the truth with a mirage of linguistic understanding. Deceptions and illusions thus

[57] Doniger 2006: 110.

[58] She does of course subsequently come to recognize his true identity, for which see Doniger 2006: 112.

continue to delight, and what is an illusion is made to be real: it threatens with an ephemeral but palpable danger, though not assassination or usurpation but only an angry wife.

The play continues. A monkey arrives and disturbs the garden, and the two women flee, leaving behind their painting but not before glimpsing the mynah bird freed from its cage by the monkey. Inevitably enough, the mynah repeats the secret of the portrait and this within earshot of Udayana and his *vidūṣaka*; and although they have yet to see the image and thus don't yet know it is the king who is painted in for Kāma, they quickly grasp the gist of the scheme just revealed.[59]

Soon after, they find the painting, and all is revealed. In the same moment Susaṃgatā and Sāgarikā return to collect their art, having tried before in vain to recover the bird. Hearing the voice of the *vidūṣaka* as they approach, they realize the king is near, and so they conceal themselves and watch them from hiding—more spying, disguise, another hidden intent, but in the Sanskrit drama it is all in fun. In a manner similar to what was portrayed in the *Abhijñānaśākuntala*, the men observe that the painter showed her passion for the person she painted, teardrops from Sāgarikā's eyes appearing like sweat on the body of the king-depicted-as-Kāma, as if smeared off the palm of her hand.[60] Sāgarikā in turn comes to know of the king's passion for her, because she spies on him as he expresses it. He, in turn, also infers hers from the pressed lotus leaves that cover her bed: they show the impression of her slender body and large breasts, and—more to the point—reveal her stirring discomfort, no doubt for the reason of her theretofore unfulfilled love, of her beloved whom she figured on canvas.[61] The subtle inferences described in the *Arthaśāstra*—royal discernment used in the audience hall to judge the honesty of plaintiffs, ever used as well in the palace to detect the dangers of deceit—here are put to happier use.

[59] Indeed, the king divines it perfectly (*Ratnāvalī* 2.70, Doniger 2006: 140): *vayasyaivaṃ tarkayāmi | kayāpi hṛdayavallabho 'nurāgād ālikhya kāmadevavyapadeśena sakhī purato 'pahnutaḥ | tat sakhyāpi pratyabhijñāya vaidagdhyād asāv api tatraiva rativyapadeśenālikhiteti* |. "My friend, this is what I deduce. Some woman sketched the darling of her heart, because she was in love with him, and then passed him off in front of her friend under the pretext that it was the god Kāma. But that friend was worldly enough to see through this trick and sketched her, too, in that picture, under the pretext of Rati." Translation Doniger's.

[60] See *Ratnāvalī* 2.130 (Doniger 2006: 152): *bhāti patito likhantyās / tasyā bāṣpāmbuśīkarakaṇāughaḥ | svedodgama iva karatala- / saṃsparśād eṣa me vapuṣi* ||. "The flood of spraying tear-drops / that fell from her as she sketched / seems like sweat breaking out on my body / from the touch of the palm of her hand." Translation Doniger's.

[61] See *Ratnāvalī* around 2.135 (Doniger 2006: 152).

Susaṃgatā emerges from hiding to collect the painting and threatens to tell the queen of the matter, so the *vidūṣaka* coaxes the king to bribe her silence with a gift of earrings. But this is in jest, and she brings the king to Sāgarikā. Time, however, proves short. Aside the chiding of Susaṃgatā, which mirrors the perennial, playful dialogue of the king and the *vidūṣaka*, Queen Vāsavadattā soon appears to inspect the jasmine flowers that the king under the guidance of a visiting horticultural master had learned to cultivate. And so Udayana's partner in crime, the *vidūṣaka*, hides the painting from the queen.

Kāñcanamālā, the queen's attendant, nevertheless notices it after the *vidūṣaka*, always the fool, drops the incriminating art.[62] The queen immediately recognizes both her husband and Sāgarikā, whom (we remember) she had wished to keep from the king. Concealing her sadness—that her husband found a new (younger) lover (to be)—she departs the scene on the excuse of a headache. Of course, all of this has to be explained to the *vidūṣaka*, Vasantaka, who could not divine her true, and obvious—and predictable—feelings. No true minister could possibly have failed so plainly to read the signs of human intention; but the king in the garden needs a companion, not counsel—this ironically being precisely what renders these dramas as counsel to the king, to trust a Brahmin of service behind the scenes, so as to find and cherish a moment of reprieve.

The interlude before act 3 sets the heart of the play's course of action. The queen is having none of the affair, and so she sequesters Sāgarikā; but, of course, kings just want to have fun. And so Vasantaka concocts a plan with the help of Madanikā, a palace maid: she was left in charge of Sāgarikā and was given some clothes of the queen's as payment for the same. They connive to dress Sāgarikā in those clothes, so she can escape her lock-up in disguise and meet the pining king.

But the plan of the interlude does not come off in practice so easily in the third act: deception colludes with illusion anew. The king, led by the *vidūṣaka* Vasantaka, awaits Sāgarikā, who is dressed as the queen and accompanied by Susaṃgatā (herself dressed as Kāñcanamālā). But then in comes Queen Vāsavadattā herself, accompanied by Kāñcanamālā herself.

[62] See the stage instructions after *Ratnāvalī* 2.200 (Doniger 2006: 166): *iti bāhū prasārya nṛtyati* | *nṛtyataḥ kakṣāntarāt phalakaḥ patati* | *rājāpavārya vidūṣakam aṅgulyā tarjayati* |. "As he [the *vidūṣaka*] says this [i.e., 'we've won'], he stretches out his two arms and dances, and as he dances the painting board falls from under his arm. The King, aside, threatens the Jester with his finger." Translation Doniger's.

Vasantaka is fooled—of course!—believing Vāsavadattā is not herself but is Sāgarikā dressed as her. So he directs her to the *rendez-vous* in the picture gallery, her true identity hidden by way of being mistaken for Sāgarikā in disguise as she, the queen. In this doubly false appearance she meets her husband, who addresses her in adulterous words:

> Your face is the moon with its cool rays,
>   your eyes two blue lotuses,
> your hands are like day-lotuses, your two thighs
>   like the inner surface of plantains,
> and your arms like lotus filaments.
> All of your limbs are a source of delight.
> But my limbs are wasting away in the fever
>   of [Kāma,] the god who has no limbs.
> So come, come, embrace me fiercely,
>   without hesitation, and soothe them.[63]

His poetic courting proves to be too much, and the first time Vāsavadattā speaks she unveils her disguise in a burst of accusation: "My husband, I am truly Sāgarikā. For your heart is so entirely carried away by Sāgarikā that you see *everything* as made of Sāgarikā."[64] His desire rendered the illusion as if real: the woman, disguised only inasmuch as she looks the part of the person disguised as her, is rendered not herself, but the woman who took on her likeness as a disguise. The mistaken identities reflect dizzyingly inward, like two mirrors facing one another.

Vāsavadattā departs without relenting; the king stands unforgiven. He thus fears she will in depression choose to take her own life. And Vasantaka the *vidūṣaka* is as always comically unable to grasp the situation: he worries not for the queen, but for Sāgarikā's well-being.

Just then enters Sāgarikā herself, but dressed as Vāsavadattā. Distraught that the queen had come to know her intended transgression, she prepares to hang herself. Vasantaka and the king quickly intervene, but they do

[63] *Ratnāvalī* 3.11 (Doniger 2006: 198): *śītāṃśur mukham utpale tava dṛśau padmānukārau karau / rambhāgarbhanibhaṃ tathoruyugalaṃ bāhū mṛṇālopamau | ity āhlādakarākhilāṅgi rabhasān niḥśaṅkam āliṅgya mām / aṅgāni tvam anaṅgatāpavidhurāṇy ehy ehi nirvāpaya* ||. Translation a slight modification of Doniger's.

[64] *Ratnāvalī* 3.98 (Doniger 2006: 202): *ajjautta saccaṃ evva ahaṃ sāariā | tumaṃ uṇa sāariokkhitahiao savvaṃ evva sāariāmaaṃ pekkhasi* |. (*Chāyā*: *āryaputra satyam evāhaṃ sāgarikā | tvaṃ punaḥ sāgarikotkṣiptahṛdayaḥ sarvam eva sāgarikāmayam prekṣase* |.) Translation Doniger's.

so thinking Sāgarikā is in fact Vāsavadattā herself, despondent over her husband's adulterous love. Sāgarikā is rescued while appearing in disguise; illusion—her false appearance as the queen whom the king had wronged—motivates the king to save her life.

And then Udayana recognizes her and rescues her; and then Vāsavadattā returns with Kāñcanamālā, because she, the queen, wishes finally to reconcile with her husband. But she spies her husband with Sāgarikā, still dressed as the queen herself, and Vāsavadattā loses her sense of conciliation. Misdirection again, for Udayana and Vasantaka were only with Sāgarikā because they thought they were saving the queen. A conciliatory intention (for once) gone wrong, the result being that Vāsavadattā has Sāgarikā bound and taken away, and the *vidūṣaka* Vasantaka too. King Udayana is left only the option of seeking to appease his angry wife, who directs her prisoners to be taken to the palace.

Prelude to act 4. Sāgarikā despairs for her life, and so gives her jewel necklace to Susaṃgatā, so that she could gift it to a Brahmin, which is of course a *dharmic* and merit-making act.[65] The queen, the audience is told, will in the meantime have Sāgarikā taken away to Ujjayinī. Susaṃgatā then spots Vasantaka, just then let free by the queen, and she approaches to give him the necklace. He is, after all, a Brahmin, fool though he may be.

The play's core disguise is revealed, then, to these characters, at least in part. Vasantaka says, "Indeed, this ornament, which would be impossible for any ordinary person to get, tells the story—that [Sāgarikā] must come from an altogether great family. Susaṃgatā, where is my dear friend now?"[66] That is, Vasantaka asks for the king. Perhaps a moment of good counsel is in the cards for him, after all, for any good minister would inform his king of the presence of a princess in the court. And so Vasantaka sets himself to finding Udayana to share what he, with Susaṃgatā, had divined. Sāgarikā is no mere beauty, though of course she is that as well. Vasantaka can happily report that Udayana's amorous emotions offer more than the usual temptations; they promise to bring the wealth of a royal alliance as well.

Thus comes this *nāṭikā*'s fourth and final act. It begins with Udayana relieved that he had finally managed to appease the queen, leaving him only

[65] See, e.g., Brick 2015 and Brick 2018.

[66] *Ratnāvalī* 4.20 (Doniger 2006: 226): *ṇaṃ kahidaṃ jjeva sāmaṇṇajaṇadullaheṇa imiṇā paricchadeṇa savvahā mahākulappasūdāe tāe hodavvaṃ tti | susaṃgade piavaasso dāṇiṃ kahiṃ |*. (*Chāyā*: *nanu kathitam eva sāmānyajanadurlabhenānena paricchadena sarvathā mahākulaprasūtayā tayā bhavitavyam iti | susaṃgate priyavayasya idānīṃ kutra |*.) Translation Doniger's.

to worry for his would-be beloved, Sāgarikā. The *vidūṣaka* shares that the queen has sent her to Ujjayinī. She was not executed, after all—and as he had thought. And he dons the necklace on Udayana's command, this to remind him of his exiled beloved.

But then business intervenes. The king, who has indulged the part of the playboy across every scene of the drama, suddenly is presented with work: he must greet Vijayavarman, the nephew of Rumaṇvat, the king's commander-in-chief. Vijayavarman arrives to share good news, that the king of Kosala had been subdued. Indeed, it transpires that Rumaṇvat himself had slain the enemy "with a hundred arrows" (*śaraśata*).[67]

And then Kāñcanamālā appears, bringing with her Sarvasiddhi, a magician (*aindrajālika*) from Ujjayinī, whom the queen thought should see the king, and he puts into verse the key to the drama, which is to know one is trapped in the play of illusion.

> "Bow to the feet of Indra,
> whose name is closely bound up
> in the very name of magic, 'the Net of Indra,'
> and of Śambara, whose fame in illusion is
> well-established."[68]

For magic can produce anything:

> "This is my promise: Whatever you wish
> in your heart to see
> I will show you, by the power of my teacher's
> *mantra*."[69]

Echoes again of the *Kathāsaritsāgara*, mantric causation and with it a faint echo of tantric power. And the magician does not disappoint: he begins by displaying in the sky all the gods. But Vasantaka scolds him, telling him that

[67] *Ratnāvalī* 4.6 (Doniger 2006: 240).

[68] *Ratnāvalī* 4.7 (Doniger 2006: 242): *paṇamaha calaṇa indassa indajālaapiṇaddhaṇāmassa* | *taha jjevva saṃbarassa māāsupariṭṭhidajasassa* ||. (*Chāyā: praṇamata caraṇāv indrasyendrajālakapinaddhanāmnaḥ* | *tathaiva śambarasya māyāsupratiṣṭhitayaśasah* ||.) Translation Doniger's.

[69] *Ratnāvalī* 4.9: *majja paiṇṇā eṣā jaṃ jaṃ hiadeṇa ihasi saṃdaṭṭum* | *taṃ taṃ daṃsemi ahaṃ guruṇo mantappabhāveṇa* ||. (*Chāyā: mama pratijñaiṣā yad yad hṛdayenehase saṃdraṣṭum* | *tat tad darśayāmy ahaṃ guror mantraprabhāveṇa* ||.) Translation Doniger's.

if he really wishes to satisfy the king, he should show him Sāgarikā. The *vidūṣaka* miraculously offers a moment of lucidity, if with a slanted sarcasm!

But the magic show is interrupted, again so the king may tend to the business of the state. A minister of Vikramabāhu, the king of Siṃhala, has appeared. Named Vasubhūti, he has news, and on being led to see the king—for him a highly anticipated privilege—he notices the necklace around Vasantaka's neck and announces his recognition of it to Bābhravya, the attendant of Udayana who led him in. But then he hesitates in his judgment, because any great royal palace is stocked with jewelry, and it is possible to confuse one item for another.

Focus returns to the matter to hand: he had come to the king to share some sad news. Vikramabāhu's daughter was lost at sea, this after having been promised to Udayana on the (false) understanding that his first wife, Vāsavadattā, had died in a fire. This news saddens Vāsavadattā—not the false story of her demise, which she passes off with a sarcastic remark, but that of the loss of her "sister,"[70] Ratnāvalī, by marriage to whom her husband would have won a powerful alliance.

Precisely in that moment, a great fire erupts, this in the women's quarters, scorching the palace grounds! It inspires an irrational fear in the king, who worries that Vāsavadattā is burned up, even as she stands just beside him. Again, emotion serves the good, because it directly reveals his care for her, which is music to her ears. She too is concerned with the fire, but her lament is not for what threatens her own belongings or well-being, as her emotional and confused husband had thought, but for Sāgarikā, whom she had chained down in the women's quarters—now with regret for her cruelty in doing just that. Again, the (illusory) calamity they see unleashes helpful emotion: Vāsavadattā softens on Sāgarikā while simultaneously seeing her husband's softness for her. Illusion and misdirection are put not to dangerous deceit, as in the "real world," but to good use.

Udayana heroically rushes into the fire to save the woman he loves, and Vāsavadattā, miserable for her husband's valiant but sorrowful heroism, chooses, in an echo of the *satī*, to follow him in, as does—comically, this time, it seems—the *vidūṣaka*, Vasantaka. Then follows Vasubhūti, Vikramabāhu's emissary, and following him Bābhravya, Udayana's attendant. Humor marches into the scene: what was the king's heroic foolishness, followed by a

[70] On use of this appellation, "sister," see Doniger 2006: 491–492, note at 4.150.

satī-like concern for her husband, becomes a comical serial pursuit, one fool rushing after another, stumbling into the fires.

Udayana soon locates Sāgarikā—bound in chains—who finds new hope for life on seeing him and asks him to save her. But all of a sudden, the fire is gone! Vāsavadattā rejoices that her husband is not hurt. And they quickly divine the illusion: the fire was the magician's last trick. And with it comes the play's resolution.

It is asked wherefrom this lady has come, and the queen responds that the minister, Yaugandharāyaṇa, handed her over for safekeeping after she nearly perished at sea. Vasubhūti, the visiting minister, then addresses her by name, as Ratnāvalī, decisively removing any veil of false identity. All the facts are out, and the king exclaims, "Why, she is the daughter of Vikramabāhu, the king of Siṃhala, and he has an exalted lineage."[71]

All that is to be finally resolved are not events but emotions. Sāgarikā regrets her transgression against the queen. Queen Vāsavadattā reciprocates by welcoming her, herself regretting her own fit of anger, as well as her inability quickly to play her role and forgive the king.[72] She wishes to blame Yaugandharāyaṇa for her transgression—that of jailing the princess Ratnāvalī in chains—this for his not having revealed to her the maiden's true identity. Yaugandharāyaṇa, in turn, regrets moving Queen Vāsavadattā to a distance from the king, facilitating thereby Udayana's plan to get together with another wife (*kalatrasaṃghaṭanā*).[73] But what else was he to do, he laments, for it is the duty of a minister to serve his king in this manner: "Such is the vow of devotion to one's master that it will not swerve even for people who deserve the greatest respect."[74] Ministers must help kings, even when their wishes are passions, their intentions indulgences. In the drama, the king is freed to play and this by the aid of his Brahminical counselor.

Soon though, this minister, a sort of Wizard of Oz, reveals his entire plot, for the entire series of events experienced in the play was structured by his conniving. A seer predicted that whoever took Ratnāvalī's hand in marriage would conquer the entire universe, but Ratnāvalī's father would not give his daughter to Udayana on account of wanting to avoid

[71] See Doniger 2006: 270: *katham, udāttavaṃśasya siṃhaleśvarasya vikramabāhor ātmajeyam.* Translation Doniger's.

[72] Indeed, it is this imperative in the third act at 3.110 that leaves Udayana unable to fathom that his wife could depart without "relent" (*prasāda*).

[73] See *Ratnāvalī* 4.20.

[74] *Ratnāvalī* 4.225 (Doniger 2006: 272): *īdṛśam atyantamānanīyeṣv api niranurodhavṛtti svāmibhaktivratam* |. Translation Doniger's.

distressing Vāsavadattā. Emotions are dangerous, after all; but they can be soothed by benevolent Brahminical cunning. And so Yaugandharāyaṇa invented the story of her demise in the fire, and Ratnāvalī was betrothed. And then Yaugandharāyaṇa handed her over to the queen's harem so the king might see her. The fire too, from the magician, was meant to create a reason for the king to find the princess, and for Vasubhūti to confirm her true identity.

Of course, it works: the queen, her sentiments tempered by the near miss from fiery death (her husband's, Sāgarikā's, and her own), asks that Udayana care for Sāgarikā, since she will be far from her family. Yaugandharāyaṇa then inquires as to how he could otherwise serve his king, who replies there is nothing left to do:

> "Vikramabāhu is now my second self.
> I have won Sāgarikā,
> the very essence of all that there is
> on the surface of the earth,
> *and the means of gaining the earth*
> *bounded by the ocean.*
> The queen is pleased because she's gotten a sister.
> I've conquered Kosala. And as long as you,
> a bull among ministers,
> are there, what could I long for that I do not have?"[75]

Emotion and Illusion

The predominant concern of the *Ratnāvalī* is thus emphasized in the play's conclusion: there is inestimable value in a good relationship between king and minister. We here see recast the core narrative trope of the *Kathāsaritsāgara*, evoked by way of the drama's reference to the characters of the outer frame of that story—King Udayana and Yaugandharāyaṇa, his minister—such intertextuality being a well-known desideratum of dramatic

[75] *Ratnāvalī* 4.21 (Doniger 2006: 278): *nīto vikramabāhur ātmasamatāṃ prāpteyam urvītale / sāraṃ sāgarikā sasāgaramahī prāpty eka hetuḥ priyā | devī prītim upāgatā ca bhaginīlābhāj jitaḥ kosalāḥ / kiṃ nāsti tvayi saty amātyavṛṣabhe yasmai karomi spṛhām* ||. Translation Doniger's. Emphasis mine.

works.[76] Also present in Udayana's summation is the notion, so common in the narratives that entertain, that pleasure (*kāma*)—love—can secure the wealth (*artha*) of kingdoms. Sāgarikā is the means to win the whole earth and to preserve *dharma* there in the form of righteous political rule.

Two other major themes also define the drama. First, as noted extensively, is that of the problem and delight of illusion and the ways of navigating the same, which has been carefully examined by Doniger in the introduction to her translation of the play. Indeed, her analysis has closely informed my own.[77] Second is the simple power of emotion. Both themes are of a provenance that is rooted in the genre in question, as we have argued, already; the play is evidently self-conscious of the abiding presence of both. What, then, are we to make of this pairing *by a playwright who also is a king*—a drama that makes an explicit play on emotions with the deployment of illusion?

Against the reality that misperception was generally speaking dangerous and presented reason for caution among kings, the drama here rather depicts it as a minister's principal tool in dealing with the royal sovereign. Yaugandharāyaṇa deploys deception to guarantee the success of the king he serves, not, as was ever possible in the royal courts of South Asia's premodernity, to threaten his suzerainty or even his life. The dramatic effects of illusion—disguises and the misidentifications of the characters in disguise—rather delight the audience with a comedy of errors.

So too the web of crossed emotions and desires, pursued with false identities and concealments, which could ruin a king in the "real world," are offered as delights, not impediments to the security and prosperity of the kingdom and the safety and well-being of the king. Indeed, as with the *Abhijñānaśākuntala*, it is the king's desire that leads to his reward. No mention of addiction; no fear of distraction from his duties; no danger in cavorting with a foolish minister, the *vidūṣaka*. The drama sidesteps the dangers of vice; it unravels any residual hurt feelings. Udayana may inherit the earth through marriage and yet keep his first wife harmoniously. Here, then, we have a drama written by a king, its story one of a king playing carefree, with—because he has—a talented minister safely directing events from behind the drama onstage. This drama is the king's happy dream, an illusion indeed.

[76] Thus, for example and as is well known, Daṇḍin says this of the *mahākāvya* at *Kāvyādarśa* 1.15ab: *itihāsakathodbhūtam itarad vā sadāśrayam* |. "It [the *mahākāvya*] arises from Itihāsa, Kathā, or elsewhere [i.e., from other works] whose basis is true."

[77] See, esp., Doniger 2006: 44–47.

A Counterpoise

The Sanskrit drama thus offers a happy escape. And so it may here be useful to look at an opposing view offered in yet another literary work, albeit a poem, not a play. The item in question is the *Kuṭṭanīmata* of Dāmodaragupta, recently rendered in a refreshing English translation by Csaba Dezső and Dominic Goodall.[78] The text and its author are of a Kashmirian provenance: Dāmodaragupta is mentioned as a minister (*dhīsaciva*) of King Jayāpīḍa in Kalhaṇa's *Rājataraṅgiṇī*.[79] The text offers as a frame story the parable of a woman of the night seeking counsel from an elderly bawd to better know the ways of her profession. Mālatī is said to be very beautiful, young, and early in her work in the trade (verse 18). She lived in Benares,[80] when she by chance hears a verse one day uttered by some passerby:

> "The Loveliness of youth breeds pride,
> Harlots! Cast it far aside:
> Diligently learn the arts
> With which to inveigle lovers' hearts."[81]

Inspired by this, she visits the experienced "madam," Vikarālā, who is depicted as past her prime: "her jutting teeth were sparse, her jaw was sunk, her nose-tip broad and flat—projecting nipples, withered breasts—and skin hung loose from her body."[82] How could the beautiful Mālatī profit from the advice of this old hag, the poem implicitly asks?

The counsel given is offered by way of a pair of stories set into this frame narrative, an emboxing of stories that mirrors the practice more heavily and intricately used in both the *Pañcatantra* and the *Kathāsaritsāgara*, but this while elaborating a narrative of romantic intrigue that is more easily associable with the Sanskrit dramas. Vikarālā conveys both these stories in a serial fashion, which respectively furnish positive and negative examples of how to

[78] Dezső and Goodall 2012.

[79] See *Rājataraṅgiṇī* (RT) 4.496. Cf. Bronner 2013: 167–169. See also the appendix to Chapter 3 of the present volume.

[80] See the description of Mālatī, from head to toe, found in *Kuṭṭanīmata*, verses 44–57.

[81] *Kuṭṭanīmata* 23: *yauvanasaundaryamadaṃ dūreṇāpāsya vāravaṇitābhiḥ* | *yatnena veditavyāḥ kāmukahṛdayārjanopāyāḥ* ||. Translation that of Dezső and Goodall.

[82] *Kuṭṭanīmata* 27: *atha viralonnatadaśanāṃ nimnahanuṃ sthūlacipiṭanāsāgrām* | *ulbaṇacūcukalakṣitaśuṣkakucasthānaśithilakṛttitanum* ||. Translation that of Dezső and Goodall.

engage the work of a courtesan. With them she offers didactic instruction to Mālatī in order to counsel her in the ways of their chosen profession.

The first is the sad story of Hāralatā, who foolishly falls in love with the son of a Brahmin named Sundarasena. It is love at first sight: on glimpsing him, traveling with his companion Guṇapālita on Mount Abū (verses 176*ff.*), she is lost in love. Hāralatā, like Mālatī, is beautiful, and Sundarasena falls for her on their first meeting (see verses 258–262 and following). She swoons in equal portion for him, which prompts Hāralatā's friend, Śaśiprabhā, to offer her prudent, cautionary advice:

> "Hāralatā, ah please restrain
> This outburst caused by him whose form
> Was burnt to ash by Śiva's rage.
> True love, with feelings truly felt,
> Is no commodity at all
> For girls who sell themselves."
>
> "Despise the pauper! Only those
> With pockets full, deserve respect!
> My simple girl, for those like us,
> Beauty's for making money."[83]

She has an objective, we are told. She is to slip past him the agreement to which he is not to know he has assented: an exchange of his wealth (*artha*) for the pleasure (*kāma*) she embodies. She is, quite simply, to take him for all he is worth. Far from the idealized world of the dramas, where kings indulge pleasure but easily win wealth and power in doing so, the *Kuṭṭanīmata* quickly presents the battle of the sexes as a zero-sum game: pleasure subtracts the male counterpart's wealth.

Hāralatā, however, forgetting her place in society, has fallen madly for her mark, and in mutual attraction she and Sundarasena indulge in bouts of deeply felt lovemaking (verses 375–391).[84] This goes on for a time, until

[83] *Kuṭṭanīmata* 277–278: *ayi hāralate saṃhara harahuṅkṛtidagdhadehasaṃkṣobham* | *sadbhāvajānuraktir na hi paṇyaṃ paṇyanārīṇām* || *avadhīraya dhanavikalaṃ kuru gauravam akṛśasampadaḥ puṃsaḥ* | *asmādṛśāṃ hi mugdhe dhanasiddhyai rūpanirmāṇam* ||. Translation that of Dezső and Goodall.

[84] Here, we note in an aside, the poet colorfully illustrates something of the cultural life of the world's "oldest profession." The chatter of prostitutes is heard, including complaints about the stupidity of their clients, a Brahmin, for example, who was nothing much more than a pest (verse 393), or a man who had a desire for love but no stamina (verse 394).

Sundarasena's father hears of the affair and sends him a disapproving missive by a courier who delivered the scathing letter:

> "How could one think to juxtapose
> The chant '*vaṣaṭ*', filling the ears,
> —An ornament to all six rites—,
> With eagerness to hear the moans
> Of common women making love?"[85]

The life of a ritually compliant, chastened Brahmin cannot square with the young man's galivanting with a woman of the night. A young man "sowing his oats," he is called back to the family. Sundarasena slowly comes to realize the danger of his folly (as it is conceived by his family and according to the norms of his day, caste prejudices also being clearly at play). Though he does not like his father's counsel nor does he wish for the consequences it promises, he ultimately chooses to follow his order: Sundarasena quits his beloved and returns to the Brahminical fold. As his friend advises:

> "The senses' objects can't, it's true,
> Be wholly shunned, but all the same
> People of sense don't make themselves
> The butt of denigrating slurs.
>
> Attending to one's guru's need,
> A marriage to a well-born wife,
> The company of caring friends,
> Observing Vedic rituals
> —These are the means for prudent men
> For triumph in the here and now,
> And in the world hereafter."[86]

[85] *Kuṭṭanīmata* 417: *kva vaṣaṭkāradhvānaḥ ṣaṭkarmavibhūṣaṇaṃ śravaṇapūraḥ* | *kva ca sādhāraṇ avanitāratimaṇitākarṇanautsukhyam* ||. Translation that of Dezső and Goodall.

[86] *Kuṭṭanīmata* 435–436: *no parihartuṃ viṣayāḥ śakyāḥ satyaṃ tathāpi nipuṇadhiyaḥ* | *abhidheyatāṃ na gacchanty apavādaviśeṣitābhidhānasya* || *guruparicaryā jāyā kulodgatā snigdhabandhusamparkaḥ* | *brāhme karmaṇi saktir lokadvayasādhanaṃ sudhiyām* ||. Translation that of Dezső and Goodall.

Thus is the Brahmin's world. And:

> "It's by the force of previous deeds
> That men become attached to whores.
> But happiness in worldly life
> Is found beside a well-born wife."[87]

Under the influence of his family, Sundarasena separates from Hāralatā with a heavy heart, this for the presence of what is simply described as a kind of attachment (*ko 'py anubandhaḥ*, verse 454, Dezső and Goodall translate with "*karmic* obstacle"). He leaves her despite their real affections and intentions. It is a touchingly tearful separation, moreover, precisely because their love was sincere. Hāralatā failed to maintain a hardened heart, and failed also to keep to the proper manner of performing the duties of her occupation. It is in this way that her story counsels a warning: unable to endure the separation from her client who is her beloved, she dies of utter despondency.

Sundarasena returns soon after their farewell, somehow, and quickly realizes what has become of her, upon which he himself sets her to the funeral pyre (verse 490). He even contemplates suicide by joining her on the fire, a gender reversal of the rite of *satī*, and though he comes close to it, he finally chooses not to commit himself to her fate (verses 491–493). But his life cannot simply go on as before, as though Hāralatā had never been known to him: while he returns with a certain fidelity to the Brahminical norms on which he was raised, he opts for world renunciation over and against the married life of a ritualist householder (verse 495), an acceptable if alternative course of action, and, we can speculate, perhaps not what his father would have wanted for him (though it partially echoes Rāma's chastened nature who, though remaining in the world, never remarried after having lost his one true love).

Following this is narrated a string of advice from the bawd: how to look in the morning so as to appeal to one's man, how to make jealous comments, how to orchestrate a fight with her madam in order to convince her mark of her faithfulness—these and other tricks of the trade. The moral of this story is clear, of course: the courtesan should extract wealth and never fall disastrously in love, though she might enjoy the sex along the way.

[87] *Kuṭṭanīmata* 440: *prāktanakarmavipākaḥ kṣudrāsu śarīriṇāṃ yadāsaktiḥ* | *āyatanaṃ tu sukhānāṃ saṃsārabhuvāṃ kulodgatā rāmā* ||. Translation that of Dezső and Goodall.

Mālatī, however, instinctively rejects this counsel, suggesting nobly to Vikarālā that love is a greater treasure than wealth (verses 546–555). So the bawd continues with her counsel, explaining to Mālatī how to catch a man and succeed in her profession, as well as how to break up with the spent man when he has lost his wealth (see verses 615–625 and up to verse 663).[88] She also explains how to win back a discarded man should he recover his means.

Vikarālā subsequently narrates the other story, that of a successful concubine, illustrating therewith the possibilities for Mālatī, because, she implicitly explains, wealth is more important than love for those in her profession. Thus the story of the prostitute Mañjarī, who takes a royal prince named Samara for all he is worth.

It is of significance that Mañjarī is set to play the part of an actress in her effort to hook the rich prince (see verses 801–805). In fact, she takes up a part in the drama of Harṣa we have placed under study already: the *Ratnāvalī*. The prince is drawn into watching some of the performance (verse 879), and the first act is put on with Mañjarī taking the role of Sāgarikā/Ratnāvalī (see verse 803), which the prince enjoys well. The illusion of the drama is fun, but the reality reflected in the bawd's counsel cautions against easy love.

Then another verse is floated and overheard, which suggests to him another favored distraction: the hunt.

> "Standing one's ground on battle-fields,
> And keeping up-to-date with plays,
> Delighting in a well-turned verse,
> Devotion to the chase—it's these
> That are the perquisites [*kulavidyā*] of princes."[89]

Samara the rich prince wishes then to hunt, but the dinner hour intervenes, and by the time he gets to his meal he is head over heels in love with Mañjarī. "Keeping up-to-date with plays," at least those cast with beautiful women, trumps the battlefield, the hunt, and even delighting in a well-turned verse. And yet the danger facing him is plainly evident, if not to him: it is by the

[88] See also, e.g., verse 305, where Guṇapālita explains to Sundarasena that what is at stake in the battle of the sexes is entirely a matter of wealth: *pradyumnaḥ pradyumno / virūpakaḥ khalu virūpakaḥ satatam* | *susnigdhaḥ susnigdho / rūkṣo rūkṣas tu gaṇikānām* ||. "To courtesans, *a wealthy man* / Becomes *the God of Love* himself; / And *one who hasn't got a cent* / Will always be an *ugly mug*; / A *well-greased cove's* a "*dear old friend*"; / But *one (whose wealth has) shrivelled up* / *Is deemed an uncouth oaf*." Translation that of Dezső and Goodall.

[89] *Kuṭṭanīmata* 949: *saṃgrāmād anapasṛtiḥ prekṣābhijñā subhāṣitābhiratiḥ* | *ācchodanabhiyogaḥ kulavidyā rājaputrāṇām* ||. Translation that of Dezső and Goodall.

"perquisites" of princes (*kulavidyā*) that he risks it all, for danger lurks where *kṣatriyas* play beyond watchful Brahminical eyes.

Now Mañjarī's go-between turns up in the story (verse 989), and after her convincing Samara assents to a *rendez-vous* with that young courtesan (verse 1044).

> When thus the house was all their own,
> He started gradually to lift
> Her veil of natural reserve,
> While she, displaying fear and shame,
> Cried out: "What are you doing?"
>
> "O simple girl! What I'm about
> Is striving for the very core
> Of all four goals of human life."
> Smiling at what he'd said, deranged
> By Kāma, he then launched himself
> Upon the battleground of sex.[90]

Here we are given little detail of Mañjarī's tactics in pursuing her mark, but readers are left plainly to understand that she deployed the various schemes that Vikarālā had recommended to Mālatī. This she does to great effect, for Samara is totally hooked, and by the end of Mañjarī's story, and with it the end of both the course of advice given by Vikarālā to Mālatī and the *Kuṭṭanīmata* itself, we are told this:

> That prostitute treated the prince
> With various modes of making love,
> Consumed entire his worldly wealth,
> And not long after let him go,
> Nothing but skin and bones.
>
> So using these techniques I've taught
> Of getting wealth from paramours

[90] *Kuṭṭanīmata* 1054–1055: *iti śūnyīkṛtaveśmani harati śanaiḥ sahajam aṃśukaṃ tasmin | darśitasādhvasalajjā jagāda sā kiṃ karoṣīti || ayi mugdhe tat kriyate puruṣārthacatuṣṭayasya yat sāram | iti nigaditasasmeraḥ smaravidhur ita ātatāna ratikalaham ||*. Translation that of Dezső and Goodall.

You'll thrive in great prosperity
With riches taken from your lovers.

Pleased with the insights she'd received
From listening to this homily,
Delusion lifted, Mālatī,
Revering Vikarālā's feet,
Set off to go back home.

Whoever hears this poem through
And heeds its moral carefully
Will never find himself deceived
By rakes and trulls and rogues and bawds.[91]

How are we to *interpret* this text? Similar to the famed *Cauraśāstra*, the "Scientific Treatise on Thievery," we here see articulated a normative order for a socially transgressive course of action. On the face of it, the work directs the trull to execute her proper role, and in this manner it speaks to the normativity of roles as such, the notion that (quoting Coulson on the formation of the heroic characters of *nāṭakas*) "the characters in these [works] are types rather than individuals. The method of the Indian poet was not to elevate particular people to universal status but to take universal types and then infuse them with individual human life."[92] This is to say the *Kuṭṭanīmata* articulates a "model for" prostitution as a profession, not merely a "model of" the same.[93] There is a normative way of doing things, an order and structure, a reality that is present *as such*, not in an ad hoc manner but because it always would and should be thus—even so far as something like prostitution goes.

Some eeriness sets in on acceding to this interpretation, however. The normative structures of *dharmic* discourse are evoked—of this there is no doubt. But the *dharma* of prostitution leaves one cold. Obviously, the two "types" of courtesans, embodied by Hāralatā and Mañjarī, present respectively

[91] *Kuṭṭanīmata* 1056–1059: *nānāsuratavišeṣair ārādhya cakāra bhuktasarvasvam | gaṇikāsau rājasutaṃ tvagasthiśeṣaṃ mumoca nāticirāt || tad yanmayopadiṣṭaṃ kāmijanārthāptikāraṇam tena | mahatīṃ samṛddhim eṣyasi kāmukalokāhṛtena vittena || ity upadeśaśravaṇaprabodhatuṣṭā jagāma dhāma svam | mālatyapagatamohā vikarālāpādavandanām kṛtvā || kāvyam idaṃ yaḥ śṛṇute samyakkāvyārthapālanenāsau | no vañcyate kadācid viṭaveśyādhūrtakuṭṭanībhir iti ||*.

[92] Coulson 1981: 18–19. See also footnote 3.

[93] This is, of course, Clifford Geertz's distinction, for which see Geertz 1973: 87–125, esp. 92*ff.* (The same is cited in Pollock 1985: 504, fn. 26.) See also the Introduction, footnote 86.

wanting and successful articulations of that normative practice. Certainly one must read the former's story as a warning to the prostitute, as to what can go wrong when sentiment interferes with what is the work of playing the client's emotions: always be the hunter, never, even inadvertently, the prey. With Mañjarī, in turn, is issued not only a recommendation to ladies of the night but also a warning to those who might fall to the temptation of the cultivated consort, who is so deeply cultured in the ways of making the body appealing, as well as her words, gestures, moods, and emotions. All this—her knowledge of food and pleasant conversation and everything else one might love to love with a lover—sets a trap for the unguarded, emotionally unchastened gentleman. Of this there can be no doubt, if one is to take in the final line of the poem.[94]

The problem, one senses then, is a fundamental one. The poem itself stitches together the mundane and corporeal and utterly pragmatic world of the paid lover with the culturally and religiously valorized world of the normative order as bound by *dharmic* stricture:

> How strange! Her girdle suddenly
> Has slithered from her buttocks. Yet,
> *Consorting with one's guru's wife . . .?*
> (No:) *clinging to an ample rear*
> Must always lead to downfall.[95]

A struggle is identified, one that pits pleasure against the threatened penalties of pursuing too zealously the same.

> "This is the prize of being born,
> This is the fruit of human life,
> When men allow their youth to pass

[94] One might question whether the closing verses should figure too strongly in our interpretation of the text, given that they are present only in some of the manuscript witnesses, about which see Dezső and Goodall 2012: 394, footnote at verse 1056. The point made, however, is elsewhere reinforced, as, for example, at *Kuṭṭanīmata* 657: *kleśāya durgatānāṃ mānastutigātrabhaṅgavinyāsam* | *gaṇikābhinayacatuṣṭayam ākṛṣṭyai svāpateyapuṣṭānām* ||. "Her injured pride, her blandishments, / Her postures and her ornament / —A harlot's four expressive means / (Corporeal, sartorial, / Linguistic and involuntary) / Are meant to taunt the hapless poor / And draw the well-to-do." Translation that of Dezső and Goodall.

[95] *Kuṭṭanīmata* 296: *raśanāguṇena vigalitam ekapade tannitambataś citram* | *patanāya niyatam athavā niṣevaṇaṃ gurukalatrasya* ||. Translation that of Dezső and Goodall.

In blissful union with girls
Of lovely callipygian type."[96]

There is true value in pursuing love—sex—in human life. *Kāma* is of course one of the four human aims (*puruṣārtha*s) and a vital one at that: it helps to make life worth living, and in the right contexts and on the right occasions it may be pursued righteously, *dharmically*, and to the end of—for the king—prosperity in obtaining rich alliances and a rightful heir to the throne. It is nevertheless a dangerous pursuit, as the *Kuṭṭanīmata* cautions. It is no coincidence that the poem speaks of "the battleground of sex," for as in war, one's counterpart in sex can bite back.

We have here, then, a realism and a playfulness married in a poem that looks at a fundamental human concern from a reversed perspective. The high language of Sanskrit poetry brings to life the language and lives of prostitutes, who speak in Sanskrit and explain the ways of their trade. All are warned, but all are enticed as well. The pleasure is in spite of the danger, not in its absence, which is a circumstance utterly unlike those of the *Abhijñānaśākuntala* and the *Ratnāvalī*. The humor of the poem, which is, indeed, beautiful—and a joy to read—is found in its uncommon angle on the dynamic (uncommon for Sanskrit literature, gendered as it is), one presented from the woman's point of view (and the surprising and therefore playful one of the elderly bawd at that). But the concerns are deadly real. Pleasure has its place in life, but its dangers as well. Hāralatā's Brahmin lover escapes, barely, the trap of falling for the wrong woman (in this case, as so often is tragically the case in premodern South Asia, caste being deemed an element of what renders Hāralatā unsuitable); but Mañjarī's *kṣatriya* prince loses everything. The position of counterpoise offered in this poem against the dramas reviewed in the present chapter, then, is this, that passion is not to be indulged easily, but with skill and a cognizance of the potential dangers thereto. While not in the dramas, for certain in reality: fun may come at a price.

Dharma points to obligation. But the obligation pursued in the *Kuṭṭanīmata* does not produce what is right or moral, for "*dharma*, for [the prostitute], is realized / By sex with some lovelorn young man, / Deserving but necessitous; / The aim of Wealth can be attained / By congress with a wealthy man; / Kāma, the third of human goals, / She satisfies by savouring /

96 *Kuṭṭanīmata* 327: *idam eva hi janmaphalaṃ jīvitaphalam etad eva yat puṃsām* | *laḍahanitambavatījanasambhogasukhena yāti tāruṇyam* ||. Translation that of Dezső and Goodall.

A man whose lusts suit hers."[97] Instead, it produces what are nothing less than modes of domination, modes of deception, the results of which devastate the lover's prey. The positive and negative examples of the *Kuṭṭanīmata* furnish proof for both *fille de joie* and her client, that certain actions are bound to produce certain results, and which example, which "model for" prostitution, one pursues will determine one's fortunes—in love and in holding onto one's fortune alike. *Dharma* in Dāmodaragupta's poem is thus reduced to *karman*, to actions that, if executed to the letter, invariably produce a certain result, but it is a cold instance of action; it is action issuing consequence, nothing less, certainly nothing more. Emotions have power and can lead astray—as all would know but as the dramas deny.

Conclusion

What the positive and negative examples of the *Kuṭṭanīmata* therefore ultimately advise is that *dharma* offers a model for action in the world that, at the extremes, turns onto itself. It is not that Dāmodaragupta speaks in an *adharmic* mode, as Doniger has shown the *Kāmasūtra* to do, but that he speaks, again to paraphrase Doniger, of *adharma* in terms of *dharma*.[98] The very limits of *dharma* are found thereby, for it is clearly possible to stray from the path, and in so doing one may be met with an order by which one's actions inexorably and invariably are led to wrong ends; there is a regular order to falling out of order. Thus the *Kuṭṭanīmata* offers advice that cuts both ways: it counsels trulls on how to win their mark, *and* it warns men of the predictable dangers of their trade in doing so—danger diagnosed in beautiful poetic verse. It is this regular order, standing apart but within the structure of *dharma*, that is utterly removed from the purview of the plays, the elision by which the Sanskrit dramas are freed to entertain, for they are escapist in scope.

Or are they? The dramas also issue an implicit counsel for kings: trust your trustworthy advisors, for pleasure, prosperity, and power may be found thereby. Thus, the relationship of Brahmins to kings is clearly rendered in the plays, even if the Brahmin most frequently consulted on the stage is the *vidūṣaka* clown, foolish but reliably loyal. Be it a kindly fate or destiny, as

[97] *Kuṭṭanīmata* 652: *dharmaḥ kāmād abhinavaguṇavanniḥsvasya madanarogavataḥ* | *artho 'rthavato 'bhigamāt kāmaḥ samaratanaropabhogena* ||. Translation that of Dezső and Goodall.

[98] See Doniger 2016. Cf. Nemec 2018.

in the *Abhijñānaśākuntala*, where virtue ethics are intrinsic to kings, or the guiding hand of a wise and effective minister, as in the *Ratnāvalī*, the Sanskrit dramas direct kings to actions that promise pleasure, and the kingdom's prosperity thereby.

Caste, again, is held in mind. In Kālidāsa's play *dharma* predetermines that no caste transgression could ever cross Duṣyanta's mind; and the *brāhmaṇa-kṣatriya* bond is pivotal to the events of the *Ratnāvalī* (the minister orchestrating the action for his king); finally, the *Kuṭṭanīmata* ranks Brahmins and *kṣatriya*s in order, for no coincidence explains why the poem narrates a Brahmin escaping the worst fate of falling for a concubine of low social status, while Mañjarī traps a *kṣatriya* with her arts of seduction. These works of *belles lettres* preserve not just a regard for the bond between Brahmins and kings but for normative Brahminical notions of caste hierarchy as well.

Finally, by their intertextuality the dramas in their composition and performance self-consciously play on expectations and the social realities of their historical moments, which are more realistically or at least more somberly represented in the works they echo, the *Rāmāyaṇa* for depicting the high costs of the chastened emotions of kingship, for example, or the *Kuṭṭanīmata* for exposing the real dangers of the illusions of love. Sanskrit dramas by conformity to their genre idealize *both* the representations of the feelings, actions, thoughts, and emotions of a host of character types *and* the results they may produce. But the dramatic genre in creating an illusion of human relations simultaneously reflects the mirror image of the reality of the "battleground of sex," which is defined by threats of misdirection, illusion, the wagering and losing of wealth and influence—even one's own life—in the course of the pursuit of pleasure. The very convention of the drama, only to present a happy ending, is palpably felt to be the photographic negative of the hard knocks of human intention.

Thus one may ultimately need to understand this genre—the Sanskrit drama—not as *merely* escapist but *also* as offering what their authors saw as a realist, honest-to-life "model of" and "model for" being in the world (at the least for a king, at least in the social milieu of the royal court). The texts, that is, may best be read as offering themselves as counsel. In the Sanskrit dramas, so often but not always composed by Brahminical authors, it is regularly under the advice of a learned and chastened Brahminical advisor that a prince or king might find his way to the safety the dramas depict. Certainly, conformity to Brahminical norms is ever implicitly recommended.

This, however, *is* the Brahmin's view of the matter, the drama's Brahminical counsel for kings. In a play written by a king not only is love easily rewarded but also, more than this, *his advisors are as reliable as the Brahmins say they are and should be.* In the *Ratnāvalī*, the king is permitted to pursue pleasure (*kāma*) with reckless abandon, winning prosperity (*artha*) along the way. It's *a king's play* about a king, the king's fantasy of what can be real. Such fantasy also projects a photographic negative of the reality facing kings of the day in the court, which was hardly a garden but rather a forest of mirrors. Light reflected on sharp and returning angles is exceedingly difficult to track; reality is echoed in the escapism of a king's dramatic counsel for kings. Yes, Harṣa depicts the story of a poorly counseled (by his *vidūṣaka*), reckless, and lovelorn king, who happily chases his beloved with the help of a hapless clown; but that king also *implicitly* relies on his masterful minister, who doesn't explicitly counsel him at all but instead fruitfully takes matters into his own hands, *all to the good for king, queen, and kingdom.* This, above all, proves to be the natural conceit for an escapist and entertaining genre, especially a play about illusion that was written by a king. Harṣa's play is a happy distraction into an unreality of reliability, it having been said to have been written by the royal sovereign and staged for princes and kings, a dramatic spectacle guided by the reliable minister of the king, performed in a world where anyone with access to power—Brahmins included—could be relied upon frequently *not* to do what *dharma* dictates, but what *karman*s forebodingly threaten. The virtue ethic of the Sanskrit narratives thus is not simply a call to *dharma*, for in the political arena no simple call to proper action could always suffice. Kings do well by being good; and being good demands *dharmic* action; but the consequences matter, and sometimes the ends shape the contours of the means. Being good means being wise in action above all, and sometimes wisdom requires a worldliness nowhere demanded in the happy escape of the dramas.

6

The Wisdom of Animals

Kingship and the *Pañcatantra*

Introduction

Whatever serious notes they may sound or echo, the works examined in Chapters 4 and 5 are nothing if not entertaining, explicitly and intentionally so. Three modes or genres of entertainment, moreover, may be found, respectively, in the *kathā* literature of the *Kathāsaritsāgara*; the narrative poem, the *Kuṭṭanīmata*; and the two plays of the *Abhjñānaśākuntala* and the *Ratnāvalī*. The *Kathāsaritsāgara* offers a kind of fantasy narrative and an adventure, replete with haunting stories from the cremation grounds and fantastical turns of events, exploits on the high seas and far away from home. These stories also are meant to entertain, as their own metanarrative suggests, but they do so with stories from worlds far away. They are in their contents similar to horror movies, which also can marry serious social messages to ghoulish fun, or else similar to the action-adventure film, the movie-epic.

The *Kuṭṭanīmata*, in turn, is whimsical in a way and beautiful and entertaining for its subject matter, love and sex, and also for its perspective on the same—words of wisdom from women who speak Sanskrit, the wisdom of bawds and trulls. (There is an unfortunate sexism implicit here, of course, in that a certain entertainment is derived from the novelty of eliciting learning from female protagonists, who in the dramas are depicted as non-Sanskrit speakers who rarely know best.)

Finally, the dramas offer an escapist entertainment, albeit while being able to deliver a serious message in the echo of subsequent reflection. They are fun and for fun, and they show beauty and intrigue in their performance. (Consider the depiction of the performance of the *Ratnāvalī* in the *Kuṭṭanīmata*, which was an occasion for seduction.) Yes, they reflect the world outside the drama's escape; but while the dramas work in a narrative realism of a kind, dealing with real characters and issues familiar to members of the royal court, it is an idealized presentation of events, realism in the sense

Brahmins and Kings. John Nemec, Oxford University Press. © Oxford University Press 2025.
DOI: 10.1093/oso/9780197791998.003.0007

that human characters and "real" events (magic aside) are represented and explored. They do not dwell on the difference between the easy world of the spectacle and the hardened world it more easily represents. As we have seen, many of the hard truths of the Indian court and society are simply sidelined in the dramas to open a space for unencumbered romantic intrigue, even if self-consciously so.

Here in the last close reading of the present volume will be taken up a work that in some sense offers the inverse of the dramas: it presents a series of stories about animals that are clearly represented as fictions, for animals do not talk and act as humans do, however clever they might be. They are nevertheless stories that accurately represent the deadly serious realities of life in the premodern South Asian political realm. While the dramas represent an idealized and therefore fictional—illusory—world of easy pleasure, presented in a realistic mode, the animal stories present hard-bitten realities, but within an imagined world—the illusory world—of talking animals.

Thus, stories about animals are also both fun and serious. They are enjoyable because stories about animals are charming and can be deceptively simple; they are easy entertainment, perhaps even suitable for children. But the stories deal lessons on issues of life and death, and the framing narrative makes clear their vital, indispensable, pedagogic value: they are light and heavy at the same time.

First, their lightness. The evident accessibility of the *Pañcatantra* suggests, *prima facie*, little that demands nuanced or sustained interpretation. The text is written in a lucid, relatively simple, and comprehensible Sanskrit. The narrative itself similarly signals facility in understanding, with its purpose announced in the preamble: the *Pañcatantra* offers an efficient pedagogical tool that all but guarantees success.

But their lightness gives them weight. Viṣṇuśarman, the introductory frame narrative explains, was a wise and elderly Brahmin of eighty years, who answered the call of a king named Amaraśakti to teach his three dullard sons—Vasuśakti, Ugraśakti, and Anekaśakti—who were simply unable to learn the science of statecraft (*arthaśāstra*). This, then, is most fundamentally a story of a Brahmin who successfully counsels those who will be kings. Like all the works examined in this book, it narrates the giving of counsel, it offers itself as a work of counsel, it reinforces the *brāhmaṇa-kṣatriya* alliance, and it supports the virtue ethic identified as central to Sanskrit-language narrative literatures.

And so the story proceeds. The princes' father summoned his ministers to inquire as to how his incapable sons possibly could be educated, to which they reply by citing the famed dictum, that any student must work for twelve years to master Sanskrit grammar. Only after this may one go on to study the various learned works on *dharma*, *artha*, and *kāma*. The task is difficult even for clever students, only the more so for the dim-witted.[1] The ministers nevertheless hold out hope that the doyen of the subject might succeed where the traditional methods could not, and they recommend that Amaraśakti call on Viṣṇuśarman's aid, which of course he does.

Viṣṇuśarman quickly presents himself to the court like a fresh breeze, promising not only to teach the three foolish sons without regard for financial reward but also to do so in a foreshortened period of only six months. He has reason for his confidence, the narrative suggests: his teachings will be delivered by way of charming and lucid stories about animals, whose natures and courses of action offer easily comprehensible lessons for negotiating human relations in and around the royal court. The simplicity of the stories ensures their profound effect.

What one should glean from these lessons has been the subject of some scholarly debate, however, and I argue that there is good reason for this. The *Pañcatantra* stories resist the sort of simple messaging that Hertel, for example—and as Patrick Olivelle noted—understood them to offer, namely, an undiminished Machiavellianism.[2] Hertel was in good company in maintaining this position, however, for Edgerton followed him on the matter (though not without caveats), suggesting that the stories are "generally unmoral, and at times positively immoral, in the political lessons they inculcate."[3] Falk, on the other hand, went the other way. He argued that many of the stories of the collection were adopted from the *Mahābhārata* and *Jātakas* and adapted to a normative understanding of *dharma*, such that any "Machiavellian" elements were, as Olivelle puts it, intended only "to show how the other half lives, with the message 'don't be like them.' "[4]

[1] See Edgerton 1924 (vol. 1): 4, (6): *tatra kecid āhuḥ deva, dvādaśabhir varśāiḥ kila vyākaraṇaṃ śrūyate | tad yadi katham api jñāyate, tato dharmārthakāmaśāstrāṇi jñeyāni | tad etad atigahanaṃ dhīmatām api, kiṃ punar mandabuddhīnām |*. Note that Edgerton (1924: xv) harbors doubts as to whether this passage "literally corresponds to the original text" and is unsure "that the original contained even the equivalent in general sense."

[2] See Olivelle 1997: xxxi–xxxii.

[3] See Olivelle 1997: xxxi–xxxii. The quotation here offered is cited by Olivelle. See also Edgerton 1924 (vol. 2): 5. See Olivelle 1997: xxxii, fn. 33 for his misgivings regarding this view.

[4] See Falk 1978: 185; cf. Olivelle 1997: xxxii.

Banerjee, in turn, took a different approach in an essay whose title—"In Life's Maze"—best captures the import of the work, though he ultimately argued somewhat narrowly that the narratives were structured on the model of the classical syllogism of the Nyāya, further arguing that the text indicates one should rely predominantly on what can be known for oneself by direct observation (*pratyakṣa*) and this in preference to the other means of knowing.[5] Next, Olivelle suggested that the work does not recommend paths of action in matters of governance that accord with the strictures of *dharma*, for, he notes, the stories that do offer *dharmic* morals are conveyed by the "losers," not the "winners," in particular disputes. He therefore proposes instead that "the central message of the *Pañcatantra*, with the possible exception of Book II, is that craft and deception constitute the major art of government."[6]

Olivelle's position is sympathetic with an extended argument that Wendy Doniger has recently prosecuted in a pair of books, in which she claims that various texts on *artha* and *kāma* work against the principle that *dharma* should govern human action in these domains, or more generally.[7] Finally, Mark McClish has demonstrated that a similar phenomenon may be unearthed by excavating the compositional history of the *Arthaśāstra*: an earlier, more pragmatic, and less overtly Brahminical stratum of the work is interlaced with later redactions that promote Brahminical notions of *dharma* as the guiding force in politics and governance.[8]

If asked to boil the matter down, I would partially assent to Olivelle's proposition but also adopt Keith's summary view of the *Pañcatantra*. The latter argued that the core purpose of its stories was "to give advice of a useful character," not advice that was essentially or exclusively immoral, which is to say *adharmic*.[9] Indeed, the text is at base concerned with judicious action, *tout court*, not "moral" or "immoral" acts per se, and on my view the question of *dharmic* action is ultimately adventitious to the overall intention of the work's lessons. In this sense the animal fables are closer to the *Arthaśāstra* than to the Dharmaśāstras and the *Nītisāra*, though without being opposed to the influences of the latter.

[5] See Banerjee 1996.
[6] Olivelle 1997: xxxv.
[7] See Doniger 2016 and Doniger 2018.
[8] See McClish 2019.
[9] See Keith 1928: 249.

The line of inquiry I wish to explore in the present chapter, however, concerns not an endeavor simply or narrowly to identify any single, overarching lesson of the text, moral or otherwise, nor to identify any unidirectional pedagogical impulse of the work. Rather, I wish to explore the *various* lessons offered in the *Pañcatantra* by way, as is the wont of the present volume, of tending closely to the turns in its narrative. If the lessons that this "utterly charming" (*sumanohara*) "scientific work" (*śāstra*) on statecraft are meant to offer just might be summarized obviously enough[10]—that kings must make, and may be taught (by Brahmins) to make, judicious decisions—the manners in which these dicta are communicated are not so simply discerned. Rather, the stories in a manner similar to biblical parables are not facile but subtle, and the work of reading this narrative on Indian political life *as a narrative* uncovers a fascinating web of interpretation, which structures a lesson in the complexity of the same, a complexity of human choice in action that any political leader must master in order to succeed in governance. (So much also explains the scholarly disagreement regarding the true purport of the text.)

It should come as no surprise that a text seemingly pellucid and simple conceals or misdirects in conveying the complex messages of its stories. This fact not only underscores the nature of working in "life's maze," where decision-making requires one to negotiate the cunning of others, but also sets in clear relief the importance of the position and role of the readers or hearers of the stories in question—notably, princes and kings—who were meant by the author of the *Pañcatantra* to apply the text's lessons in lived experience. If good judgment, in the end, is paramount, hard-and-fast rules—that one's minister is to be trusted or not to be trusted, for example, or that nature always trumps nurture (or vice versa)—are impossible indelibly to write. Indeed, the stories in various places narrate mutually contradictory lessons, taking respectively each side of such binary maxims. Sometimes they claim to narrate one lesson while in fact offering another one altogether. It is up to readers who *use* the text to discern the lessons—to know which applies in the particular situations they face—and to be prepared to make similar, parallel discernments in their real-world interactions with others.

[10] See Olivelle 1997: x, where he notes the work identifies itself as a *śāstra*, "that is, a technical or scientific treatise, and more specifically as a *nītiśāstra*, a treatise on government or political science." Indeed, so much is found in the *maṅgala* verses themselves: *manave vācaspataye śukrāya parāśarāya sasutāya | cāṇakyāya ca viduṣe namo 'stu nṛpaśāstrakartṛbhyaḥ* || 1 || *sakalārthaśāstrasāraṃ jagati samālokya viṣṇuśarmāpi | tantraiḥ pañcābhir etaiś cakāra* ***sumanoharaṃ śāstraṃ*** || 2 ||.

Cunning and deception are in the end said to be integral to the workings of government, as not only Olivelle's view of the *Pañcatantra* indicates but also virtually all the evidence we can muster of premodern Indian political life also makes plain.[11] But not always. And it is precisely because of this that not simply inerrant preference for cunning but rather real discernment in directing a course of action—the virtue ethic of being chastened in emotion and restrained in desire so as properly to be able to act in the world—is what is required, encompassing sometimes even the offering of one's confidence to and placing one's trust in a "natural" enemy. The imperative of governance par excellence, then, though simply stated—"act wisely," and do well in the world thereby—is not so simple in practice. Whatever summary statement regarding the purport of the *Pañcatantra* one might favor, the proverbial devil is in the details.

Textual Sources

And the details are abundant, for the *Pañcatantra* is perhaps better understood as an eponymous genre than a single literary work. Like the *Bṛhatkathā*, multiple versions were produced, even while the text is no longer available to us in its original form. It is, moreover, a work that drew interest across sectarian religious boundaries. The author of the urtext was likely to have been a Brahmin, but two important Jain versions from northern India were also penned and are extant to the present day.[12]

Where the text was first produced is disputed. Hertel has proposed Kashmir, the Kashmiri recension being to his mind the closest to the original work that is currently available to us. Edgerton, however, suggested that repeated mention in the frame narratives of a southern Indian kingdom indicates a provenance from that part of the subcontinent. Olivelle tends

[11] I have particularly in mind here the historically oriented *Rājataraṅgiṇī*, examined earlier in Chapter 3, and Daud Ali 2004, a seminal and careful consideration of the structure of works on court culture in premodern South Asia. The same also calls to mind Olivelle's claim that the core lesson of the *Arthaśāstra* may be summed up with a single term: *atisaṃdhāna*, or "outwitting." See Olivelle 2013: 50, cited also in the Introduction at footnote 9.

[12] One of these two, we should more precisely say, was likely to have been composed by a Jain monk. It is labeled by scholars as the "simplicitor" or, sometimes, the *Pañcākhyānaka*. There can be no doubt that it was extant by 1199 CE, because a(nother) Jain monk, Pūrṇabhadra, elaborated a longer *Pañcatantra* that drew on both it and the Kashmiri recension, called the *Tantrākhyāyikā*, as well as on some now-lost versions of the text. (The "simplicitor," in turn, draws on a now-lost, earlier version of the *Tantrākhyāyikā*, the so-called *Ur-Tantrākhyāyikā*.)

closer to Hertel's view than Edgerton's, arguing that "in narrating fabulous tales from the distant past it would be more natural to place them in a distant exotic land than in one's own backyard."[13] Regardless—for the record, I favor Olivelle's view on this matter—there can be no doubt that several versions of the text were composed in South India, including not only the so-called "Southern *Pañcatantra*" but also a pair of longer versions based on it, respectively authored by Vasubhāga and Durgasiṃha.

Also produced was a Nepalese version of the text that extracts the verses from the southern version. The famed *Hitopadeśa* of Nārāyaṇa, who hailed from Bengal, in turn, similarly recasts that recension of the text. Finally, one of the two Kashmiri retellings of the *Bṛhatkathā*, the *Kathāsaritsāgara* of Somadeva (examined in Chapter 4), offers a fully elaborated *Pañcatantra* narrative.

There can be no doubt that an *Ur-Pañcatantra* was composed no later than the year 550 CE, this *terminus ante quem* being firmly established by the production of a Pahlavi translation by that date (though it is now lost), one from which all premodern translations in the West were derived.[14] One can say with a certain confidence, moreover, that the text was first composed in Sanskrit.

Following Olivelle, I here examine the stories as presented in Edgerton's reconstruction of the text, this being an edition which, as Olivelle argues, "comes as close to the original as we are going to get without the discovery of new evidence, certainly closer than any of the extant versions."[15] Of course, the analysis of other versions of the text, with their additional or alternatively ordered stories, would present further opportunity for interpreting *Pañcatantra* narratives. One particular desideratum is a thoroughgoing study of the Jain contributions to the corpus, for example. Regardless, these stories often present with a sort of concealed complexity that requires one carefully to read for their consequences, which is also to say that not all Indian animal stories are the same or may be read in the same manner.[16] In

[13] See Olivelle 1997: xiii.

[14] See Olivelle 1997: xii.

[15] He goes on immediately following this (Olivelle 1997: xliv–xlv) to say: "Most scholars would concede at least the following: (1) The reconstructed text contains *every story* that was found in the original, and the original contained *no stories* other than those included in the reconstructed text. (2) The vast majority of the verses given in the reconstructed text were found in the original, which may have contained a limited number of additional verses. (3) The narrative sequence of the original was the same as it is in the reconstructed version."

[16] The *Pañcatantra*—this *Pañcatantra*, at least (particularly the first book)—cannot be read like Jātaka stories, for example (or even the *Hitopadeśa*), that is, with an easily discernable purport and moral to the story.

the present instance, the wisdom of animals is much more subtle than the form of the stories initially suggests.

The Aim of Proper Instruction: Proper Discernment

Governance, the *Pañcatantra* argues, involves properly managing those with whom one is necessarily engaged. The trick is to deploy human resources to good effect:

> Be it a horse, a science, or a sword,
> A lute, a voice, a woman, or a man—
> Whether they become capable or not
> Depends on the competence of the man
> to whom they belong.[17]

For ministers, the caution or ambition to be exercised concerns the very perils involved with serving a king, a person whom the *Pañcatantra* compares to a mountain that is full of risks, or to a snake, embodying danger.[18] For the king, in turn, the danger is one of misunderstanding the nature of those around him:

> Be careful in how you assess
> The merits of your kingdom and your men.
> On this alone will your success depend—
> Discerning the relative worth of men.[19]

Indeed:

> When a king is unwise,
> dimwits will surround him;
> When such men come to power,
> the wise soon disappear;

[17] *Pañcatantra* 1.44 (Edgerton 1924 [vol. 1]: 31): *aśvaḥ śastraṃ śāstraṃ vīṇā vāṇī naraś ca nārī ca | puruṣaviśeṣaṃ prāptā bhavanty ayogyāś ca yogyāś ca* ||. Translation Olivelle's.

[18] See Edgerton 1924 (vol. 1): 25, lines 3–7.

[19] *Pañcatantra* 1.33 (Edgerton 1924 [vol. 1]: 28): *viśeṣajño bhava sadā rāṣṭrasya ca janasya ca | tadantarajñānamātrapratibaddhā hi saṃpadaḥ* ||. Translation Olivelle's. Note that Edgerton (1924 [vol. 1]: xv) doubts whether this passage "literally corresponds to the original text," and he encloses the entire second half-verse in crux marks.

When the wise leave the realm,
policies go askew;
When his policies have come to ruin,
The line perishes along with the king.[20]

One must be clever to do well in the world, and the discerning we find in the text requires one to be good at figuring who is reliable and to what ends.

We thus are a far cry from the world of the Sanskrit dramas, where the king may frolic carefree because he is served faithfully by his ministers, including the *vidūṣaka* who—yes—is an idiot, but pleasantly and pleasingly so, because he is without question a friend. Set in relief against the *Pañcatantra*, one can see ever more clearly the joyful escape of the Sanskrit dramas: it involves not only the playboy's carefree cavorting but also the tremendous privilege of doing so under the watchful *and faithful* care of trustworthy ministers and friends. It is not just that women are more prominently featured in the plays than they are in the *Pañcatantra*, the latter of which, as Olivelle has noted, was "a male domain,"[21] but it is also that the privilege of true (male) friendship is eminently and implicitly possible in the dramas, even to be expected, even while it cannot be thus without caution and care in the "real world" that is depicted in Viṣṇuśarman's animal fables.

The First Book

Simple morals, simple disciplines to be practiced in complex circumstances, all of it conveyed by way of stories that often seem simple. *What* to do is clear: trust the trustworthy, root out the unscrupulous, act with control and proper care. But *how*? I would like to argue that the task the reader or hearer of the *Pañcatantra* faces precisely mirrors the task facing both the three princes for whom the narratives are conveyed and the contemporaneous royal sovereign working in the world outside the text (who may have been among those for whom the text was composed in the first place): to discern the true natures of those whom one encounters, to recognize the elements of their intentions and actions that are never explicitly announced but that

[20] *Pañcatantra* 1.50 (Edgerton 1924 [vol. 1]: 32): *avijñānād rājño bhavati matihīnaḥ parijanas / tatas tatprādhānyād bhavati na samīpe budhajanaḥ | budhais tyakte rājye bhavati na hi nītir guṇavatī / pranaṣṭāyāṃ nītau sanṛpam avaśaṃ naśyati kulam ||*. Translation Olivelle's.

[21] Olivelle 1997: xxvi.

define the opportunities and dangers they present. The text fundamentally offers itself as a work of counsel, a mode for practicing the art of discerning. Readers and hearers of the work must find the way forward, through hidden complexity, just as kings and princes (and others) needed to negotiate with wisdom and cunning the possible deceptions and misdirection of others to be able to seize opportunity, when occasioned, for fruitful alliances and other modes of cooperation, even with unlikely friends.

Nowhere in the *Pañcatantra* is this pattern of reading for the hidden message more possible, nor more necessary, than with the first book. The first is the most elaborated and the longest of the five books, and it is perhaps the preeminent illustration of the major theme of *Brahmins and Kings*, that a certain interaction of Brahminical advisors and the kings they serve is thought positively to shape the cultural landscape of premodern Indian political life. I propose that the *Pañcatantra*'s first book, entitled "On Causing Dissension among Allies," is in fact intentionally misnamed, because virtually every lesson in it is presented a step out of place. (I also wonder whether it originally stood alone, given the degree to which it functions as a coherent narrative of a more complex and intricate quality than is found in the other four books.)

Its outermost story is perhaps the best known of all the *Pañcatantra* narratives. A lion named Piṅgalaka, who is king, one day is frightened by a sound, which is in fact the howling of a harmless bull name Saṃjīvaka. A clever jackal named Damanaka decides to capitalize on Piṅgalaka's anxiety to ingratiate himself with the king and install himself as a minister in the upper echelon of his court. Karaṭaka, another jackal, plays the role of contrarian, questioning constantly the viability of Damanaka's schemes but nowhere interacting with Piṅgalaka directly. In the end, Damanaka achieves his objective: the book ends with him working in the court at the king's side, in a position of utter privilege.

Piṅgalaka is not presented in much of a favorable light, it must be said.[22] He is manipulable and is repeatedly manipulated by Damanaka, the clever jackal-minister. The first and fundamental lessons of the book, that is to say, are never explicitly mentioned: a lion by nature should be brave, and it is Piṅgalaka's failing for not being so; a king should be capable of harnessing the power of his office, but Piṅgalaka—and many kings in the world outside

[22] Indeed, and as Olivelle has noted already, the kings of the *Pañcatantra* are often depicted negatively.

the text—cannot. Thus, while it is true that Damanaka ultimately wins his ambition to serve at the side of the king, this by way of "causing dissension" between Piṅgalaka and Saṃjīvaka, the very occasion to do so results from the presence of fundamental shortcomings in the king, his misplaced fear for one, as well as his credulous acceptance of Damanaka's advice in the first place.

Let us survey in greater detail the major narrative turns of the story. The lion-king is afraid of the sound he hears, as already noted, which is of course only the bellowing of a harmless bull that had been abandoned by his owner. Damanaka then presents himself to the king, and though he is an otherwise insignificant person in the court, Piṅgalaka accepts his offer to investigate the source of the sound on his behalf. Discovering the harmless bull, Damanaka arranges for Saṃjīvaka to meet the king, after which the two develop a fast friendship.

In fact, their friendship becomes a danger to the kingdom: Piṅgalaka so enjoys Saṃjīvaka's company that he neglects his royal duties and, failing therefore to kill prey at a sufficient rate, leaves to starve those among his subjects who feast on the leftovers (as do his jackal-ministers). To rectify this problem, which as Karaṭaka readily notes Damanaka himself created, the jackal-minister Damanaka cultivates dissension between Piṅgalaka and Saṃjīvaka, this toward the end of the book. Convincing each that the other is an enemy, he drives them to a battle that wounds the lion-king and kills the bull, only after which is Damanaka established as the most trusted of Piṅgalaka's ministers.

Subtly signaling the fact that the core lesson of the first book is not the how-to of "causing dissension among allies," however, but rather consists in an admonition to guard oneself against evil and to cultivate good counsel, the text passingly notes that Saṃjīvaka knew many *śāstra*s and taught them to Piṅgalaka, which surely is to be seen as a commendable quality, given the outermost frame narrative of the *Pañcatantra* itself, in which Viṣṇuśarman promises to train the young princes in the art of statecraft.[23] Indeed, if one

[23] See Edgerton 1924 (vol. 1): 46, lines 3–8 (noting that Edgerton judges that the equivalent to parts of this passage were not represented in the original *Pañcatantra*, while other parts also had no literal correspondence in the same): *tatas tayoḥ piṅgalakasaṃjīvakayoḥ pratidinaṃ parasparaprītipūrvakaṃ kālo 'tivartate | anekaśāstrārthapraṇihitabuddhitvāc ca saṃjīvakenānabhijño 'pi vanyatvāt piṅgalako 'lpenaiva kālena dhīmān kṛtaḥ | kiṃ bahunā, pratyahaṃ piṅgalakasaṃjīvakāv eva rahasyāni mantrayete, śeṣaḥ sarvo 'pi mṛgajano dūrībhūtas tiṣṭhati* |. "From that time onwards, every day Piṅgalaka and Saṃjīvaka spent their time together in mutual affection. Piṅgalaka, because he had lived his entire life in the wild, was not a learned person.

enters into the perspective of the frame narrative, the contradiction is readily evident, because the *Pañcatantra*'s outermost story records a promise: efficiently to teach three princes how to become effective kings. Yet, the first book centers a narrative about a king who is duped by a minister. To imagine the incongruity that the first book's narrative would necessarily present to the three princes of the frame narrative (if they are paying any attention) is to weigh the value of the book to any *kṣatriya* prince worth his salt: the book claims to teach how to sow dissension, but that very lesson is dependent on the credulity of a duped king. This sort of misstep in counsel also characterizes the remainder of the book's narrative. Consider, for example, the following sequence of embedded stories.

Damanaka quickly comes to regret his intervention, which facilitated the friendship of Piṅgalaka and Saṃjīvaka, a regret he shares with his more cautious jackal colleague, Karaṭaka the contrarian. He seeks in dialogue with his companion both consolation and a way forward, lamenting that the problem they face involves precisely what he was warned against, namely, getting involved in a matter that should not have concerned him. Weighing his error, Damanaka compares his difficult situation to the stories of an ascetic and his friend, a jackal and two rams, and an unfaithful wife and a weaver. Karaṭaka asks after these three stories, and we have them as told to him by Damanaka, these stories embedded in the narrative just recounted of Damanaka's inapt intervention in Piṅgalaka's court.

First, the story of the ascetic, a man named Devaśarman. He is too trusting and allows into his company someone he meets casually, one Āṣāḍhabhūti, who steals his money when the ascetic leaves for the river to perform ablutions. Now, the obvious moral of this story, *prima facie*, suits Damanaka's current situation: the ascetic introduced a problem into his life by allowing an untrustworthy person to get close to him, which furnishes an apt lesson for Damanaka, who facilitated the introduction of a new companion into Piṅgalaka's inner circle, creating thereby a problem in his own life. Remember, Damanaka is starving as a result of the king's distraction with his new friend—the type of eventuality against which Damanaka's companion Karaṭaka had warned him. And yet, the story is not so simply curated, as we shall presently see.

Saṃjīvaka, however, who had mastered the subject matter of many a branch of knowledge, made him erudite in a very short time. To make a long story short, every day Piṅgalaka and Saṃjīvaka discussed secret matters by themselves, while all the other animals were kept far away." Translation that of Olivelle.

The second story is encased by that of the credulous ascetic. In the course of going to the river and prior to discovering that Āṣāḍhabhūti robbed him, Devaśarman spots two rams butting heads, spilling between them a pool of blood in the course of battle. Devaśarman there witnesses a jackal who, seeing the blood, seeks to taste it during a pause in the fight; but the next butting of heads catches that jackal between the two rams, and he is crushed.

At first blush, the story may perhaps be said aptly to have been proffered to the ascetic Devaśarman, who took to the company of a dangerous individual; but it is most plainly (also) a story whose moral applies to Damanaka, who ill-advisedly and voluntarily involved himself with a pair of giant animals, the mighty lion-king and the fearsome bull. There can be no mere coincidence in it being a jackal who is harmed in the story and by two large beasts, at that, when Damanaka encouraged the friendship of two large animals whose association has caused him harm. Here too, then, a lesson is clearly offered: don't join the company of dangerous individuals; don't stick one's nose where it doesn't belong.

On further reflection, though, is the moral of the Devaśarman story so straightforwardly presented? The danger warned against, that of befriending untrustworthy people or involving oneself with violent opponents, does not offer any perfect analog to the problem faced in the case of Damanaka's relationship with Piṅgalaka, the danger threatening Damanaka (and because of his actions Karaṭaka) being overinvolvement in the lives and business of *others*, not the inviting of a dangerous person into their own lives. That is Piṅgalaka's problem, not Damanaka's, though perhaps it is Karaṭaka's too, for his association with Damanaka. After all, Damanaka's friendship with Piṅgalaka does him no *direct* harm in a manner similar to Devaśarman and Āṣāḍhabhūti. The king's distraction has the side effect of leaving him off the hunt; but Piṅgalaka does not target Damanaka with mischief as the thief Āṣāḍhabhūti does the ascetic Devaśarman.

Neither is it the case that the friendship Piṅgalaka formed with Saṃjīvaka harmed the lion-king per se—again, not in the manner that Āṣāḍhabhūti harmed Devaśarman. As noted already, the text clearly indicates that Saṃjīvaka is well educated, that he imparts *sāstric* learning to Piṅgalaka, and that they share in a true friendship, none of which finds parallel in the false friendship Devaśarman invites with the mischievous Āṣāḍhabhūti. Piṅgalaka's is, to repeat, a friendship that leads him to neglect his royal duties—the danger par excellence for a king is self-indulgence—but this is not the danger warned of by Devaśarman's story. In fact, it is rather the opposite: Saṃjīvaka offers too much of a *good* thing: real friendship and learning. By contrast, Āṣāḍhabhūti gives Devaśarman nothing but grief, because he is a false friend. The analogy with the credulous (and evidently wealthy) ascetic is inexact, vis-à-vis both Damanaka's difficulties and those of King Piṅgalaka.

Nor does Damanaka's situation find any perfect analogy in the story of the rams, which describes a jackal's Icarian flight too close to conflict. This is nothing like what transpires with the fast friendship of Piṅgalaka and Saṃjīvaka, who rather than fighting live together harmoniously. It is rather that a *successful* liaison between Piṅgalaka and Saṃjīvaka harmed the one who arranged it, and in the story of the rams the jackal arranged nothing but only turned up from the margins to the scene of a conflict already under way. The story of the rams is inaptly applied as a warning to Damanaka, then, because it highlights the dangers associated with two large beasts at battle, but does so precisely when Damanaka innovates his intention to "sow dissension" between two large beasts. More importantly, by sowing such dissension at the end of the first book, he is not harmed as is the jackal by the two rams, but he rather attains his ultimate goal of wielding unrivaled influence over the king.

Again, the question of questionable liaisons, which the ascetic's story invokes, was evoked early in the first book's narrative, not in considering what Damanaka can win from friendship with Piṅgalaka or what Piṅgalaka can win from friendship with Saṃjīvaka, but rather in pondering what Piṅgalaka should guard against in welcoming any liaison with Damanaka. Here is the *real* lesson, and the most apt target of the morals of Damanaka's stories—that is, if only the hearers of the stories (the three princes; we the readers) are careful enough to notice it. It was Piṅgalaka who needed to protect himself, just as Devaśarman should have done against Āṣāḍhabhūti the ascetic, not Damanaka. The story Damanaka tells his jackal companion Karaṭaka in response to his own difficulties is one whose moral is better applied to the target of his own dishonesty, the lion-king Piṅgalaka, and the moment when the story would have been most suitably narrated had already passed (without mention) by the time the story is told. And perhaps the jackal in the story of two rams got exactly what Piṅgalaka should have realized Damanaka deserves.

Now, King Piṅgalaka does ponder the wisdom of inviting a distant person, Damanaka, into his life, and this he does at the time of the invitation. But he questions the matter only in passing, without any guiding story to help his thinking, and thus he does so in a manner that slips from narrative focus just as easily as it peeks in. It is only an incipient concern; it fades imperceptibly, as any glimmer of warning not heeded would and does outside the text, in "life's maze." One can wager one's own good fortune and one's very life without even knowing it; the misjudgment slips across one's attention unnoticed, unless one is discerning.

In the first book, it happened like this: at the moment when Damanaka first sought to ingratiate himself with Piṅgalaka, the jackal asks why the lion won't approach the water, but Piṅgalaka brushes off the question. Damanaka then signals that he detects an underlying problem, prompting Piṅgalaka to query of himself whether he can confide in Damanaka. But he quickly and precipitously assures himself that the jackal is both capable and loyal, precisely what a king should seek in good counsel.[24]

After a discourse on when and where fear is justified, Damanaka agrees to go out to see what has caused the noise. On his departure, the lion-king becomes concerned that Damanaka could become a double agent or become hostile.[25] This, of course, is something of the right line of questioning, though the concern implicitly expressed—and wrongly so—is that Damanaka left his company as a loyal aide but could become a double agent on meeting whomever it is who is making the frightening noise. Questioning Damanaka's trustworthiness, however, is appropriate, and it is precisely the line of questioning recommended by Devaśarman's story, told later to Karaṭaka by Damanaka; but Piṅgalaka never revisits the concern. The readers and hearers of the *Pañcatantra* narrative, however, have heard Damanaka and can do so. Thus may the three princes, also the external audience, be educated by such stories, the lessons of which are set out of place.

What of the third story that Damanaka tells Karaṭaka, that of the unfaithful wife and the weaver? It is narrated like this: robbed of his wealth, the ascetic

[24] Indeed, Damanaka introduces himself, in part, as follows (*Pañcatantra* 1.49, Edgerton 1924 [vol. 1]: 32): *kiṃ bhaktenāsamarthena kiṃ śaktenāpakāriṇā* | *bhaktaṃ śaktaṃ ca māṃ rājan yathāvaj jñātum arhasi* ||. "Now, what is the use of a faithful man, / if he is without skill? / And what is the use of a skillful man, / if he is ill-disposed? / But know, O my King, and this is the truth, / I am faithful and I do have the skill!" Translation that of Olivelle.

[25] See Edgerton 1924 (vol. 1): 39, line 7-40, line 2, where Piṅgalaka says the following to himself on Damanaka's departure: *aho na śobhanaṃ kṛtaṃ mayā, yat tasya viśvāsaṃ gatvātmābhiprāyo niveditaḥ* | *kadācid damanako 'yam ubhayavetano bhūtvā mamopari duṣṭabuddhiḥ syāt* |. "Come to think of it, I may not have been wise to place my trust in him and to reveal what was in my mind. It could well happen that Damanaka will turn into a double agent and become hostile toward me." Translation that of Olivelle. Note that Edgerton (1924 [vol. 1]: xv) harbors doubts as to whether much of this passage "literally corresponds to the original text" and for some of it is unsure "that the original contained even the equivalent in general sense."

Devaśarman wanders listlessly in an effort to locate the false friend and thief Āṣāḍhabhūti, when he finds himself at sunset in a village where a weaver lives. There, the ascetic comes to witness a stunning series of events. From the corner of the weaver's house, where he was permitted to spend the night, Devaśarman sees that man leave his wife alone at home so he might visit his friends in town, which is far from their secluded house. Soon, a bawd visits and coaxes the weaver's wife, who was promiscuous, to meet her lover. But her husband soon returns—drunk—and intercepts his wife, beats her with a club, and ties her to the central post of the house, after which he stumbles into a drunken sleep. When the bawd returns to collect the wife for the planned *rendez-vous*, she finds her bound and offers to take her place so the weaver's wife can meet her desperate lover after all. The plan is agreed to and the bawd adorns the wife's clothes as disguise and takes her place tied to the post.

When the weaver awakens, however, he returns to punishing her, berating her again, though this time in a more sobered state. The bawd is terrified and says nothing, but her silence only provokes him further, and to punish her he cuts off her nose. On her return, the wife sees the bawd in this sorry state, the weaver—her husband—having somehow fallen once again asleep (out of shock for what he did?). She acts quickly, swiftly switching places with the bawd. When her husband awakens yet again, she has occasion to makes a scene, asking the "guardians of the universe" to restore her nose if she is sexually pure. Her husband of course finds her there, "restored" to her uncut self, and he thus comes—wrongly—to trust in her fidelity. All the while Devaśarman silently stands witness to the entire series of events from the corner of the house.

Meanwhile, the unfortunate bawd—obviously still with her nose cut off—returns home and is met by her own testy and impatient husband, who is a barber. He yells to her to bring the shaving kit from another room, in response to which she throws only the razor to him, which he in anger hurls back across the threshold. Of course, she claims he cut her nose off in doing so and accuses him of an unjust punishment. The police are called, and they beat the barber bloody. But just as they are about to impale him for abusing his wife, Devaśarman intervenes (somehow, he is there too, to witness the events in the bawd's house), recounting for them the entire series of stories—that of his own victimization at the hands of Āṣāḍhabhūti the robber, of the jackal and the rams, and of the bawd and the weaver. The barber who was beaten for the supposed crime of harming his wife is thus released on the basis of Devaśarman's direct witness of the events.

How do we interpret this story? Banerjee is right to suggest that the use of repetition here of the verse that introduces the stories told, as elsewhere in the *Pañcatantra*, may fruitfully be compared with the *nigamana* of the Nyāya syllogism,[26] and the present episode may be understood to support his argument that the stories of the *Pañcatantra* reassert the preference, also found in Nyāya epistemology, for *pratyakṣa* over *śabda* (or *āptopadeśa*), direct witnessing over testimony, the latter presented as of a questionable reliability in the *Pañcatantra* narratives (this on the caveat that we overlook the fact that it is the *testimony* of his direct witness that allows Devaśarman to exculpate the barber from the crime of spousal abuse).[27] I would argue, however, that the question nevertheless remains as to *for whom* the moral of this story is most aptly suited, for, as we have repeatedly noted above, the fact that the narratives are emboxed means that the hearers of the stories are themselves also nested: the three princes, so too we the hearers of the *Pañcatantra* who are external to the frame narrative, take in *all* the stories; characters down the line hear some but not all, and so on.

Bearing the nesting of audiences in mind, one might say that the story of the weaver, his wife, the bawd, and her husband offers a useful lesson to Devaśarman, the ascetic who was too trusting of his friend the thief, Āṣāḍhabhūti, who robbed him blind. He saw with his own eyes how ones with whom one is intimate can lie. But there is a certain uncomfortable irony in what the weaver's story offers Devaśarman, in that a presumably celibate and unmarried ascetic is given occasion to stand as the unfettered witness to the travails of adultery in marriage—not, one may presume and by definition given his station in life, his immediate concern.

More importantly, the events in the weaver's house offer little in the way of a germane parable of advice to Damanaka, who in this moment needs no lesson in the intrigues of promiscuous women, nor the value of the direct witness, nor the dangers of credulity, but rather a lesson in the virtues of *nonintervention* in the affairs of others. And yet—and again, ironically—the narrative of the weaver and his wife chronicles Devaśarman's entirely successful intervention on behalf of the barber, who is saved from execution by his voluntary testimony. Indeed, this is the very concluding move in the narrative. Devaśarman stands witness to all the repeatedly violent events and yet is left entirely unmolested by them and unharmed by his intervention, an

[26] See Banerjee 1996: 42.
[27] Banerjee 1996: 47.

intervention that, like Damanaka's with Piṅgalaka, is entirely adventitious in the sense that if he did not present himself, no one would have asked for his participation in the events to hand.

It is true that from another point of view this story licenses Damanaka's next intended move, to sow dissension among allies, for the story suggests with the example of Devaśarman that an intervention judiciously made *can* prove to be fruitful, and Damanaka is plotting just such a move. But the advice the story embeds is also inapt, or at least inexact. Devaśarman intervenes on the behalf of another—the barber—not for his own sake, while Damanaka has personal interests in mind. And the need for Damanaka's further intervention is precisely to remedy his previous, improperly executed intervention, which fashioned the alliance between Piṅgalaka and Saṃjīvaka in the first place. In the story of the weaver, Devaśarman is an innocent bystander. Finally, and most importantly, Devaśarman's role is to make evident the real presence of a deception where none was seen prior to his intervention, while Damanaka intends to create an aura of deception where none is actually present.

Read from the point of view of the three princes, who may wish to know how Piṅgalaka might act, he being the character of the core narrative of the first book who holds a social position analogous to theirs, the weaver's story offers a warning and not a recommended path of action. There is a perfect analogy in the weaver's story with the threat faced by Piṅgalaka: Devaśarman clarifies that no harmful action was intended or enacted in a circumstance where another—the barber's wife, the bawd—falsely claims there was, just as Piṅgalaka is to be presented with the false claim that Saṃjīvaka intends harm even while he harbors no such intent. And kings are supposed to keep spies in their kingdom to know the actions of their subjects, agents of the crown who are to perform the very role that Devaśarman plays in the narrative here offered—to offer seeing eyes on events, witnesses who can discover how events have actually transpired, so the authorities may know how properly to act.

The parable of the rams and the jackal, in turn, tells Damanaka that proximity to warring titans is dangerous. But, despite this warning, shared by him with Karaṭaka in noting the problems he himself has created, he proceeds to elect to generate just such a battle between the two large beasts. The readers outside—above—the frame of the Piṅgalaka-Damanaka narrative, however, can see the more fundamental message of the entire Devaśarman narrative and its substories. The story of the rams warns one against sticking one's nose into any risky place, and the core lessons of this entire cycle of three narratives are, first, that deception may ever and always be operative, particularly where and when it is least expected, and, second, that either danger or good fortune can enter with characters who emerge from outside one's circle of trust. This is what all the stories have in common: Āṣāḍhabhūti is an outsider, the jackal between the rams comes from outside their fight, and Devaśarman saves the barber from unjust capital punishment as an outside witness to the events that transpired. The matter, then, is double-edged; for, properly read, it suggests Piṅgalaka should meet the outsider Damanaka with caution while also suggesting the opposite, for the outsider Saṃjīvaka is no ill influence but someone who, properly managed, could fruitfully be engaged as an ally. Discerning is difficult in "life's maze": the warning that the three princes could find in these stories for Piṅgalaka—and for themselves—also invites occasion to welcome new friends.

Karaṭaka asks Damanaka how he will create the conflict, in reply to which Damanaka offers another story, in which is nested yet another. The outer of these two stories tells of how a murder of crows killed their enemy. The crows lived otherwise happily in a tree, in the hollow of which lived a snake. Whenever the crows hatched chicks, the black cobra would emerge slowly from the hollow and eat them before they could learn to fly. In despair the crows consulted a jackal, who explained to them what they should do. They needed cunning to defeat the snake, as did, the jackal says, the heron who ate a lot of fish. "How did that happen?" ask the crows, and the emboxed tale is then told as follows.

A heron had grown old and no longer could catch fish, so he concocts a story. He tells a crab, who is friends with the fish he likes to eat, that he overheard some human fishermen saying they will soon cast their nets in the pond in which they live, capturing them all and also depriving the heron thereby of any chance at a livelihood. The crab conveys the news to the fish, and all agree that the only way out is to have their theretofore enemy, the heron, fly them to the safety of another pond. An enemy might be an ally, after all, in the face of a threat from an even more powerful foe. The heron begins to take the fish one by one from the pond, but instead of offering a rescue he drops them on the rocks and eats them. This he does happily and invariably until it is the crab's turn. He lifts the crab with the same intentions, but the crab spots the bones of his erstwhile friends and decides to fight back, clawing off the heron's head. The crab then returns and explains to the surviving fish the heron's ruse, as well the heron's demise by his claw.

With this narrative and the advice it embeds in mind, the crows are told they must steal a gold chain from someone in the local king's court in order to plant it in the snake's hollow, which they do. Of course, this leads the king's men to the hollow in searching out the gold chain. Once there, they kill the snake in order to recover it.

What is evident is that the story of the crows and the snake indicates a means for a weaker party to win through cunning, precisely what Damanaka needs to do in the moment, for the bull and the lion are his physical superiors. In this sense the story is aptly curated. The inset story of the heron, however, presented to the crows to illustrate the tactic of using cunning, is only of limited use to the crows for whom it is supposedly narrated. It does not teach them how to use a stratagem to defeat a stronger opponent but only how a heron used cunning, while weak, to trick nimbler but not stronger prey to fall to his wishes. Yet, the heron story is defined not only by the general stratagem it narrates but also by the twin dangers it exposes, first that of being duped by a ploy—the warning of the slaughtered fish—and, second, that of being unintentionally afflicted by one's own cunning, this being a danger the heron should have heeded when he instead applied his strategy too cavalierly and picked up the clawing crab. The story is in this sense of use to both the crows and Damanaka, then, in that it suggests one must be careful when deploying a stratagem.

More importantly, however, the story of the heron and the fish carries with it an irony if we are to understand it to guide either the crows or Damanaka to act well, for it involves the use of wile to create an alliance—albeit a false one—in the context of the presence of a greater external threat, which is imagined. The crows, by contrast, need a real external intervention, and they seek to create no alliance, whether false or otherwise, but to sow dissension among those who are as yet unknown to one another: the humans don't even know of the snake they will be led to kill. Damanaka, on the other hand, will create a false external threat, as did the heron; but like the crows and unlike the heron he does so to sow dissension, not to forge a false alliance between those who to that point had been mortal foes.

The readers or hearers of the entire set of nested narratives—the three princes, the readers and hearers of the *Pañcatantra* itself—remain better served by the heron story than are either the crows or Damanaka himself, the essential lesson of which is, at base, that one who presents oneself as a friend often is not. The story in this sense would have been more suitable to Piṅgalaka, and for that matter to Saṃjīvaka, than it is to Damanaka. Indeed, the story Damanaka comes to tell Piṅgalaka will not only be a lie, one deceptively suggesting Saṃjīvaka is disloyal and conniving, but it will also cover over the very fact that it is he himself who is self-serving, loyal only to himself.[28]

The story of the crows and the snake that frames the story of the heron and the crab, as noted, does suggest the usefulness of a stratagem for defeating a stronger foe, and this advice *is* applicable to Damanaka's situation. The crows manage to cultivate dissension between the humans they lure to the scene, on the one hand, and the snake that is their mortal enemy, on the other hand, the humans ridding the crows of the snake without knowing they were serving to doing so. Yet one must also question whether power—strength—really is the issue to hand, for while the snake is actively killing the crows' chicks, Damanaka is instead faced with an overly pacific and *neglectful* king. And however fierce Piṅgalaka may be (despite the bout of cowardice that defines the very occasion for his alliance with Damanaka), he also is overly credulous, and this is his defining character trait. His relationship with Damanaka is therefore partially unlike that of the heron and the fish, who are natural enemies, but partially similar in that the fish too are overly credulous. Piṅgalaka's situation is also unlike that of the snake and the crows, who are at mortal odds, which is not true of his relationship to

[28] What's more, the very place where Damanaka seeks to convince Piṅgalaka of Saṃjīvaka's disloyalty reads precisely as a lesson in how Piṅgalaka should have measured the reliability of Damanaka himself. Yet the king, when he pondered the trustworthiness of Damanaka and feared his becoming a double agent, this shortly after meeting him (and as noted already), fails properly to weigh the concern to hand. Reciting what is likely an untraced quotation from a heretofore unidentified treatise on government that has parallels at *Arthaśāstra* 1.14.2–5 (for which see Olivelle 1997: 168, endnote on p. 19 of his translation), Piṅgalaka considered that two classes of people pose danger to a king: those who have been marginally harmed by him, who can be overcome with cunning, and, secondly, those who are invariably opposed to him, this for reasons of overtaxation, suffering poverty or forced exile, or being overshadowed by their peers or overworked, or because they are pretenders to the throne who hail from the king's own family. These two classes of possible opponents in mind, Piṅgalaka determined (on wobbly grounds) that he could not but pass time close to Damanaka, because withdrawal could have turned Damanaka against him, even to the point where Damanaka could have allied himself with a stronger opponent in a burgeoning opposition to him. Of course, the right solution would have been to exercise proper discretion vis-à-vis Damanaka in the first place, that or Piṅgalaka could have used cunning to separate himself from him under a ruse, or rid himself of him altogether. Instead, he determined that circumstances demanded passive acquiescence: "Now Damanaka, thinking honours have been withdrawn from him, could well become hostile towards me. Or, because he is himself powerless, he may ally himself with someone powerful and show neutrality towards me. In either case, I am certainly doomed. I have no option but to leave this place and go somewhere else until I find out what he intends to do." See Edgerton 1924 (vol. 1): 40, line 8-41, line 4: *so 'yaṃ pratyāhṛtamāno 'ham iti matvā mamaivopari kadācid vikāraṃ bhajeta, athavāsamarthyād balavatā pratyanubaddho mamaiva madhyenāgacchet | tathāpi ahaṃ vinaṣṭa eva | tat sarvathāsmāt sthānāt anyat sthānam āśrayāmi, yāvad asya mayā vijñātaṃ cikīrṣitam iti*... Translation that of Olivelle.

either Saṃjīvaka or Damanaka. Saṃjīvaka has similarly shown no ill will as yet toward Damanaka, unlike the snake with the crows and the heron with the fish.

By analogy, Damanaka might wish to understand Piṅgalaka to be most like the humans in the story of the crow and the snake, with the snake being an analog for Saṃjīvaka—the proximate enemy who must be destroyed. Yet Damanaka already has an alliance with Piṅgalaka, unlike the crows with the humans, and Saṃjīvaka is not afflicting his kin with violence, while the snake was eating the chicks. Also, the alliance between the crows and the humans was episodic and not enduring, while Damanaka, taken as an analog for the story's protagonist crows, is already aligned with Piṅgalaka, the analog of the humans in that story.

In the end, then, all these two stories really suggest to Damanaka is that one may bring an outside force to bear when dealing with a proximate opponent (or prey). For the *readers and hearers* of the Piṅgalaka-Damanaka narrative, in turn, the message of the heron's story is overpowering. It is not primarily one recommending cunning where power is scarce; it is more simply an admonition: don't be a sucker.

What neither story addresses is the core quality of Damanaka's relationship with Piṅgalaka in the first place, for one may question how impeachable the lion-king is in his friendship with Saṃjīvaka. Damanaka does claim that the "evil [of kings] is just one; it is called addiction" (*ekam evedaṃ vyasanaṃ prasaṅgākhyaṃ*).[29] Yet when he subsequently charts the range of types of addiction, friendship and immersion in learning are not offered as among them, which is all Piṅgalaka has with Saṃjīvaka, though, as noted already, he does neglect to provide for his people for indulging the friendship.[30] Simply put: why pursue dissension among allies at all? Is this really the proper course of action for a minister so situated as Damanaka is? Couldn't this jackal-minister have applied another, less drastic remedy to the problem, some method to ease the king back to the work to hand? After all, what was he learning in those *śāstric* lessons in the first place? And couldn't Piṅgalaka the king, in turn, have more carefully questioned Damanaka's sincerity in announcing Saṃjīvaka's disloyalty?

Let us turn now to the endgame of the first book and consider the story Damanaka deploys to convince Piṅgalaka of Saṃjīvaka's disloyalty, for it too

[29] See Edgerton 1924 (vol. 1): 61, lines 7–8.
[30] See footnote 23.

is an ironic narrative for the lessons it offers. In it a louse allows a bug into the bed in which he lives, which is the king's. But he tells the bug only to bite the king when he is drunken and asleep or exhausted from lovemaking, moments when he would not easily be awoken to their presence. The bug, of course, ignores the louse's direction and bites the king at will, who is disturbed and takes action, demanding from his attendants that the culprit be eliminated.

The king's men tear up his bed, but by that time the bug had jumped out, and only the slow-moving louse was found and destroyed. The moral of the story, at least from Damanaka's perspective, is clear: allowing into one's house a supposed friend can invite harm; and this is what happened *to him* with the introduction of Saṃjīvaka into Piṅgalaka's court, precipitating the lack of fresh kills on which he and Karaṭaka could feast. In narrating the story for the king, moreover, Damanaka means the story to suggest the same, that allowing the wrong person into *his* company can cause him harm—thus the purported need to eliminate Saṃjīvaka. Damanaka tells Piṅgalaka that he is, by analogy, the louse who allowed the bug into the bed.

But the lion-king, if he were a careful interpreter of the story, would have noticed the imperfection in the analogy. If he could see through with wisdom, he would have found his obvious analog in the story to be the human king whose bed was infested, not the louse. This is to say that while the story stands as a lesson for Piṅgalaka, because it aptly suggests the need to practice caution in managing one's kingdom and court (by analogy the bed where the story's infestation occurs)—a lesson of use too to the three princes listening to the narrative—it could also have raised Piṅgalaka's sense of caution in measuring the quality of the relations of his ministers *with one another* (as with the bug and the louse). The real lesson of the story, if Piṅgalaka were thoughtful enough to discern it, was that two of his courtly underlings could not live fruitfully together, and that *both* of them were wrongly sapping his resources—Damanaka having eyes on a totalizing influence, Saṃjīvaka monopolizing his time.

With this we see the narrative force and pedagogic significance of the entire first book. Lessons in "life's maze" might easily be misapplied or misunderstood, and only discerning—supported by the careful reading of text—can make one aware of this fact. Finally, and most importantly, there is the ultimate irony of the story of the bug and the louse, ironic in particular in light of the fact that Damanaka offers it to Piṅgalaka in order to turn him against Saṃjīvaka: the story is one of a king whose men fail to eliminate all the offending pests. The one who precipitated the confrontation in the first place—the bug, whose bites are felt and who thus stands as Damanaka's true analog in the story—escapes before the cleansing has begun.[31]

On Money, Fate, and Friendship: The Second Book

As Olivelle notes, the first is the largest of the five books of the *Pañcatantra*, making up some forty-five percent of the entire text.[32] It also is the most sophisticated, for the reasons indicated: no other book is as subtle or complex in its narration of the lessons it offers. The remaining four books of the *Pañcatantra* do nevertheless communicate various complexities in navigating "life's maze," and inviolable rules of conduct or mechanical methods of discernment are difficult to come by in them, because judgment—in particular judgment of the character of others—is presented more as an art than a science.

Perhaps no book makes this more plainly evident than the second, the core narrative of which explicitly contravenes what one would have expected to be a bedrock principle of statecraft: that "nature (birth, pedigree) rather than upbringing determines behaviour," as Olivelle put it, subsequently citing a maxim of the *Pañcatantra* itself that, as it happens, is found in the second book: "there can be no friendship between grass-eaters and meat-eaters, between a food and its eater."[33] And yet, the core narrative of the second book itself works explicitly against this position.

Entitled "On Securing Alliances," the second book illustrates the proper measure of friendship. Friends offer not just comfort but also committed support in times of difficulty, and friendship is a matter of the heart:

> A favour does not signify a friend,
> An injury does not reveal a foe;
> Whether a man's heart is virtuous or vile,
> Determines whether he is friend or foe.[34]

[31] This would suggest, however, that Piṅgalaka is right to eliminate Saṃjīvaka, just as the king's men are right to rid the bed of the louse, the pest in the story analogous with him. I continue to think, however, that another manner of dealing with Saṃjīvaka could have been engaged, to modify his behavior rather than to eliminate his presence altogether.

[32] It measures to forty-five percent of the Edgerton edition of the text, that is. See Olivelle 1997: xiv.

[33] Olivelle 1997: xxxvi.

[34] *Pañcatantra* 2.23 (Edgerton 1924 [vol. 1]: 203): *nopakāraḥ suhṛccihnaṃ nāpakāro 'rilakṣaṇam* | *praduṣṭam apraduṣṭaṃ vā cittam evātra kāraṇam* ||. Translation that of Olivelle.

The second book does not present the morals to its stories out of step, as it were, as the first book does, nor for that matter do any of the books after the first. The emboxed stories of the second book offer fitting analogies and lessons to those for whom they are told. Indeed, the embedded stories are often those of the very characters who tell them: the second book narrates stories of friends confiding in friends, sharing their personal stories in openness and trust. *Trust*, in fact, defines the message of the second book, in which no act of trust in friendship anywhere results in betrayal.

Particularly noteworthy is that the core alliance of the book is one of a crow with a mouse, animals that are in fact natural enemies. This produces a mood in the second book that stands as the mirror opposite to that of the first. One may be forgiven for anticipating—at least toward the beginning of the second book—a ruinous end to the alliance between these natural enemies, between "food and its eater." Even Hiraṇyaka, the mouse, fears as much at first, citing as he does the very dictum Olivelle did in tracing the nature of alliances.[35] But the moment of betrayal never arrives. So the reader, if naturally haunted by a tension emanating from this book's narrative—also the betrayals of the first book—nevertheless finds the concern ultimately to be one that is unwarranted.

If the dynamic of the first book is one in which one is easily lulled into a false sense of security, one of trusting those who should not be trusted, in the second book the mood is one of a haltingly growing confidence in loyal friendship. Rather than demanding the reader seek out the hidden cautions of the text, as does the first book, the second book brings the reader gradually to a certain place of comfort, uneasy at first because something certainly could go wrong—by the maxim of natural enemies, something *should* go wrong—but comfort all the same for the book's happy ending. Thus, the path through to prosperous action here is again one of understanding that good judgment—so too hard work—is paramount in guaranteeing success. It's just that sometimes a good judgment is one that places confidence in one's friends, and it really can be as simple as that.

The book's framing story is charming and relatively simple. A crow named Laghupatanaka witnesses something that makes a deep impression on him. He saw a flock of crows land themselves in a fowler's net, enticed as they were to go there by the grain he laid out as bait for his trap. The king of the

[35] *Pañcatantra* 2.9 (Edgerton 1924 [vol. 1]: 196): *yad yena yujyate loke budhas tat tena yojayet* | *aham annaṃ bhavān bhoktā kathaṃ prītir bhaviṣyati* ||.

doves too, one Citragrīva, was captured this way with his bevy. Sensing only one way to escape, their king set his dule of doves to coordinated work, and though trapped in it together they lifted the net and flew off.

The fowler, however, followed them, knowing they would eventually tire and have to land. Laghupatanaka was curious as to what would transpire—after all, he himself was potentially the fowler's victim—so he too followed at a safe distance. Citragrīva, though, soon recognized the fowler's plan and encouraged his companions to fly high into the sky and over hills, out of his sight. Eventually, the fowler gave up chase and turned back, allowing the doves to land themselves near a friend. Citragrīva knew Hiraṇyaka, a mouse who would help them, and when they landed themselves by his home, Hiraṇyaka quickly chewed through the net and released them from the fowler's trap.

Laghupatanaka is immediately enamored with the possibility of having a friend like Hiraṇyaka, and he seeks him out and establishes just that—despite the fact that the mouse is his habitual prey. Indeed, the text specifies that the crow is not Hiraṇyaka's merely "incidental" enemy but a "natural" one, the latter being subdivided into "enmity from just one side and enmity coming from both sides."[36] (Here we have the former.) Nevertheless convincing Hiraṇyaka of his honest heart, Laghupatanaka befriends the mouse, and the two pass many happy days together.

Through the medium of their friendship the book explores two twined themes. The first is that of power and the intoxicating pull of wealth, of money. The second is that the power of discernment and good judgment—in a word, a virtuous character—can lead one through life's inevitable difficulties. The best judgment to have, evidently, is in friendship, because

[36] See Edgerton 1924 (vol. 1): 198, line 10-199, line 1: *tac ca svābhāvikaṃ vairaṃ dvividhaṃ bhavati, ekāṅgavairam ubhayavairaṃ ca* |. Note, however, that Edgerton doubts whether this passage corresponds perfectly with what was to be found in the *Ur-Pañcatantra*.

The matter is further elaborated as follows (Edgerton 1924 [vol. 1]: 199): *yo vihanyāt parasparam, anyonyena bhakṣate, parasparāpakārāt tad ubhayavairam, yathā siṅhagajānām | yaḥ pūrvam eva hatvā bhakṣayati, na cāsau tasyāpakaroti, na hinsati, na bhakṣyati, tad ekāṅgavairam, akasmāt, yathā, aśvamahiṣāṇāṃ mārjāramūṣakāṇām ahinakulānām* |. "When each would kill the other and each would eat the other, then there is enmity from both sides, because each can cause harm to the other. Such, for example, is the enmity between lions and elephants. When without provocation the one kills and eats the other, while the other does no harm to him, does not injure him, and does not eat him, that is enmity from just one side and for no reason. Such, for example, is the enmity between horses and buffaloes, between cats and mice, and between snakes and mongooses." Translation Olivelle's. (Note, however, that Edgerton also doubts whether this extended passage literally corresponds to the original text, and of several small elements of it he doubts whether the original contained even the equivalent in a general sense, for which see Edgerton 1924 [vol. 1]: xv, where his rubric for marking these doubts is defined, and the passage of text here cited is thus annotated with italics and parentheses.)

friends stand by their companions in the tough times and not just when luck is with them. The vicissitudes of life are often mentioned in the second book. Fate is emphasized in the context of underscoring the value of hard work, which is strongly praised but only in the context of a promise that no individual entirely escapes misfortune in life.

Money, fate, and friendship might make for a *prima facie* incidental juxtaposition, but the second book implicitly and gradually proves their necessary association, for money motivates many people above all:

> "He is my friend!"—is that any reason
>   to trust a scoundrel?
> "I have done him a great many favours"—
>   that counts for nothing!
> "This man is my own relative"—
>   that's an old folk tale!
> People are driven by money alone,
>   No matter how small.[37]

Indeed:

> When you have wealth, you have friends!
> When you have wealth, you have kin!
> When you have wealth, you're a man,
> You're a pundit in this world.[38]

These words we receive from Hiraṇyaka in the course of relating his own life's experiences to Laghupatanaka. And he would know. His personal history is punctuated first by a time when he was riding high: he was a mouse who easily and always could steal the food of an ascetic, even when it was secured in a bowl hung high up on a peg on the wall. This is as it was until one day a close friend of that ascetic, another peripatetic, set out to help his companion. This man dug out Hiraṇyaka's fortress with a spade and found his hidden talisman, a bit of gold he had once stolen and squirreled away.

[37] *Pañcatantra* 2.16 (Edgerton 1924 [vol. 1]: 200): *suhṛd ayam iti durjane 'sti kāśā, bahu kṛtam asya mayeti luptam etat | svajana iti purāṇa eṣa śabdo, dhanalavamātranibandhano hi lokaḥ ||*. Translation that of Olivelle.

[38] *Pañcatantra* 2.31 (Edgerton 1924 [vol. 1]: 232): *yasyārthās tasya mitrāṇi yasyārthās tasya bāndhvaḥ | yasyārthāḥ sa pumān loke yasyārthāḥ sa ca paṇḍitaḥ ||*. Translation that of Olivelle.

After that, just as the friend of the ascetic promised, Hiraṇyaka could no longer jump high enough to reach the food, much as he would try. He had lost his "confidence and vigour"[39] by way of the loss of his wealth. By the next day all the mice who had followed him went over to his adversaries, cheerfully and openly taunting him in doing so.

It was fate, Hiraṇyaka said, that brought this turn of events to him, though the astute reader will note that his fate befell him by way of the advice and aid of the ascetic's *friend*. And yet, what is also suggested is that anyone can experience—everyone will experience—a sour turn of luck in life. The mouse Hiraṇyaka is in no sense unique. He works, however, to rectify the situation: he tried and tried but could not steal back his gold and could not regain his old confidence. So he settled on what he could manage, saying this:

> "When it is altogether impossible to obtain wealth, discernment is surely the best course. As it is said:
>
> What's righteousness? Compassion on all beings.
> What's happiness for creatures in this world?
> Freedom from sickness.
> What's affection? A true disposition.
> What's erudition? True discernment."[40]

We here sense the weight of Hiraṇyaka's name, which means "eagerness for gold" (or perhaps better, the "little golden one"), as he relates his story to his friend the crow, and with him the crow's friend, Mantharaka the turtle. His good luck—at least his luck with money and with attracting those kinds of acolytes who are attracted to money—had run out, but he had used his judgment to agree to an unlikely friendship with a "natural enemy," Laghupatanaka the crow, who brought him to the hometown of his old friend the turtle.

Mantharaka lived on an island to which Laghupatanaka retreated in a depression, one caused by having always to negotiate fowlers and their traps, a constant threat on his life. When he retreated, he brought Hiraṇyaka with him. Mantharaka quickly endeavors to cheer his new friend Hiraṇyaka, who

[39] That is, he was *nijaśaktihīna* and *sattvotsāharahita*. (See Edgerton 1924 [vol. 1]: 231, line 2.) The translations cited of these adjectival terms are those of Olivelle.

[40] *Pañcatantra* 2.50 (Edgerton 1924 [vol. 1]: 239): *tat sarvathā 'sādhye 'rthe pariccheda* [corr: *paricheda*, ed.] *eva śreyān. uktaṃ ca: ko dharmo bhūtadayā kiṃ saukhyam arogatā jagati jantoḥ | kaḥ snehaḥ sadbhāvaḥ kim pāṇḍityaṃ paricchedaḥ* ||. Translation that of Olivelle.

was still despondent over his losses in life, by reminding him that wealth is "like bubbles on the water":

> The shadow of a cloud, and a new crop,
> A young woman, and friendship with a rogue;
> One enjoys these only for a moment
> as also youth and wealth.[41]

Fate is fate, but friendship is the ultimate salve:

> Friends who enjoy the company of friends,
> In mutual affection and delight;
> They drink deeply at the fountain of joy;
> they alone are true men;
> they alone truly live.[42]

Soon after, a deer rushes onto the scene, and after checking against any imminent danger, Laghupatanaka, Mantharaka, and Hiraṇyaka come out of hiding to speak to him. The deer, Citrāṅga, was in retreat, hiding from the hunters ever on his track. The three welcome him to their island, and he stays on for some time in friendship, until one day he fails to return home at the habitual hour. The friends grow worried, so Laghupatanaka flies skyward to search for him, and finds him trapped in a hunter's snare. He quickly brings Hiraṇyaka there, and Citrāṅga, after blaming fate for his being captured, begs the mouse to bite through the snare and set him free. This he does, but not before hearing the deer's story, and not before Mantharaka manages slowly to amble at his turtle's pace onto the scene.

They all share a feeling of gratitude for friendship, Mantharaka again speaking the most wholesome words about it:

> "If it weren't for that splendid medicine,
> the company of friends,

[41] *Pañcatantra* 2.67 (Edgerton 1924 [vol. 1]: 245): *abhrachāyā khalaprītir navasasyāni yoṣitaḥ | kiñcitkālopabhogyāni yauvanāni dhanāni ca ||*. Translation Olivelle's. (Edgerton doubts the originality of the term *abhra* in *abhrachāyā*, however. See his edition, Edgerton 1924 [vol. 1]: 245.)

[42] *Pañcatantra* 2.73 (Edgerton 1924 [vol. 1]: 247 *sukhasya maṇḍaḥ paripīyate tair, jīvanti te satpuruṣās ta eva | hṛṣṭāḥ suhṛṣṭaih suhṛdaḥ suhṛdbhiḥ, priyāḥ priyair ye sahitā ramante ||*. Translation Olivelle's. (Edgerton doubts the originality of the term *maṇḍaḥ paripīyate*, however. See his edition, also at Edgerton 1924 [vol. 1]: 245.)

Is there a man who could endure the loss
Of wealth or of loved ones?"[43]

And:

"By telling your troubles
To a faithful friend or a virtuous wife,
Or a master who's known adversity,
Your heart will find some rest."[44]

But they dally too long, and the hunter returns to the scene, prompting Laghupatanaka to retreat to the sky, Hiraṇyaka to a burrow, and the deer Citrāṅga to escape into the woods. The hunter believes it a miracle—in fact, an act of fate—that the deer somehow freed himself, but then he captures Mantharaka, who could not so quickly escape, and he sees the turtle as a consoling reward.

The friends regroup and lament the fate of their friend, that eloquent turtle, and then choose to act without delay. The plan is hatched. Citrāṅga will be the bait, appearing within sight of the hunter, who will forget the cheap turtle and seek the bigger prize. Laghupatanaka will mime the act of pecking Citrāṅga's eyes, to convince the hunter his prey is killed and therefore easy to retrieve. When he will do the inevitable—leave Mantharaka so as to get to Citrāṅga—Hiraṇyaka will have an opportunity to cut through the turtle's snares, and Laghupatanaka can fly off and Citrāṅga run off in time to evade capture.

All this they do. And "then the four friends, all freed from their troubles and whole in body, came together again and returned to their own place. Living in mutual affection, they spent time in comfort."[45] They lived happily ever after, that is to say.

[43] *Pañcatantra* 2.81 (Edgerton 1924 [vol. 1]: 260): *dayitajanaviprayogo vittaviyogaś ca kasya sahyāḥ syuḥ* | *yadi sumahauṣadhakalpo vayasyajanasaṃgamo na syāt* ||. Translation that of Olivelle. See the same page of Edgerton's edition for his sense of how much of this verse may reliably be attributed to the *Ur-Pañcatantra*.

[44] *Pañcatantra* 2.83 (Edgerton 1924 [vol. 1]: 261): *suhṛdi nirantaracitte guṇavati dāre prabhau ca duḥkhajñe* | *viśrāmyatīva hṛdayaṃ duḥkhasya nivedanaṃ kṛtvā* ||. Translation that of Olivelle. Edgerton doubts whether *antara* of *nirantaracitte* literally corresponds to what was present in the original text of the *Pañcatantra*.

[45] See Edgerton 1924 (vol. 1): 270, lines 3–6: *atha catvāro 'pi te sarve vimuktāpadaḥ kalyaśarīrāḥ punar ekasthībhūya svasthānaṃ gatvā parasparaṃ snehena vartamānāḥ kālena yathāsukham āsthitāḥ* |. Translation that of Olivelle.

It is no narrative coincidence that the final episode of the story required all the friends to play a role in order to execute their plan. All the friends must act and in unison, and all are uniquely capable of playing the parts to which they are assigned. These friends need one another, and as friends they are there for one another in the time of need. And having reached the end of the narrative and as the circle of friends had grown, one can hardly remember any longer the trepidation with which the first two "natural enemies" had formed the original alliance. Friendship, we are taught, trumps fate, trumps the naked pursuit of material gain—it lasts longer than one's grip on money—and it makes for an easy way, where necessary, to accomplish the hard work that might be called for. Yet another maxim sums it up well:

> An evil man is like an earthen pot,
> easy to break, hard to restore;
> A virtuous man is like a golden pot,
> hard to break, easy to restore.[46]

Sometimes good judgment requires trust, that is, because friendship has its place in the realpolitik of the *Pañcatantra*, even friendship found in unexpected or *prima facie* impossible places. In the end, friendship is simple, but invaluable: a virtuous person—a practitioner of the virtue ethic of the Sanskrit narratives—makes for a good friend, and good friends are not only like golden pots, hard to break, but also worth their weight in gold.

Friendship and wealth go together, moreover, because wicked people so frequently pursue the latter at the cost of the former, while the former facilitates the acquisition of the latter; and one can know true friends by whether they will sell their companions out or not. Most importantly, one can have no true friends without the power to spot one and then to trust in those worthy of trust, this in the context of a world where others can well be expected to practice cunning, to pursue their own ends, to harm others in order to help themselves. Friendship, in a word—true, invaluable friendship—can only be born of judgment.

[46] *Pañcatantra* 2.22 (Edgerton 1924 [vol. 1]: 201): *mṛdghaṭavat sukhabhedyo duḥsaṃdhānaś ca durjano bhavati | sujanas tu kanakaghaṭavad durbhedyaḥ saṃdhanīyaś ca ||*. Translation that of Olivelle.

The Other Books

This lesson is repeated often in the remaining three books, that good judgment is the king's most precious commodity, his most precious talent. The interpretation of the last three books can become more mechanical, however, opening to a manner of reading by which the entire collection has often been read—straightforwardly, by way of finding easy morals in simple stories about animals.

The third book deals with "war and peace," and we see in it a statement regarding the nature of counsel and the dangers of credulity in accepting it too easily. It offers a master class in utter and devastating cunning. Other lessons are found in book three, as well, to be sure, one of them being that cutting words never heal:

> Struck by an arrow or cut by an axe,
> Even when a forest fire burns it up,
> A tree mends itself;
> But a wound that is caused by cutting words
> Can never be healed.[47]

Avoiding bad and accepting good counsel, however, figures as the core lesson, because bad counsel is simply deadly:

> Counsel wrongly applied, like a vampire (*vetāla*)
> Improperly invoked (*duriṣṭa iva*),
> Is not pacified until he has killed
> The man who employs it.[48]

The story of the book is one of combat between owls and crows. The crows are in a bad way, having been mauled by the owls' attack, and they decide to deploy a ruse to win the war. Ciraṃjīvin, the minister of Meghavarṇa, king of the crows, hatches a plan whereby he will have his feathers plucked and his body covered with the blood of crows already killed, then set himself in the

[47] *Pañcatantra* 3.53 (Edgerton 1924 [vol. 1]: 310): *saṃrohatīṣuṇā viddhaṃ vanaṃ paraśunā hatam | dagdhaṃ dāvānalenāpi na prarohati vākkṣatam ||*. Translation that of Olivelle.

[48] *Pañcatantra* 3.30 (Edgerton 1924 [vol. 1]: 284): *mithyā praṇihito mantraḥ prayoktāram asaṃśayam | duriṣṭa iva vetālo nānihatyopaśamyati ||*. Translation that of Olivelle. Note also that Edgerton marks the entire verse as perhaps not literally corresponding with what was found in the original *Pañcatantra* text.

sights of the owls. The other crows will retreat to a safe harbor and wait for him to signal that the plan is afoot.

The owls soon find the battered minister, who claims that he had advised his king to submit to the owls—essentially, to sue for peace—so as to mitigate the problem of facing down their much stronger opponent. Meghavarṇa, he claims, took the counsel for treason and had him reduced to the feeble state in which he is found, lucky to get away with his life. The owl king, (ironically, as we shall see) named Arimardana or "Enemy Crusher"—what issues an echo of the narrative of the *Kathāsaritsāgara*[49]—is then set to decide what to do with him, and in weighing options he takes the advice of five of his long-serving ministers: Raktākṣa, Krūrākṣa, Dīptākṣa, Vakranāsa, and Prākārakarṇa. Raktākṣa goes first and gives the simple (and ultimately correct) advice: kill the opponent while he is weak and vulnerable. Krūrākṣa offers the opposite counsel, suggesting that those who are wounded and vulnerable deserve shelter, and all the other ministers agree with him.

Ciraṃjīvin has his prey on the hook, then; but he seeks to set it deep. Now that Arimardana the king has decided with the majority of his ministers to offer him refuge, he feigns refusal of just that, claiming he is worthless in his present state and that he wishes to die by self-immolation so that he might be reborn an owl, which would give him a means to take revenge on the crows for mistreating him as they did. Raktākṣa is having none of it, but the flourish in his story eases Ciraṃjīvin's way into the confidence of the other owls, and they bring him to their fortress where he is to recover his health. Raktākṣa, meanwhile, predicts the decision will be ruinous, collects his family, and abandons the king and the kingdom he had served in preference for a safer harbor at a distance from his erstwhile countrymen. Kings should value good (Brahminical) ministers, who can vote with their feet, and at great cost to the king!

That predicted ruin is quickly delivered on the owls for the credulousness of their king, abetted as he was by the misguided counsel of all but one of his ministers. Ciraṃjīvin over a period of time regrows his feathers and regains his vigor, and in the meantime learns the strengths and vulnerabilities of the owls' fortress, his temporary home. At the right time he quickly plugs the entrances to the fortress with cow dung, and then retrieves Meghavarṇa, his

[49] It is interesting too that this is the name of the king of the *vidyādharas*, for as we just noted, reference to *vetālas* is found in this narrative, and *vetālas* of course figure prominently in the stories of the *Kathāsaritsāgara*, the ultimate end of which is immortality as a *vidyādhara*.

king, to recruit his help and that of the other crows to complete the final step in his plan: he and the crows set sticks into the fortress and burn down the entire army of owls all at once.

The book is rounded out with a long dialogue between minister and king, Ciraṃjīvin explaining the virtues of the counsel he offered and the nature of the failing judgment of Arimardana's four foolish owl-ministers. These passages are chock-full of anecdotes that refer to the principal characters of the two Hindu epics and with gnomic verses pointing to the need to stamp out an enemy when one can, the sufferings of living with one's foes, and the like. Simply and clearly put, the lesson of the third book is that good judgment can be aided or impeded by the counsel one keeps. Wisdom again determines the nature of the counsel and, as importantly, the capacity of the sovereign discerningly to be guided thereby. The story and the book thus offer a straight narration of a key, fundamental lesson regarding a king's good counsel, as well as the power of ruthless cunning when so much is called for.

The last two books, in turn, are each exceedingly short. Book 4 concerns "Losing What You Have Gained," book 5 "Hasty Actions." The former is introduced by a verse recited directly in the presence of the three princes of the frame story.

> When someone gives up something he has gained,
>   fooled by soothing words,
> That fool is deceived just the same way as
> The foolish crocodile by the monkey.[50]

It happened that an old monkey who had lost his vigor had become friends with a crocodile, which led the crocodile's wife to become suspicious of her husband because she became jealous of him for his absences from the home. Thinking he was having an affair with a female monkey, because a companion wrongly suggested as much, she chose her course of action: dressed in the worst rags, she smeared her body with oil and presented herself as if she were on death's door. Only one remedy for her grave illness could be found, she told her husband: the heart of a monkey, if she could consume it, would save her life.

[50] *Pañcatantra* 4.1 (Edgerton 1924 [vol. 1]: 371): *prāptam arthaṃ tu yo mohāt sāntvataḥ pratimuñcati | sa tathā vañcyate mūḍho jalajaḥ kapinā yathā* ||. Translation Olivelle's.

Her death was imminent, her husband thought, and the crocodile weighed the relative value of friend and spouse, because he knew of and thought of no way to gain a monkey's heart other than by taking his companion's. In preference for his wife he hatched a plan. He put on a grand lament—that he never invited his friend to dinner as true friends do—and with it he convinced the monkey to climb onto his back for the trip to his home. The monkey agreed with alacrity to travel with him, because he trusted their friendship. But in the course of crossing the waters, the crocodile, whose heart was conflicted about the action he had resolved to undertake, began muttering to himself in his sorrow over the need to betray his friend. The monkey, no fool, quickly came to understand the situation, and so he somehow convinced the crocodile that he had forgotten his heart back in the fig tree where they used to meet. Credulously, the crocodile let the monkey off his back to collect his heart (presumably on the foolish understanding that his friend could share it without losing his life, given he was purportedly traveling to dinner without it and happily so), and thus he lost the monkey he had had in hand, as it were, for his wife, and thus is seen to be a fool.

This little parable has the obvious lesson, announced too by the book's title: it is easy to lose what one has already won. But in one sense it is like the first book of the *Pañcatantra*, because the fourth book conceals other, probably truer, lessons, though unlike the first book the concealed lessons here are sympathetic in that they show no dissonance with the obvious one. The implicit lessons here are these, namely, that it is foolish to surrender a true friendship, particularly when one is tricked into doing so, as the crocodile was by his wife. As Olivelle has noted,[51] women in general are not well positioned in this *Pañcatantra*, and here another lesson, half-concealed and, alas, gendered though it unfortunately is, is that one must guard against too easily trusting one's "better half." Finally, there is the implicit but unstated proposition that the crocodile's wife could have avoided all the problems the story narrates if she had just discovered the true nature of her husband's activities: he had no mistress but only passed time happily with a true friend—not a lover but an elderly male monkey who had lost his vigor to age. In the end, all these implicit morals of the story share with the primary one the notion that poor judgment can lead one to lose things of

[51] Olivelle 1997: 26. In particular he argues that "a pattern emerges from these animal stories: wife-mother is the only positive role for a female, while other females, even wives, who do not play maternal roles always pose a threat to the males either as sexual objects or by their nefarious activities."

value, so too that good judgment alone guards against losing what it is one has already gained.

Then the last book, "On Hasty Action." The fifth book narrates the very lesson announced by its title, this and a closely related one involving "counting one's chickens before they hatch." The latter is framed in particular around the lesson that one should not act with any confidence on an expected but not yet-realized bit of fortune. Like the fourth book, this fifth and final one is presented as a story that Viṣṇuśarman delivers directly to the three young princes. The core story is of a poor Brahmin who anticipated the birth of a son with such joy that his wife admonished him not to be too sure he would get what he wants—the expected child could be a girl and not a boy, after all(!). But a son *is* born, and the Brahmin loves him and cares for him, not being able to afford to pay any servant to care for the child.

One day an occasion arises for him to serve as a priest in a ritual that he cannot pass up for need of the promised compensation, and he accepts the engagement but is forced thereby to place the care of his son in the hands of his mongoose. (Where his wife is in the moment in question is not explained.) He does so, of course, and a snake emerges when the Brahmin is away. The mongoose kills it swiftly, and when his master is seen returning home, he emerges from the house with alacrity, joyously to share the news of his brave and loyal act. But the Brahmin, seeing the blood still on his mouth and paws, believes the mongoose had mauled his son, and so he beats it to death with a stick. His wife then returns, comes to understand the situation—they find their son peacefully asleep—and utters this following verse, which is itself alone the single most important contribution of the fifth book:

> "No person should ever do anything
> he has not properly seen,
> nor properly understood;
> he has not properly heard,
> nor properly examined;
> One should never do what the barber did."[52]

What the barber did was swiftly and thoughtlessly to imitate what he saw a merchant do. That merchant was told in a prophecy that he would meet

[52] *Pañcatantra* 5.3 (Edgerton 1924 [vol. 1]: 405): *kudṛṣṭaṃ kuparijñātaṃ kuśrutaṃ kuparīkṣitaṃ* | *puruṣeṇa na kartavyaṃ nāpitena yathā kṛtam* ||. Translation that of Olivelle. (See Edgerton's edition for his sense that *yathā* is not certain to correspond with what was present in the original text.)

three mendicants, and if he clubbed them to death they would turn to piles of gold. The barber saw him do this but without having heard the prophecy. When he quickly tried the same thing on another trio of monks, he was met with a disastrously different result.

Conclusion

Proper care in examining the facts as they are, then, a proper check of the reality of a given situation, defines good action, all good action, in the *Pañcatantra*. Again we see that the cultivation of a virtue ethic, a cultivated spontaneity for wisdom, is the key to discerning and taking up good counsel. And so the task to hand is simple. Make good decisions, act judiciously, discern whom to trust and who is untrustworthy. But in "life's maze" the application, the actual work of making the right decisions, is harder to do than to describe. There can be no hard-and-fast manner of acting. Invariant adherence to moral ideals or *dharma*, unceasing application of cunning, an unreconstructed Machiavellianism—all of these offer models of behavior too doctrinaire for the panoply of circumstances with which one may be faced in negotiating the intentions and motivations of others.

Yes, at base the *Pañcatantra* is concerned with ways of negotiating others, precisely the concern that is diminished in the Sanskrit dramas, where the motivations of others at worst are inconvenient, never truly dangerous, nor—what is more important—ultimately disappointing. This is the realism of the *Pañcatantra*, that what others do or plan to do is of such limitless possibility that to govern is to manage all expected and unexpected possibilities of human engagement. This is why no single instruction for action may be drawn from the text, so too why scholars might reasonably narrow onto one among the variously articulated morals of the stories. We have sometimes Machiavellianism recommended, sometimes thoroughly uncomplicated—even innocent—loyalty, sometimes caution, and sometimes bold action. The only simple or singular moral of the stories, that is, is that no simple, hard-and-fast principle may account for all the possible ways in which those with whom one communes might choose to act, and therefore which actions those relations might require of the judicious royal sovereign.

What this renders is a form of subjectivity that is proper in thinking: rational and reasonable. One must *engage with the evidence* to hand. And this text, *as counsel*, leads its audience to learn the very mode of engagement at hand. But it is also a subjectivity that is proper in feeling: instinct can lead one correctly to trust a "natural enemy" as a friend. Taking and enacting counsel cannot be understood as a system of inviolable rules or invariant dogmas, and sometimes cunning is required, though an invariably ruthless dogma of "every man for himself" can hardly define wisdom in the political realm. "Life's maze" is difficult to navigate. The range of options is open, because the range of possible challenges one might face is limited in scope only by the limits of human activity and imagination. What is needed in every case—and what is uniquely conveyed by the example of stories, textured as they are with all the personal quirks and particular circumstances that only narratives can fully relate—is the right deployment of the right stratagem, cultivable by maintaining a proper personal disposition and with the support of virtuous counsel and counselor, all depending too on the nature of one's counterparts, be they friend or foe, cunning or honest, of pure heart or cynical, wise in counsel or fools.

Conclusion

The present volume has engaged at length the task of reading Sanskrit-language narratives as literary works that in their very composition constitute a form of counsel. Taking seriously the literary qualities[1] of the texts to hand and coupling the same with both the suggestion in the *Arthaśāstra* that political learning may be gleaned from story and the fact that texts such as the *Pañcatantra* are often explicitly constructed as narratives of advice, I have argued that the works examined in this book repeatedly offer a particular form of political counsel. Sanskrit narrative works, read for the implicit influence thereon of the technical works on Dharma and Artha, show that the royal sovereign is regularly directed in story to act in accordance with the ethical and moral values of the Brahminical tradition—to be good, as it were—and this is so because by being so he (or, where queens are involved, she) can do well, that is, achieve his (or her) desired aims in the world and beyond. Yes, cunning sometimes is needed, but wisdom comes first, because cunning itself is properly applied only with the wisdom born from proper, chastened behavior, inasmuch as restraint opens a clear-mindedness that permits for measured and therefore fruitful action.

Collectively and individually, the works examined in this book consistently and repeatedly represent the claim that a virtue ethics ultimately also consists in a pragmatic consequentialism, for *being good to do well* suggests that a chastened way of being, a controlling of desire and the cultivation of the virtue of personal restraint—this virtue ethic is the way to effect all the results one would wish for, including those of keeping the order of the world and the propriety of one's personal actions (*dharma*), producing prosperity (*artha*), facilitating and inviting moments of delight (*kāma*), and even directing oneself to felicity in the hereafter. This is so, moreover, such that

[1] Indeed, it is a core and implicit argument of this book that Sanskrit literary works may fruitfully be read for their narrative intent, with the grain of their stories as it were, rather than merely resorting to the kind of mechanical interpretation that Tieken 2000, for example, argues is found when contemporary scholars deploy *rasa* theory as an interpretive skeleton key.

Brahmins and Kings. John Nemec, Oxford University Press. © Oxford University Press 2025.
DOI: 10.1093/oso/9780197791998.003.0008

the royal sovereign may flourish individually while leading the kingdom's subjects simultaneously to prosper along the way.

Each of the principal texts examined in this book both constitutes a work of counsel and narrates instances of counsel being given, indirectly or more often directly, by Brahmins and engaged by kings and princes, and this is so minimally and invariably because each explicitly features the mutual relations of the first two of the four *varaṇas*: *brāhmaṇas* and *kṣatriyas*, Brahmins and kings. All the narratives examined in this book, some of the most well-known and most widely circulated works of India's premodernity, exhibit in their very structures and framing narratives the major theme here placed under question, which reflects the mores of the Dharmaśāstras and Arthaśāstras, namely, that the *brāhmaṇa-kṣatriya* bond is vital to the political order, because it engenders the virtue ethic that produces wisdom and successful action thereby. I further have argued that this constitutes a central and organizing theme of the works examined in this book, even while it is not their sole narrative concern.

The texts in question further made this core act of offering counsel readily accessible by way of their particular narrative mode—that of telling stories in a kind of realist mood. These texts, I have argued, all speak in the language of genric verisimilitude, which I have suggested reflects a cultural verisimilitude in that their stories exhibit and seek to shape and influence the actions and decisions "on the ground" of key figures in their contemporaneous histories. To do so, they not only work to present didactic teachings in a manner that is deeply intertextually formed but also further seek to interpolate their audiences into their narratives and to open the way for the characters of their stories to enter back into the world of their audiences. The stories these texts tell thus offer not only models of action in the world, the model of the actions of the characters of the narratives, but also models for action in the world, the model offered as the counsel the texts impart.

Working in a world in which the model of government was defined by the whims and decisions of a single royal sovereign who wielded extraordinary power, these texts, read together, illustrate the degree to which politics in premodern South Asia was largely a personal matter. The narratives in question supported a comprehensive virtue ethic that amounted to a political "theology of ordinary life," which was a comprehensive political ethics expressed in the emotive nuances of story that put metaphorical flesh on the bare bones of the strictures of the Arthaśāstras and the Dharmaśāstras. They counsel the royal sovereign and members of the royal court to engage in a virtue ethics precisely because the matter to hand for the Brahmins who are responsible for composing the narratives in question was precisely this, to chasten the one figure who could wield unrivaled discretion in political action. It is also for this reason that the texts may be said each to direct the force of the counsel they implicitly and explicitly offer toward tending to the individual human ends of life, the *puruṣārtha*s, for in that politics in kingship is personally directed, the royal sovereign's private aims were simultaneously also of social consequence, which is best but hardly exclusively exemplified by the fact that whom the king married did much to determine who would inherit royal power. It was to capture not only the emically sourced intertextuality of these narratives, then, but also the affective range of application of the counsel here perennially offered that the selection of works found in this book was made.

The *Mahābhārata*, I have argued, deals with *dharma* in the breach. It explores the inexorable consequences of action based not in the chastened restraint of *dharmic* rectitude but in the failure that is a favoritism of familial preference. The text narrates a remembrance of ancestral indiscipline to counsel a turn away from the same and a return to the peaceful sanctity furnished by upholding the *brāhmaṇa-kṣatriya* bond. Janamejaya is presented with occasion for the very act of favoritism that precipitated the devastation wrought by and on his ancestors in the fratricidal Bhārata war, the retelling of the Bhāraṭa narrative being meant to chasten him to *dharma*, discourage the naturally human but ultimately devastating preference against discretion of one's closest kin. Brahmins recede from the scenes in which advice is counseled in the epic's narration, precisely because the text recounts nothing less than a breach in *dharmic* norms. *Kṣatriya*s counsel *kṣatriya*s, but the counselors have been made wise by hard lessons, born of *kṣatriya* transgressions—or in the case of Kṛṣṇa, a *kṣatriya* counsels transgression on a divine mandate, restoring *dharma* by the "law of the fishes," total destruction being the only means in a dog-eat-dog world. *Dharma* nevertheless is and may be restored, we are told, and so much requires nothing more or less than a return to the chastened restraint, the virtue ethic, that produces and is produced by wisdom, that is supported by the *brāhmaṇa-kṣatriya* bond, and that furnishes the material rewards of kingship.

The *Rāmāyaṇa* too deals with the nature of *dharma*, as well as the personal dispositions required to maintain the same. Here, however, the cosmic eon in play is not the deteriorating and decrepit Kali Yuga of the *Mahābhārata* but an earlier age of relative virtue and sanctity. This epic explores slips from *dharma* and most of all the here uncommon (given the eon of the epic) failure to face up to any shortcoming in upholding the strictures of chastened action, the latter most notably including the inexhaustibly inexcusable acts of Rāvaṇa, the antagonist and villain of Vālmīki's *Rāmāyaṇa*. The two epics in an intertextual sympathy thus respectively map the internal states and externalized values and preferences of familial relations, which together define the subjective nature of kingship and on their own justify the nature of the counsel offered across the Sanskrit narrative literatures: counsel needs and must emphasize virtue ethics if it is to influence a model of governance that is individual and subjective in its application.

Kings, princes, and queens, however, can hardly act alone in government administration, a fact reflected in the theoretical literature's very assessment of a properly functioning kingdom, ministers being counted as the second of seven vital elements of the same (as noted already in the Introduction). The *Rājataraṅgiṇī*, I have argued, reflects this fact with particular poignance by narrating stories about kings but primarily, if not exclusively, for members of the Brahminical community that had historically advised them. Kalhaṇa engages with what feels and appears to be the nearly inevitable turn of events that is the royal sovereign slipping badly away from *dharmic* rectitude. The mood of his historical poem is explicitly said to be one articulating the need to cultivate the *śānta rasa*, the sentiment of peace or resignation. I argue, however, that what this entails is not a surrender to the inevitable destruction of any stable social order that can be formed in and by adherence to *dharma* but rather a steady dispassion—the virtue ethic—in the face of oft-met challenges to the same that are nevertheless by no means inevitably to arrive. Here I read against received scholarly wisdom, finding a consonance with the same message I find in the *Mahābhārata*, namely, not a recommendation of world renunciation in the face of inevitable moral decay, but a call (for Brahmins and sympathetic kings, princes, and queens) to retrench in the very values that are so under threat. The *Rājataraṅgiṇī* sometimes narrates stories that offer hope for a restoration of the very personal virtues that make that properly functioning social order, and Brahmins can—and the text argues should—cleave to *dharma* and the possibility of living it successfully, even in the Kali age. Thus, as I argue the *Rājataraṅgiṇī* itself argues, the virtue ethic recommended in the Sanskrit narrative literatures is prescribed not (just) to princes, queens, and kings but also to the Brahmins who counsel them, for it can effect the same in the royals they counsel and serve.

In a political theology of ordinary life, however, kingship involves much more than the difficult disciplines of maintaining the moral order. Yes, actions do have consequences, but some are more desirable than others. The legitimate ends of human endeavor also include the pursuit of pleasure, and of wealth and power and fame. And immortality. Thus, the *Kathāsaritsāgara* can elaborate a fantastic web of tales with a culturally resonant narrative frame involving adventuresome princes cavorting through life in pursuit of wives and riches, accompanied by prudent Brahminical companions all along the way. Recasting a narrative formed around the cultural context of merchants and enterprising traders, Somadeva transforms the "Ocean of Rivers of Stories" from a tale of Vaiśyas to one that is framed by the *brāhmaṇa-kṣatriya* bond and defined by the counsel of the former, given as it is in a key narrative moment of the text. Explicit echoes of Śaiva tantra in a popularized imagination serve to texture this massive narrative and justify and encapsulate the capacity of the tale successfully to marry worldly pursuits with soteriological ends, wealth and women being harmoniously sought in the text's stories even while the protagonist follows the path to becoming the immortal king of the *vidyādhara*s. With the aid of royal counsel, the Sanskrit narrative literatures suggest it is well possible that one may do good and do well simultaneously, both here in the world of affairs and in the hereafter. Even if it is true that the *Kathāsaritsāgara* spins its narrated web to allow a queen to forget the extreme difficulties of her day, the relief the story offers her is found in its tantra-made-popular tale, which marries and makes consonant and fruitful spiritual, material, and political pursuits. Any royal sovereign of sound mind would want all of these, and the royal counsel of the Sanskrit narrative literatures envisions all being achievable, allowing simultaneously, and thereby, for the kingdom's subjects to prosper as well.

A shift of genric norms, and with it a modification of conceptual expectations around the virtue ethic, is to be found with the Sanskrit dramas examined in this book. The adjustment, however, while it transforms the audience's engagement with the works in their performance, does nothing to diminish the innately expressed value of the *brāhmaṇa-kṣatriya* bond and the counsel to act in accordance with its mores. It is only that the spectacle of the drama and the contents of the same reflect the moment of pause and reprieve that is available to any royal sovereign who properly engages the world of affairs (and it is kings in particular who are presented as the protagonists of these dramas, who benefit from the events that are set to the stage). Thus, the pleasure of watching the performances of the dramas examined in this book is reflected in their very message and contents.

Kings in the dramas are set to cavort freely, to live unconcerned by the difficulties of governance and the dangers posed by enemy armies or spies. They are free, most importantly, to indulge emotional impulses, for as the *Abhijñānaśākuntala* suggests, a good king's affection for a woman would not occur if it were barred by caste restrictions. And as the *Ratnāvalī* narrates, kings can just have fun, because good kings may rely on the hard work of a faithful chief minister, who, like the Wizard of Oz, directs events from behind the scenes, and always to the benefit of both the king and his subjects. Indeed, in the dreamworld of these Sanskrit dramas, pleasure is left alone, is left only to be pleasurable, just as the dangers of romantic entanglement, such as the obvious ones that are documented delightfully but seriously in the *Kuṭṭanīmata*, are set aside in the royal lives of the dramatic performance. The unsettling truth, that the order of the world has a dark side, that a proper way of engaging the art of seduction involves the entrapment of the beloved and this entirely in accord with the hard-and-fast rules of human nature—all this is precisely what kings and princes and members of the royal court can forget by way of the genric rules of the pleasurably escapist Sanskrit dramas.

And so the lesson the dramas offer, not in the moment of their performance but in a studied reflection on the same—in tracing the shadings set in relief by their photographic negative print, as it were—is also implicitly sober and meant to be true to life: pleasure may arrive in fleeting moments of reprieve, but this is so most of all and most enduringly only if *dharmic* norms and their Brahminical representatives are implicitly held in regard. *Kāma* and *artha*, the latter being the product of the former when it comes to the biological fruits of the royal sovereign's lucky marriage, are freely enjoyed under the implicit guarantees of the *brāhmaṇa-kṣatriya* bond, but they are by no means guaranteed. While being good allows one to do well enough in the world truly to enjoy it, it is also the case that the escapism articulated in the *Ratnāvalī*, the drama that is written *by a king*, saw through to offer as its happy illusions both the notion that Brahminical advisors could always be relied upon and the proposition that the women of the court would respond to royal indulgence (in taking another wife), however strategic and fruitful the indulgence might be, with idyllic and virtuous restraint. Indeed, actions have consequences, and the virtue ethic as royal counsel calls above all for being wise to the ways of the world: sometimes the inescapable results of actions must be taken into account—for example, what inevitably happens when one hopelessly falls for the wrong lover. Sometimes, that is, one must act on just such inextricably bound actions of difficult cause and effect—those driven by human emotions—just not in the spectacle of the drama, where such concerns may be left off the stage, or reduced by the illusion of the performance.

Finally, there is the *Pañcatantra*, a narrative that strikes to a central concern of the present book, and echoes the dramas' complications. The text's framing explicitly evokes the *brāhmaṇa-kṣatriya* bond and explicitly seeks to offer counsel by way of relating stories. It does so by aligning the work's internal audience (namely, the princes) with its external audience (namely, the text's hearers and readers): both hear the stories simultaneously, just as Rāma heard the story of the final events of his life alongside the epic's external audience; both audiences must puzzle out the sometimes-crooked lessons of the animal fables. The *Pañcatantra*, however, counsels first of all rational, consequential action in the world of political affairs, wisdom born from a chastened discretion, a knowing when and which rules apply and why. Natural enemies can be friends, advice can miss the mark, and awareness of all possible perspectives and possible problems counts above all.

So yes, the virtue ethic is active in the *Pañcatantra*, because restraint is implicitly accepted as that which cultivates wisdom. But as the dramas signal in absences, here wisdom is signaled with positive exemplification, sometimes to call on one to brook in the work of cunning. The *Pañcatantra* is concerned with effective action *tout court*, sometimes even the kind of dastardly action recommended in the *Arthaśāstra*. Here we see emerge a slight conceptual difference between the virtue ethic collectively counseled by the narrative literatures and *dharma* pure and simple. Or to put the matter differently, here we see the difference between a "theology of ordinary life" governed solely by the Dharmaśāstras, on the one hand, and the royal one offered in the narratives, on the other hand, which is leavened by Arthaśāstric thinking. The king must produce results. Virtue thus is held as the implicit and explicit norm, and *dharmic* behavior is universally recommended, for precisely this makes one wise and able properly to act. But wisdom also sometimes calls for acts of "outwitting," or extreme acts such as those recommended by Kṛṣṇa, for—again—the royal sovereign must produce results, and as the *Kuṭṭanīmata* makes clear, actions always have their consequences and this in a world that is no place for the simply naïve. And yet, and even so, the virtue ethic, while distinguishable from it, is asymptotically close to *dharma*, for wisdom and discretion in action—even dastardly acts of outwitting—are only to be born from restraint.

The political ethic recommended implicitly or explicitly by all the narratives examined in this book in fact is flavored by just this sort of rational wisdom. All offer up a path of action that may be said to be "religious" in the sense that they call those who wield political power respectfully to engage the Brahmins who are said to embody *dharma* and chastened individual action. And while those Brahmins may be said in the theoretical literatures as in the narratives themselves to have sacerdotal power, the narratives examined in this book drive their stories first of all by way of the very worldly, even quotidian choices its protagonists make and put into action. It is reasoned discretion in action that so often directs the narratives and furnishes the successes or the suffering witnessed therein.

In this one may say that the Brahminical authors who shaped this counsel understood their religiously sanctioned influence to find application in a context that, measured by a static and stereotyped model of Enlightenment dichotomies, has sometimes been taken to stand on the "secular" side of a religion-versus-secular divide, this divide also being defined by a parallel dichotomizing of "faith," on the one hand, and "reason," on the other hand. The counsel charted in these narratives is, in no small part, a kind of reasoned "Confucian" wisdom,[2] a logic in measured action, rather than an investment in "faith," be it faith in divine agency or the necessity of recognizing and succumbing to fate or destiny, all of which in an important sense lie beyond the control of the agents who are depicted in the works in question as innately influenced by Brahminical counsel. While of course faith and belief and the effects of fate are to be found and sometimes in abundance in the narratives examined in this book (notably including fate as defined by the *karmic* consequences of actions taken by one in a previous birth),[3] it is pragmatism—first of all by way of being good—that constitutes the fundamental narrative strand that frames and plays a central role in the narrative structures and narrative force of these texts. One cannot but be left with the clear understanding that it is precisely the kind of feet-on-the-ground pragmatic choice in action here described that stands at the heart of these Sanskrit narratives, and this across varying genres of works, signaling thereby the fact that the same constituted a fundamental cultural value and desideratum in India's premodern political life.

[2] I am thankful to one of the anonymous readers of this manuscript for suggesting this interpretation may be expressed in this manner.

[3] Consider, to offer but one example, the various aphorisms concerning fate and destiny to be found in the *Kathāsaritsāgara*, which are collected in Sternbach 1980: 67–75. The *Mahābhārata* too brooks in deep discussions of *karmic* fate, as is well known.

There is something truly admirable in the contents of the lessons offered thereby, for they seek to bind royal sovereigns to choices and actions that do not merely serve themselves—though they do—but also, we are repeatedly told, all the subjects of the kingdom. Any call to restraint at the level of personal indulgence and action may be welcomed in texts that deal with political rulers, for we live in a world in which the very kinds of indiscipline that threaten harm in the Sanskrit narratives are perennially to be found, even to the present day: avariciousness, exploitation, selfishness and self-dealing, favoritism and nepotism, mendaciousness, indiscipline, unseriousness of purpose, lack of intellectual rigor, rashness in action, spitefulness, vengefulness, the pursuit of desires pure and simple—and probably more. To mute these human tendencies and check these human vices, the Sanskrit narratives counseled as they did, and still can do. Doing well by being good is admirable and to be emulated.

There are also glaring limitations to the narratives that must be acknowledged and were surely recognized and felt by the texts' inaugural audiences, if in inevitably varying degrees and in ways that induced differing levels of concern, depending on who read or heard these narratives or witnessed them being performed—depending, that is, on how members of their audiences were located hierarchically by the slanted favors set to story in the texts in question. First is the gendered quality of the counsel and the works that offer them. The advice that Brahmins offer kings is set in a pervasively male-gendered aspect: in considering the choices and actions of the royal sovereign, one may easily speak of "his" choices and actions precisely because it is primarily to the male *kṣatriya* king that Brahmins directed their political counsel, and the texts are regularly written accordingly. Our readings have shown how Sanskrit story literatures frequently and implicitly favor men over women and others in setting and explaining their narrative turns of events. Simply, the gendered quality of these works is persistent, if less than inevitable.

Caste (*varṇa*) too is of a fundamental concern in reading these works, as *varṇa*-based bias, often unspoken and unmarked, is similarly pervasive in Sanskrit textual sources. This is so not only in the narratives examined in the chapters of this book but also in the Arthaśastric and Dharmaśāstric works that historically helped to shape the major narrative theme traced herein.[4]

[4] This is, of course, also a well-known fact. But to offer one example, consider Parasher 1991: 116–117, which notes Kauṭilya's differential treatment of *mlecchas* as regards their behavior toward offspring and like concerns. The setting of differential standards by caste (and outcaste) status is of course also a hallmark of the *Mānavadharmaśāstra* and many other works as well.

These texts, across their various genres, work to reaffirm norms of capacity, social role, and proper action as defined by *varṇa*, which innately sets the first two classes of the tetradic hierarchy apart. If, then, one may rightly find inspiration in the positive moral of the stories narrated in these texts, the one that argues that those who wield unusual social and political influence must exercise self-restraint in order to bring about not only their own prosperity but also that of the subjects of the kingdom, one can only do so together with the recognition of and sensitivity to the separations and discriminations also found therein—of caste, of gender, even of religious identity and affiliation—which probably would not have greatly concerned the (male) Brahmins and *kṣatriya*s who inevitably were well represented in the contemporaneous audiences of the texts here examined, but which would have presented as troubling to those not so favorably socially situated as they were.

The question of how these works serve socially to separate, empower, transform, and discriminate, moreover, is one that strikes to the very heart of the question of the power of literary works, in particular their power persuasively to deliver advice. This book, after all, has sought first and foremost to read literary works as literature and to discern the power inherent therein. What, then, does reading these texts *as counsel* have to tell of how they would have been and sometimes still are engaged by their historically located audiences, particularly those who lived and engaged these works in a place and time when their full intertextual range could have been observable—the Kashmir Valley of the twelfth century, for example? How, we must ask, does the content of the counsel in question—the admonition to engage one's choices in the world not with the reckless abandon made available to those with extraordinary social influence and power but with a reasoned restraint—color *not only* logical decision-making *but also* the lives lived of those who conducted a model of governance that renders the entire gamut of the political ruler's subjective formation, not just the logical-rational element, to be vital to the affairs of the state?

How can all the four goals of human endeavor—*dharma*, *artha*, *kāma*, and *mokṣa*—be promised by a counsel that brooks in a logical and chastened dispassion, this counsel also being offered in various genric modes that sought to appeal not just to the intellect but also to the emotions, to humor, to the somatic, and the gamut of cultural tastes and values? How, that is, was the conveyance of this counsel in diverse genres intended to facilitate, support, and cultivate a virtue ethics that constituted not a mere mindset but a full-blown "theology of ordinary life"? Finally and ultimately, this is to ask how the subjective identities of the audiences of these texts were and still can be shaped and engaged and challenged by narratives that recognized as vital and real what they understood to be a host of subjective identities, be they genealogical (the Bhāratas; the inhabitants of the Kashmir Valley); caste or *varṇa* based; gender based; grounded in social status and position (as kings, as ministers to the king); situated by a sense of history and time that suggests, as we saw in the *Rājataraṅgiṇī*, that neither is a neutral field for action; or based in a sense of a transmigratory subjective identity that spans births and therefore does not offer the *tabula rasa* of a singular and unique—or sociologically or ontologically equal—human entrance into the world.

The answers to these questions, I wish to argue in conclusion, lie with the very dynamic modality of the texts examined in this book, the high degree of interaction between text and audience fashioned by these works, what constitutes both a dialogical and dialectical encounter between text and audience. After all, it stands to reason that the Sanskrit narrative tradition must be read in terms of the emotional (and other) effects the works have on their audiences when the Sanskrit-language works on aesthetics, the Alaṃkāraśāstra and its *rasa* theories and *dhvani* theories, have placed a persistent emphasis on conceptualizing the effects of literary works on the subjective states of their audiences.

Let us couple awareness of this causal quality of these works with another observation regarding a literary quality of these stories: they were not built on suspense. Unlike what is found, for example, in contemporary film theory,[5] there is little emphasis in the Sanskrit narratives on suspending the audience in anticipation of unknown or unpredictable events. It is a dictum of Indian culture that the *Mahābhārata* is never heard for the first time; one has little doubt that Rāma ultimately will defeat Rāvaṇa;[6] the *Kathāsaritsāgara* offers no cliffhanger of a story, only fantasy—the fantastic (about which more in a moment); the Sanskrit drama famously offers only a happy ending; and no reader would reasonably doubt that Viṣṇuśarman would with his *Pañcatantra* narrative ultimately succeed in educating the three dullard princes in record time. Yes, the *Rājataraṅgiṇī* presents with a certain uncertainty regarding the end of the reign of the last of its kings, but

[5] See Neale 1980: 25–30.

[6] Yes, the audience can be excited by the suspenseful drama of witnessing battles and like narrative events, as I myself witnessed in the performance of the *Rāmāyaṇa* in Rāmnagar in 2002. But the suspense is similar to that found in watching the fight scenes in a Marvel superhero movie: the action is exciting, but the final outcome of the epic war is never in doubt.

the uncertainty does not suspend the audience to waiting on future events, I have argued, but instead calls them to the chastened discipline that could have an influence on the outcome of the same.

Nor can the subject who engages these Sanskrit narrative literatures easily be labeled a voyeur, as is the subject in the audience of a contemporary film.[7] Nor again is there an exhibitionism to these narratives, as is also often found in film, for these stories do not look at their audiences from a distance, simply watching them watch their narratives, which is precisely what exhibitionism entails.[8] The Sanskrit narratives are not meant to be "mere" stories, recognizing in their presentation the "the fiction's obvious fictionality,"[9] but are meant to draw their audiences in and stretch the world of the story out into that of its audiences, as the pages of this book have repeatedly endeavored to show: the narratives examined in this book inspire not a suspension of the audience's agencies but rather demand their personal and engaged participation.

Thus, while the *Mahābhārata* is a story about the idea of *dharma* in the breach and the difficulties of conforming to morally sanctioned action in a world corrupted by those who refuse to do the same, simultaneously it also is a deeply emotionally difficult narrative, so much so that many today refuse to keep copies of it in their homes. There is emotional pain in knowing the utter trauma that Janamejaya was led to know, of one's ancestors' dramatic failure to adhere to the most common-sense and measured ways of engaging the world, even to the point of paying the costs of total war. It is not just a story but an admonition, one that would have burrowed through the members of its audience who counted themselves a part of the larger Bhārata family, they being thus chastened personally by the disaster of their ancestors, as was Janamejaya.

Similarly, the *Rāmāyaṇa* is not merely a story of a good prince done a wrong turn, who loved his wife but lost her ultimately to the obligations he held for the people his office and position in life called him to maintain. It also is a deeply felt reassurance—for those to whom it speaks—conveying as it does a sense that what is right and proper is possible, even likely, when one is with one's kith and kin, for they are those on whom one can count, because one always counts in their communal measure of the world. Sorrow may palpably be felt with such a story, but the sorrow is also beautiful—*śoka*

[7] Neale 1980: 33.
[8] Neale 1980: 34.
[9] Neale 1980: 38.

becomes well-made *śloka*s—because it is a shared sentiment, a kind of comfort of family in hard times, the comfort of being among those who share one's values and in one's successes, those who will continue to stand by one's side all the way through to the best days to come. Both epics evoke feelings about how to live with family and loved ones, then, as well as—particularly in the case of the *Rāmāyaṇa*—how to feel right about drawing boundaries that define the borders of inclusion in *and exclusion from* the community.

The *Rājataraṅgiṇī* too is more than an analytical work of history. It offers more than just a chronicle of the lives of kings long gone. It is also a shared recollection that offers the shared prospect of perhaps making a difference in one's homeland, the Kashmir Valley—land inhabited for generations by the ancestors of the text's inaugural audience. It speaks of the sentiment of dispassion, yes, to the *śānta rasa*, because little is as painful as seeing one's native land set to ruin by those *from* there who nevertheless cannot hold it in favor. But—as I argued in Chapter 3—this *śānta* involves not a renunciatory world weariness but a palpable resignation to maintain the duties to hand, for few who are so rooted for generations in the beautiful valley, whose ancestors advised those royal sovereigns who could make or break the political and social life thereof, would simply have let go the endeavor to preserve it. The text thus defines a deeply felt disposition toward proper action in the world, as much as the two epics do, one that the text's audiences would have intuited as much as they would have understood it conceptually.

And what of the pleasurable ends of life? The narratives examined in this book offer different modes of pursuing just this through story. First is the "Ocean of Rivers of Stories," which explicitly offers an escape to a queen whose life in the Kashmir Valley is said to be so awful as to demand a pure escapism. The tantra-valanced narrative evokes the adventures of the mercantile class, allowing the fantastic to be explored in a way that takes one away from the realities of regular events in quotidian life and explicitly so, both in the notion that the narrative involves adventure and in that the adventures that ensue enmesh the protagonists in a web of tales that describe *yoginī*s and *vidyādhara*s and *vetāla*s, portals through space and across oceans, and other wonderful beings and events.

Simultaneously, however, the tale is built around the notion of a return, Naravāhanadatta's winning of wives and bringing them home, ever also in the caring hands of his wise and loyal Brahmin minister. It is tempting therefore to read the narrative for its historical context, Kashmir after the turn of the second millennium, a world in which travelers could visit the valley from across Eurasia and did. The tale not only echoes narratives told in the historical *Rājataraṅgiṇī*, as we have seen—not least a story associated with the life of Ananta's wife, Queen Sūryamatī, for whom the *Kathāsaritsāgara* is said to have been composed—but also suggests that all the wonder that the wider world can bring may (only) be fruitfully encountered under the supervision of a conservative cultural hand, that of the learned, and partly tantricized and therefore powerful, Brahminical minister. Here, then, the contents of the metanarrative and those of the narrative are married. Sūryamatī needed distraction from the disasters developing in the kingdom, and this is provided in the fantastic tale that features female lead characters of great power—"witches," *yoginīs*, queens, and others. But it simultaneously suggests that the male-dominated, sacrosanct bond between Brahmins and kings is indispensable to engaging in that very fantastic escape, because just and only this frames all the narratives of the compendium. And that bond must be policed and guarded, as the last of the twenty-five *vetāla* stories cautions. The fantastic is thus set to wonder only in the able hands of what conserves the normative social order. The pleasure, for the reader—and this explicitly so in the metanarrative of the text—is *only* an escape, and is felt and intuited as such. And this would have been known in the audience's experience, as much as—perhaps more than—it is known in the dry logic of the idea. Escape if you will—to a world of powerful wizards and female *yoginī* forces, to distant lands and foreign kingdoms—but escape under the watchful care of a properly functioning *brāhmaṇa-kṣatriya* bond. The genre of fantasy *feels* titillating and ephemeral, because the escape is only a fantasy.

Then, the dramas. While the *Kathāsaritsāgara* evokes a pleasurable remove from the problems of the "real world" by way of entry into a fantasy world, the dramas give relief by imagining just and only a perfected, ideal version of the "real world" of its audience. These plays also offer an escape, but this time the reprieve is not fantastic but offered in a more realist, if sometimes magical-realist, voice. Fantasy is fine for a while, and this is what the "Ocean of Rivers of Stories" can offer. The dramas instead gesture to the claim that the world off the stage itself can be perfect, under the right circumstances—just as is representing in the spectacle of the drama, which merely perfects the normative social order as defined in the technical works that shape Sanskrit narratives and define the idea outside the world of texts. *For a time*, perhaps for a long time—perhaps to the end of one's life—all may function well and without fail. The two modes of producing pleasure in their audiences thus both promise love and wealth in a context supported by the normative order of things. The *Kathāsaritsāgara*, however, also embeds a warning as to the dangers of what lies outside of just that, while the dramas reinforce the notion that the normative order is right and good and can function to just that ideal end. Both are meant to leave their audiences feeling enraptured in a happy and entertaining escape, precisely because both hold the fixed norms of gender and above all *varṇa*, the proper functioning of the *brāhmaṇa-kṣatriya* bond.

Finally, the *Pañcatantra* frames with the *brāhmaṇa-kṣatriya* bond a work that entertains, cultivating thereby the capacity to win *artha*, the fruits of judicious wisdom, and this in pleasing fashion. But the stories offer this in a manner that affectively touches their audiences by forcing them deeply to think—if they are attentive to the modality of the text. The *Pañcatantra*'s animal stories are tremendously entertaining; they also do more than set their audiences at an abeyance, in observation of the various turns of events. They require tremendous intellectual work—of the princes for whom the framing narrative says the stories are written and for the external audience of the work set right behind them in their learning. The genre is in no small part a cerebral one, asking for hard thinking even—especially—when one is set to the task of harshly outwitting opponents. And yet, this work can open into deeply felt and intuited trust, for example, in friendship.

This is the point: the line between the rational and the nonrational is a communicative line, with causal movement in both directions. These narratives are not just stories that entertain, but stories that work on and for their audiences, imparting in sentiment what their narratives represent in their contents, counseling sentimentally the courses of action their narratives impart. These works shape and challenge and occasion their readers to think, to feel, and imaginatively—and intuitively—to enact the strictures of the technical works on Dharma and Artha, all in the textured complexities of lived experience, all in a manner that both intuits and recognizes on rational grounds the social and economic and caste-based and gendered mores of the *brāhmaṇa-kṣatriya* bond.

The storyline I have identified in this book must therefore be said to be a decidedly conservative one, seeking as it does to cultivate a socially circumscribed effect—to make individuals feel, and feel to be normal, the strictures and practices bound by the bond between the two most privileged castes, and gendered at that. This is so, moreover, precisely inasmuch as the core theme examined in this book is defined and informed by the Arthaśāstras and Dharmaśāstras, technical works concerned with directing and restraining action. It is indeed of no coincidence, then, that the thematic I here trace maps the counsel—the influence—that the most well placed of all caste-identified peoples in India's premodernity wished to impart.

The methodology engaged in this book, however, is transportable to other narrative themes and concerns, to be found in these or other texts. Narrative analysis that is sensitive to genre, which is fully cognizant of the dialogic and dialectic quality of the works examined, and which reads narratives in mutual relation for the reason that stories and texts containing stories were intertextual from day one in premodern South Asia—such an approach to South Asian story literatures can be engaged to chase down not just this, what I argue is a core narrative concern of the Sanskrit literary works here examined, but also other major narrative themes that sought to evoke and provoke subjective identifications in their audiences. Surely, for example, there also are feminist and anti-casteist elements to be evoked and examined in these texts as read in mutual relation. Surely this is all the more the case in other Sanskrit narratives and in texts written in other South Asian languages, which perhaps were not as directed by the core theme exhibited in the works here examined. Perhaps there also are other models of counsel to be found in narratives than the one here studied.

More generally than this, one may perhaps go so far as to stipulate, by way of the example of interpreting Sanskrit narratives as dialogical and dialectical texts that work to fuse the horizon of internal and external agents and worlds, that the intention and capacity to effect transformation in their audiences is central to what defines any narrative we may properly label "religious." To think of religious narrative involves not just identifying stories that speak of faithful personages and gods and such like. It should also entail the recognition that narratives have the capacity to function in a dynamic mode, which can shape and evoke the full and transformational participation of their audiences across the spectrum of subjective experience, this, in turn, sometimes, by narrating stories whose contents are other than what has classically been counted as religious.

Finally, and perhaps most importantly, surely those of us who are scholars of religion must recognize that the logical or rational element of the counsel here offered—as with (religious) counsel in general—progresses beyond mere abstraction for being embedded in stories, which can lead it to solidify as common sense precisely because ideas are enmeshed by narrative with complex subjective modes of living and being, such that an idea about ethics and morals can emerge as feeling—as an instinct—which is perhaps best exemplified in Chapter 2 by the uninhibited and puzzled question that Kaikeyī innocently asked, before Mantharā led her to folly: why lament Rama's rise to the throne, over and against that of her own son? The Brahmins who wrote law and guided kings in matters of state sought to win not just the thoughts but also the hearts of both kings and their ministers *and* the audiences of the texts they deployed to effect the same, as would and do all religious authors.

Just as religion engaged in worldly affairs is *also* a matter of the head, of cultivating a reasoned, idealistic pragmatism to achieve material and measurable ends, so too do ideas *also* live in human contexts, in the dynamic complexity of the human subject—not just thought but felt, driven by instinct, shared in community, embodied. Narrative literatures in their religious modes dialogically and dialectically put flesh on the bare bones of doctrinal ideals and ideas by engaging, by actively shaping and evoking in their audiences, not just thoughts but also emotions, cultivated instincts, and somatic habits. The vital power and the hegemony of narratives of a religious valence are found in the fact that they take in and engage their audiences in a full embrace—as it were in body, mind, and spirit. The metaphorical flesh that narrative puts on the proverbial bare bones of doctrine is the flesh of the body as well as the text.

Bibliography

Sanskrit Editions

Abhijñānaśākuntala of Kālidāsa. Edited by M. R. Kāle. [1898] 1980. *The Abhijñānaśākuntalam of Kālidāsa, with the Commentary of Rāghavabhaṭṭa, Various Readings, Introduction, Literal Translation, Exhaustive Notes and Appendices*. Second Reprint of the Tenth Edition of 1969. Delhi, Varanasi, and Patna: Motilal Banarsidass.

Abhijñānaśākuntala of Kālidāsa. See Vasudeva 2006.

Abhijñānaśākuntala of Kālidāsa. Edited by Dilīp Kumār Kanjilāl. 1980. *A Reconstruction of the Abhijñānaśākuntalam*. Calcutta Sanskrit College Research Series 90. Calcutta: Calcutta Sanskrit College.

Arthaśāstra of Kauṭilya. Edited and translated by R. P. Kangle. 1969. *The Kauṭilīya Arthaśāstra*. (Part I: Sanskrit Text; Part II: Translation.) Delhi: Motilal Banarsidass.

Kathāsaritsāgara of Somadeva. 1839. *Katha Sarit Sagara. Märchensammlung des Sri Somadeva Bhatta aus Kaschmir. Erstes bis fünftes Buch. Sanskrit und Deutsch*. Edited and translated by Hermann Brockhaus. Leipzig: F. A. Brockhaus.

Kathāsaritsāgara of Somadeva. 1862. *Kathâ Sarit Sâgara. Die Märchensammlung des Somadeva. Buch vi. vii. viii*. Edited and translated by Hermann Brockhaus. Abhandlungen für die Kunde des Morgenlandes 2. Leipzig: F. A. Brockhaus.

Kathāsaritsāgara of Somadeva. [1866] 1966. *Kathâ Sarit Sâgara. Die Märchensammlung des Somadeva. Buch ix–xviii*. Edited by Hermann Brockhaus. Reprinted ed. In *Abhandlungen für die Kunde des Morgenlandes* 4. Nendeln, Liechtenstein: Kraus Reprint Ltd.

Kathāsaritsāgara of Somadeva. Edited by Paṇdit Durgāprasād and Kāśīnāth Pāndurang Parab. 1930. 4th ed. Revised by Wāsudev Laxmaṇ Śāstrī Paṇśīkar. Bombay: Nirnaya Sagar Press.

Kāmasūtra of Vātsyāyana, with the commentary of Yaśodhara. Edited with the Hindi "Jaya" commentary by Devadatta Shastri. 1964. Varanasi: Chaukhambha Sanskrit Sansthan.

Kālidāsagranthāvalī [Complete Works of Kālidāsa]. Edited by R. P. Dwivedī. 1976. Varanasi: Banaras Hindu University.

Kuṭṭanīmata of Dāmodaragupta. Edited and translated by Csaba Dezső and Dominic Goodall. 2012.

Dāmodaraguptaviracitaṃ Kuṭṭanīmatam. The Bawd's Counsel: Being anī. Groningen Oriental Series 23. Groningen: Egbert Forsten.

Chāndogya Upaniṣad. Edited and translated by Patrick Olivelle. 1998. *The Early Upaniṣads: Annotated Text and Translation*. 166–287. New York and Oxford: Oxford University Press.

Nāṭyaśāstra of Bharatamuni. Edited by R. S. Nagar and K. L. Joshi. 2012. *Nāṭyaśāstra of Bharatamuni with the Commentary Abhinavabhāratī by Abhinavaguptācārya*. 4 vols. Fourth Reprint Edition. Delhi: Parimal Publications.

Pañcatantra. See Edgerton 1924, vol. 1.

Pañcatantra. Edited by M. R. Kale. [1912] 2005. *Pañcatantra of Viṣṇuśarman: Edited with a Short Sanskrit Commentary, a Literal English Translation of Almost all the ślokas Occurring in it, and of Difficult Prose Passages, and Critical and Explanatory Notes in English*. Reprinted ed. Delhi: Motilal Banarsidass.

Mahābhārata. Critically edited by V. S. Sukthankar, with the cooperation of S. K. Belvalkar, A. B. Gajendragadkar, V. Kane, R. D. Karmarkar, P. L. Vaidya, S. Winternitz, R. Zimmerman, and other scholars and illustrated by Shrimant Balasaheb Pant Pratinidhi. 1927–1959. 19 vols. Pune: Bhandarkar Oriental Research Institute.

Mānavadharmaśāstra. Edited and translated by Patrick Olivelle. With the editorial assistance of Suman Olivelle. 2005. *Manu's Code of Law: A Critical Edition and Translation of Mānava-Dharma-śāstra*. Oxford: Oxford University Press.

Ratnāvalī of Harṣa. Edited and translated by Moreshvan Ramchandra Kale. 1921. *The Ratnāvalī of Śrī Harṣa-deva. Edited with an Exhaustive Introduction, a new Sanskrit Commentary, Various Readings, a Literal English Translation, Copious Notes and Useful Appendices*. Delhi: Motilal Banarsidass.

Ratnāvalī of Harṣa. Edited and translated by Asoknath Bhattacharya and Maheshwar Das. 1967. Calcutta: Modern Book Agency.

Ratnāvalī of Harṣa. See Doniger 2006.

Rājataraṅgiṇī of Kalhaṇa. Edited and translated by M. A. Stein. [1900] 1988 (vol. 3) and 1989 (vols. 1 and 2). *Kalhaṇa's Rājataraṅginī: A Chronicle of the Kings of Kaśmīr*. 3 vols. Delhi: Motilal Banarsidass.

Rājataraṅgiṇī of Kalhaṇa. Edited by Vishva Bandhu. 1963. *Rājataraṅgiṇī of Kalhaṇa: Edited Critically and Annotated with Text-comparative Data from Original Manuscripts and Other Available Materials*. 2 vols. Woolner Indological Series, vols. 5 and 6. Hoshiarpur: Vishveshvaranand Vedic Research Institute.

Rāmāyaṇa of Valmīki. Edited by J. M. Mehta, G. H. Bhaṭṭ, P. C. Divanji, G. C. Khala, D. R. Mankhad, U. P. Shah, and P. L. Vaidya. 1960–1975. *Rāmāyaṇa: Critically Edited for the First Time*. Baroda: Oriental Institute.

Secondary Sources and Translations

Adluri, Vishwa, and Joydeep Bagchee, Eds. 2016. *Argument and Design: The Unity of the Mahābhārata*. Brill's Indological Library 49. Leiden: Brill.

Aiyangar, K. V. R. 1935. *Considerations on Some Aspects of Ancient Indian Polity*. 2nd ed. Patna: Eastern Book House.

Ali, Daud. 2004. *Courtly Culture and Political Life in Early Medieval India*. Cambridge Studies in Indian History and Society 10. Cambridge: Cambridge University Press.

Ali, Daud. 2010. "The *Subhāṣita* as an Artifact of Ethical Life in Medieval India." In *Ethical Life in South Asia*, edited by A. Pandian and D. Ali, 21–42. Bloomington: Indiana University Press.

Ali, Daud. 2011. "Rethinking the History of the 'Kāma' World in Early India." *Journal of Indian Philosophy* 31.1: 1–13.

Ali, Daud. 2013. "Temporality, Narration and the Problem of History: Shifting Historical Discourse in Western India *c.* 1100–1400." *Indian Economic and Social History Review* 50.2: 237–259.

Allen, Michael S. 2016. "Dueling Dramas, Dueling Doxographies: The *Prabodhacandrodaya* and *Saṃkalpasūryodaya*." *Journal of Hindu Studies* 9.3: 273–297.

Alles, Gregory D. 1989. "Reflections on Dating 'Vālmīki.'" *Journal of the Oriental Institute, Baroda* 38.3–4: 217–244.

Altekar, A. S. [1949] 1962. *State and Government in Ancient India*. 4th ed. Delhi, Patna, and Varanasi: Motilal Banarsidass.

Ananta Murthy, U. R. [1976] 1978. *Samskara, A Rite for a Dead Man*. Translated by A. K. Ramanujan. New York: Oxford University Press.

Anderson, Benedict R. 1991. *Imagined Communities: Reflections on the Origin and Spread of Nationalism*. 2nd ed. London: Verso.

Andrijanić, Ivan, and Sven Sellmer, Eds. 2016. *On Growth and Composition of the Sanskrit Epics and Purāṇas: Relationship to Kāvya. Social and Economic Context. Proceedings of the Fifth Dubrovnik International Conference on the Sanskrit Epics and Purāṇas, August 2008*. Zagreb: Croatian Academy of Sciences and Arts.

Asad, Talal. 2003. *Formations of the Secular: Christianity, Islam, Modernity*. Stanford, CA: Stanford University Press.

Auerbach, Erich. 1953. *Mimesis: The Representation of Reality in Western Literature*. Translated from German by Willard R. Trask. Princeton, NJ: Princeton University Press.

Austin, Christopher R. 2009. "Janamejaya's Last Question." *Journal of Indian Philosophy* 37.6: 597–625.

Bakker, Hans. 2006. "A Theatre of Broken Dreams: Vidiśā in the Days of Gupta Hegemony." In *Interrogating History: Essays for Hermann Kulke*, edited by Martin Brandtner and Shishir Kumar Panda, 165–187. New Delhi: Manohar Press.

Bakker, Hans. 2010. "Royal Patronage and Religious Tolerance: The Formative Period of Gupta-Vākāṭaka Culture." *Journal of the Royal Asiatic Society* 20.4: 461–475.

Baldissera, Fabrizia. 2011. "Tradition of Protest: The Development of Ritual Suicide from Religious Act to Political Statement." In *Boundaries, Dynamics and Construction of Traditions in South Asia*, edited by Federico Squarcini, 515–568. New York: Anthem Press.

Balkaran, Raj. 2019. *The Goddess and the King in Indian Myth: Ring Composition, Royal Power, and the Dharmic Double Helix*. London: Routledge.

Balkaran, Raj. 2021. "Synchronic Strategy: Rules of Engagement for Sanskrit Narrative Literature." *Journal of Dharma Studies* 2.1: 1–23.

Balkaran, Raj, and A. Walter Dorn. 2012. "Violence in the Vālmīki *Rāmāyaṇa*: Just War Criteria in an Ancient Indian Epic." *Journal of the American Academy of Religion* 80.3: 659–690.

Balogh, Dániel, and Eszter Somogyi, Trans. 2009. *Málavika and Agni•mitra. By Kali•dasa*. Clay Sanskrit Library. New York: NYU Press and JJC Foundation.

Banerjee, Ron D. K. 1996. "In Life's Maze: The *Pañcatantra*." *Journal of the Institute of Asian Studies, Madras*: 39–54.

Banerji, S. C. 1968. *Kālidāsa-kośa: A Classified Register of the Flora, Fauna, Geographical Names, Musical Instruments and Legendary Figures in Kālidāsa's Works*. The Chowkhamba Sanskrit Series LXI. Varanasi: Chowkhamba Sanskrit Series Office.

Bansat-Boudon, Lyne. 1992. *Poétique du théâtre indien: Lectures du Nāṭyaśāstra*. Paris: École française d'Extrême-Orient.

Bansat-Boudon, Lyne. 1994. "Le texte accompli par la scene: Observations sur les versions de Śakuntalā." *Journal Asiatique* 282: 280–333.

Bansat-Boudon, Lyne, Ed. 1998. *Théâtres indiens*. Paris: Éditions de l' École des hautes études en sciences sociales. http://books.openedition.org/editionsehss/26032

Barnett, Steve, Lina Fruzzetti, and Akos Ostor. 1976. "Hierarchy Purified: Notes on Dumont and His Critics." *Journal of Asian Studies* 35.4: 627–646.

Basham, A. L. 1948. "Harṣa of Kashmir and the Iconoclast Ascetics." *Bulletin of the School of Oriental and African Studies* 12.3–4: 688–691.

Basham, A. L. 1961. "The Kashmir Chronicle." In *Historians of India, Pakistan and Ceylon*, edited by C. H. Philips, 57–65. Oxford: Oxford University Press.

Basham, A. L. 1963. *Aspects of Ancient Indian Culture*. The Heras Memorial Lectures. Bombay, Calcutta, New Delhi, Madras, Lucknow, Bangalore, London, and New York: Asia Publishing House.

Basham, A. L., Ed. 1975. *A Cultural History of India*. Delhi: Oxford University Press.

Bellah, Robert Neelly. 1975. *The Broken Covenant: American Civil Religion in a Time of Trial*. New York: Seabury Press.

Berreman, Gerald. 1971. "The Brahmannical View of Caste." *Contributions to Indian Sociology* 5: 16–23.

Bhattacharyya, Narendra Nath. 1975. *History of Indian Erotic Literature*. New Delhi: Munshiram Manoharlal.

Bhattacharya, Ramakrishna. 2011. *Studies on the Cārvāka/Lokāyata*. London and New York: Anthem Books.

Biardeau, Madeleine. 1976. "Études de mythologie hindoue (IV)." *Bulletin de l'École française d'Extrême-Orient* 63: 111–263.

Biardeau, Madeleine. 1978. "Études de mythologie hindoue (V)." *Bulletin de l'École française d'Extrême-Orient* 65.1: 87–238.

Biardeau, Madeleine. 1981a. "The Salvation of the King in the *Mahābhārata*." *Contributions to Indian Sociology* (new series) 15: 75–97.

Biardeau, Madeleine. 1981b. "Śakuntalā dans l'épopée." *Indologica Taurinensia* 7: 115–125.

Biardeau, Madeleine. 1984. "Nala et Damayantī: Héros Épiques." *Indo-Iranian Journal* 27.4: 247–274.

Bisgaard, Daniel James. 1994. *Social Conscience in Sanskrit Literature*. Delhi: Motilal Banarsidass Publishers.

Black, Brian. 2007. "Eavesdropping on the Epic: Female Listeners in the *Mahābhārata*." In *Gender and Narrative in the Mahābhārata*, edited by by Simon Brodbeck and Brian Black, 53–78. London: Routledge.

Blackburn, Stuart H. 1988. *Singing of Birth and Death: Texts in Performance*. Philadelphia: University of Pennsylvania Press.

Bloomfield, Maurice. 1917. "On the Art of Entering Another's Body: A Hindu Fiction Motif." *Proceedings of the American Philosophical Society* 56.1: 1–43.

Bloomfield, Maurice. 1924. "On False Ascetics and Nuns in Hindu Fiction." *Journal of the American Oriental Society* 44: 202–242.

Bollée, Willem. 2015. *A Cultural Encyclopaedia of the Kathāsaritsāgara in Keywords: Complementary to Norman Penzer's General Index on Charles Tawney's Translation*. Studia Indologica Universitatis Halensis 8. Halle an der Saale: Universitätsverlag Halle-Wittenberg.

Bollée, Willem. 2015/2016. "Addenda et Corrigenda to 'Bollée, Willem B., *Cultural Encyclopaedia of the Kathāsaritsāgara*.'" *Zeitschrift für Indologie und Südasienstudien* 32/33.2015/2016: 175–202.

Bose, Mandakranta, Ed. 2004. *The Rāmāyaṇa Revisited*. New York: Oxford University Press.

Bowles, Adam, Trans. 2006. *Mahābhārata*. Bk. 8, *Karṇa*. Vol. 1. Clay Sanskrit Library. New York: NYU Press and JJC Foundation.

Bowles, Adam. 2007. *Dharma, Disorder and the Political in Ancient India: The Āpaddharmaparvan of the Mahābhārata*. Leiden: Brill Press.

Bowles, Adam, Trans. 2008. *Mahābhārata*. Bk. 8, *Karṇa*. Vol. 2. Clay Sanskrit Library. New York: NYU Press and JJC Foundation.

Brick, David. 2015. *Brahmanical Theories of the Gift: A Critical Edition and Annotated Translation of the Dānakāṇḍa of the Kṛtyakalpataru*. Harvard Oriental Series. Vol. 77. Cambridge, MA: Harvard University Press.

Brick, David. 2018. "Gifting: *dāna*." In *Hindu Law: A New History of Dharmaśāstra*, edited by Patrick Olivelle and Donald R. Davis Jr., 197–207. The Oxford History of Hinduism. Oxford: Oxford University Press.

Brockington, John L. 1985. *Righteous Rāma: The Evolution of an Epic*. Delhi: Oxford University Press.

Brockington, John L. 1988. *The Sanskrit Epics*. Leiden: Brill.

Brockington, John L. 2000. *Epic Threads: John Brockington on the Sanskrit Epics*. Edited by Greg Bailey and Mary Brockington. New Delhi: Oxford University Press.

Brockington, John L. 2004. "The Concept of *Dharma* in the *Rāmāyaṇa*." *Journal of Indian Philosophy* 32.5–6: 655–670.

Brockington, Mary. 2002. *Stages and Transitions: Proceedings of the Second Dubrovnik International Conference on the Sanskrit Epics and Purāṇas*. Zagreb: Croatian Academy of Sciences and Arts.

Brockington, Mary, and Peter Schreiner, Eds. 1999. *Composing a Tradition: Concepts, Techniques and Relationships, Proceedings of the First Dubrovnik International Conference on the Sanskrit Epics and Purāṇas, August 1997*. Zagreb: Croatian Academy of Sciences and Arts.

Brodbeck, Simon Pearse. 2016. *The Mahābhārata Patriline: Gender, Culture and the Royal Hereditary*. London and New York: Routledge.

Bronkhorst, Johnnes. 2007. *Greater Magadha: Studies in the Culture of Early India.* Delhi: Motilal Banarsidass.

Bronkhorst, Johnnes. 2016. *How the Brahmins Won: From Alexander to the Guptas.* Handbook of Oriental Studies Section Two South Asia 30. Leiden and Boston: Brill.

Bronkhorst, Johnnes. "Brahmanism: Its Place in Ancient Indian Society." *Contributions to Indian Sociology* 51.3: 361–369.

Bronner, Yigal. 2013. "From Conqueror to Connoisseur: Kalhaṇa's Account of Jayāpīḍa and the Fashioning of Kashmir as a Kingdom of Learning." *Indian Economic and Social History Review* 50.2: 161–177.

Brough, John. 1978. *Selections from Classical Sanskrit Literature, with English Translation and Notes.* 2nd ed. London: University of London, School of Oriental and African Studies.

Brown, W. Norman. 1972. "Duty as Truth in Ancient India." *Proceedings of the American Philosophical Society* 116.3: 252–268.

Bühler, Georg. 1885. "Über das Zeitalter des kaśmîrischen Dichters Somadeva." *Sitzungsberichte der Philosophisch-Historischen Classe der Kaiserlichen Akademie der Wissenschaften, Wien* 110: 545–558.

Bühler, Georg, Trans. 1886. *The Laws of Manu: Translated with Extracts from Seven Commentaries.* Sacred Books of the East. Vol. 25. Oxford: Clarendon Press.

Buitenen, J. A. B. van. 1958. "The Indian Hero as Vidyādhara." *Journal of American Folklore* 71.281: 305–311.

Buitenen, J. A. B. van. 1959. *Tales of Ancient India.* Phoenix Books. Chicago and London: University of Chicago Press.

Buitenen, J. A. B. van. 1973. *The Mahābhārata.* Vol. 1. Chicago: University of Chicago Press.

Buitenen, J. A. B. van. 1974. "The Indian Epic." In *The Literatures of India: An Introduction,* edited by Edward C. Dimock Jr., Edwin Gerow, C. M. Naim, A. K. Ramanujan, Gordon Roadarmel, and J. A. B. van Buitenen, 47–80. Chicago: University of Chicago Press.

Buitenen, J. A. B. van. 1975. *The Mahābhārata.* Vol. 2. Chicago: University of Chicago Press.

Buitenen, J. A. B. van. 1981. *The Bhagavadgītā in the Mahābhārata: Text and Translation.* Chicago: University of Chicago Press.

Bulcke, Camille. 1960. "The *Rāmāyaṇa*: Its History and Character." *Poona Orientalist* 25: 36–66.

Calhoun, Craig, Mark Juergensmeyer, and Jonathan Van Antwerpen, Eds. 2011. *Rethinking Secularism.* New York and Oxford: Oxford University Press.

Casanova, José. 1994. *Public Religions in the Modern World.* London and Chicago: University of Chicago Press.

Chatterjee, Partha. 1993. *The Nation and Its Fragments: Colonial and Postcolonial Histories.* Princeton, NJ: Princeton University Press.

Cherniak, Alex, Trans. 2008. *Mahābhārata.* Bk. 6, *Bhishma.* Vol. 1, *Including the "Bhagavad Gita" in Context.* Clay Sanskrit Library. New York: NYU Press and JJC Foundation.

Cherniak, Alex, Trans. 2009. *The Mahābhārata.* Bk. 6, *Bhishma.* Vol. 2. Clay Sanskrit Library. New York: NYU Press and JJC Foundation.

Clooney, Francis X. 2001. *Hindu God, Christian God: How Reason Helps Break Down Boundaries between Religions.* New York: Oxford University Press.

Collins, Brian. 2020. *The Other Rāma: Matricide and Genocide in the Mythology of Paraśurāma.* Albany: State University of New York Press.

Coomaraswamy, Ananda Kentish. 1942. *Spiritual Authority and Temporal Power in the Indian Theory of Government.* New Haven, CT: American Oriental Society.

Coulson, Michael. 1981. *Three Sanskrit Plays.* Harmondsworth, England: Penguin Books.

Cox, Oliver Cromwell. 1959. *Caste, Class, and Race: A Study in Social Dynamics.* New York: Monthly Review Press.

Cox, Whitney. 2013. "Literary Register and Historical Consciousness in Kalhaṇa: A Hypothesis." *Indian Economic and Social History Review* 50.2: 131–160.

Crosby, Kate, Trans. 2009. *Mahābhārata*. Bk. 10, *Dead of Night*; bk. 11, *The Women*. Clay Sanskrit Library. New York: NYU Press and JJC Foundation.

Datta, Pradip Kumar, and Sanjay Palshikar, Eds. 2013. *Indian Political Thought*. Political Science. Vol. 3. New Delhi: Indian Council of Social Science Research and Oxford University Press.

Davis, Donald R., Jr. 2005. "Intermediate Realms of Law: Corporate Groups and Rulers in Medieval India." *Journal of the Economic and Social History of the Orient* 48.1: 92–117.

Davis, Donald R., Jr. 2007. "Hinduism as a Legal Tradition." *Journal of the American Academy of Religion* 75.2: 241–267.

Davis, Donald R., Jr. 2010. *The Spirit of Hindu Law*. Cambridge: Cambridge University Press.

Davis, Donald R., Jr., and John Nemec. 2016. "Legal Consciousness in Medieval Indian Narratives." *Law, Culture, and the Humanities* 12.1: 106–131.

De, Sushil Kumar. 1924. "The Akhyayika and the Katha in Classical Sanskrit." *Bulletin of the School of Oriental Studies, University of London* 3.3: 507–517.

Deheja, Vidya. 1998. "The Very Idea of a Portrait." *Ars Orientalis* 28: 40–48.

Derrett, J. Duncan M. 1973. *Dharmaśāstra and Juridicial Literature*. A History of Indian Literature. Vol. 4, Scientific and Technical Literature, pt. 1. Wiesbaden: Otto Harrassowitz.

Derrett, J. Duncan M. 1976. "*Rājadharma*." *Journal of Asian Studies* 35.4: 597–609.

Dezső, Csaba. 2005. *Much Ado about Religion, by Bhaṭṭa Jayanta*. Clay Sanskrit Library. New York: NYU Press and the JJC Foundation.

Dezső, Csaba. 2010. "Encounters with Vetālas: Studies on Fabulous Creatures I." *Acta Orientalia Academiae Scientiarum Hung* 63.4: 391–426.

Dhand, Arti. 2002. "The *Dharma* of Ethics, the Ethics of *Dharma*: Quizzing the Ideals of Hinduism." *Journal of Religious Ethics* 30.3: 347–372.

Dhand, Arti. 2004. "The Subversive Nature of Virtue in the *Mahābhārata*: A Tale about Women, Smelly Ascetics, and God." *Journal of the American Academy of Religion* 72.1: 33–58.

Dhand, Arti. 2009. *Woman as Fire, Woman as Sage: Sexual Ideology in the Mahābhārta*. Albany, NY: State University of New York Press.

Dikshitar, V. R. R. [1948] 2008. *War in Ancient India*. Delhi: Motilal Banarsidass.

Dirks, Nicholas. 1988. *The Hollow Crown: Ethnohistory of an Indian Kingdom*. Cambridge: Cambridge University Press.

Dirks, Nicholas. 1989. "The Original Caste: Power, History, and Hierarchy in South Asia." *Contributions to Indian Sociology* 23.1: 59–77.

Dirks, Nicholas. 2001. *Castes of Mind: Colonialism and the Making of Modern India*. Princeton, NJ: Princeton University Press.

Doniger, Wendy. 2006. *'The Lady of the Jewel Necklace' and 'The Lady Who Shows Her Love' by Harṣa*. Clay Sanskrit Library. New York: NYU Press and JJC Foundation.

Doniger, Wendy. 2016. *Redeeming the Kāmasūtra*. New York: Oxford University Press.

Doniger, Wendy. 2017. *The Ring of Truth: Myths of Sex and Jewelry*. New York and Oxford: Oxford University Press.

Doniger, Wendy. 2018. *Against Dharma: Dissent in the Ancient Indian Sciences of Sex and Politics*. The Terry Lectures Series. New Haven and London: Yale University Press.

Doniger, Wendy, and Sudhir Kakar, Trans. 2002. *The Kāmasūtra*. Oxford and New York: Oxford University Press.

Doniger O'Flaherty, Wendy, Ed. 1980. *Karma and Rebirth in Classical Indian Traditions*. Berkeley, Los Angeles, and London: University of California Press.

Doniger O'Flaherty, Wendy. 1984. *Dreams, Illusion, and Other Realities*. Chicago: University of Chicago Press.

Doniger O'Flaherty, Wendy. [1988] 1995. *Other People's Myths: The Cave of Echoes*. Chicago: University of Chicago Press.

Dumézil, Georges. 1968, 1971, and 1973. *Mythe et Épopée*. Vols. 1, 2, and 3. Paris: Gallimard.

Dumont, Louis. 1980. *Homo Hierarchicus: The Caste System and Its Implications*. Complete rev. English ed. Translated by Mark Sainsbury, Louis Dumont, and Basia Gulati. Chicago and London: University of Chicago Press.

Dunham, John. 1985. "Manuscripts Used in the Critical Edition of the *Mahābhārata*: A Survey and Discussion." Special Issue entitled "Part 1: Essays on the *Mahābhārata*." *Journal of South Asian Literature* 20.1: 1–15.

Dutt, Michael Madhusudan, Trans. [1858] 1904. *Ratnāvalī: A Drama in Four Acts. Translated from the Bengali*. Calcutta: G. A. Savielle.

Dutt, M. N., Ed. and Trans. 1895–1905. *A Prose English Translation of the Mahabharata (Translated Literally from the Original Sanskrit Text)*. 18 vols. Calcutta: H. C. Dass, Elysium Press.

Dutt, Nripendra Kumar. 1931. *Origin and Growth of Caste in India*. Calcutta: Mukhopadhyay.

Edgerton, Franklin. 1924. *The Panchatantra Reconstructed: An Attempt to Establish the Lost Original Sanskrit Text of the Most Famous of Indian Story-Collections on the Basis of the Principal Extant Versions*. 2 vols. American Oriental Series 2 and 3. New Haven: American Oriental Society.

Edgerton, Franklin. 1944. *The Bhagavad Gītā*. New York: Harper and Row.

Erndl, Kathleen M. 1991. "The Mutilation of Śūrpaṇakhā." In *Many Rāmāyaṇas: The Diversity of a Narrative Tradition in South Asia*, edited by Paula Richman, 67–88. Berkeley and Los Angeles: University of California Press.

Falk, Harry. 1978. *Quellen des Pañcatantra*. Freiburger Beiträge zur Indologie 12. Wiesbaden: Otto Harrassowitz.

Fitzgerald, James L. 1983. "The Great Epic of India as Religious Rhetoric: A Fresh Look at the *Mahābhārata*." *Journal of the American Academy of Religion* 51.4: 611–630.

Fitzgerald, James L. 1985. "India's Fifth Veda: The *Mahābhārata*'s Presentation of Itself." Special Issue entitled "Part 1: Essays on the *Mahābhārata*." *Journal of South Asian Literature* 20.1: 125–140.

Fitzgerald, James L. 2002. "The Rāma Jāmadagnya 'Thread' of the *Mahābhārata*: A New Survey of Rāma Jāmadagnya in the Pune Text." In *Stages and Transitions: Proceedings of the Second Dubrovnik International Conference on the Sanskrit Epics and Purāṇas*, edited by Mary Brockington, 89–132. Zagreb: Croatian Academy of Sciences and Arts.

Fitzgerald, James L. 2003. "'The Many Voices of the *Mahābhārata*." *Journal of the American Oriental Society* 123.4: 803–818.

Fitzgerald, James L., Trans. 2004. *Mahābhārata*. Vol. 7, bk. 11, *The Book of the Women*; bk. 12, *The Book of Peace*, pt. 1. Chicago: University of Chicago Press.

Fitzgerald, James L. [2004] 2005. "*Mahābhārata*." In *The Hindu World*, edited by Sushil Mittal and Gene Thursby, 52–74. New York: Routledge Press.

Ganguli, Kisan Mohan, Trans., and Pratap Chandra Roy, Publisher. [1884–1896] 1970. *The Mahabharata, trans.* New Delhi: Munshiram Manoharlal.

Garbutt, Kathleen, Trans. 2006. *Mahābhārata*. Bk. 4, *Viráta*. Clay Sanskrit Library. New York: NYU Press and JJC Foundation.

Garbutt, Kathleen, Trans. 2008a. *Mahābhārata*. Bk. 5, *Preparations for War*. Vol. 1. Clay Sanskrit Library. New York: NYU Press and JJC Foundation.

Garbutt, Kathleen, Trans. 2008b. *Mahābhārata*. Bk. 5, *Preparations for War*. Vol. 2. Clay Sanskrit Library. New York: NYU Press and JJC Foundation.

Geertz, Clifford. 1973. *The Interpretation of Cultures: Selected Essays*. New York: Basic Books.

Gellner, Ernest. 1983. *Nations and Nationalism*. Ithaca, NY: Cornell University Press.

Gerow, Edwin. 1971. *A Glossary of Indian Figures of Speech*. The Hague: Mouton.

Gerow, Edwin. 1977. *Indian Poetics*. A History of Indian Literature. Vol. 5, pt. 3. Wiesbaden: Otto Harrassowitz.

Gerow, Edwin. 1979. "Plot Structure and the Development of Rasa in the Śakuntalā. Pt. 1." *Journal of the American Oriental Society* 99.4: 559–572.

Gerow, Edwin. 1980. "Plot Structure and the Development of Rasa in the Śakuntalā. Pt. 2." *Journal of the American Oriental Society* 100.3: 267–282.

Gerow, Edwin, Trans. 1985. "*Ūrubhaṅga*: The Breaking of Thighs, A One-Act Play Attributed to Bhāsa, Based on Episodes from the *Mahābhārata*." Special Issue entitled "Part 1: Essays on the *Mahābhārata*." *Journal of South Asian Literature* 20.1: 57–70.

Ghosal, Sibendra Nath, Trans. 1969. *The Indian Drama (The Sanskrit Drama): Translated from the Original German*. (Translation of Konow 1920.) Calcutta: General Printers & Publishers.

Ghoshal, Upendra Nath. 1923. *A History of Hindu Political Theories: From the Earliest Times to the End of the First Quarter of the Seventeenth Century A.D.* London, Bombay, Madras, and Calcutta: Oxford University Press.

Glucklich, Ariel. 1988. "The Royal Sceptre (*daṇḍa*) as Legal Punishment and Sacred Symbol." *History of Religions* 28.2: 97–122.

Glucklich, Ariel. 1994. *The Sense of* Adharma. New York: Oxford University Press.

Goldman, Robert P. 1976a. *Gods, Priests, and Warriors: The Bhṛgus of the Mahābhārata*. New York: Columbia University Press.

Goldman, Robert P. 1976b. "Vālmīki and the Bhṛgu Connection." *Journal of the American Oriental Society* 96.1: 97–101.

Goldman, Robert P. 1977. *Gods, Priests, and Warriors: The Bhṛgus of the Mahābhārata*. New York: Columbia University Press.

Goldman, Robert P. 1978. "Fathers, Sons, and Gurus: Oedipal Conflict in the Sanskrit Epics." *Journal of Indian Philosophy* 6.4: 325–392.

Goldman, Robert P. 1980. "Rāmaḥ Sahalakṣmaṇaḥ: Psychological and Literary Aspects of the Composite Hero of Vālmīki's '*Rāmāyaṇa*'." *Journal of Indian Philosophy* 8.2: 149–189.

Goldman, Robert P. 1982. "Matricide, Renunciation, and Compensation in the Legends of Two Warrior Heroes of the Sanskrit Epics." *Indologica Taurinensia* 10: 117–131.

Goldman, Robert P. 1984. *The Rāmāyaṇa of Vālmīki: An Epic of Ancient India*. Vol. 1, *Bālakāṇḍa*. Princeton Library of Asian Traditions. Princeton, NJ: Princeton University Press.

Goldman, Robert P. 1995. "Gods in Hiding: The *Mahābhārata*'s Virāṭa Parvan and the Divinity of the Indian Epic Hero." In *Modern Evaluation of the Mahābhārata* (R. K. Sharma Felicitation Volume), edited by S. P. Narang, 73–100. Delhi: Nag Publishers.

Goldman, Robert P., and Sally J. Sutherland Goldman. 1996. *The Rāmāyaṇa of Vālmīki: An Epic of Ancient India*. Vol. 5, *Sundarakāṇḍa*. Princeton Library of Asian Traditions. Princeton, NJ: Princeton University Press.

Goldman, Robert P., and Sally J. Sutherland Goldman. 2017. *The Rāmāyaṇa of Vālmīki: An Epic of Ancient India*. Vol. 7, *Uttarakāṇḍa*. Princeton Library of Asian Traditions. Princeton, NJ: Princeton University Press.

Goldman, Robert P., Sally J. Sutherland Goldman (Introduction, Translation, and Annotation), and Barend A. van Nooten (Translation and Annotation). 2009. *The Rāmāyaṇa of Vālmīki: An Epic of Ancient India*. Vol. 6, *Yuddhakāṇḍa*. Princeton Library of Asian Traditions. Princeton, NJ: Princeton University Press.

Gonda, Jan. 1965. *Change and Continuity in Indian Religion*. The Hague: Mouton.

Gonda, Jan. 1969. *Ancient Indian Kingship from the Religious Point of View. Reprinted from Numen III and IV with Addenda and an Index*. Second, Photomechanical Reprint. Leiden: E. J. Brill.

González-Reimann, Luis. 2006. "The Divinity of Rāma in the *Rāmāyaṇa* of Vālmīki." *Journal of Indian Philosophy* 34.3: 203–220.

Goodall, Dominic. 2020. "Dressing for Power: On *vrata*, *caryā*, and *vidyāvrata* in the Early Mantramārga, and on the Structure of the *Guhyasūtra* of the *Niśvāsatattvasaṃhitā*." In *Śaivism and the Tantric Traditions: Essays in Honour of Alexis G. J. S. Sanderson*, edited by Dominic Goodall, Shaman Hatley, Harunaga Isaacson, and Srilata Raman, 47–83. Leiden and Boston: Brill.

Grünendahl, Reinhold. 2002. "On the Frame Structure and 'Sacrifice Concept' in the Nārāyaṇīya and Tīrthayātrā Sections of the *Mahābhārata*, and the Craft of Citation." *Zeitschrift der Deutschen Morgenländischen Gesellschaft* 152: 309–340.

Hacker, Paul. 1960. "Zur Entwicklung der Avatāralehre." *Wiener Zeitschrift für die Kunde Sud- und Ostasiens* 4: 47–70.

Halbfass, Wilhelm. [1981] 1988. *India and Europe: An Essay in Philosophical Understanding*. 1st Indian ed. Delhi: Motilal Banarsidass.

Hall, Stuart, Ed. [1997] 2003. *Representation: Cultural Representations and Signifying Practices*. London, Thousand Oaks, and New Delhi: Open University.

Hara, Minoru. 1973. "The King as Husband of the Earth (Mahī-pati)." *Asiatische Studien* 27.2: 97–114.

Hara, Minoru. 1979. "Hindu Concepts of Teacher: Sanskrit Guru and Acārya." In *Sanskrit and Indian Studies: Essays in Honour of Daniel H. H. Ingalls*, edited by M. Nagatomi, B. K. Matilal, J. Moussaieff Masson, and E. Dimock, 93–118. Dordrecht: D. Reidel Publishing Company.

Hatley, Shaman. 2007. "The *Brahmayāmalatantra* and Early Śaiva Cult of Yoginīs." PhD diss., University of Pennsylvania.

Hawley, Nell Shapiro, and Sohini Sarah Pillai, Eds. 2021. *Many Mahābhāratas*. SUNY Series in Hindu Studies. Albany: State University of New York Press.

Heesterman, Jan C. 1957. *The Ancient Indian Royal Consecration: The Rājasūya Described According to the Yajus Texts and Annotated*. 's-Gravenhage: Mouton.

Heesterman, Jan C. 1971. "Kauṭalya and the Ancient Indian State." *Wiener Zeitschrift für die Kunde Süd- und Ostasiens* 15: 5–22.

Heesterman, Jan C. 1978a. "The Conundrum of the King's Authority." In *Kingship and Authority in South Asia*, edited by J. F. Richards, 1–27. Madison: University of Wisconsin—Madison, Department of South Asian Studies.

Heesterman, Jan C. 1978b. "Veda and Dharma." In *The Concept of Duty in South Asia*, edited by Wendy O'Flaherty (Doniger) and J. Duncan M. Derrett, 80–95. New Delhi: Vikas Publishing House.

Heesterman, Jan C. 1979. "Power and Authority in Indian Tradition." In *Tradition and Politics in South Asia*, edited by Robin James Moore, 60–85. New Delhi: Vikas Publishing House.

Heesterman, Jan C. 1985. *The Inner Conflict of Tradition: Essays in Indian Ritual, Kingship, and Society*. Chicago and London: University of Chicago Press.

Heesterman, Jan C. 1993. *The Broken World of Sacrifice: An Essay in Ancient Indian Ritual*. Chicago and London: University of Chicago Press.

Hegarty, James M. 2006. "Encompassing the Sacrifice: On the Narrative Construction of the Significant Past in the Sanskrit *Mahābhārata*." *Acta Orientalia Vilnensia* 7.1–2: 77–118.

Hegarty, James M. 2009. "On Platial Imagination in the Sanskrit *Mahābhārata*." *International Journal of Hindu Studies* 13.2: 163–187.

Hegarty, James M. 2012. *Religion, Narrative, and Public Imagination in South Asia: Past and Place in the Sanskrit Mahābhārata*. London: Routledge.

Hertel, Johannes. 1912. *The Panchatantra-Text of Purnabhadra: Critical Introduction and List of Variants*. Harvard Oriental Series 12. Cambridge, MA: Harvard University Press.

Hertel, Johannes. 1914. *Das Pañcatantra: seine Geschichte und seine Verbreitung*. Leipzig and Berlin: Teubner.

Hiltebeitel, Alf. 1976. *The Ritual of Battle: Krishna in the Mahābhārata*. Ithaca, NY: Cornell University Press.

Hiltebeitel, Alf. 1979. "Kṛṣṇa and the *Mahābhārata* (A Bibliographical Essay)." *Annals of the Bhandarkar Oriental Research Institute* 60.1/4: 65–107.

Hiltebeitel, Alf. 1980a. "Draupadī's Garments." *Indo-Iranian Journal* 22.2: 97–112.

Hiltebeitel, Alf. 1980b. "Śiva, the Goddess, and the Disguises of the Pāṇḍavas and Draupadī." *History of Religions* 20.1/2: 147–174.

Hiltebeitel, Alf. 1981. "Draupadī's Hair." *Puruṣārtha* 5: 179–214.
Hiltebeitel, Alf. 1982–1983. "Sītā *Vibhūṣitā*: The Jewels for Her Journey." *Indologica Taurinensia* 8–9: 193–200.
Hiltebeitel, Alf. 1985. "Two Kṛṣṇas, Three Kṛṣṇas, Four Kṛṣṇas, More Kṛṣṇas: Dark Interactions in the *Mahābhārata*." Special Issue entitled "Part 1: Essays on the *Mahābhārata*." *Journal of South Asian Literature* 20.1: 71–77.
Hiltebeitel, Alf. 1999. "Reconsidering Bhṛguization." In *Composing a Tradition: Concepts, Techniques, and Relationships: Proceedings of the First Dubrovnik International Conference on the Sanskrit Epics and Purāṇas*, edited by Mary Brockington and Peter Schreiner. Zagreb: Croatian Academy of Sciences and Arts.
Hiltebeitel, Alf. 2000. "The Primary Process of the Hindu Epics." *International Journal of Hindu Studies* 4.3: 269–288.
Hiltebeitel, Alf. 2001. *Rethinking the Mahābhārata: A Reader's Guide to the Education of the Dharma King*. Chicago: University of Chicago Press.
Hiltebeitel, Alf. 2005. "Not Without Subtales: Telling Laws and Truths in the Sanskrit Epics." *Journal of Indian Philosophy* 33.4: 455–511.
Hiltebeitel, Alf. 2011a. *Dharma: Its Early History in Law, Religion and Narrative*. New York: Oxford University Press.
Hiltebeitel, Alf. 2011b. *Reading the Fifth Veda: Studies on the Mahābhārata. Essays by Alf Hiltebeitel*. Vol. 1. Edited by Vishwa Adluri and Joydeep Bagchee. Leiden: Brill.
Hiltebeitel, Alf. 2011c. *When the Goddess Was a Woman: Mahābhārata Ethnographies. Essays by Alf Hiltebeitel*. Vol. 2. Edited by Vishwa Adluri and Joydeep Bagchee. Leiden: Brill.
Hocart, A. M. 1941. *Kingship*. The Thinker's Library 82. London: Watts & Company.
Hocart, A. M. 1970. *Kings and Councillors: An Essay in the Comparative Anatomy of Human Society*. Edited and with an Introduction by Rodney Needham. Foreword by E. E. Evans-Pritchard. Chicago: University of Chicago Press.
Hopkins, E. J. 1882–1885. "On the Professed Quotations from Manu Found in the *Mahābhārata*." *Journal of the American Oriental Society* 11: 239–275.
Hopkins, E. Washburn. [1901] 1969. *The Great Epic of India: Its Character and Origin*. Reprinted ed. Calcutta: Punthi Pustak.
Hopkins, Washburn. 1900. "On the Hindu Custom of Dying to Redress a Grievance." *Journal of the American Oriental Society* 21: 146–159.
Huang, Po-chi 2009. "The Cult of *Vetāla* and Tantric Fantasy." In *Rethinking Ghosts in World Religions*, edited by Mu-Chou Poo. Studies in the History of Religions 123. Leiden and Boston: Brill.
Hudson, Emily. 2013. *Disorienting Dharma: Ethics and the Aesthetics of Suffering in the Mahābhārata*. New York: Oxford University Press.
Huizinga, Johan. 1955. *Homo Ludens: A Study of the Play-Element in Culture*. Boston: Beacon Press.
Hultzsch, Eugen. 1911. "Critical Notes on Kalhana's Seventh Taranga." *Indian Antiquary* 40: 97–102. [Reprinted in Stein 2013: 179–186.]
Hultzsch, Eugen. 1913. "Critical Notes on Kalhana's Eighth Taranga." *Indian Antiquary* 42: 301–306. [Reprinted in Stein 2013: 187–194.]
Hultzsch, Eugen. 1915. "Kritische Bemerkungen zur *Rājataraṅgiṇī*. Nr. IV." *Zeitschrift der Deutschen Morgenländischen Gesellschaft* 69: 129–167, 271–282. [Reprinted in Stein 2013: 195–248.]
Ikari, Yasuke, Ed. 1994. *A Study of the Nīlamata: Aspects of Hinduism in Ancient Kashmir*. Report of the Research Project: Studies in Traditional Cultures in the Context of Ancient Indian and Indo-European Societies. Kyoto: Institute for Research in Humanities, Kyoto University.
Inden, Ronald. [1990] 2000. *Imagining India*. Bloomington and Indianapolis: Indiana University Press.

Inden, Ronald, Jonathan Walters, and Daud Ali. 2000. *Querying the Medieval: Texts and the History of Practices in South Asia.* New York: Oxford University Press.

Ingalls, Daniel H. H. 1965. *An Anthology of Sanskrit Court Poetry: Vidyākara's Subhāṣitaratnakoṣa.* Harvard Oriental Series 44. Cambridge, MA: Harvard University Press.

Ingalls, Daniel H. H. 1976. "Kālidāsa and the Attitudes of the Golden Age." *Journal of the American Oriental Society* 96.1: 15–26.

Ingalls, Daniel. H. H., and Daniel H. H. Ingalls Jr. 1985. "The *Mahābhārata*: Stylistic Study, Computer Analysis, and Concordance." Special Issue entitled "Part 1: Essays on the *Mahābhārata.*" *Journal of South Asian Literature* 20.1: 17–46.

Jain, Kamta Prasad. 1929. "The *Ādipurāṇa* and *Bṛhatkathā*." *Indian Historical Quarterly* 5: 547–548.

Jamison, Stephanie. 1996. *Sacrificer's Wife, Sacrificed Wife: Women, Ritual, and Hospitality in Ancient India.* New York: Oxford University Press.

Jefferds, Keith N. 1981. "Vidūṣaka versus Fool: A Functional Analysis." *Journal of South Asian Literature* 16.1: 61–73.

Jha, D. N. [1977] 1998. *Ancient India: In Historical Outline.* Rev. and enlarged ed. New Delhi: Manohar Publishers.

Johnson, William J., Trans. 1998. *The Sauptikaparvan of the Mahābhārata: The Massacre at Night.* New York: Oxford University Press.

Johnson, William J., Trans. 2005. *Mahābhārata.* Bk. 3, *The Forest.* Vol. 4. Clay Sanskrit Library. New York: NYU Press and JJC Foundation.

Jowett, B., Trans. 1885. *The Politics of Aristotle, Translated into English with Introduction, Marginal Analysis, Essays, Notes, and Indices.* Vol. 1, Containing the Introduction and Translation. Oxford: Clarendon Press.

Juergensmeyer, Mark. 1993. *The New Cold War?: Religious Nationalism Confronts the Secular State.* Berkeley, Los Angeles, and London: University of California Press.

Juergensmeyer, Mark. [1993] 2011. *Global Rebellion.* Berkeley: University of California Press.

Kane, Pandurang Vaman. 1930–1962. *A History of Dharmaśāstra: Ancient and Mediaeval Religious and Civil Law.* 5 vols. Pune: Bhandarkar Oriental Research Institute.

Kangle, R. P. 1963. *The Kauṭilīya Arthaśāstra.* Vol. 1, *Text.* Vol. 2, *An English Translation with Critical and Explanatory Notes.* Delhi: Motilal Banarsidass.

Kapferer, Bruce, Ed. 1976. *Transaction and Meaning: Directions in the Anthropology of Exchange and Symbiotic Behavior.* Philadelphia: Institute for the Study of Human Issues.

Karashima, Noboru, Ed. 1999. *Kingship in Indian History.* Japanese Studies on South Asia 2. New Delhi: Manohar.

Kaul, Shonaleeka. 2014. "'Seeing' the Past: Text and Questions of History in the *Rājataraṅgiṇī*." *History and Theory* 53.2: 194–211.

Kaul, Shonaleeka. 2018. *The Making of Early Kashmir: Landscape and Identity in the Rajatarangini.* New Delhi: Oxford University Press.

Keith, A. Berriedale. 1914. "The Brahmanic and Kshatriya Tradition." *Journal of the Royal Asiatic Society of Great Britain and Ireland* 46.1: 118–126.

Keith, A. Berriedale. 1924. *The Sanskrit Drama in Its Origin, Development, Theory and Practice.* Oxford: Oxford University Press.

Keith, A. Berriedale. [1920] 1966. *A History of Sanskrit Literature.* Oxford: Oxford University Press.

Kern, Hendrik. 1867. "Remarks on Professor Brockhaus' Edition of the *Kathāsarit-Sāgara*, Lambaka IX-XVIII." *Journal of the Royal Asiatic Society of Great Britain and Ireland* (New Series) 3.1: 167–182.

Knutson, Jesse Ross. 2021. *The Essence of Politics.* Murty Classical Library of India. Cambridge, MA, and London: Harvard University Press.

Kölver, Bernhard. 1971. *Textkritische und philologische Untersuchungen zur Rājataraṅgiṇī des Kalhaṇa.* Wiesbaden: Franz Steiner Verlag.

Konow, Sten. 1920. *Das Indische Drama*. Berlin and Leipzig: De Gruyter.

Konow, Sten. 1969. *The Indian Drama (The Sanskrit Drama)*. Translated from original German by Dr. S. N. Ghosal. Calcutta: General Printers & Publishers.

Kosambi, D. D. 1965. *The Culture and Civilization of Ancient India in Historical Outline*. London: Routledge and Kegan Paul.

Koskikallio, Petteri, Ed. 2005. *Epics, Khilas and Purāṇas: Continuities and Ruptures. Proceedings of the Third Dubrovnik International Conference on the Sanskrit Epics and Purāṇas, September 2002*. Zagreb: Croatian Academy of Sciences and Arts.

Koskikallio, Petteri. 2009. *Parallels and Comparisons: Proceedings of the Fourth Dubrovnik International Conference on the Sanskrit Epics and Purāṇas, September 2005*. Zagreb: Croatian Academy of Sciences and Arts.

Kramrisch, Stella. 1981. *The Presence of Śiva*. Princeton, NJ: Princeton University Press.

Krishnamachariar, M. [1937] 1974. *History of Classical Sanskrit Literature*. 3rd ed. Delhi, Varanasi, and Patna: Motilal Banarsidass.

Kuiper, Franciscus Bernardus Jacobus. 1979. *Varuṇa and Vidūṣaka: On the Origin of the Sanskrit Drama*. Amsterdam, Oxford, and New York: North-Holland Publishing Company.

Kulke, Hermann, and Dietmar Rothermund. 1988. *A History of India*. 3rd ed. London: Routledge Press.

Lacôte, Félix. 1908. *Essai sur Guṇāḍhya et la Bṛhatkathā, suivi du texte inédit des chapitres XXVII à XXX du Nepāla-Māhātmya*. Paris: Ernest Leroux.

Lefeber, Rosalind. 1994. *The Rāmāyaṇa of Vālmīki: An Epic of Ancient India*. Vol. 4, *Kiṣkindhākāṇḍa*. Princeton Library of Asian Traditions. Princeton, NJ: Princeton University Press.

Leslie, Julia. 1998. "A Bird Bereaved: The Identity and Significance of Vālmīki's *krauñca*." *Journal of Indian Philosophy* 26.5: 455–487.

Lévi, Sylvain. [1890] 1963. *Le théâtre indien*. Bibliothèque de l'École des hautes études. IVe Section, Sciences Historiques et Philologiques 83. Paris: Collège de France.

Lienhard, Siegfried. 1984. *A History of Classical Poetry: Sanskrit-Pali-Prakrit*. Wiesbaden: Harrassowitz.

Lincoln, Bruce. 1999. *Theorizing Myth: Narrative, Ideology, and Scholarship*. London and Chicago: The University of Chicago Press.

Lingat, Robert. 1962. "Time and the Dharma, on Manu 1.85–6." *Contributions to Indian Sociology* 6: 7–16.

Lingat, Robert. 1973. *The Classical Law of India*. Translated from the French with additions by J. Duncan M. Derrett. Berkeley and Los Angeles: University of California Press.

Long, J. Bruce. 1980. "The Concepts of Human Action and Rebirth in the Mahābhārata." In *Karma and Rebirth in Classical Indian Traditions*, edited by Wendy Doniger O'Flaherty, 38–60. Berkeley, Los Angeles, and London: University of California Press.

Macdonell, A. A. [1900] 1962. *A History of Sanskrit Literature*. Delhi: Motilal Banarsidass.

Madan, T. N., Ed. 1982. *Way of Life: King, Householder, Renouncer—Essays in Honour of Louis Dumont*. Delhi: Vikas Publishing House.

Majumdar, Bimal Kanti. [1955] 1960. *The Military System in Ancient India*. 2nd ed. Calcutta: Firma K. L. Mukhopadhyay.

Majumdar, R. C. [1918] 1969. *Corporate Life in Ancient India*. 3rd ed. Calcutta: Firma K. L. Mukhopadhyay.

Mallinson, James, Ed. and Trans. 2005. *The Emperor of the Sorcerers by Buddhasvāmin*. Vols. 1 and 2. Clay Sanskrit Library. New York: NYU Press and the JJC Foundation.

Mallinson, James, Trans. *Messenger Poems by Kali•dasa, Dhoyi & Rupa Go•svamin*. Clay Sanskrit Library. New York: NYU Press and the JJC Foundation.

Marasinghe, E. W. 1989. *The Sanskrit Theatre and Stagecraft*. Sri Garib Dass Oriental Series 78. Delhi: Sri Satguru Publications.

Marriott, McKim. 1976. "Hindu Transactions: Diversity without Dualism." In *Transaction and Meaning: Directions in the Anthropology of Exchange and Symbolic Behavior*, edited by Bruce Kapferer, 109–142. Philadelphia: Institute for the Study of Human Issues.

Masson, J. 1969. "Who Killed Cock Krauñca? Abhinavagupta's Reflections on the Origin of Aesthetic Experience." *Journal of the Oriental Research Institute, Baroda* 18: 207–224.

Masson, J. Moussaieff. 1975. "Fratricide among the Monkeys: Psychoanalytic Observations on an Episode in the *Vālmīkirāmāyaṇam*." *Journal of the American Oriental Society* 95.4: 672–678.

Masson, J. Moussaieff, and M. V. Patwardhan. 1969. *Śāntarasa and Abhinavagupta's Philosophy of Aesthetics*. Poona: Bhandarkar Oriental Research Institute.

Maten, Erik. 1973. *Buddhasvāmin's Bṛhatkathāślokasaṃgraha: A Literary Study of an Ancient Indian Narrative*. Orientalia Rheno-Traiectina 18. Leiden: Brill.

Matilal, Bimal K. 1989. *Moral Dilemmas in the Mahābhārata*. New Delhi: Indian Institute of Advanced Study.

Matilal, Bimal K. 2002. "The Throne: Was Duryodhana Wrong?" In *Ethics and Epics: The Collected Essays of Bimal Krishna Matilal*, edited by Jonardon Ganeri, 109–122. Delhi: Oxford University Press.

McClish, Mark. 2014. "The Dependence of Manu's Seventh Chapter on Kauṭilya's *Arthaśāstra*." *Journal of the American Oriental Society* 134.2: 241–262.

McClish, Mark. 2019. *The History of the Arthaśāstra: Sovereignty and Sacred Law in Ancient India*. Cambridge and New York: Cambridge University Press.

McCrea, Lawrence. 2013. "*Śāntarasa* in the *Rājataraṅgiṇī*: History, Epic, and Moral Decay." *Indian Economic and Social History Review* 50.2: 179–199.

Mehta, T. 1995. *Sanskrit Play Production in Ancient India*. Delhi: Motilal Banarsidass.

Meiland, Justin, Trans. 2005. *Mahābhārata*. Bk. 9, *Śalya*. Vol. 1. New York: NYU Press and the JJC Foundation.

Meiland, Justin, Trans. 2007. *Mahābhārata*. Bk. 9, *Śalya*. Vol. 2. New York: NYU Press and the JJC Foundation.

Meister, Michael. 2006. "Mountain Temples and Temple-Mountains: Masrur." *Journal of the Society of Architectural Historians* 65.1: 26–49.

Miller, Barbara Stoler, Ed. 1984. *Theater of Memory: The Plays of Kālidāsa*. New York: Columbia University Press.

Miller, Barbara Stoler. 1985. "*Karṇabhāra*: The Trial of Karṇa: A One-Act Play Attributed to Bhāsa, Based on Episodes from the *Mahābhārata*." Special Issue entitled "Part 1: Essays on the *Mahābhārata*." *Journal of South Asian Literature* 20.1: 47–56.

Minkowski, Christopher Z. 1989. "Janamejaya's *Sattra* and Ritual Structure." *Journal of the American Oriental Society* 109.3: 401–420.

Minkowski, Christopher Z. 2001. "The Interrupted Sacrifice and the Sanskrit Epics." *Journal of Indian Philosophy* 29.1–2: 169–186.

Mlecko, Joel D. 1982. "The Guru in Hindu Tradition." *Numen* 29.1: 33–61.

Monier-Williams, M. Monier. 1891. *Brāhmanism and Hindūism; Or, Religious Thought and Life in India, as Based on the Veda and Other Sacred Books of the Hindūs*. 4th ed. New York: Macmillan and Co.

Moore, Robin James, Ed. 1979. *Tradition and Politics in South Asia*. New Delhi: Vikas Publishing House.

Mukherjee, Prabhati. 1974. "Toward Identification of Untouchable Groups in Ancient India, as Enumerated in Sanskrit Lexicons." *Journal of the Asiatic Society of Bengal* 16: 1–14.

Narang, Satya Pal, Ed. 1995. *Modern Evaluation of the Mahābhārata: Prof. R. K. Sharma Felicitation Volume*. Delhi: Nag Publishers.

Narayana Rao, Velcheru, David Shulman, and Sanjay Subrahmanyam. 2001. *Textures of Time: Writing History in South India, 1600–1800*. New Delhi: Permanent Black.

Neale, Stephen. 1980. *Genre*. London: British Film Institute.

Nelson, Donald. 1974. "The *Bṛhatkathā*: A Reconstruction from *Bṛhatkathāślokasaṃgraha, Peruṅkatai* and *Vasudevahiṃdi*." Doctoral diss., University of Chicago.

Nelson, Donald. 1978. "*Bṛhatkathā* Studies: The Problem of an Ur-text." *Journal of Asian Studies* 37.4: 669.

Nemec, John. 2007. Review of Sheldon Pollock, *The Language of the Gods in the World of Men: Sanskrit, Culture, and Power in Premodern India. Journal of the American Academy of Religion* 75:1: 207–211.

Nemec, John. 2009. "When the Paramparā Breaks: On Gurus and Students in the *Mahābhārata*." In *The Anthropologist and the Native: Essays For Gananath Obeyesekere*, edited by H. L. Seneviratne, 35–64. Firenze: Società Editrice Fiorentina.. Reprinted ed. (same title and pagination): London: Anthem Press, 2011.

Nemec, John. 2013. "On the Structure and Contents of the *Tridaśaḍāmaratantra*, a Kaula Scriptural Source of the Northern Transmission." *Journal of Hindu Studies* 6.3: 297–316.

Nemec, John. 2014. Review of Christian Wedemeyer, *Making Sense of Tantric Buddhism: History, Semiology, and Transgression in the Indian Traditions. Journal of Religion* 94.2: 271–273.

Nemec, John. 2017a. Review of Walter Slaje (ed. and trans.), *Kingship in Kaśmīr (AD 1148–1459): From the Pen of Jonarāja, Court Paṇḍit to Sulṭān Zayn al-ʿĀbidīn. Journal of the American Oriental Society* 137.2: 404–406.

Nemec, John. 2017b. "Dying to Redress the Grievance of Another: On *prāya/prāyopaveśa(na)* in Kalhaṇa's *Rājataraṅgiṇī*." *Journal of the American Oriental Society* 137.1: 43–61.

Nemec, John. 2018. Review of Wendy Doniger, *Redeeming the Kāmasūtra. Religion* 48.1: 142–144.

Nemec, John. 2020a. "Innovation and Social Change in the Vale of Kashmir, circa 900–1250 C.E." In *Śaivism and the Tantric Traditions: Essays in Honour of Alexis G. J. S. Sanderson*, edited by Dominic Goodall, Shaman Hatley, Harunaga Isaacson, and Srilata Raman, 283–320. Gonda Indological Studies, no. 22. Leiden: Brill.

Nemec, John. 2020b. Review of Walter Slaje, *Brahmā's Curse: Facets of Political and Social Violence in Premodern Kashmir. Journal of the American Oriental Society* 140.4(2020): 974–976.

Nemec, John. 2020c. "Toward a Volitional Definition of Religion." *Journal of the American Academy of Religion* 88.3: 664–692.

Nemec, John. 2020d. "Hindu Law and Society." Review article of Patrick Olivelle and Donald R. Davis Jr., Eds., *Hindu Law: A New History of Dharmaśāstra. Journal of the American Oriental Society* 140.1(2020): 207–219.

Nemec, John. 2023. "Religion, Law, and Governance in Premodern Hindu Political Theory." Online publication in *Canopy Forum*. Published July 25, 2023. Accessed September 2, 2023. https://canopyforum.org/tag/nemec-john/.

Oberlies, Thomas. 2003. *A Grammar of Epic Sanskrit*. Berlin: Walter de Gruyter.

Obrock, Luther. 2012. "Abhinanda's *Kādambarīkathāsāra* and the Development of a Kashmiri Style." In *Highland Philology: Results of a Text-Related Kashmir Panel at the 31st DOT, Marburg 2010*, edited by Roland Steiner, 107–119. Studia Indologica Universitatis Halensis 4. Halle an der Saale: Universitätsverlag Halle-Wittenberg.

Obrock, Luther. 2013a. "History at the End of History: Śrīvara's *Jainataraṅgiṇī*." *Indian Economic and Social History Review* 50.2: 223–238.

Obrock, Luther, Ed. 2013b. *Marc Aurel Stein: Illustrated Rājataraṅgiṇī, Together with Eugen Hultzsch's Critical Notes and Stein's Maps*. In Collaboration with Katrin Einicke. Studia Indologica Universitatis Halensis 6. Halle an der Saale: Universitätsverlag Halle-Wittenberg.

Obrock, Luther. 2015. "Translation and History: The Development of a Kashmiri Textual Tradition from ca. 1000–1500." PhD diss., University of California, Berkeley.

Obrock, Luther. 2020. "Landscape in Its Place: The Imagination of Kashmir in Sanskrit and Beyond." *History and Theory* 59.1: 156–164.

O'Flaherty, Wendy (Doniger) and J. Duncan M. Derrett, Eds. 1978. *The Concept of Duty in South Asia*. New Delhi: Vikas Publishing House.

Oldenberg, Hermann. 1922. *Das Mahābhārata: Seine Entstehung, sein Inhalt, seine Form*. Göttingen: Vandenhoeck and Ruprecht.

Olivelle, Patrick. 1993. *The Āśrama System: The History and Hermeneutics of a Religious Institution*. New York: Oxford University Press.

Olivelle, Patrick. 1997. *The Pañcatantra: The Book of India's Folk Wisdom*. The World's Classics Series. Oxford and New York: Oxford University Press.

Olivelle, Patrick. 1998. "Caste and Purity: A Study in the Language of the Dharma Literature." *Contributions to Indian Sociology* 32.2: 190–216.

Olivelle, Patrick. 1999. *Dharmasūtras: The Law Codes of Ancient India, A New Translation*. Oxford World's Classics. Oxford: Oxford University Press.

Olivelle, Patrick. [2000] 2003. *Dharmasūtras: The Law Codes of Āpastamba, Gautama, Baudhāyana, and Vasiṣṭha, Annotated Text and Translation*. Reprinted ed. Delhi: Motilal Banarsidass.

Olivelle, Patrick. 2004a. "Manu and the *Arthaśāstra*: A Study in Śāstric Intertextuality." *Journal of Indian Philosophy* 32.2/3: 281–291.

Olivelle, Patrick, Trans. 2004b. *The Law Code of Manu: A New Translation Based on the Critical Edition*. Oxford World's Classics. New York: Oxford University Press.

Olivelle, Patrick. 2005. *Manu's Code of Law: A Critical Edition and Translation of the Mānava-Dharmaśāstra*. South Asia Research Series of the University of Texas Center for South Asian Studies. New York: Oxford University Press.

Olivelle, Patrick, Ed. 2006. *Between the Empires: Society in India, 300 BCE to 400 CE*. New York: Oxford University Press.

Olivelle, Patrick. 2013. *King Governance, and Law in Ancient India: Kauṭilya's Arthaśāstra, A New Annotated Translation*. New York: Oxford University Press.

Olivelle, Patrick, Trans. and Ed. 2017. *A Dharma Reader: Classical Indian Law*. New York and Chichester, West Sussex: Columbia University Press.

Olivelle, Patrick, and Donald R. Davis Jr., Eds. 2018. *Hindu Law: A New History of Dharmaśāstra*. The Oxford History of Hinduism. Oxford: Oxford University Press.

Onians, Isabelle, Trans. 2005. *What Ten Young Men Did*. Clay Sanskrit Library. New York: NYU Press and the JJC Foundation.

Pandit, R. S. [1935] 1968. *Rājataraṅgiṇī: The Saga of the Kings of Kaśmīr*. New Delhi: Sahitya Akademi.

Parasher, Aloka. 1991. *Mlecchas in Early India: A Study in Attitudes Towards Outsiders up to A.D. 600*. Delhi: Munshiram Manoharlal.

Pathak, Shubha. 2006. "Why Do Displaced Kings Become Poets in the Sanskrit Epics? Modeling *Dharma* in the Affirmative *Rāmāyaṇa* and the Interrogative *Mahābhārata*." *International Journal of Hindu Studies* 10.2: 127–149.

Pathak, Shubha. 2014. *Divine yet Human Epics: Reflections of Poetic Rulers from Ancient Greece and India*. Hellenic Studies Series. Cambridge, MA: Harvard University Press.

Patton, Laurie L. 2007. "How Do You Conduct Yourself?: Gender and the Construction of a Dialogical Self in the *Mahābhārata*." In *Gender and Narrative in the Mahābhārata*, edited by Simon Brodbeck and Brian Black, 97–109. London: Routledge Press.

Penzer, N. M., Ed. 1968. *The Ocean of Story: Being C. H Tawney's Translation of Somadeva's Kathā Sarit Sāgara, Or, Ocean of Streams of Story, Now Edited with Introduction, Fresh Explanatory Notes and Terminal Essay*. Indian ed. 10 vols. Delhi: Motilal Banarsidass.

Philips, C. H., Ed. 1961. *Historians of India, Pakistan and Ceylon*. Oxford: Oxford University Press.

Pickering, Michael, Ed. 2008. *Research Methods for Cultural Studies*. Edinburgh: Edinburgh University Press.

Pilikian, Vaughan, Ed. and Trans. 2006. *Mahābhārata*. Bk. 7, *Droṇa*. Vol. 1. Clay Sanskrit Library. New York: NYU Press and JJC Foundation.

Pilikian, Vaughan, Ed. and Trans. 2009. *Mahābhārata*. Bk. 7, *Droṇa*. Vol. 2. Clay Sanskrit Library. New York: NYU Press and JJC Foundation.

Pollock, Sheldon. 1984a. "*ātmānaṃ mānuṣyam manye*: Dharmākūtam on the Divinity of Rāma." *Journal of the Oriental Institute, Baroda* 33.3–4: 231–243.

Pollock, Sheldon. 1984b. "The Divine King in the Indian Tradition." *Journal of the American Oriental Society* 104.3: 505–528.

Pollock, Sheldon. 1985. "The Theory of Practice and the Practice of Theory in Indian Intellectual History." *Journal of the American Oriental Society* 105.3: 499–519.

Pollock, Sheldon. 1986. *The Rāmāyaṇa of Vālmīki: An Epic of Ancient India*. Vol. 2, *Ayodhyākāṇḍa*. Princeton Library of Asian Traditions. Princeton, NJ: Princeton University Press.

Pollock, Sheldon. 1989. "Mīmāṃsā and the Problem of History in Traditional India." *Journal of the American Oriental Society* 109.4: 603–610.

Pollock, Sheldon. 1990. "The Idea of *Śāstra* in Traditional India." In *Shastric Traditions in Indian Arts*, edited by A. L. Dallapiccola. Stuttgart: Steiner.

Pollock, Sheldon. 1991. *The Rāmāyaṇa of Vālmīki: An Epic of Ancient India*. Vol. 3, *Āraṇyakāṇḍa*. Princeton Library of Asian Traditions. Princeton, NJ: Princeton University Press.

Pollock, Sheldon. 1993. "*Rāmāyaṇa* and Political Imagination in India." *Journal of Asian Studies* 52.2: 261–297.

Pollock, Sheldon. 1996. "The Sanskrit Cosmopolis, 300–1300: Transculturation, Vernacularization, and the Question of Ideology." In *Ideology and Status of Sanskrit: Contributions to the History of the Sanskrit Language*, edited by Jan E. M. Houben, 197–247. Leiden: Brill.

Pollock, Sheldon. 2001. "The Death of Sanskrit." *Comparative Studies in Society and History* 43.2: 392–426.

Pollock, Sheldon. 2006. *The Language of the Gods in the World of Men: Sanskrit, Culture and Power in Premodern India*. Berkeley and Los Angeles: University of California Press.

Pollock, Sheldon. 2007. "Pretextures of Time." *History and Theory* 46: 364–381.

Pollock, Sheldon, Ed. 2010. *Epic and Argument in Sanskrit Literary History: Essays in Honor of Robert P. Goldman*. Delhi: Manohar.

Pollock, Sheldon, Trans. and Ed. 2016. *A Rasa Reader: Classical Indian Aesthetics*. Historical Sourcebooks in Classical Indian Thought. New York: Columbia University Press.

Proudfoot, Ian. 1979. "Interpreting *Mahābhārata* Episodes as a Sources for the History of Ideas." *Annals of the Bhandarkar Oriental Research Institute* 60.1/4: 41–63.

Pusalker, A. D. 1952. "The Brāhmaṇa Tradition and the Kṣatriya Tradition." In *Professor M. Hiriyanna Commemoration Volume*, edited by Mysore Hiriyanna, N. Sivarama Sastry, and G. Hanumantha Rao, 151–155. Mysore: M. Hiriyanna Commemoration Volume Committee.

Radhakrishnan, S. 1953. *The Principal Upaniṣads*. New York: Harper Brothers.

Raghavan, V. 1978. *Bhoja's Śṛṅgāraprakāśa*. 3rd rev. enlarged ed. Adyar, Madras: Vasanta Press of the Theosophical Society.

Rajan, Chandra. [1993] 2006. *Viṣṇu Śarma: The Pañcatantra, Translated from the Sanskrit with an Introduction*. Penguin Classics. London: Penguin Books.

Raman, Srilata, and István Keul, Eds. 2022. *Religious Authority in South Asia: Generating the Guru*. London and New York: Routledge Press.

Ramanujan, A. K. 1999. "Three Hundred *Rāmāyaṇas*: Five Examples and Three Thoughts on Translation." In *The Collected Essays of A. K. Ramanujan*, edited by Vinay Dharwadker, 131–160. New Delhi: Oxford University Press.

Ramaswami Sastri, K. S. 1944. *Studies in Ramayana*. Kirti Mandi Lecture Series 9. Baroda: Baroda State Department of Education.

Raychaudhuri, H. 1923. *Political History of Ancient India*. Calcutta: University of Calcutta.

Richards, J. F., Ed. 1978. *Kingship and Authority in South Asia.* University of Wisconsin Publication Series, Publication No. 3. 2nd ed. Madison: South Asian Studies, University of Wisconsin—Madison.

Richman, Paula, Ed. 1991. *Many Rāmāyaṇas: The Diversity of a Narrative Tradition in South Asia.* Berkeley and Los Angeles: University of California Press.

Ricoeur, Paul. 1979. "The Human Experience of Time and Narrative." *Research in Phenomenology* 9: 17–34.

Ricoeur, Paul. 1981. *The Rule of Metaphor: Multidisciplinary Studies of the Creation of Meaning in Language.* Toronto: University of Toronto Press.

Ricoeur, Paul. 1990. *Time and Narrative.* 3 vols. Chicago and London: University of Chicago Press.

Rocher, Ludo. 1975. "Caste and Occupation in Classical India: The Normative Texts." *Contributions to Indian Sociology* 9.1: 139–151.

Rocher, Ludo. 1980. "Karma and Rebirth in the Dharmaśāstras." In *Karma and Rebirth in Classical Indian Traditions,* edited by Wendy Doniger O'Flaherty, 61–89. Berkeley, Los Angeles, and London: University of California Press.

Rocher, Ludo. 1986. *The Purāṇas.* A History of Indian Literature. Vol. 2, Fasc. 3. Wiesbaden: Verlag Otto Harrassowitz.

Rocher, Ludo. 2002. Review of *Kingship and Authority in South Asia,* edited by J. F. Richards. *Journal of the American Oriental Society* 122.1: 186–187.

Rossella, Daniela. 2009. "Satire, Wit and Humour on Kings and Ascetics in *Kāvya* Literature: 'He Who Laughs Last Laughs Best.'" In *Kings and Ascetics in Indian Classical Literature,* edited by by Paola M. Rossi and Cinzia Pieruccini, 117–133. Milan: Cisalpino..

Roy, Kumkum. 1994. *The Emergence of Monarchy in North India, Eighth-Fourth Centuries B.C., as Reflected in the Brahmanical Tradition.* Delhi: Oxford University Press.

Said, Edward. 1979. *Orientalism.* New York: Vintage Books.

Saletore, Bhasker Anand. 1963. *Ancient Indian Political Thought and Institutions.* New York: Asia Publishing House.

Salomon, Richard. 1987. "Notes on the Translations of Kalhaṇa's *Rājataraṅgiṇī* (I-IV)." *Berliner Indologische Studien* 3: 149–179.

Samozantsev, A. M. 1984. "Some Remarks on the Land Relations in the Kauṭilīya *Arthaśāstra.*" *Indo-Iranian Journal* 27.4: 275–289.

Sanderson, Alexis. 2009. "Kashmir." In *Brill's Encyclopedia of Hinduism.* Vol. 1, *Regions, Pilgrimage, Deities,* edited by Knut A. Jacobsen, 99–126. Leiden and Boston: Brill. Handbuch der Orientalistik. Zweite Abteilung, Indien, Vol. 22.

Sanderson, Alexis. 2015. "Tolerance, Exclusivity, Inclusivity, and Persecution in Indian Religion during the Early Mediaeval Period." In *Honoris Causa: Essays in Honour of Aveek Sarkar,* edited by John Makinson, 155–224. London: Allen Lane.

Sandhu, Major-General Gurcharan Singh. 2000. *A Military History of Ancient India.* New Delhi: Vision Books.

Sathaye, Adheesh A. 2007. "How to Become a Brahmin: The Construction of *varṇa* as Social Place in the *Mahābhārata*'s Legends of Viśvāmitra." *Acta Orientalia Vilnensia* 8.1: 41–67.

Sathaye, Adheesh A. 2010. "The Other Kind of Brahman: Rāma Jāmadagnya and the Psychosocial Construction of Brahman Power in the *Mahābhārata.*" In *Epic and Argument in Sanskrit Literary History: Essays in Honor of Robert P. Goldman,* edited by Sheldon Pollock, 185–207. Delhi: Manohar.

Sathaye, Adheesh A. 2015. *Crossing the Lines of Caste: Viśvāmitra and the Construction of Brahmin Power in Hindu Mythology.* New York: Oxford University Press.

Sathaye, Adheesh A. 2022. "How the Guru Lost His Power: Public Anxieties of Tantric Knowledge in the Sanskrit Vetāla Tale." In *Religious Authority in South Asia: Generating the Guru,* edited by Srilata Raman and István Keul, 8–37. London and New York: Routledge Press.

Scharfe, Harmut. 1989. *The State in Indian Tradition*. Handbuch der Orientalistik. Leiden, New York, København, and Köln: E. J. Brill.

Scharfe, Harmut. 1993. *Investigations in Kauṭilya's Manual of Political Science*. Wiesbaden: Harrassowitz.

Scharfe, Harmut. 2002. *Education in Ancient India*. Leiden: Brill.

Scharpé, Adriaan. 1954–1964. *Kālidāsa-lexicon: Basic Text of the Works*. Pt. 1, *Abhijñānaśākuntala*. Pt. 2, *Mālavikāgnimitra and Vikramorvaśī*. Pt. 3, *Kumārasaṃbhava, Meghadūta, Ṛtusaṃhāra and incerta*. Pt. 4, *Raghuvaṃśa*. Brugge: De Tempel.

Scharpé, Adriaan. 1975. *Kālidāsa-lexicon*. Vol. 2, *References*. Pt. 1, *Poetical Works*; Pt. 2: *Dramatic Works*. Brugge: De Tempel.

Schetelich, Maria. 1997/1998. "Traces of Early *Purohita* Knowledge in the Kauṭilīya *Arthaśāstra*." *Indologica Taurinensia* 23/24: 653–661.

Schilbrack, Kevin. 2010. "Religions: Are There Any?" *Journal of the American Academy of Religion* 78.4: 1112–1138.

Schilbrack, Kevin. 2014. *Philosophy and the Study of Religions: A Manifesto*. Chichester, West Sussex, UK, and Malden, MA: John Wiley & Sons.

Schuyler, Montgomery, Jr. 1899. "The Origin of the Vidūṣaka and the Employment of This Character in the Plays of Harṣadeva." *Journal of the American Oriental Society* 20: 338–340.

Sen, Amartya. 2005. *The Argumentative Indian: Writings on Indian History, Culture, and Identity*. New York: Farrar, Straus and Giroux.

Sharma, Arvind, Ed. 1991. *Essays on the Mahābhārata*. Leiden: E. J. Brill.

Sharma, Arvind. 2000. "Of *śūdras*, *sūta*s and *śloka*s: Why Is the *Mahābhārata* Preeminently in the *anuṣṭubh* Metre?" *Indo-Iranian Journal* 43.3: 225–278.

Sharma, Arvind. 2003. *Hinduism and Its Sense of History*. New Delhi, Oxford, and New York: Oxford University Press.

Sharma, Ram Sharan. [1965] 1980. *Indian Feudalism, c. 300–1200*. New Delhi: Macmillan.

Sharma, Ram Sharan. 1983. *Material Culture and Social Formations in Ancient India*. Delhi, Mumbai, Calcutta, and Madras: MacMillan India Limited.

Sharma, Ram Sharan. 1989. *The Origin of the State in India*. D. D. Kosambi Memorial Lectures. Bombay: University of Bombay, Department of History Publication.

Sharma, Ram Sharan. [1990] 2002. *Śūdras in Ancient India: A Social History of the Lower Order Down to Circa A.D. 600*. 3rd rev. ed. Reprint. Delhi: Motilal Banarsidass.

Sharma, Ram Sharan. 2003. *Perspectives in Social and Economic History of Early India*. Delhi: Munshiram Manoharlal.

Sharma, Ram Sharan. 2005. *Aspects of Political Ideas and Institutions in Ancient India*. 5th rev. ed. Delhi: Motilal Banarsidass.

Sharma Sastri, Rudrapatna, Ed. 1929. *Kauṭilya's Arthaśāstra*. 5th ed. Mysore: Raghuveer Printing Press.

Shulman, David. 1985. *The King and the Clown in South Indian Myth and Poetry*. Princeton, NJ: Princeton University Press.

Shulman, David. 1991. "Fire and Flood: The Testing of Sītā in Kampaṉ's *Irāmāvatāram*." In *Many Rāmāyaṇas: The Diversity of a Narrative Tradition in South Asia*, edited by Paula Richman, 89–113. Berkeley and Los Angeles: University of California Press.

Shulman, David. 2013. "Preface: Kalhaṇa's *Rājataraṅgiṇī: What Is It?*" *Indian Economic and Social History Review* 50.2: 127–130.

Siegel, Lee. 1983. *Fires of Love, Waters of Peace: Passion and Renunciation in Indian Culture*. Honolulu: University of Hawaii Press.

Siegel, Lee. 1987. *Laughing Matters: Comic Tradition in India*. Chicago: University of Chicago Press.

Silk, Jonathan A. 2020. "A Resurgent Interest in 'Hindu Fiction': On and around the *Kathāsaritsāgara*." *Indo-Iranian Journal* 63.3: 263–306.

Singh, Upinder. 2017. *Political Violence in Ancient India*. Cambridge, MA, and London: Harvard University Press.

Sircar, D. C. 1971. *Studies in the Religious Life of Ancient and Medieval India.* Delhi: Motilal Banarsidass.

Slaje, Walter. 2004. *Medieval Kashmir and the Science of History.* Austin: South Asia Institute of the University of Texas.

Slaje, Walter. 2008. "In the Guise of Poetry—Kalhaṇa Reconsidered." In *Śāstrārambha: Inquiries into the Preamble in Sanskrit*, edited by Walter Slaje, 207–244. Preface by Edwin Gerow. Abhandlungen für die Kunde des Morgenlandes LXII. Wiesbaden: Harrassowitz Verlag.

Slaje, Walter. 2014. *Kingship in Kaśmīr (AD 1148–1459), from the Pen of Jonarāja, Court Paṇḍit to Sulṭān Zayn al-'bidīn, Critically Edited with Annotated Translation, Indexes and Maps.* Studia Indologica Universitatis Halensis 7. Halle an der Saale: Universitätsverlag Halle-Wittenberg.

Slaje, Walter. 2019. *Brahmā's Curse: Facets of Political and Social Violence in Premodern Kashmir.* Studia Indologica Universitatis Halensis 13. Halle: Universitätsverlag Halle-Wittenberg.

Smith, Brian K. 1987. "Exorcising the Transcendent: Strategies for Defining Hinduism and Religion." *History of Religions* 27.1: 32–55.

Smith, Brian K. 1989. *Reflections on Resemblance, Ritual, and Religion.* New York: Oxford University Press.

Smith, Brian K. 1994. *Classifying the Universe: The Ancient Indian Varṇa System and the Origins of Caste.* New York: Oxford University Press.

Smith, David, Trans. 2005. *The Birth of Kumára. By Kali•dasa.* Clay Sanskrit Library. New York: NYU Press and JJC Foundation.

Smith, John. 1989. "Scapegoats of the Gods: The Ideology of the Indian Epics." In *Oral Epics in India*, edited by Stuart H. Blackburn, Peter J. Claus, Joyce Burkhalter Flueckiger, and Susan Wadley, 176–194. Berkeley: University of California Press.

Smith, John, Trans. 2009. *The Mahābhārata, An Abridged Translation.* Penguin Classics. New York and London: Penguin.

Smith, Jonathan Z. 1978. *Map Is Not Territory: Studies in the History of Religions.* Chicago: University of Chicago Press.

Smith, Jonathan Z. 1982. *Imagining Religion: From Babylon to Jonestown.* Chicago: University of Chicago Press.

Sooklal, Anil. 1990. "The Guru-Shishya Parampara: A Paradigm of Religio-Cultural Continuity." *Journal for the Study of Religion* 3.2: 15–30.

Spellman, John W. 1964. *Political Theory of Ancient India: A Study of Kingship from the Earliest Times to circa A.D. 300.* Oxford: Clarendon Press.

Speyer, Jacob Samuel. 1908. *Studies about the Kathāsaritsāgara.* Amsterdam: Johannes Müller.

Sreekantaiyya, T. Nanjundaiya. 1980. *'Imagination' in Indian Poetics and Other Literary Studies.* Mysore: Geetha Book House.

Sreekantaiyya, T. Nanjundaiya. 2001. *Indian Poetics.* Translated from the Kannada by N. Balasubrahmanya. New Delhi: Sahitya Akademi.

Staal, Frits. 1959. "Über die Idee der Toleranz im Hinduismus." *Kairos: Zeitschrift für Religionswissenschaft und Theologie*: 215–218.

Stein, Burton. 1960. "The Economic Function of a Medieval Hindu Temple." *Journal of Asian Studies* 19.2: 163–176.

Stein, Marc A. 2013. *Marc Aurel Stein: Illustrated Rājataraṅgiṇī: Together with Eugen Hultzsch's Critical Notes and Stein's Maps.* Edited by Luther Obrock in collaboration with Katrin Einicke. Halle: Universitätsverlag Halle-Wittenberg.

Steiner, Roland, Ed. 2012. *Highland Philology: Results of a Text-Related Kashmir Panel at the 31st DOT, Marburg 2010.* Studia Indologica Universitatis Halensis 4. Halle an der Saale: Universitätsverlag Halle-Wittenberg.

Sternbach, Ludwik. 1953. *Gaṇikā-vṛtta-saṅgraha, Or Texts on Courtezans in Classical Sanskrit.* Vishveshvaranand Indological Series 4. Hoshiarpur: Vishveshvaranand Institute Publications.

Sternbach, Ludwik. 1973a. *Bibliography of Kauṭilīya Arthaśāstra*. Hoshiarpur: Vishveshvaranand Institute.

Sternbach, Ludwik. 1973b. *Bibliography on Dharma and Artha in Ancient and Mediaeval India*. Wiesbaden: Otto Harrassowitz.

Sternbach, Ludwik. 1974. *Subhāṣita, Gnomic and Didactic Literature. A History of Indian Literature*. Vol. 4, pt. 1. Weisbaden: Otto Harrassowitz.

Sternbach, Ludwik. 1971–1976. *The Kāvya-Portions in the Kathā-Literature*. 3 vols. New Delhi: Meharchand Lachhmandas.

Sternbach, Ludwik. 1980. *Aphorisms and Proverbs in the Kathā-Sarit-Sāgara*. Lucknow: Akhila Bharatiya Sanskrit Parishad.

Stoller Miller, Barbara, Ed. [1984] 1999. *The Plays of Kālidāsa: Theater of Memory*. Delhi: Motilal Banarsidass.

Sukthankar, S. V. 1936. "Epic Studies 6: The Bhṛgus and the Bhārata: A Text-Historical Study." *Annals of the Bhandarkar Oriental Research Institute* 18.1: 1–76.

Sullivan, Bruce M. 1990. *Kṛṣṇa Dvaipāyana Vyāsa and the Mahābhārata: A New Interpretation*. Leiden, New York, København, and Köln: E. J. Brill.

Sullivan, Bruce M. 2006. "The Ideology of Self-Willed Death in the Epic *Mahābhārata*." *Journal of Vaishnava Studies* 14.2: 61–80.

Sutton, Nicholas G. 1997. "Aśoka and Yudhiṣṭhira: A Historical Setting for the Ideological Tensions in the *Mahābhārata*?" *Religion* 27.4: 333–341.

Sutton, Nicholas G. 2000. *Religious Doctrines in the Mahābhārata*. Delhi: Motilal Banarsidass.

Tawney, C. H., Trans. 1880 and 1884. *The Kathā Sarit Sāgara or Ocean of the Streams of Story, Translated from the Original Sanskrit*. 2 vols. Calcutta: Baptist Mission Press.

Taylor, Charles. 2007. *A Secular Age*. Cambridge, MA, and London: Harvard University Press.

Taylor, McComas. 2007. *The Fall of the Indigo Jackal: The Discourse of Division and Pūrṇabhadra's Pañcatantra*. Albany: State University of New York Press.

Thapar, Romila. 1971. "The Image of the Barbarian in Early India." *Comparative Studies in Society and History* 1.4: 408–436.

Thapar, Romila. 1978a. *Ancient Indian Social History: Some Interpretations*. New Delhi: Orient Longman.

Thapar, Romila. 1978b. *Exile and the Kingdom: Some Thoughts on the Rāmāyaṇa*. Bangalore: Mythic Society.

Thapar, Romila. 1980. "State Formation in Early India." *International Social Science Journal* 32.4: 655–669.

Thapar, Romila. 1983. "Kalhaṇa." In *Historians of Medieval India*, edited by Mohibbul Hasan, 52–62. New Delhi: Meenakshi Prakashan.

Thapar, Romila. [1984] 2002. *From Lineage to State: Social Formations in the Mid-First Millennium B.C. in the Ganga Valley*. 7th impression. Delhi: Oxford University Press.

Thapar, Romila. 2002a. *Early India: From the Origins to 1300*. London: Penguin Books. Reprinted ed.: Berkeley and Los Angeles: University of California Press, 2004.

Thapar, Romila. 2002b. *Śakuntalā: Texts, Readings, Histories*. London: Anthem Books.

Thapar, Romila. 2005. "Cyclic and Linear Time in Early India." *Museum International* 57.3: 19–31.

Tieken, Herman. 2000. "On the Use of '*rasa*' in Studies of Sanskrit Drama." *Indo-Iranian Journal* 43.2: 115–138.

Todorov, Tvetan. [1973] 1975. *The Fantastic: A Structural Approach to a Literary Genre*. Translated from the French by Richard Howard. With a new foreword by Robert Scholes. Ithaca, NY: Cornell University Press.

Törzsök, Judit. 2012. "Tolerance and Its Limits in Twelfth-Century Kashmir: Tantric Elements in Kalhaṇa's *Rājataraṅgiṇī*." *Indologica Taurinensia* 38: 211–237.

Tubb, Gary. 1985. "*Śāntarasa* in the *Mahābhārata*." 1985. Special Issue entitled "Part 1: Essays on the *Mahābhārata*." *Journal of South Asian Literature* 20.1: 141–168.

Um, Janet Mijung. 2014. "Crossing the Ocean of Story: The Kashmiri *Bṛhatkathās* in Literary Context." MA thesis, University of California at Berkeley.

Vassilkov, Yaroslav. 1995. "The *Mahābhārata's* Typological Definition Reconsidered." *Indo-Iranian Journal* 38.3: 249–256.

Vasudeva, Somadeva, Trans. 2006. *The Recognition of Shakúntala. By Kali•dasa.* Clay Sanskrit Library. New York: NYU Press and JJC Foundation.

Vaudeville, Charlotte. 1961. "A Further Note on *Krauñca-vadha* in the *Dhvanyāloka* and *Kāvyamīmāṃsā*." *Journal of the Oriental Institute, Baroda* 11: 122–126.

Venkatasubbiah, A. 1929. "The *Ādipurāṇa* and *Bṛhatkathā*." *Indian Historical Quarterly* 5: 31–35.

Warder, A. K. [1974] 1990. *Indian Kāvya Literature.* Vol. 2, *The Origins and Formation of Classical Kāvya.* Delhi: Motilal Banarsidass.

Warder, A. K. 1990. *Indian Kāvya Literature.* Vol. 3, *The Early Medieval Period.* 2nd rev. ed. Delhi: Motilal Banarsidass.

Wedemeyer, Christian. 2013. *Making Sense of Tantric Buddhism: History, Semiology, and Transgression in the Indian Traditions.* South Asia across the Disciplines Series. New York: Columbia University Press.

Wells, Henry W. 1963. *The Classical Drama of India: Studies in Its Values for the Literature and Theatre World.* Bombay, Calcutta, Madras, New Delhi, Lucknow, London, and New York: Asia Publishing House.

Whitaker, Jarrod L. 2000. "Divine Weapons and *Tejas* in the Two Indian Epics." *Indo-Iranian Journal* 43.2: 87–113.

Whitaker, Jarrod L. 2002. "How the Gods Kill: The *Nārāyaṇa Astra* Episode, the Death of Rāvaṇa, and the Principles of *Tejas* in the Indian Epics." *Journal of Indian Philosophy* 30.4: 403–430.

White, David Gordon. 1984. "Why Gurus Are Heavy." *Numen* 31.1: 40–73.

White, Hayden. 1987. *The Content of Form.* Baltimore, MD: Johns Hopkins University Press.

Wilmot, Paul, Trans. 2006. *Mahābhārata.* Bk. 2, *The Great Hall.* Clay Sanskrit Library. New York: NYU Press and JJC Foundation.

Wilson, H. H. 1825. "An Essay on the Hindu History of Cashmir." *Asiatic Researches* 15: 1–119.

Winternitz, Maurice. 1908. *Geschichte der indischen Literature.* 3 vols. Leipzig: C. F. Amelang.

Winternitz, Maurice. 1927. *A History of Indian Literature.* Vol. 1, *Introduction, Veda, National Epics, Purāṇas, and Tantras. Translated from the Original German by Mrs. S. Ketkar and Revised by the Author. Only Authorized Translation into English.* Calcutta: Calcutta University Press.

Winternitz, Maurice. 1933. *A History of Indian Literature.* Vol. 2, *Buddhist Literature and Jaina Literature. Translated from the Original German by Mrs. S. Ketkar and Miss H. John, B.A. and Revised by the Author. Only Authorized Translation into English.* Calcutta: Calcutta University Press.

Winternitz, Maurice. [1963, 1965] 1985. *History of Indian Literature.* Vol. 3, pt. 1, *Classical Sanskrit Literature;* pt. 2, *Scientific Literature. Translated from German into English by Subhadra Jha.* Reprinted ed. (Vol. 3, pt. 1, Delhi, 1963; Vol 3, pt. 2, Delhi, 1967). Delhi: Motilal Banarsidass.

Witzel, Michael. 1987. "On the Origin of the Literary Device of the 'Frame Story' in Old Indian Literature." In *Hinduismus und Buddhismus: Festschrift für Ulrich Schneider,* edited by Harry Falk, 173–213. Freiburg: Hedwig Falk.

Witzel, Michael. 1990. "On Indian Historical Writing: The Role of the *Vaṃśāvalīs*." *Journal of the Japanese Association of South Asian Studies* 2: 1–57.

Witzel, Michael. 1994. "The Brahmins of Kashmir." In *A Study of the Nīlamata: Aspects of Hinduism in Ancient Kashmir,* edited by Yasuke Ikari, 237–294. Kyoto: Institute for Research in Humanities, Kyoto University.

Witzel, Michael. 2016. "Kashmiri Brahmins under the Kārkoṭa, Utpala, and Lohara Dynasties, 625–1151 CE." In *Around Abhinavagupta: Aspects of Intellectual History of Kashmir from the Ninth to the Eleventh Century* (Leipziger Studien zu Kultur und Geschichte Sud- und Zentralasiens 6), edited by Eli Franco and Isabelle Ratié, 609–644. Leipzig: Lit Verlag.

Wulff, Donna Marie. 1984. *Drama as a Mode of Religious Realization: The Vidagdhamādhava of Rūpa Gosvāmin*. American Academy of Religion Academy Series. Chico, CA: Scholars Press.

Wynne, Alexander, Trans. 2009. *Mahābhārata*. Bk. 12, *Peace*. Vol. 3, *The Book of Liberation*. Clay Sanskrit Library. New York: NYU Press and JJC Foundation.

Yajnik, R. K. 1933. *The Indian Theatre: Its Origins and Its Later Developments under European Influence*. London: George Allen & Unwin Ltd.

Zutshi, Chitralekha. 2011. "Translating the Past: Rethinking *Rajatarangini* Narratives in Colonial India." *Journal of Asian Studies* 70.1: 5–27.

Zutshi, Chitralekha. 2013. "Past as Tradition, Past as History: The *Rajatarangini* Narratives Kashmir's Persian Historical Tradition." *Indian Economic and Social History Review* 50.2: 201–219.

Zutshi, Chitralekha. 2014. *Kashmir's Contested Pasts: Narratives, Sacred Geographies, and the Historical Imagination*. New Delhi: Oxford University Press.

Index

For the benefit of digital users, indexed terms that span two pages (e.g., 52–53) may, on occasion, appear on only one of those pages.

Abhijñānaśākuntala 3, 18, 23, 178, 180–196, 200, 208, 217, 219, 264, 277, 293
Abhinanda 108n., 290
Abhinavagupta 114n., 118n., 140, 278, 289, 297
abhiṣeka (royal consecration) 82n., 83n., 113, 115, 162n.
ācārya 36, 39n., 53
adharma 73
Āgama(s) 142
Agastya 97
agniṣṭoma rite 76, 77n.
agrahāra (royal donation of land) 25, 118n., 123
Aiyangar, K. V. R. 5n., 6n., 10, 278
ākhyāyikā (factually grounded narrative) 17, 22n.
Alaṃkāraśāstra 118n., 138, 269
Ali, Daud ix, 5n., 18n., 19, 105n., 108n., 172n., 179n., 226n., 278
Altekar, A. S. 8n., 278
Ambā 50, 188
Ānandavardhana 108n., 114, 118n., 123n., 139
Ananta (Kashmiri King) 26, 130, 160, 161, 168, 272
Anuśāsanaparvan 12
āpaddharma 14, 66, 280
Āraṇyakāṇḍa 85, 88, 292
Arjuna 25, 42, 43, 44, 45, 46, 49, 50, 51–55, 59n., 60, 62, 73n., 80n., 81n., 86n., 103, 111, 114
artha 4, 8, 10n., 11, 30, 84n., 96, 142, 169, 174, 176, 192, 197, 208, 210, 220, 223, 224, 254n., 259, 264, 268, 273, 295
Arthaśāstra(s) 4n., 5, 6, 7, 8, 9n., 10, 13, 14, 15n., 18n., 23, 27, 28, 54, 129, 200, 222, 224, 225n., 226n., 241n., 259, 260, 265, 273, 277, 287, 289, 291, 293, 294, 295
Arthaśāstra 4n., 5n., 6, 7, 8, 9n., 10, 13, 14, 15n., 18n., 23, 27, 28, 54, 129, 200, 224, 226n., 241n., 251, 265, 277, 287, 289, 291, 293, 294, 295
ascetic(s) 10n., 46n., 71, 85n., 95, 120, 143, 155, 166, 167, 170, 173, 174, 180, 181, 184, 185, 186, 188, 193, 232, 233, 234, 236, 237, 247, 248, 279, 280, 282, 293
āśrama (stage of life) 38, 75, 82n., 180, 181n., 182, 183, 188, 290
Āstīka 63, 64, 131
aśvamedha sacrifice 76
Aśvatthāman 49
Atharvaveda 14
atirātra rite 76
atisaṃdhāna ("outwitting") 6, 226n.
ātman 47
Aucityavicāracarcā of Kṣemendra 125n., 138
Avantivarman 120, 121n., 123, 130
Avantisvāmin temple 121
Avantīśvara temple 121
avatāra 66, 68, 69, 285
Ayodhyā 84, 94, 101
Ayodhyākāṇḍa 84, 88, 292

Bakker, Hans 156n., 178n., 279
Bālakāṇḍa 69n., 73n., 85n., 103, 284
Balarāma 4n., 51n.
Balog, Dániel 178n., 279
Bāṇa 108n., 155n.
Banerjee, Ron D. K. 224, 237, 279
Basham, A. L. 180n., 279
Bhagavadgītā 51–55, 86n., 111, 114, 123, 281
Bhairavatantras 143
bhakti 53, 55
Bharata 25, 29, 34, 35, 50, 51n., 58, 59, 63, 73, 82, 83, 84, 85, 88, 90, 105, 130, 261, 270,
Bhaṭṭa Kallaṭa 121, 140
Bhaṭṭa Udbhaṭa 138
Bhīṣma, a.k.a. Devavrata 11n., 35n., 44n., 50, 52, 57, 58, 60, 64, 84n., 85n., 130, 188
Bhīṣmaparvan 33
Bisgaard, Daniel 23n., 280
Bloomfield, Maurice 16n., 280

boon(s) 57, 63, 64, 70, 83, 84, 85, 94n., 131, 144n., 150, 170, 173
Bose, Mandakranta 68n., 280
Bowles, Adam 35n., 280
Brahmā 76, 94n., 96, 97, 98, 99, 149, 150, 290, 295,
brāhmaṇa-kṣatriya alliance 9, 10, 11, 13, 15, 23, 28, 29, 30, 31, 34, 35, 44, 47, 52, 59, 60, 64, 65, 66, 67, 105, 120, 124, 131, 132, 145, 146, 153, 160, 219, 222, 260, 261, 263, 264, 265, 272, 273, 292
Brahmayāmalatantra 143n., 285
brahminicide 71, 95, 149
Bṛhadāraṇyaka Upaniṣad 6n., 48n.,
Bṛhaspati 26n., 139
Bṛhatkathā 18, 31, 142, 143, 144, 145, 146n., 147, 151, 152, 154n., 226, 227, 287, 288, 289, 296
Bṛhatkathāmañjarī of Kṣemendra 142
Bṛhatkathāślokasaṃgraha of Buddhasvāmin 145n., 152n., 159n., 171n., 289,
Brick, David 203n., 280
Brockington, John 46n., 51n., 280
Bronner, Yigal 18n., 123, 130, 209n., 281
Brueck, Laura x
Buddhasvāmin 145n., 288, 289
Buddhiśarīra (minister of first *vetāla* story) 164, 165, 166, 167
Buddhism/Buddhist 61, 118, 139, 142, 143, 290, 297
Bühler, Georg 24n., 26n., 37n., 38n., 39n., 40n., 48n., 281
Bühnemann, Gudrun ix
Buitenen, J.A.B. van 46n., 48n., 51., 52n., 159, 174, 281
Bulcke, Camille 89n., 281

Candragupta II 156
Candrāpīḍa (King of Kashmir) 119
carmakāra (tanner) 119
caste/*varṇa* 9n., 11, 12, 13, 15, 30, 35n., 36, 40, 41, 42, 45, 46, 47, 48, 51, 65, 71, 72, 102, 103, 110n., 112, 119, 127, 135, 145, 146n., 179, 181, 182, 183, 184, 195, 211, 217, 219, 264, 267, 268, 269, 273, 274, 279, 281, 282, 293, 290, 293, 295
casteism/casteist 274
Chāndogyopaniṣad 47, 48n., 277
Chatterjee, Indrani 10
Clines, Gregory x, 100n.
Clooney, Frank x, 70, 281
Collins, Brian 9n., 45n., 46n., 57n., 125n., 281
Confucian(ism) 266
conquering the senses 5n., 6n.
consequentialism 7, 18n., 28, 54, 259
Coulson, Michael 177n., 180n., 181n., 182n., 184n., 185n., 186n., 187n., 188n., 189n., 191n., 193n., 194n., 195n., 215, 281
Cox, Whitney 18n., 107, 108, 109, 110, 281
cremation ground See also: *śmaśāna* 21n., 120n., 143, 146, 148, 149, 150, 151, 155, 156, 157, 166, 167, 171, 174

ḍākinī(s) 143, 144n., 145, 151n.
dakṣiṇā 40, 42, 43, 187n.
Dalit(s) 45
Damanaka 230, 231, 232, 233, 234, 235, 237, 238, 239, 240, 241, 242, 243, 244
ḍāmara(s) 160, 290
Dāmodaragupta 3, 16, 18, 24, 31, 139, 209, 218, 277
daṇḍanīti (administration of justice) 13
Daṇḍin 17n., 167n., 208n.
Daśakumāracarita of Daṇḍin 167n.
Daśaratha 8n., 81n., 82, 83, 84, 85, 86, 92, 103,
Davis, Donald R. ix, 6, 7, 22, 23n., 93n., 135, 144, 280, 282, 290, 291
De, S. K. 17n., 282
deontology 7, 28
Devīcandragupta of Viśākhadatta 156
Dezső, Csaba 18n., 24n., 151n., 155, 156, 157, 176, 209, 210n., 211n., 212, 213n., 214n., 216n., 217n., 218n., 277, 282
Dhand, Arti 58, 282
dharma 4, 5, 8, 10n., 11, 12, 18n., 29, 30, 31, 33, 34, 35, 36, 40, 41, 43, 48n., 50, 51, 52, 53, 54, 55, 58, 59, 60, 61, 62, 63, 64, 65, 66, 67, 69, 71, 72, 73, 74, 75, 77, 78, 80, 81, 82, 83, 84, 85, 86, 87, 88, 89, 91, 92, 93, 94, 97, 89, 99, 100, 101, 102, 103, 104, 111, 112, 119, 126, 127, 129, 132, 133, 134, 135, 136, 137, 142, 162n., 174, 176, 179, 182, 185, 188, 191, 192195, 196, 197, 208, 215, 217, 218, 219, 220, 223, 224, 257, 259, 261, 262, 265, 266, 268, 270, 273, 280, 282, 285, 286, 288, 290, 291, 295
Dharmaśāstra(s) 4n., 5, 6, 7, 8, 13, 14, 60, 71, 224, 260, 265, 273, 280, 282, 287, 290, 291, 293
Dharmasūtra(s) 4n., 9n., 291
Dhṛṣṭadyumna 44
Dhṛtarāṣṭra 34, 52, 58
dhvani 269
Dhvanyāloka 118, 296
Diddā (a Kashmiri Queen) 112n.

Dīrghadarśin (minister of king Yaśaḥketu in twelfth *vetāla* story) 158, 159
Doniger (O'Flaherty), Wendy 2n., 4n., 15n., 23n., 178n., 190n., 196n., 197n., 198n., 199n., 200n., 201n., 202n., 203n., 204n., 205n., 206n., 207n., 208, 218, 224, 278, 282, 285, 288, 290, 293
Draupadī 97, 285
drinking (of intoxicants) 5, 179, 181
Droṇa 41, 42, 43, 44, 45, 46, 47, 48, 49, 50, 51, 52, 57, 60, 64, 291
Droṇaparvan 43
Drupada 44
Durgasiṃha 227
Durlabhakaratāpāditya II (Kashmiri king) 163
Durvāsas 187, 188, 194, 195
Duryodhana 34, 46n., 50, 51, 60, 80n., 131, 134, 289
Duṣyanta 180, 181, 182, 183, 184, 185, 186, 188, 189, 190, 191, 192, 193, 194, 196, 219
Dvāpara Yuga 46n.

Edgerton, Franklin 51n., 52, 223, 226, 227, 228n., 229n., 231n., 235n., 241n., 242n., 244n., 245n., 246n., 247n., 248n., 249n., 250n., 251n., 252n., 254n., 256n., 277, 283
Ekalavya 41, 42, 43, 44, 45, 46, 47, 48, 56, 57, 60, 64
Erndl, Kathleen 70n., 283
ethics See: consequentialism, deontology, virtue ethics
external audience(s) (of stories) 21, 24, 25, 27, 74, 75, 80, 99, 168, 169, 175, 235, 265, 273

Falk, Harry 223, 283, 297
fantasy/the fantastic 20, 26, 45, 187, 188, 199, 220, 221, 269, 271, 272, 286
father-son bond 35, 56, 57, 75
film theory 10, 2n., 20n., 269, 270, 289
Fitzgerald, James 35n., 283
framing narrative(s) 3, 4n., 9, 15n., 21n., 22, 25, 27, 61, 72, 76, 78, 152, 153, 154, 222, 245, 260, 265, 273

gambling 5, 179, 181, 190
Gāndhārī 54, 55
Geertz, Clifford 29, 215n., 283
gender/gender-bias 14, 93n., 102, 135, 158, 212, 217, 255, 267, 268, 269, 273, 280, 291
genre(s) 16, 17, 20, 21n., 108n., 176, 177, 208, 219, 220, 221, 226, , 266, 267, 268, 272, 273, 274, 289
Gerow, Edwin 116, 281, 283, 284, 294
Ghoshal, Upendra Nath 5, 7n., 9n., 12n., 284
Goldman, Robert 23n., 66n., 67n., 69n., 70n., 71n., 72n., 73n., 75n., 76n., 77n. 99n., 81n., 82n., 87n., 91n., 92, 93, 94, 95, 96n., 97n., 98n., 284, 292, 293
Goldman, Sally J. Sutherland 70n., 73n., 75n., 76n., 77n., 81n., 82n., 87n., 91n., 92, 93, 94, 95, 96n., 97n., 98n., 284
Gomukha (minister of Naravāhanadatta) 153, 154, 171
Gonda, Jan 36, 39, 40n., 41n., 42n., 43n., 51n., 56, 284,
González-Reimann, Luis 69n., 284
Goodall, Dominic 18n., 24n., 140n., 151n., 209, 210, 211n., 212, 213n., 214n., 216n., 217n., 218n., 277, 284 290
gosava rite 76, 77n.
Guṇāḍhya 142, 143n., 151, 152, 169n., 174, 288
guru(s) ix, 8n., 33–65, 66, 78, 85n., 104, 120n., 144n., 174n., 187n., 204n., 211, 216, 284, 285, 289, 292
guru-student relationship See: teacher-student relationship

Haladhara (advisor to Kashmiri king Ananta) 160
Halbfass, Wilhelm 8n., 285
Hall, Stuart 20n., 285
Hanumān 22n., 70n., 75, 87, 192
Haracaritacintāmaṇi 151n.
Hāralatā 210, 212, 215, 217
Hāridrumata Gautama 47
Harṣa (author of the *Ratnāvalī*) 23, 178, 196, 213, 220, 278, 282
Harṣa (king of Kashmir) 130, 131, 140, 279
Harṣacarita of Bāṇa 155n.
Hatley, Shaman 143, 144, 167n., 284, 285, 290
Heesterman, Jan 9n., 20n., 285
Hegarty, James 25n., 285
Hertel, Johannes 17n., 223, 226, 227, 285
Hiltebeitel, Alf 23n., 34n., 39n., 49n., 50n., 51n., 54, 55n., 62n., 62n., 75n., 285, 286
Himālaya 150
Hindu/Hinduism/Hindus 4n., 7, 16n., 22, 68, 72, 134, 254, 277, 278, 279, 280, 281, 282, 283, 284, 285, 286, 288, 289, 290, 291, 293, 294, 295, 297
historiography 106, 112, 113, 136
Hitopadeśa 227
Hopkins, E. Washburn 18n., 37n., 38n., 286
horror (movie genre) 20n., 27, 221
Huang, Po-chi 155n., 286
Hueckstedt, Robert 10

Hultzsch, Eugen 115n., 120n., 121n., 122n., 126n., 140n., 286, 290, 295
hunting 5, 62, 99, 179, 181, 184

Ikṣvāku(s) 85, 88
imaginaire, cultural, religious, and literary 19, 175
Indra 8n., 45, 73n., 98, 192, 193, 204
indriyajaya See also : conquering the senses 5n., 6n.
Ingersoll, Julie xi
internal audiences (of stories) 101, 168
Itihāsa ("Epic" poems) 16, 208n.

Jabālā (mother of Satyakāma) 47
Jain/Jainism 17n., 108n., 142, 146n., 154n., 226, 227, 297
Jamadagni 46
Jamison, Stephanie 77n., 287
Janamejaya 25, 35, 36, 47, 49, 54, 59n., 62, 63, 64, 72, 73, 131, 261, 270, 279, 289
Jātaka(s) 223, 227n.
Jayā (wife of Puṣpadanta) 147, 148n.
Jayantabhaṭṭa 108n.
Jayāpīḍa (king of Kashmir) 24n., 123, 124, 130, 139, 209, 281
Jayasiṃha (king of Kashmir) 106, 130, 131
Jonarāja 106, 131, 132n., 290, 294

Kaikasī (mother of Rāvaṇa) 95, 96
Kaikeyī 81n., 82, 83, 84, 85, 86, 92, 275
Kalaśa (prince, son of king Ananta) 130, 140, 160
Kālasaṃkarṣiṇī 143, 144n.
Kāle, M. R. 180n., 181n., 182n., 183n., 184n., 185n., 186n., 187n., 188n., 189n., 190n., 191n., 193n., 194n., 195n., 277
Kalhaṇa x, 3, 9, 18, 24, 59, 104, 105, 106, 107, 108, 109, 110, 111, 112, 113, 114, 115, 117, 118, 119, 123, 124, 126, 127, 128, 129, 130, 131, 132, 133, 134, 135, 136, 137, 209, 262, 278, 281, 286, 287, 290, 293, 294, 296
Kālidāsa 3, 18, 23, 178, 180, 183, 185, 196, 219, 277, 279, 287, 289, 293, 296
Kali Yuga 12, 51, 59, 60, 63, 64, 66, 105, 129, 132, 134, 135, 261
Kāma (god of love) 198, 199, 200, 202, 214
kāma 4, 8, 10n., 11, 30, 31, 39, 52n., 85n., 92n., 96, 122, 142, 169, 174, 176, 179, 185, 192, 198n., 208, 210, 218n., 220, 223, 224, 259, 264, 268, 278
Kāmandaki 5n., 6n., 7n., 8n., 10, 23
Kāmaśāstra 14, 223
Kāmasūtra 4n., 15n., 218, 277, 282, 290
Kāṇabhūti 148, 149, 150, 151,
Kanauj 178
Kāñcanamālā (female friend of Vāsavadattā) 199, 201, 203, 204
Kangle, R. P. 5n., 8, 10n., 277, 287
Kaṇva 173, 182, 183, 184, 187
Kāpālika(s) 172, 173
Karaṭaka 230, 231, 232, 233, 234, 235, 238, 239, 243
Kārkoṭa Dynasty 130
Karṇa 45, 46, 47, 48, 49, 51, 60, 64, 80, 95, 280, 289
Karṇotpala (king in first *vetāla* story) 164, 167, 168
Kashmir, Kashmiri(s), Kashmirian, the Kashmir Valley ix, 3, 18, 19, 24, 30, 59n., 104–140, 142, 143, 146n., 154n., 163, 172n., 179, 209, 226, 227, 268, 269, 271, 279, 281, 286, 287, 290, 293, 294, 295, 296, 297, 298
Kaśyapa 172, 187n., 193, 194, 195,
kathā (fictive narrative) 17, 108, 144n., 163, 172n., 208, 221
Kathāpīṭha 147, 153n.
Kathāsaritsāgara ix, x, 3, 15, 18, 21, 24, 26, 27, 30, 31, 62, 93n., 96, 108n., 141, 142, 143, 144, 145, 146, 147, 150, 151n., 152, 153, 154, 155, 156, 159, 160, 161, 163n., 168, 169, 171, 172, 173, 174, 175, 176, 178, 179, 185, 197, 204, 207, 209, 221, 227, 253, 263, 266n., 269, 272, 273, 277, 294
Kaul, Shonaleeka 18n., 106, 112, 113n., 136, 137, 287
Kauravas 41, 50, 61
Kausalyā 82
Kauśāmbī 143, 151n., 196, 198
Kauṭilya 5n., 6, 7, 10, 13, 14, 22, 23, 267n., 277, 289, 291, 293, 294
kavi (poet) 113n., 116
kāvya (poetry) 108, 109, 137, 215, 278, 293, 295, 296, 297
Kāvyādarśa of Daṇḍin 208n.
kāyastha(s) 118n.
Keith, A. B. 16n., 224, 287
kingship 4, 9n., 12, 13, 14, 15, 17, 18n., 19, 20n., 21n., 67, 80, 91, 104, 109n., 123, 135, 136, 145, 172n., 174, 176, 177, 180, 184, 185, 192, 196, 197, 219, 221, 261, 262, 284, 285, 286, 287, 290, 292, 293, 294, 295,
Kiṣkindhākāṇḍa 73n., 88, 288
Knutson, Jesse 4n., 5n., 7n., 24n., 26n., 287
Konow, Sten 178n., 284, 288

Kosala 204, 207
Kosambi, D. D. 22n., 287, 294
krauñca bird 79, 80n., 86, 94, 101, 288, 296
Kṛṣṇa 33, 35, 41n., 45, 48, 49, 50, 51, 53, 54, 55, 56, 60, 64, 65, 66, 67, 80n., 81n., 86n., 103, 104, 111, 114, 261, 265, 285, 286, 296
kṣatriyadharma 11, 89
Kṣemendra 18n., 108n., 113n., 125n., 138, 139, 140, 142
Kuntī 45
Kuṭṭanīmata 3, 16, 18, 24, 25, 31, 139, 209, 210, 211n., 212n., 213n., 214, 215, 216n., 217, 218, 219, 221, 264, 265, 277
Kuvera/Kubera 96, 149, 159n.

Lacôte, Félix 18n., 142, 143n., 144n., 145n., 150n., 153n., 154n., 172n., 175n., 288
Lakṣmaṇa 70, 80n., 88, 89, 90
Lalitāditya (King of Kashmir) 130
Laṅkā 82, 85, 87, 94, 96
Lefeber, Rosalind 73n., 89, 90n. 288
Leslie, Julia 80n., 288
Lomapāda 8n.
loyalty 36, 38, 39, 41, 42, 43, 46, 49, 52, 53, 55, 56, 57, 58, 59, 60, 62, 63, 80n., 85n., 86, 87, 89, 91, 92, 93, 103, 120, 134, 161, 168, 257

Machiavelli 54, 104, 223, 257
Madanamañjukā / Madanamañcukā 146n., 153, 173
Mādhavya (*vidūṣaka* of *Abhijñānaśākuntala*) 184, 185, 190, 19,
Mahābhārata ix, 3, 4n., 5n., 6n., 8n., 11, 12, 13n., 15, 17n., 18, 23, 25, 26, 29, 30, 33–65, 66, 67, 72, 73, 74, 78, 80, 81n., 83n., 84, 86–88, 92, 97n., 99, 101n., 102, 103, 104, 105, 108, 110, 111n., 112, 114, 120, 129, 130, 131, 132, 134, 135, 137, 185, 188, 223, 261, 262, 266n., 269, 270, 277, 278, 280, 281, 282, 283, 284, 285, 286, 287, 288, 289, 290, 291, 292, 293, 294, 295, 296, 297
makarandodyāna ("garden of nectar") 199
Mālatī 192, 209, 210, 213, 214, 215
Mallinson, James 178n., 288
Mālyavān (aide to Puṣpadanta) 96, 148, 151, 152
Mānavadharmaśāstra (Manusmṛti, Manu) 4n., 5n., 6n., 7, 8n., 11, 14., 21n., 23, 34, 36, 37, 38, 39, 40, 41, 42, 43n., 46, 48, 53, 54, 55, 56, 60, 61, 62, 64, 78, 267n., 278, 281, 286, 288, 291
Mañjarī 18n., 145n., 213, 215, 214, 216, 217, 219
Mantharā 82, 83, 84, 86, 248, 249, 250, 275
mantra(s) 8, 143, 144n., 204
Marasinghe, E. W. 178n., 288
Mārīca 87n.
marriage 27, 37n., 59, 80, 144n., 146n., 154, 161, 172, 197, 205, 206, 208, 211, 237, 264
Marriott, McKim 22n., 288
Marvel (movies) 269n.
Masson, Moussaief 70n., 89, 285, 288, 289
Mātali 192
Matilal, B. K. 52n., 58n., 185n., 285, 289
Mātṛgupta (Brahmin become vassal king in Kashmir) 125, 126, 130, 138
mātsyanyāya ("law of the fishes") 35n., 55, 261
Maurya/Mauryan Kings 61
McClish, Mark x, 8n., 224, 289
McCrea, Lawrence 18n., 107n., 108, 109, 110, 111n., 113, 114, 126, 129, 131, 289
Meister, Michael ix, 130, 289
Menakā 192
merchant(s) (*vaṇij*) 144n., 146n., 159n., 161, 163, 174, 192, 197, 256, 263
mleccha(s) 267n., 291
"models for" action 27, 29, 260
"models of" action 27, 29, 260
mokṣa 4, 11, 259, 268
Monius, Anne x
moral dilemma 58, 59, 63, 74, 185, 189, 289
Mṛgāṅkadatta 153, 154, 155, 171
Mughals, the 106
Murty Classical Library of India 4n., 287

Nārada 71, 72, 79
Naravāhanadatta 142, 143, 146n., 152, 153, 154, 159n., 171, 172, 173, 271
Nārāyaṇa (author of the *Hitopadeśa*) 227, 297
Narayana Rao, Velcheru 106, 107, 130, 289
nāṭaka (type of drama) 178, 180, 215
nāṭikā (type of drama) 178, 196n., 197, 203
Nāṭyaśāstra 16, 114, 178, 277, 279
Neale, Stephen 1n., 2n., 19n., 20n., 269n., 270n., 289
Nelson, Donald 18n., 142, 143n., 144n., 145n., 146n., 152n., 154n., 171n., 289
Nemec, John ix, 6n., 7n., 17n., 19n., 93n., 106n., 111n., 118n., 124n., 125n., 126n., 127n., 135n., 144n., 151n., 168n., 218n., 282, 289, 290
Niṣāda(s) 41, 79, 94, 99, 101
Niśvāsa corpus 143n., 155n., 284
Nītisāra 4n., 5n., 6n., 7n., 8n., 10n., 12n., 13n., 14, 23, 26n., 224
nītiśāstra 14, 168, 225n.

Nooten, Barend van 70n., 91n., 92n., 98n., 284
Nṛpāvali of Kṣemendra 113n., 138
Nyāya (school of Indian philosophy) 108n., 224, 237

Obeyesekere, Gananath ix, 289
Obrock, Luther 18n., 106n., 108, 290, 295
Olivelle, Patrick x, 4n., 5n., 6, 8n., 9n., 10, 11n., 21n., 22n., 23n., 36n., 37n., 38n., 39n., 40n., 48n., 61, 62n., 64, 223, 224, 225, 226, 227, 229, 230n., 232n., 235n., 241n., 244, 245, 247n., 248n., 250n., 251n., 252n., 255, 256n., 277, 278, 280, 290, 291
Onians, Isabelle 167n., 291
outcaste(s) 41, 42, 119, 267n.

pādāgra (office of finance ministry) 160
Padmāvatī (maiden of first *vetāla* story) 164, 165, 166, 167, 169
Pahlavi 23n., 227
Paiśācī (language), a.k.a. Piśācabhāṣā 142, 143n., 152
Pañcākhyānaka 226n.
Pañcatantra 3, 17, 18, 20, 21n., 23, 25, 31, 169n., 209, 221, 222, 223, 224, 225, 226, 227, 228, 229, 230, 231, 232, 235, 237, 240, 244, 245n., 246n., 247n., 248n., 249n., 250n., 251, 252n., 254n., 255, 256n., 257, 259, 265, 269, 273, 277, 279, 283, 285, 290, 292, 296
Pāṇḍavas 41, 42, 44, 48, 49, 50, 51, 54, 55, 285
Pandit, R. S. 115, 125, 291
Pāṇini 124, 139, 148, 150
paramparā (lineage) ix, 33, 36, 64, 78, 289, 295
Parasher, Aloka 267n., 291
Paraśurāma, a.k.a. Rāma Jāmadagnya 9n., 45, 46, 47, 56, 57, 60, 113n., 125n., 281
Parikṣit 49, 62, 63, 131
Pārvatī 147, 148, 149, 150
Patel, Deven ix, 118n.
Patel, Geeta x
Penzer, N. M. 159n., 167n., 169n., 280, 291
Persian 106, 108n., 298
Peruṅkatai 152n., 154n., 289
Philips, C. H. 112, 279, 291
Piṅgalaka 230, 231, 232, 233, 234, 235, 238, 239, 241, 242, 243, 244n.
piśāca 148, 149, 152
political philosophy 14
political theology 262
Pollock, Sheldon 5n., 19n., 37n., 68n., 69, 70n., 82n., 83n., 84n., 85n., 86n., 88, 94, 95n., 97n., 99n., 101n., 107, 110n., 215n., 289, 291, 292, 293,
prakaraṇa (type of drama) 178
Prakrit 193, 198, 288
Pratāpamukuṭa (Benarasi king of first *vetāla* story) 164
pratyakṣa (direct perception) 224, 237
prāya/*prāyopaveśa* (the fast unto death) 124, 127, 290
Purāṇa(s) 16, 20n., 247, 278, 288, 293, 297,
Pūrṇabhadra 17n., 226n., 285, 296
purohita 8n., 51n., 53n., 294
puruṣakāra ("human effort") 146n.
puruṣārtha(s) See also: *dharma*, *artha*, *kāma*, and *mokṣa* 29, 142, 214n., 217, 261
Puṣpadanta 147, 148, 149, 150, 151

queen(s) x, 3, 5, 6, 26, 28, 30, 55, 82, 84, 105, 111, 112, 118n., 133, 135, 136, 144n., 156, 160, 168, 174, 175, 185, 198, 199, 201, 202, 203, 204, 206, 207, 220, 259, 262, 263, 271, 272

Radhakrishnan, S. 47n., 292
Raghavan, 156n., 292
rājadharma 14, 282
Rājadharmaparvan 26
Rājataraṅgiṇī ix, x, 3, 17, 18, 24, 25, 30, 59n., 64n., 104–140, 142, 160, 161, 163, 168, 179, 181, 185, 190, 209, 226n., 262, 269, 271, 272, 278, 286, 287, 289, 290, 291, 293, 294, 295, 296
rākṣasa(s) ("demons") 87n., 94, 95, 97, 98, 99, 101n., 151n.
Rāma 22n., 27, 30, 33, 46n., 66–103, 104, 184, 192, 195, 196, 212, 265, 269, 280, 281, 283, 284, 291, 293
Rāma Jāmadagnya See: Paraśurāma
Raman, Srilata x, 284, 290, 292, 293
Rāma-*rājya* 77
Ramaswami Sastri, K. S. 68n., 73n., 292
Rāmāyaṇa 3, 15, 18, 22n., 23, 27, 30, 33, 59n., 66–103, 104, 134, 135, 136, 137, 185, 188, 194, 195, 196, 219, 261, 262, 269n., 270, 271, 278, 279, 280, 281, 283, 284, 288, 291, 292, 294, 296
Rāmnagar 269n.
rasa 26n., 113, 114, 115, 116, 117, 132, 177, 259n., 269, 283, 292, 296
Rati (Kāma's wife) 199, 200n.
Ratnākara 123n., 139
Ratnāvalī, a.k.a. Sāgarikā 197, 199, 200, 201, 202, 203, 204, 205, 206, 207, 208, 213

Ratnāvalī of Harṣa 3, 18, 23, 178, 196–208, 213, 217, 219, 220, 221, 264, 278, 283
Rāvaṇa 66, 70, 71, 75, 82, 84n., 86, 87, 88, 91, 92, 93, 94, 95, 96, 97, 98, 99, 100, 101, 102, 191, 192, 262, 269, 297
realism (of literary works) 10, 16, 19, 20n., 136, 217, 221, 222, 257
realpolitik 6, 251
Ṛg Veda 99n.
Richman, Paula 68n., 283, 292, 294
ritual 9n., 12, 20n., 25n., 37n., 38, 39, 56, 77, 110, 116, 117, 141, 143, 146n., 150, 155n., 157, 174n., 211, 212, 256, 279, 285, 287, 289, 295
Rocher, Ludo 16n., 293
Roy, Kumkum 4n., 9n., 28n., 293
Rumā (wife of Sugrīva) 89
rūpaka (major types of Sanskrit dramas) 16, 178

Sabhāparvan 97n.
Sāgarikā (a.k.a. Ratnāvalī) 199, 200, 201, 202, 203, 204, 205, 206, 207, 208, 213
Śaiva/Śaivism x, 143n., 151, 284, 290
śākinī(s) 143, 144n., 145, 174n.
Śakuntalā 181, 182, 183, 186, 187, 188, 189, 190, 191, 192, 193n., 194, 279, 280, 283, 296
Salomon, Richard 115n., 119n., 125n., 293
Śalyaparvan 4n.
Samara 213, 214
Saṃdhimati 120n., 125n., 139
Saṃhitā(s) 9n., 142
Saṃjaya 34n.
Saṃjīvaka 230, 231, 232, 233, 234, 238, 239, 241, 242, 243, 244n.
Śaṃtanu 57, 58, 84n.
śāntarasa 59n., 108, 114, 129, 262, 271, 289, 296
Śāntiparvan 5n., 6n., 11, 12, 35n., 61
sarvādhikāritā ("prime minister") 160
śāstra/*śāstric* 23n., 37n., 40, 113n., 119n., 136, 138, 225, 228, 231, 233, 242, 278, 291, 292
Śatapathabrāhmaṇa 9n., 99n.
Sātavāhana 151, 152
Sathaye, Adheesh 9, 293
satī 70n., 205, 206, 212
Satyakāma 47, 48
Satyavatī 57, 58, 84n.
Satya Yuga 119n.
Scharfe, Harmut 9n., 293
secular/secularism 266, 278, 281, 287, 296
self-restraint (*dama*) 5, 8, 46, 125, 268
Seneviratne, H. L. ix, 290
Shah Mir Dynasty 106
Sharma, Ram Sharan 4n., 294
Shulman, David 9n., 18n., 28n., 68n., 70, 71, 74, 76, 87, 105, 106, 107, 108, 110, 125, 130, 289, 294
Śikhaṇḍī 50, 188
Silk, Jonathan 16n., 24n., 108n., 294
Sītā, a.k.a. Jānakī / Maithilī 66, 70, 75, 77, 80n., 82, 85, 86, 87, 88, 89, 90, 91, 92, 93, 96, 97n., 100n., 101, 102, 189, 191, 195, 196, 278, 285, 294
Śiva 120, 123, 147, 148, 149, 150, 151, 153n., 155n., 173, 195, 210, 285, 288
Slaje, Walter 26n., 106n., 107n., 109n., 111n., 112, 113n., 114, 115, 116, 127 130n., 132n., 168n., 290, 294, 295
śleṣa (punning or paranomasia) 124
śloka meter 33n., 78, 79, 80, 94, 102, 108n., 119, 136, 270, 277, 294
śmaśāna See also: cremation ground 148n.
Smith, David 178n., 295
Smith, John 4n., 35n., 295
śoka ("grief") 33., 78, 79, 95n., 102, 136, 196, 270
Somadeva 3, 24, 108n., 142, 143, 145, 150n., 152, 172n., 173, 176, 227, 263, 277, 281, 291, 296
Spellman, John W. 10n., 14n., 295
Śrīvara 106, 108n., 138, 290
Stein, Marc Aurel 24n., 104, 113, 115n., 120n., 121n., 122, 123, 124n., 125n., 126, 29, 131, 132, 133n., 134, 138, 139, 140, 160, 174n., 278, 286, 290
Sternbach, Ludwik 266n., 295, 296
strīdharma 14
Subhadrā 49
Subhāṣitāvali of Vallabhadeva 125n., 138, 139
Subjectivity 2–3n., 27–28, 133, 257–258
Subrahmanyam, Sanjay 106, 107, 130, 289
śūdra(s) 40, 42, 61, 294
Sugandhā (wife of the Kashmiri Utpala king, Śaṅkaravarman) 112
Sugrīva 70n. 75, 81, 88–91
Śuka 106
Sundarakāṇḍa 70n., 75n., 87n., 284
Sundarasena 210, 211, 212, 213n.
superhero(es) 269n.
Superman 20
Śūra (minister to Kashmiri king Avantivarman) 120, 121, 123n., 140
Śūrpaṇakhā 70, 86, 283

Sūryamatī (a.k.a., Sūryavatī, Queen married to King Ananta) 26, 161, 168, 272
Susaṃgatā 199, 200, 201, 203
suspense, narrative 269–270
sūtradhāra (stage director) 196, 197
Sreenivasan, Ramya ix
Svapnavāsavadattam of Bhāsa 197n.
svarga 4, 5n., 11, 259

Taittirīyasaṃhitā 9n.
Takṣaka 62, 63
tantra/tantric/tantrism x, 31, 96, 118, 125n., 140, 141–175, 204, 263, 271, 272, 284, 285, 286, 290, 293, 296, 297
tantra, Buddhist 142, 143n.
Tantrākhyāyikā 226n.
tapas/*tapasya* 98, 184, 188n.
Tārā (Vālin's wife) 90
Taylor, McCormas 17n., 296
teacher-student relationship 34, 35, 37, 38, 44, 52, 53, 55, 56, 60, 78
Thapar, Romila 4n., 22n. 296
"theology of ordinary life," a/the 6, 7n., 262, 265, 268
Thucydides 136
Tieken, Herman 26n., 259n., 296
tīrtha(s) (pilgrimage sites) 118n.
Todorov, Tzvetan 1
Tretā Yuga 12, 46n., 66, 73
Tribhuvanasvāmin 119
Trijaṭā 70n.
Trivikramasena 156, 157, 159, 160, 161, 162, 167, 169, 170, 171
tropes, narrative 9n., 10, 28n., 187
truthfulness/truth-telling (See also: vow(s)) 6n., 39, 40, 43, 45, 47, 48, 58, 60, 62, 63, 64, 84, 85, 86, 88, 89, 93, 100, 103

Udayana 142, 152n., 153, 154, 171, 196, 197, 199, 200, 201, 203, 204, 205, 206, 207, 208
Udyogaparvan 49, 60
Ujjayinī/Ujjain 125, 143, 148, 150, 172, 203, 204
Um, Janet 142n.
Unmādinī (maiden of the 17th *vetāla* story) 161, 162, 163
untouchable/untouchability 119, 120n. 289
uparūpaka (subsidiary types of Sanskrit dramas) 16, 178
Uttarakāṇḍa 67, 69, 70, 73n., 82, 94, 97, 103, 284

Vaiśaṃpāyana 62, 63
vaiśya(s) 30, 145, 160, 161, 263
vājapeya rites 76
Vajramukuṭa (son of Pratāpamukuṭa, prince of 1st *vetāla* story) 164, 165, 166, 167
Vālin 70, 73, 75, 81, 84n. 86, 88, 89, 90, 91
Vālmīki 67, 68, 69, 70, 71, 73, 74, 75, 76, 78, 79, 80, 82, 85n., 86, 87, 88, 89, 93, 94, 96, 97, 98, 99, 100, 101, 102, 103, 193, 196, 262, 278, 279, 284, 288, 292
Vāmana 124, 139
Vaṃśāvalī(s) 17, 106n., 297
Vārāṇasī (Benares) 126, 164, 209
Vararuci, a.k.a. Kātyāyana 148, 149, 150, 151
varṇa See: caste
varṇāśramadharma 40, 42, 43, 47, 59, 60, 137
Vasantaka (*vidūṣaka* of the *Ratnāvalī*) 201, 202, 203, 204, 205
vasantotsava (spring festival) 197
Vāsavadattā 153, 171, 199, 201, 202, 203, 205, 206, 207
Vasubhāga 227
Vasudeva, Somadeva 178n., 277, 296
Vasudevahiṃdi 152n., 154n., 289
Veda/Vedic 4n., 17n., 36, 39, 41, 47, 48, 56, 283, 285, 286, 289, 297
verisimilitude (of literary works) 19, 20, 21n., 260
vetāla(s) 21n., 27, 31, 146, 151n., 152, 153, 154, 155, 156, 157, 158n., 159, 160, 161, 162, 163, 164, 167, 169, 170, 171, 172n., 174, 175, 252, 253n., 271, 272, 282, 286, 293
Vibhīṣaṇa 94n., 95, 96
vidūṣaka ("clown") 179, 180, 183, 184, 185, 190, 191, 192, 198, 200, 201, 202, 203, 204, 205, 208, 218, 220, 229, 287, 288, 294
vidyā(s) ("spells") 146n., 152n.
vidyādhara(s) 4, 27, 30, 143, 146n., 149, 152, 154n., 155n., 169, 170, 171, 172, 173, 175, 175n., 253n., 259, 263, 271, 281
Vidyāpīṭha 143
Vikarālā 209, 213, 214, 215
Vikramāditya 125, 126, 155, 156, 172
Vikramakeśarin 153, 155, 156, 171
Virāṭa 49, 284
Viṣṇu 51, 54, 66, 68, 69n., 76, 99, 123, 139
virtue ethics 6n., 7, 17, 23, 28, 32, 34, 36, 41, 44, 48, 50, 54, 56, 59, 63, 65, 67, 78, 80, 83, 86, 88, 96, 97, 99, 103, 105, 111, 112, 127, 130, 134, 160, 163, 168, 174, 175, 181, 196, 219, 220, 222, 226, 251, 257, 259, 260, 261, 262, 263, 264, 265, 268
Viśākhadatta 156
Viśvāmitra 9n., 183, 293

Viṣṇuśarman 3, 25, 222, 223, 229, 231, 256, 269, 277
voyeur/voyeurism 270
vow(s) See also: truthfulness/truth-telling 39, 44, 45, 47, 50, 57, 58, 61, 62, 64, 71, 76, 84, 149, 150, 193, 194, 207
Vyāḍi 150
Vyāsa 35n., 58, 62, 63, 72n., 74, 80n., 140n., 296

Warder, A. K. 16n., 297
Wedemeyer, Christian 151n., 290, 297
White, Hayden 127–129, 297
Winternitz, Maurice 16n., 163, 178n., 277, 297
Witzel, Michael 17n., 106n., 297
Wizard of Oz 206, 264

yakṣa(s) 148, 149, 151n.
Yaśaskara (king of the *Rājataraṅgiṇī*) 126n., 174n.
Yaśaḥketu (king of the 12th *vetāla* story) 158, 159
Yaśodhana (king of the 17th *vetāla* story) 161
Yaugandharāyaṇa (Udayana's minister) 153, 154, 197, 198, 206, 207, 208
yoginī(s) 120n., 143, 144, 166, 169, 174, 271, 272, 285
Yuddhakāṇḍa 75, 96n., 97, 98, 284
Yudhiṣṭhira 5n., 11n., 35n., 48–50, 51, 55n., 60, 61, 73n., 120, 121, 132, 296
Yuga(s) See: Dvāpara Yuga, Kali Yuga, Satya Yuga, Tretā Yuga
yugic historiography 136

Zutshi, Chitralekha 18n., 105n., 106, 298